Mediterranean Cruising Handbook

ROD HEIKELL

Imray Laurie Norie & Wilson

Published by
Imray, Laurie, Norie & Wilson Ltd
Wych House, St Ives,
Cambridgeshire, PE27 5BT, England.
☎ +44 (0)1480 462114 *Fax* +44(0)1480 496109
email ilnw@imray.com
www.imray.com
2004

Navigation consultant George Blance (Editor *Norie's Nautical Tables*)
Basic First Aid Terence J Carter (Thames Valley Medical and Rescue Unit)
Illustrations Pip Nielsen and Lucy Wilson
All photographs Rod Heikell except where stated.

ISBN 0 85288 778 7

British Library Cataloguing in Publication Data
A catalogue record for this book is available from the British Library.

CAUTION
Every effort has been made to ensure the accuracy of this book. It contains selected information and thus is not definitive and does not include all known information on the subject in hand; this is particularly relevant to the plans, which should not be used for navigation. The publisher believes that its selection is a useful aid to prudent navigation, but the safety of a vessel depends ultimately on the judgement of the navigator, who should assess all information, published or unpublished, available to him.

PLANS
The plans in this guide are not to be used for navigation. They are designed to support the text and should at all times be used with navigational charts.

Printed in Italy by Eurolitho SpA, Milan

Contents

Introduction

This new edition of *Mediterranean Cruising Handbook* incorporates much of the information that formerly made up the introductory chapters to the *Imray Mediterranean Almanac*. As much of this information does not radically change from year to year it was decided that it could be supplied in a companion volume to the *Imray Mediterranean Almanac* without being reprinted each time a new edition of the almanac came out. All of the information which changes from year to year, data on lights, radio services, weather services, and harbour information is contained within the *Imray Mediterranean Almanac*.

To the information from the introductory sections of the almanac I have added some of the text from the old edition of *Mediterranean Cruising Handbook* where I thought it relevant. Overall the style of this new edition is more factual and less expositional than previous editions of the *Mediterranean Cruising Handbook* and while some of you might find it a bit terse, it does make it easier to find the information you are looking for.

If any of you have pointers to what you would like to see in future editions of the handbook, I welcome any suggestions which can be sent to me care of the publishers.

Rod Heikell
London 2004

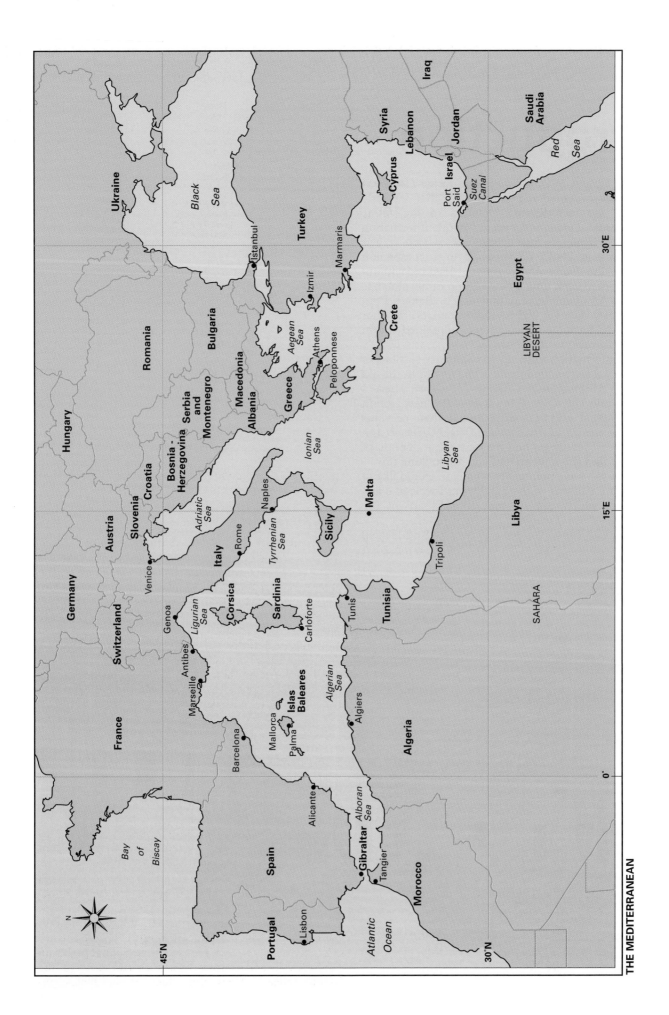

THE MEDITERRANEAN

1. The Mediterranean

1.1 Vital statistics

The Mediterranean is situated approximately between latitudes 32°N and 44°N and longitudes 05°W and 35°E.

Length is approximately 2000M (3700km) and maximum width Trieste to Gulf of Sirte 970M (1800km).

Surface area 1,145,000M² (2,974,025km²). The average depth is 1429m (4688ft). The greatest depth is 4648m (15,240ft).

Comparisons of surface area, average depth and maximum depth with the large oceans are as follows:

Ocean/Sea	Surface area M²	Average depth	Greatest depth
Pacific	64,000,000	4030m (13,215ft)	11,524m (37,784ft)
Atlantic	31,815,000	3928m (12,880ft)	9220m (30,230ft)
Indian	25,300,000	3966m (13,002ft)	9000ft (29,508ft)
Arctic	5,440,200	1206m (3953ft)	5450m (17,868ft)
Mediterranean	1,145,000	1429m (4688ft)	4648m (15,240ft)

1.2 Component seas

The Mediterranean is made up of a number of component seas, many of which have long historical associations:

Alboran Sea, Algerian Sea, Ligurian Sea, Tyrrhenian Sea, Adriatic Sea, Ionian Sea, Libyan Sea, Aegean Sea, Levantine Sea

There are also smaller named seas, particularly in the eastern Mediterranean where areas like the Aegean have smaller divisions, usually named after the nearest large island or land mass (e.g. Kithera Sea, Cretan Sea, and so on).

1.3 Component countries

The Mediterranean is bordered by 21 recognised countries and 2 inter-dependent mini-states.

Country	Area	Coastline length
Gibraltar	2·25M² (6·5km²)	6·5M (12 km)
Spain	194,329M² (504,750km²)	2680M (4964km)
France	209,836M² (545,630km²)	918M (1700km)
Italy	115,973M² (301,230km²)	2698M (4996km)
Malta	123M² (320km²)	75·6M (140km)
Slovenia	7836M² (20,296km²)	16M (26km)
Bosnia/ Hercegovina	19,781M² (51,233km²)	11M (20km)
Croatia	21,829M2 (56,538km²)	3127M (5790km)
Montenegro	5381M² (13,938km²)	107M (199km)
Albania	11,100M² (28,750km²)	195M (362km)

Country	Area	Coastline length
Greece	50,796M² (131,940km²)	7385M (13,767km)
Turkey	300,088M² (779,450km²)	3888M (7200km)
Cyprus	3561M² (9250km²)	432M (800km)
Syria	71,294M² (185,180km²)	108M (200km)
Lebanon	4004M² (10,400km²)	121M (225km)
Israel	7996M² (20,770km²)	147M (273km)
Egypt	385,558M² (1,001,450km²)	1323M (2450km)
Libya	677,423M² (1,759,540km²)	956M (1770km)
Tunisia	62,990M² (163,610km²)	620M (1148km)
Algeria	916,969M² (2,381,740km²)	648M (1200km)
Morocco	176,600M² (458,700km²)	270M (500km)
Mini-states		
Monaco	3M² (7·8km²)	2·2M (4·1km)
San Marino	23M² (60km²)	none

In addition there are the Spanish *presidos* of Ceuta and Melilla on the Moroccan coast.

1.4 Geology

The forces that formed the Mediterranean are still at work today, gently reforming the geology along the edges of the tectonic plates. The present shape of the Mediterranean took form around 9 million years ago when the continents around it pushed up into what was the great Tethys Ocean. The forces generated at the edges of the tectonic plates pushed up the high mountain ranges that surround the Mediterranean: the Pyrenees, Alps, Dinaric Alps, the Rhodope mountains, the Taurus range, and the Atlas mountains. Around 5–6 million years ago the Mediterranean was completely enclosed from the Atlantic and Indian Oceans and dried up into a series of salt lakes. This process may have occurred 15–18 times, though how the sea was refilled each time is open to speculation. Some 5 million years ago the land barrier between Spain and Morocco was breached, probably by a massive earthquake, to make a permanent connection with the Atlantic, and the Mediterranean filled for the final time.

The effect of these geological changes is visible if we take the Mediterranean in cross-section. In the Strait of Gibraltar the subterranean ridge lies 320m (1050ft) down. The ridge between the western and eastern basins between Sicily and Tunisia lies 400m (1310ft) down. In the Bosphorus, the tiny crack between Europe and Asia Minor that joins the Mediterranean to the Black Sea, the bottom is only 40m (131ft) down.

The edges of the tectonic plates can be mapped from the volcanic and seismic lines that run through the Mediterranean. Along the edges of the plates run

Vulcano in the Lipari islands in Italy. Here you anchor under an active volcano and right on top of the fault line between the African and European tectonic plates

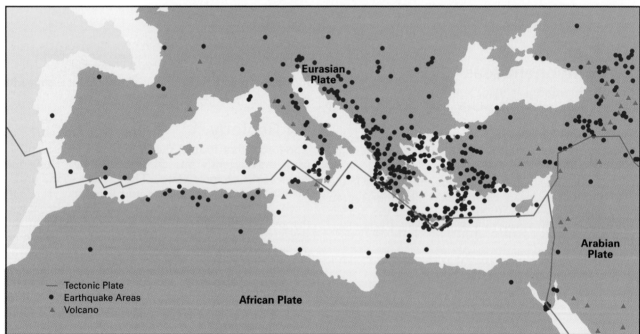

Mediterranean tectonic plates and earthquake and volcanic zones

earthquake fault lines and here and there cracks in the upper crust release magma to the surface, most notably from Vesuvius on the edge of the Bay of Naples down to Etna on Sicily. In *13. The Mediterranean countries* there is a brief description of seismic activity for each area.

1.5 Hydrology

The most striking feature of the Mediterranean for the yachtsman is the virtual absence of tides. The comparatively small mass of the sea (although it is around 1/140th of the total sea area its volume is only 1/355th of the total volume of oceans and seas on the earth's surface) is little influenced by the gravitational pull of the moon and sun. The narrow entrance between the Mediterranean and the Atlantic shuts out the Atlantic tides. Only in enclosed gulfs like the Gulf of Gabes in Tunisia or narrow channels like the Strait of Messina is there any important tidal effect.

Although there is little tidal effect, the hydrology is complex. Evaporation from the surface of the Mediterranean is the driving force for the roughly anti-clockwise circulation of water around the basin of the sea. It is estimated that rivers flowing into the Mediterranean replace only about one third of the water lost, with rainfall making it up to about half. The 50% deficit flows in through the Strait of Gibraltar, where a surface current brings in around one million cubic metres of Atlantic water every second. This surface current has an opposite bottom current flowing back out into the Atlantic. The more salty waters of the

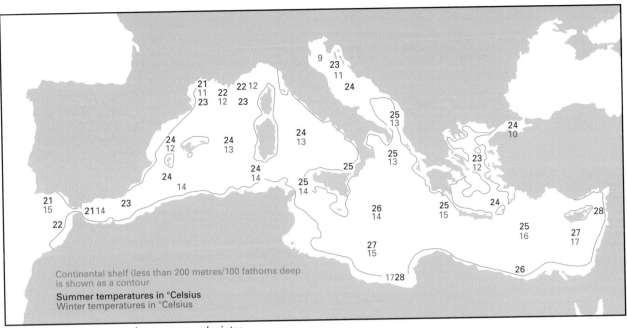

Continental shelf (less than 200 metres/100 fathoms deep
is shown as a contour
Summer temperatures in °Celsius
Winter temperatures in °Celsius

Average sea temperatures in summer and winter

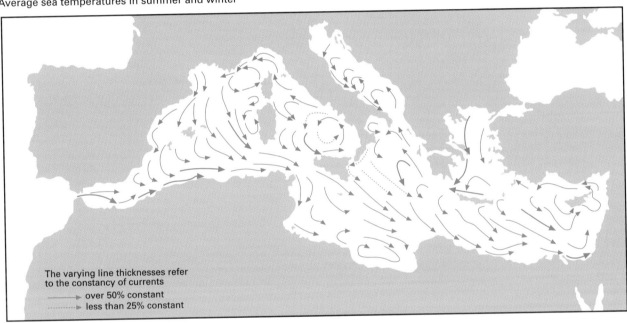

The varying line thicknesses refer
to the constancy of currents

→ over 50% constant
⤍ less than 25% constant

Surface currents - January

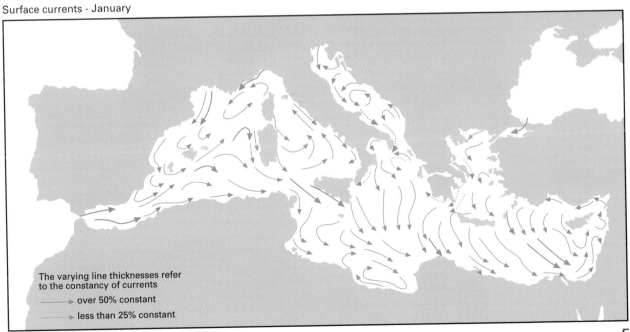

The varying line thicknesses refer
to the constancy of currents

→ over 50% constant
⤍ less than 25% constant

Surface currents - July

eastern Mediterranean (around 3·9% compared to 3·5% salt for the Atlantic) sinks and flows westwards to spill over the sill at Gibraltar into the Atlantic. Estimates vary but a best guess is that it would take 180 years to totally renew the waters of the Mediterranean. For specific detail on tides and currents see *13. The Mediterranean Countries*.

1.6 Climate

Geographers define the Mediterranean as the region between the olive tree in the north and the large palm groves in the south. The climate of this nearly land-locked sea is specific enough to earn the geographical label of the Mediterranean climate. The main feature of the geographical region is the high mountain ranges that close it off from the continental European climate,

from the Saharan desert, and from the Atlantic. In the winter the mountain barriers are more penetrable and the continental effect, the Sahara and Atlantic weather systems affect Mediterranean weather.

Summers are settled, with stable pressure gradients and few depressions. The Azores High generally deflects any depressions coming across the Atlantic up into northern Europe. Another stable high sits around the Gulf of Sirte off Libya. Weather is mostly local weather (except for the special case of the *meltemi* in the Aegean), with thermal effects generating winds. Rainfall is minimal.

In the winter depressions roll in from the Atlantic, bringing unstable weather patterns. Some of the weather caused in the Mediterranean by depressions passing over continental Europe is indirectly related to the continental weather systems such as the *tramontane*

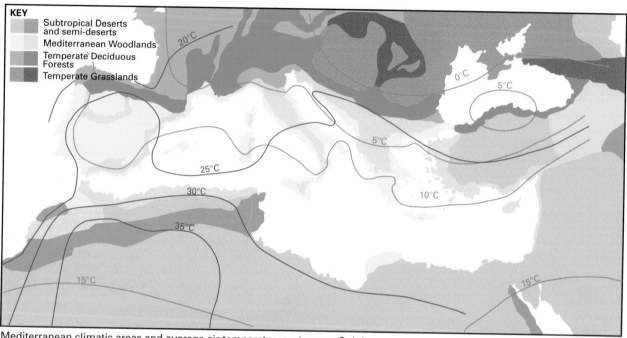

KEY
- Subtropical Deserts and semi-deserts
- Mediterranean Woodlands
- Temperate Deciduous Forests
- Temperate Grasslands

Mediterranean climatic areas and average air temperatures - January & July

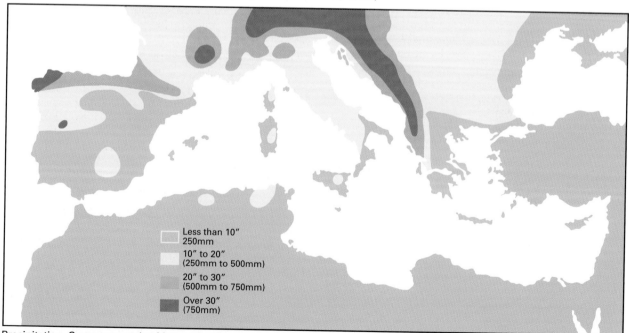

- Less than 10" 250mm
- 10" to 20" (250mm to 500mm)
- 20" to 30" (500mm to 750mm)
- Over 30" (750mm)

Precipitation. Summer months: May to October

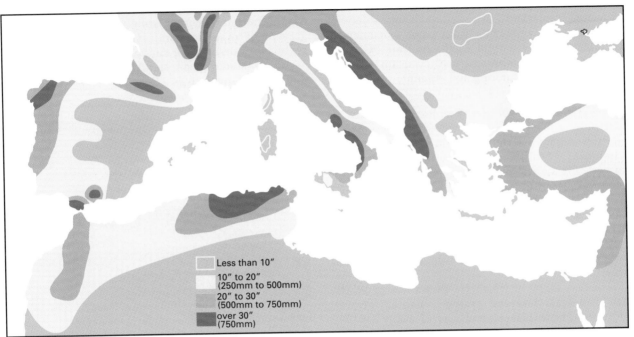

Less than 10"

10" to 20"
(250mm to 500mm)

20" to 30"
(500mm to 750mm)

over 30"
(750mm)

Precipitation. Winter months: November - April

and *mistral* (mountain gap winds) or the *bora* (coastal slope wind), but are nonetheless violent. All three have been recorded at Force 11 with gusts of Force 12. Almost all the rain in the Mediterranean, though more notably in the east than the west, falls in the winter.

For specific detail on weather see *11. Weather,* and on climate see *13. The Mediterranean Countries.*

1.7 Pollution

A sea which takes 180 years to renew its waters is vulnerable to pollution and in the Mediterranean much concern has been expressed over the environment surrounding the sea and pollution in the sea itself. One of the principal problems is that the absence of tides means there is no large scale flushing system to sweep away pollutants and dilute them as in the Atlantic or Pacific. There is also a lack of proper sewerage treatment systems, and pollutants are emptied into major rivers which flow into the Mediterranean. Add to this over-fishing for the last 40 years, which does little to help the overall ecosystem, and you have cause for concern.

Pollution in the Mediterranean can be broken down into a number of categories, but first it is useful to look at the type of sea the Mediterranean is.

The Mediterranean is a marine version of semi-desert or semi-arid land. The lack of circulating currents means that the different layers of the sea are not stirred up and mixed together as in most other seas and oceans. After 300m the water is relatively stable (13°C) and combined with the above average salt content this water can hold little oxygen and so support little in the way of marine life. This means that most marine life exists only in comparatively shallow waters, up to 200m, below which there is some life but nothing like that encountered in the Atlantic or Pacific. The lack of circulating currents and the relatively tepid water does not provide ideal conditions for plankton, the basis of all marine food chains, and in fact the much vaunted clarity of the Mediterranean is due to

this plankton poverty. A lack of plankton at the beginning of the food chain has predictable consequences at the top of the food chain, with fewer fish than in, say, the Atlantic or Red Sea.

A second and important consideration in the Mediterranean is the absence of any real continental shelf compared with the Atlantic. Although the Mediterranean is a comparatively shallow sea, paradoxically it is steep-to along much of its coast (with the exception of river deltas), dropping off to considerable depths very quickly. This steep-to coastline and the absence of tides means there is little of the important sub-littoral marine life that makes up an important part of the marine ecosystem in the Atlantic or Pacific.

Ironically a semi-desert or semi-arid sea like the Mediterranean is better placed to cope with pollution than richer seas like the Baltic or North Sea. It is less damaged and can recover more easily from human onslaught. The problem for the Mediterranean is the scale of the onslaught and there can no complacency in combatting pollution around its shores.

Hydrocarbon pollution The most obvious form of pollution, evident in oil slicks and tar along the shoreline. It is heaviest around the oil refineries and oil loading ports from spillage. There are also approximately 115 oil platforms in the Mediterranean (in Italy, Greece, Turkey, Egypt, Libya and Tunisia) where leakage occurs. Oil tankers cleaning out their tanks at sea (contrary to the MARPOL convention) also contribute to hydrocarbon pollution.

Heavy metals and toxic chemicals Much industrial effluent flowing into the major European rivers ends up in the Mediterranean. High levels of mercury, lead, cadmium, chromium and zinc have been found in Mediterranean marine life. Mercury is the worst of these, accumulating in fish and also in man. Toxic chemicals, ranging from chlorine based chemicals used for bleaching processes (especially in the production of paper products), PCBs (polychlorinated bi-phenyls) and related compounds, to acids and alkaline solutions used in cleaning processes (from paint to tanneries) have all been detected in the Mediterranean. PCBs are the worst culprits, inhibiting growth, causing birth defects and probably injuring the immune systems of larger animals.

Fertilisers and pesticides Fertiliser run-off is an increasing problem in the Mediterranean as many countries augment fertiliser use in intensive farming techniques. Fertiliser running off into rivers and subsequently the sea causes eutrophication in which an over-supply of nutrients causes a biological explosion of low level plant forms such as algaes. As a consequence all the oxygen in the water is used up, effectively killing all other marine life. The most dramatic evidence of this has been in the northern Adriatic where algal blooms covered large areas of water.

Pesticides, many of which are derivatives of PCBs, have damaged immune systems, caused growth deformities, birth defects, and very probably a whole host of still unknown problems.

Sewage Around the shores of the Mediterranean live some 132 million people, a number swollen every summer by a further 100 million tourists. Most effluent, even in the so-called developed countries of the EU, is still pumped into the sea without treatment. The effects are twofold. Toilet paper, even chopped into pieces, covers the sea floor and retards growth. The effluent itself is a natural fertiliser and adds to the effects of nitrates from fertilisers encouraging eutrophication.

Fishing techniques Contrary to popular opinion, the lack of fish in the Mediterranean is not due to 3000 years of fishing, but to fishing techniques in the last 20 to 40 years. The Mediterranean has never supported a large fish population (there were shortages in Roman times with comparatively primitive techniques), but since the war small mesh nets, dynamite and growing fleets of large trawlers have decimated the fish stocks.

There have been numerous attempts in recent years to remedy the problems of pollution in the Mediterranean. In 1975 the UN managed to get all the Mediterranean countries (except Albania and Libya) around the table to sign up to MAP, the Mediterranean Action Plan clean-up programme. The problem has been lack of implementation, either from weak political action or lack of controls and legislation, so that there have been widely varying results between the countries. More recently EU money has been put aside for environmental problems, principally for sewage treatment plants and controls on the fishing season and regulation of mesh sizes of nets. Much superficial flag waving (literally) has been evident with beaches given the EU blue pennant, principally for having a clean beach and allegedly clean water. I can't believe that blue pennants flying on some beaches have anything to do with clean water when independent tests show there is substantial pollution there.

I mention these matters on the environment and pollution not to discourage one from going to the Mediterranean, but to draw attention to what is a world-wide problem, not just one confined to the Mediterranean. Environmental movements have been growing all over the world and as independent lobby groups they deserve our support. Those of us who sail on the Mediterranean should refrain in turn from polluting it ourselves. See *6.4 Aide-memoire for yachtsmen to avoid polluting the sea.*

Geographically speaking, the Mediterranean is the area between the northern limit of the olive and the large palm groves in the south

Although Mediterranean cuisine features fish and the sea has been fished since antiquity, it has never supported a large fish population. Even the Romans complained about fish stocks in their Mare Nostrum

1.8 Flora

Over the 8000 years that man cleared and cultivated the land around the Mediterranean, it has been extensively modified. His animals have over-grazed, land was cleared by simply burning off all the vegetation, forests were felled to build fleets of ships, and trees of all kinds were cut for fuel for cooking and small industries like ore smelting and firing pottery.

The ancient writers described lush green and fertile islands that are now arid and support little more than the stunted plants of maquis and *garrigue*. Medieval writers described great forests populated by boar, wolves and bears; long ago they were driven out and

The Rock Rose, which probably gives its Corsican name (*macchia*) to the generic maquis of the Mediterranean
Lu Michell

the forests cut down so that not a trace remains. What is now desert in North Africa was a great grain-growing region. Even plants we think of as quintessentially Mediterranean turn out to be introduced species, among them the palms, loquat, oranges and lemons, bouganvillea, jasmine, cacti and quite possibly the olive. The clearing of the coniferous forests on the shores and the subsequent introduction of sheep and goats, which nibble away any new growth, radically altered the landscape. Most of the forested areas were turned into one of the two related types of vegetation that are common to this day.

Maquis is the thick, tangled vegetation typically growing on coastal regions, although it can extend a considerable distance inland. It is a mixture of low bushes and shrubs growing 2 to 4 metres high, that have adapted to survive in their exposed and windy situation. A considerable number of species are represented, including broom (*Genista cinera*), tree heather (*Erica arborea*), strawberry tree (*Arbutus unedo*), myrtle (*Myrtus communis*), kermes oak (*Quercus coccifera*) and the rock-rose (*Cistus albidus*). The latter is interesting since its Corsican name is *macchia* and it is probably a corruption of this that gave *macquis* its name. The aromatic herbs and the plants of the *macquis* give off a distinctive aroma and with an offshore wind you can often smell it several miles out to sea. Napoleon said of his native Corsica that he could recognise the island with his eyes shut, by the smell of the rock-rose alone.

These plants have adapted to their exposed habitat in a variety of ways. Because there are no tall trees to stop the wind or to shade the plants, and water is scarce in summer, the biggest danger for the plants of the maquis is water loss. To prevent this, plants like myrtle and the rock-rose secrete an oily or gummy substance over their leaves. The leaves of broom and buckthorn are very small so that the least surface area possible is presented. The plants must all be sturdy with good roots to withstand the buffeting of the wind, and the stems and branches tend to be dense and knotty. The wood of tree heather is so dense that it will not burn and is used for the bowls of pipes.

Garrigue grows on land where even the tenacious maquis cannot survive. Generally the plants are less than half a metre in height and flower briefly in the spring before the hot summer sun withers them to dry brown stems and leaves. Many common culinary herbs are found in *garrigue*: thyme, sage, rosemary, hyssop and rue. Their different flavours largely come from the aromatic oils they secrete to prevent water loss. Like *macquis*, the plants are adapted to conserve water. Some disappear underground during the summer and spend the hot dry period as bulbs in the cooler earth. The sea quill (*Urginea maritima*) exists as a large bulb in the summer, but with the first autumn rain it grows at an astonishing rate and then flowers.

In the spring the *garrigue* is transformed, many of the plants have vividly coloured flowers. Fields of red poppies have patches of other wildflowers: yellow irises, orange and yellow crocuses, white narcissus, and the delicate green and purple fritillary. Orchids are well represented, many of them of exquisite shape and colour. In some areas such as Crete, there are a large number of native orchids.

In many of the countries around the Mediterranean reafforestation has been underway for some time. Nearly all of the new pine forests are composed of Douglas fir, which grows quickly and easily. Although the planting has been undertaken for good reasons, to stop soil erosion and to provide wood for building and paper pulp, pine forests are not hospitable habitats. The dense needles prevent light getting to the ground so few plants can survive there, and the resin and dead needles decompose in the soil to form acids which prevent plants growing in it.

In a few parts of the Mediterranean, in inaccessible and relatively unpopulated areas, forest and vegetation remains that is still much like that of 2000 years ago. The holm oak (*Quercus flex*) and cork oak (*Quercus suber*) cover parts of the coasts of Sardinia and Spain. Aleppo pines (*Pinus halepensis*) and cypress grow in parts of Macedonia and the Greek islands. It is difficult to imagine most of the Mediterranean coast covered in thick deciduous forest and undergrowth, and populated by wild boar, wolves and bears. But so it was, and we can only hope that what remains is protected for the future.

Hard to believe, but these barren slopes in Greece were once described as verdant by ancient scribes. And then along came man with slash and burn and goats and sheep

2. History and culture

2.1 Historical perspectives

The geographical and geological picture is a partial view of the Mediterranean that the thinking visitor will want to fill in with the peoples and cultures around it. Such a description and history would be difficult to fit into a large book without skimping here and there. What I can do here is paint a broad canvas with the Mediterranean in the centre of it. This thin gash between the continents has historically separated completely different worlds and it still does. The divisions may be blurred by the political boundaries defining the twenty-one countries now surrounding the Mediterranean, but the overall picture is there and it takes something like the fundamentalist Islamic revolution in Iran which has spread to the Levant, or the partitioning of Cyprus in 1974, to bring these wider divisions to the surface.

The Mediterranean straddles the Occident and the Orient; taking Italy as a dividing line, everything to the west is the Occident and to the east the Orient. This is made immediately obvious in the cuisine of the two regions. In the west thick soups, ovenbaked dishes and rich sauces predominate, whereas in the east cold starters, spicy grilled kebabs and meatballs, and simple salads are the mainstay of the diet. In the 19th and early 20th centuries the division was still an accepted one referred to in travel books of the era. In *Eothen*, which means 'from the east', A.W. Kinglake describes his journey through Greece, Turkey, Cyprus and the Levant in the 1830s as an 'Oriental tour'. Most other travel writers of the period similarly described 'the Orient'. After the Second World War the division between Occident and Orient was used less, as parts of the Orient apparently became Occidental, but anyone who visits the countries in the eastern Mediterranean soon understands that under the western surface an Oriental heart still beats.

From this broad division between west and east, it is useful to reconsider the Mediterranean as a whole and this time carve it into 'three huge, thriving civilizations, three major modes of thinking, believing, eating, drinking and living' (Braudel). These divisions exist intact not only in the present, but can be traced through the convoluted history of the Mediterranean from very early on. And from this inland sea the impact of the three civilizations stretches thousands of miles, across the oceans on either side and to the continents to the north and south.

The first of these is the western culture corresponding to the Occident. It is the Christian world, formerly the Roman Catholic world, with Rome at the hub. As such it spread north to split into the Protestant church and its myriad offspring, and from there Catholic and Protestant together migrated to the New World and colonised it. So much of our current mythology – the Protestant ethic, the idea of progress as a good and worthy object, of converting those in far away lands to our western ideals – evolved from the old Latin universe centred in Rome. In Europe it can be difficult to see this, but in America the religious underpinning of western ideals is more obvious.

The second division is the Greek Orthodox world. Until quite recently western historians paid only scant attention to Byzantium and its legacy, indeed few of us comprehend the extent today of the Orthodox Church and fewer still its antecedents. From Greece the Orthodox Church covers the Balkan peninsula, Bulgaria, parts of former Yugoslavia, Romania and north up to the vastness of Russia. The barrier of the Eastern Bloc once disguised its extent, but any traveller to the region will tell you that it is alive even if not highly visible. Until the Ottoman Turks overran it in 1453, the Orthodox Church, then the Holy Roman Empire in the east, the Byzantine Empire, had its centre at Constantinople. Since then Orthodoxy has been without a centre although not without power. The central figure in the Cyprus troubles in the 1960s was Makarios, the somewhat sinister Greek Orthodox Archbishop, who in effect wanted Cyprus to be wholly part of the Greek Orthodox world. However, Islam and the Turkish Army eventually decided otherwise.

Islam is the third slice of the Mediterranean, starting at Turkey on the eastern end of the Mediterranean and running around its southern shores to Morocco. It extends from there into Africa, across the Indian Ocean to Indonesia, the Philippines and the islands in the Melanesian archipelago. Islam has recently asserted itself with the new fundamentalism centred on Iran, spreading from there to Lebanon and fomenting the bloody civil war between Muslim and Christian,

Orthodox church in Naoussa on Paros in the Greek Cyclades

Much of the geography carries a reminder of the ancients and their gods that has survived to the present day. This is Capo Palinuro on the west coast of Itay where Palinurus, the helmsman of Aeneas' ship, fell overboard and was washed ashore and murdered by the locals. Consult the *Aeneid* for more detail

and the troubles in Algeria. The effect of Islam on the Mediterranean was considerable when the Ottoman Empire held sway over all of Greece, the Balkans, and threatened Italy and Malta. From North Africa the Arab invasions of Spain introduced Islam at the western end of the Mediterranean. The legacy of Islam was not just the obvious cultural influences as seen in cuisine, music and dress, but also on agriculture with the introduction of new species and methods of irrigation, in science and in architecture, influences which spread throughout the Catholic and Orthodox worlds and remained after the Turks and Arabs left. One of our most popular beverages, coffee, was one of Islam's legacies to the west.

From these three divisions further sub-divisions can be made. Some are a part of one of the major civilizations, others combine parts of them. The Levant brings together the Orthodox islands close to Asia Minor and stretches down this coast to include Syria, Lebanon and across to Cyprus. The Mahgreb pulls together Tunisia, Algeria and Morocco, reflecting their interlocked history and cultural roots. The Balkans include northern Greece, Bulgaria, Romania and Yugoslavia as an area with much history and culture in common. In the Occidental half of the Mediterranean it is more difficult today to pick out the larger patterns that once shaped the history of these countries.

The pegs I have arranged on which to hang the multi-coloured coats of the Mediterranean countries, are there to make a broad sense of the layers of accumulated history and intermingled cultures that at first sight appears as a tangle, seemingly impossible to penetrate. Sometimes the political boundary of a country conceals a great deal more than it reveals. After all, no other region has experienced such a concentrated and lengthy period of building up civilizations and demolishing others; from the very first hunters and gatherers in the Mesopotamian valley through the Egyptians, Hittites, Assyrians, Minoans and Myceneans, Greeks, Romans, Arabs, Byzantium,

Franks, Ottomans, Venetians and Genoese, the Papal States, the Spanish, French, British and Russians, to the First and Second World Wars and the division of the Mediterranean into the 21 countries around its shores today. (Try to recite that list quickly!)

2.2 Archaeological and historical sites

A sad tale was told in a recent holiday brochure. On a yachting holiday, a charterer stumbled across a superb Roman mosaic floor on a small island off the Turkish coast. The charterers kept the discovery to themselves until they were able to tell the proper authorities about it. Somehow the news leaked out, and by the time the authorities got there the whole mosaic floor had been roughly removed, probably destroying part of it in the process.

The desire to possess a piece of the ancient world exists in most of us. Why we need an ancient coin, pottery shards, part of a mosaic, a vase or oil lamp, a scarab or some other relic is difficult to understand when most of us have only a scant knowledge of the ancient world. Why are we not satisfied with copies that even experts cannot always distinguish from originals? I have no explanation for this greed, at least no brief answers. What is more important is the vandalising of sites that occurs in the search for souvenirs from the ancient world. Such vandalism makes the work of the archaeologists nearly impossible. Just moving ancient bric-a-brac around a site makes it a hundred-fold more difficult to piece together a picture of life in those times. If unique pieces are removed, all of us are deprived of ancient works of art when they are finally housed in some private collection and not in a public museum.

All one can do is to make a plea to yachtsmen not to vandalise these sites, especially since many of them, particularly in Greece and Turkey, are accessible only by sea. The yachtsman has a special duty to refrain

from nibbling away at the bits of the ancient world still remaining and to educate his fellow users of the sea to do the same.

There are many ancient sites around the Mediterranean. A few are familiar by name to almost everyone: Pompeii, Delphi, the Parthenon in Athens, Ephesus, the Pyramids, and the Valley of the Kings at Luxor. These well known places make up a small fraction of the total number. The ancients were great colonisers as well as great builders and the Mediterranean was a busy sea crossed by merchant and naval fleets. According to Willard Bascom's *Deep Water, Ancient Ships*. 'Between 750 and 550 BC the Greeks founded some 250 colony-cities, most of which were seaport towns around the Mediterranean and Black seas and some of which have been continuously inhabited ever since. The city-state of Corinth founded Syracuse on Sicily; Miletus established Sinope and Trapezus on the Black Sea and Sybaris in the arch of the Italian boot; Megara set up Byzantium in the Turkish straits; and Sparta established Tarentum at the tip of the heel of Italy.' From Spain to Asia Minor, from Morocco across the sea to Syria, there are literally hundreds of ancient sites, many of them virtually unknown outside archaeological circles and some unexcavated. In most of their countries the finds made are displayed in museums, with models of the site to give an idea of what it originally looked like. Unfortunately the best exhibits are usually in the capital city, but there is an increasing trend to build small local museums on a site to display finds made there, or in a regional centre.

In a boat, one is in the enviable position of being able to approach an ancient site and see it as a seaman might have several thousand years ago. Often the approach from the sea is the most attractive one, as it so often is for contemporary villages and towns, and in some places you still berth in the ancient harbour. Even if you have little interest in what has been left behind since the Greeks and Romans, few are unimpressed by the brilliant engineering feats carried out, and only the hard-hearted can deny the romance

Much of the coast of the Mediterranean is littered with the remains of the ancients. Ephesus in Turkey

A Perama trading caique in Hydra in Greece. The hull form has many similarities to ancient Greek and Roman trading ships

of anchoring in a deserted bay close by the ruins of a theatre on the shore.

Apart from the cities, towns, temples and tombs of antiquity, there are numerous monuments to the civilisations that followed the churches and murals of Byzantium; the Norman cathedrals and churches and especially the fusion of Arab and Norman architecture in Sicily. The massive castles of the Knights of St John in Rhodes and Malta. The opulent palaces and the castles along the trade routes of the Venetians and Genoese. The softer rounded Moorish architecture in Spain. The massive fortifications of the Crusaders, with Krak de Chevaliers in Syria towering over them all. The pencil-thin minarets of Ottoman mosques and the opulence and indulgence of Topkapi Palace in Istanbul. The solid Romanesque and the Gothic reaction to it of the Christian world. The Baroque and neo-Gothic revival. The eccentric architecture of Gaudi in Barcelona. The Mediterranean is a treasure trove of man's attempts to raise stone, brick and mortar to leave enduring monuments to ideas and beliefs, and to keep the unbelievers out.

In the 18th century Samuel Johnson was able to state 'The grand object of travelling is to see the shores of the Mediterranean. On these shores were the four great empires of the world – the Assyrian, the Persian, the Greek and the Roman. All our religion, almost all our arts, almost all that sets us above savages, has come to us from the shores of the Mediterranean.' We can add to that list of empires, starting with the civilised court of Byzantium and progressing through the Renaissance to the legacy of the Papacy in the West and the last glimmer of the Ottoman empire in the East. Monuments from all the ages of man abound on the shores of the Mediterranean, and for those to whom sailing also means getting to interesting places – this is the place.

2.3 Food

At first glance it might appear that there is no unifying factor in the cuisine and foods of different Mediterranean countries, but there is an underlying theme and that is climate. The classic definition of the Mediterranean climate, as the area between the northern limit of the olive tree and the northern limit of the palm grove, gives us the first element of this unity, the olive. The arid summers all but rule out pasture for cows and consequently their milk products. Butter, milk and cream rarely feature in the cuisine and are replaced by olive oil. Bread is used to mop up the olive oil from salads, meat and fish, and from the numerous other dishes covered liberally with it. Sauces using olive oil with tomato paste, onion, peppers, lemon, herbs and spices replace the butter and milk-based sauces found in northern countries. Yoghurt made from goat or sheep milk is used instead of cream, which is almost never found in sauces or desserts.

A second consequence resulting from the lack of pasture is the virtual absence of beef from the diet. In recent years cheap beef has been imported and substituted for the veal, goat and lamb which have been commonly used in Mediterranean dishes. The arid land cannot sustain mature cattle and so calves are eaten as veal. Sheep and goats can survive on the sparse vegetation that remains through the summer, and their milk is used instead of cows' milk to produce yoghurt and cheese, both of which last better in a hot climate than the milk itself.

As well as the olive, wheat and vines are cultivated all around the Mediterranean. It is hard to imagine how the desert sands in Libya and Tunisia once produced vast yields of wheat, but in the heyday of the Roman Empire what is now desert was the bread-basket of Italy. Today the wheat grown is not used exclusively for bread. The hard durum wheat for making pasta is cultivated extensively in the northern Mediterranean countries, and while the Italians are the pasta wizards of the world, many other countries also use pasta as a

Wars were fought and fleets built to bring the spices of the east to the west. Spice stall in Candarli in Turkey

staple in their diet. Pastry ranges from the fancy creations of the French to the paperthin *filo* pastry of the Greeks and Turks. *Filo* is wrapped around anything from cheese and spicy minced meat to nuts and raisins soaked in honey. Rice is also an important crop, used in the *paella* of Spain, *risotto* in Italy, and the *pilav* of Turkey and the Middle East.

These, then, are the essence of Mediterranean food. Olive oil replaces the dairy products used in northern Europe. Meat is basically veal, lamb and chicken. Seafood is prized, but costly. Bread, pastry, pasta and rice provide the staple carbohydrates. Seasonal vegetables – tomatoes, aubergines, green peppers, courgettes, cucumbers, carrots, lettuce, cabbage and the essential onion and garlic – provide the variety and colour found in the dishes. It all sounds rather basic compared to the dairy-based cuisine of the north, but as Arabella Boxer points out in her excellent *Mediterranean Cookbook*, the basic ingredients are combined in appealing and interesting ways and spiked with herbs and spices. 'Taken as a whole, the average diet of the Mediterranean countries, particularly in the east, is austere but supremely healthy. Based on grilled meat and fish, raw salads, bread, fruit, herbs and yoghurt, it provides a limited but to me very appealing diet. It would be hard to suffer a liver attack or a cardiac condition in a true Mediterranean area, for the animal fats consumed by the north Europeans and the Americans simply do not exist. The potential monotony of such a limited diet is offset by the use of

herbs on the northern shores of the Mediterranean, and spices in the south.'

The different countries around the Mediterranean have different preferences for the herbs and spices most commonly used. In the North African countries spices predominate: coriander, cumin, caraway and saffron are used in Egypt and the countries of the Mahgreb, Tunisia, Algeria and Morocco. Chilli peppers are also extensively used and are most often encountered in *harissa*, a sauce made of tomato paste and hot chilli peppers. It is usually toned down for the tender palate unaccustomed to its normal fiery strength. In Spain the centuries of Arab rule significantly affected the cuisine and spices are the important additives flavouring Spanish food. *Paella* would be incomplete without saffron to give it its distinctive flavour.

In France and Italy, herbs are the important flavouring. In *bouillabaisse*, a dish Arabella Boxer describes as 'more truly typical of the Mediterranean than any other', parsley, thyme, fennel and the bay leaf are used. French cuisine utilises herbs and also spices in a rich and varied way for which it is justly famous. In Italy basil and oregano are the favourites. In Greece oregano is supreme, along with the lemon. With everything from a lamb chop to *avgolimoni* sauce, the acid juice of the lemon imparts a unique taste to the food. In Turkey, the Middle Eastern preference for certain herbs becomes evident with parsley the favourite, closely followed by chervil and dill. In the Middle East parsley and mint are used in everything

15

from meat dishes to desserts.

Fish has traditionally been part of the Mediterranean diet and figures in the cuisine of all the countries around its shores. But lately it has become something of a luxury and prices, especially for shellfish and lobster, have rocketed. The reason has to do not so much with a depletion of fish stocks in the Mediterranean, but with the increased demand for fish by both local people and the increasing numbers of foreign tourists. This is a great shame as many countries, France and Italy especially, have novel and delicious fish dishes.

In recent years the exodus of sun-starved northerners to the shores of the Mediterranean has dented the traditional cuisine. In the popular tourist spots snack bars serve up hamburgers that taste like cardboard and miserly portions of cold chips. Pizza restaurants have sprung up from Gibraltar to Greece. And Coca Cola and Pepsi slug it out for the lion's share of the market from the Mahgreb to Syria. The traveller can ignore or embrace this food pollution according to his or her tastes. More insidious is the faking of food that is becoming more widespread as demand grows for expensive and popular dishes in a country. Food faking is easiest where rich sauces are used, such as in veal marsala and coq au vin, or in dishes where the main ingredient is mixed with other dominant ingredients such as lobster mornay and *bouillabaisse*. Pork and chicken can be used instead of the more expensive veal, monkfish instead of lobster, white fish for scampi, and a *bouillabaisse* made up from seafood leftovers. Most of such passing-off goes on in the restaurants of Spain, France and Italy, and tends to occur in the richer and more complicated dishes. Plainer fare is more difficult and less profitable to fake.

2.4 Wine

The Greeks and the Romans were both fond of a good tipple. Odysseus on his travels pined for what he described as 'the best of all occasions' when the guests and feasters were assembled and 'the wine steward draws wine from the mixing bowl to pour into each cup in turn'. The Romans were famous for their excessive feasts washed down with copious quantities of wine. Their love of wine was such that wherever Roman rule spread viticulture quickly followed, providing wine to slake the thirst of foot soldier and general alike. In this way the vine spread from a few isolated parts of the Mediterranean across to the far boundaries of the Roman Empire.

Wine in the Mediterranean varies tremendously in quality from one country to another. The Côtes du Rhône and Côtes du Provence of France can be superb and reasonably priced wines. The vin ordinaire has probably been blended with wine from Sicily, though the French vehemently deny it. Italy produces excellent wines and gives the best value for money in the cheaper range. The vino corriente of Spain is eminently drinkable, but Spain produces excellent quality wines as well, not to mention the fine sherries of Jerez, its distinctive brandy and good liqueurs.

As you move farther east to Croatia, Greece and Turkey the quality deteriorates. Yugoslavia produces some excellent white wines in the north, from Macedonia come some good reds, and in Turkey a few good reds can be found from the vineyards on the Aegean coast. To some extent this is changing as modern methods are introduced to the eastern Mediterranean. Greece in particular now produces some very good wines using a large number of grape varieties unfamiliar to those more used to French, Italian or Spanish wines. But overall the quality and consistency cannot match the wines of France and Italy. You can drink a bottle of excellent wine, order another identical bottle and find it virtually undrinkable. The ingredients and the enthusiasm are there, but not the expertise to turn the grapes into consistently good wine.

In North Africa the wines of Tunisia, Algeria and Morocco vary immensely and again are not consistent. When the French administered this part of the world they planted extensive vineyards and produced some good wine. After the French departed the vineyards deteriorated and the expertise to turn the grapes into good wine was, alas, lost. Some quaffable wine at reasonable prices is bottled, but don't expect the variety and consistency of the products from the countries directly across the Mediterranean.

Individual and distinctive wines such as the *retsina* of Greece can be an acquired taste. *Retsina* is made by adding pine resin to the wine during fermentation, giving it a distinctive resiny flavour described by some as imparting a taste not dissimilar to certain brands of turpentine; others consider it a unique tangy wine. You either like it or hate it. The ancient Greeks appear to have liked it, or perhaps all wine then tasted of resin. In ancient amphorae and wine jugs traces of pine resin have been found, and it may have been used to seal the containers to prevent the wine going off, imparting the unique sappy taste. At the other end of the Mediterranean, the blended wines of the Jerez region in Spain are known world-wide. The various sherries – more than just the familiar dry pale *fino*, dark nutty *amontillado*, and the sweeter *oloroso* and cream sherry – are produced from subtle blends of wines of different types and ages. They are made on the *solera* system, where some of the oldest wine is mixed with the next oldest and so on down to the new, so that the newest wine absorbs some of the flavour and character of the older ones.

In the oldest wine producing area in the world, you will have no difficulty finding wine of some description. There are few countries around the Mediterranean that don't produce large quantities of wine for their own consumption and some of it is excellent; and whatever its merits or demerits, it is all comparatively cheap.

Cheers, Santé, Yammas, Sharife, Saluté!

2.5 A short history of yachting in the Mediterranean

Such is our insular historical perspective that we like to think that yachting began with the restoration of the monarchy in 1660 and the pleasure craft of Charles II and his cronies, not in the warm waters of the Mediterranean some fifteen hundred years earlier. Certainly the word yacht from the Dutch 'jaghte' meaning a small, fast ship, was introduced in this period to describe the royal pleasure boats, but yachting in this sense and in the meaning it picked up later has been around for longer than this.

Royal yachts have been around since the Egyptians with the earliest known royal pleasure craft belonging to the Pharaoh Cheops. At around forty-four metres (143ft) he used it on the Nile and liked it so much he had it buried with him in the Great Pyramid at Giza. When the Ptolemies came along in the fourth century BC a whole fleet of royal yachts were built. Ptolemy IV had big ideas about the sort of royal pleasure craft he wanted and had a catamaran constructed that was ninety-two metres (300ft) long with a deck nearly fourteen metres (45ft) wide and what can only be described as a miniature palace eighteen and a half metres (60ft) high erected upon it. This construction was towed up and down the Nile so that Ptolemy IV could survey and rule his kingdom in some comfort and style when on the move.

For flair and dramatic effect none of the rulers of Egypt could top the performance of Cleopatra. When she was summoned to Tarsus by Antony, Cleopatra intended to create an entrance he wouldn't forget. Plutarch describes Cleopatra's approach to Tarsus in 41 BC:

'She came sailing up the Cyndus on a galley whose stern was golden; the sails were purple, and the oars were silver. These, in their motion, kept tune to the music of flutes and pipes and harps. The Queen, in the dress and character of Aphrodite, lay on a couch of gold brocade, as though in a picture, while about her were pretty boys, bedight like cupids, who fanned her, and maidens habited as nereids and graces, and some made as though they were rowing, while others busied them about the sails. All manner of sweet perfumes were wafted ashore from the ship, and on the shore thousands were gathered to behold her'.

Cleopatra invited Antony on board for dinner and from there on in he was captivated by the Egyptian Queen and they were rarely separated. They died together, after Antony failed to wrest the Roman Empire from Octavius.

The Roman Emperors showed the same predilection for royal pleasure craft as had the Egyptians. The demented Caligula had several, the largest of which was over sixty metres (200ft) long. It was a well made craft sheathed in lead to stop teredo and gribble getting at the planking, and boasted such amenities as dining halls, a garden, baths, a brothel, and private chambers. After Caligula was dispatched Nero continued the tradition of opulent royal craft with a resplendent gilt and ivory creation on which he held lavish banquets.

What of lesser mortals in this era of gradiose royal pleasure craft? It is likely that there were rich aristocrats around who had sailing yachts constructed or converted one of the small tubby trading boats for pleasure use. The problem is that nobody wrote about it, or if they did it was lost as happened to so many of the ancient works. That is except for one important exception. The first concrete reference we have of sailing for pleasure comes from the Roman poet Catullus.

Catullus is not widely read today, but in his time he instigated something of a revolution in poetic circles writing lyrical and passionate poems with a gut feeling to them, pungent epigrams that can still shock, and poems of descriptive verse that is both evocative and accurate. He was born around 84 BC and died at an early age in 54 BC. Catullus began writing when he was fifteen or sixteen, but the period describing his yachting endeavours occurred a few years before his death. His brother died in the Troad and Catullus went to visit his grave. While he was in Bithynia on the Asiatic shores of the Black Sea he decided, for whatever reasons, to have a yacht built.

> near Cytorus
> before you were a yacht
> you stood
> part of some wooded slope
> where the leaves speak continuously in sibilants together.
> Pontic Amastris
> Cytorus
> - stifled with box-wood -
> these things
> my boat affirms
> are common knowledge to you both.

He calls his yacht a 'bean-pod boat' and in common with most boat owners assets 'that she's been the fastest piece of timber under oar or sail afloat'. The sailing boats of this period looked much the same over a thousand year period - short and broad double-ender, a twenty metre boat would have had a beam of around six metres and carried a square sail on a stubby mast. Essentially they were not too far removed from the double-ended caique, the trehandiri, seen in Greece today. The sail was set on a yard nearly twice as long as the mast, the yard itself being constructed from two saplings lashed together and with a sheet from either end led back to the steering oars. The sail could be reefed by brailing it upwards to the yard in strong winds. Some of these boats also carried a small sail, the artemion, on a steep bowsprit, and in very strong winds this would have been the only sail up. It also aided stability downwind and would have helped with the boat on a broad reach. These boats could be rowed in a calm or into harbour, but they were not anywhere near as fast under oars as the sleek galleys of the time.

In his yacht Catullus sailed out of the Black Sea, through the Bosphorus and Dardanelles into the Aegean. Here he sailed to Rhodes and through the Cyclades and probably around the Peloponnesus where he turned north to sail up the Adriatic to the river Po.

> Call as witness
> the rough Dalmatian coast
> the little islands of the Cyclades
> Colossan Rhodes
> the savage Bosphorus
> the unpredictable surface of the Pontic Sea.

He then sailed up the Po and the Mincio to a short distance from Lake Garda. He must have had the yacht hauled overland because he describes her as lying under his villa at Sirmio on the lake:

Finally,
no claim on the protection of any sea god
on the long voyage up to this clear lake.

These things have all gone by.
Drawn up here
fathering quiet age.

Poem 4 transl. Peter Whigham

Catullus was not just a passenger on these trips. In various poems he accurately describes the winds, navigation, storms, and his boat in a manner only someone intimately acquainted with the sea could do. In this fragment he describes the afternoon breeze getting up in the Aegean:

Zephyr
flicks the flat water into ridge
with a morning puff,
the sloped waves
loiter musically,
later the wind rises
& they rise,
they multiply
they shed the sun's sea purple as they flee.

Poem 64 transl. Peter Whigham

And in this fragment reveals an awareness of the basics of navigation by the times of sunrise and sunset and the appearance of certain stars:

Who scans the bright machinery of the skies
& plots the hours of star-set & star-rise,
this or that planet as it earthward dips,
the coursing brightness of the sun's eclipse.

Poem 66 transl. Peter Whigham

Catullus died at Sirmio with his yacht drawn up on the shore of Lake Garda when he was only thirty years old. For over a thousand years his poetry was lost until the codex was discovered, so the story goes, wedging a wine barrel in Verona at the end of the thirteenth century. How many more works have been lost describing innocent pleasures on the water in those long ago times is something we will never know. Catullus himself would no doubt have made further voyages had he lived longer - he had that hunger to break loose and go travelling that a yachtsman needs.

Now spring burst
with warm airs
now the furor of March skies
retreats under Zephyrus...
and Catullus will forsake
these Phrygian fields
the sun-drenched farm-lands of Nicaea
& make for the resorts of Asia Minor,
the famous cities.
Now, the trepidation of departure
now lust of travel,
feet impatiently urging him to be gone.
Good friends, good-bye.

Poem 46 transl. Peter Whitham

Not until the nineteenth century do we again have a record of yachting in the Mediterranean. It is likely that in Byzantium, Venice, Genoa, and other centres of wealth in the intervening period, the aristocracy and rich eccentrics had sailing boats constructed and sailed them for pleasure, but there are no records of adventures such as those of Catullus.

We know, of course, that poor Shelley was drowned while sailing with friends in Italy. Percy Bysshe Shelley was at La Spezia and set out to sail to Leghorn with Edward Williams, a sailor Charles Vivian, and Captain Daniel Roberts who had built the boat. They arrived safely and five days later set out to sail back. A storm blew up in the evening and the boat was seen to sink off Viareggio, the bodies were washed ashore ten days later on 17 July 1822. Byron and Leigh Hunt who were in Leghorn hurried down and made the funeral arrangements, the bodies had to be burnt because of quarantine laws, and that is about as much as we know of Shelley's yachting endeavours or of Roberts who had the boat built. Byron himself liked boats but knew little about them, being as interested in the flamboyant captains and crew of the ships he chartered when in Greece as in the boats themselves.

In the middle and late nineteenth century the Victorians took to yachting in a big way. One of the first accounts of a yachting cruise is to be found in E. M. Grosvenor's *Narrative of a Yacht Voyage in the Mediterranean during the years 1840-41*. Grosvenor and his family cruised in the 217-ton RYS *The Dolphin* for a year exploring many of the harbours and islands from Gibraltar to Turkey. The Americans, always keen to visit decadent and ailing Europe, sailed a number of large yachts across to the Mediterranean, sometimes with odd notions about the object of the cruise. In 1816-17 George Crowninshield Jr sailed the opulent *Cleopatra's Barge* to the Mediterranean. George Jr was obsessed with Napoleon and intended in a mercy mission to convey Napoleon's wife, the Empress Marie Louise who was ensconced in Rome, to the erstwhile Emperor exiled on St Helena in the middle of the Atlantic. As it turned out Marie Louise was quite happy in Rome with a large part of the fortune amassed by Napoleon and a lover to help her spend it - she declined the offer and poor George Jr sailed back home where he died not long after. In 1835 Vanderbilt visited the Mediterranean in his paddle-wheel schooner, but was little impressed and returned home after a short stay and rarely ventured onto a yacht again. Not long afterwards the eccentric and extravagant newspaper owner, Gordon Bennet Jr, the man whose name became an exclamation for anything outrageous, cruised around Europe and the Mediterranean for an extended period. Bennet Jr's eccentricities became a by-word in his own time. He abhorred playing cards and would have his crew and passengers' baggage searched for any offending pack. If he found a pack of cards he extracted a sly revenge by taking out the four aces and throwing them away before returning the pack to the bag. He didn't like beards and no-one on board was allowed to have one. One of his newspaper editors who stubbornly refused to shave his beard off followed the boat from port to port until he finally resigned from the paper in disgust.

In one port when a troupe of actors came abroad he was so delighted with their performance that he sailed off with them and would not return until they had performed their entire repertoire.

Most visitors to the Mediterranean were rather more restrained than this. In 1895 *With the Yacht, Camera, and Cycle in the Mediterranean* by the Earl of Cavan was published. In it he details his voyage from Gibraltar to Turkey in the 200-ton schooner Roseneath and has reproduced a considerable number of remarkably crisp photographs. His book is typical of several of the period and reflects the ideas of the well-heeled aristocracy and what they considered to be the proper way to go cruising. These are the Earl's ideas on the proper yacht for such a cruise:

> Two or three strong, good masts, in proportion to the size of the vessel – masts, I mean, upon which leg of mutton sails of tanned or waterproof canvas could be set – will be necessary of course. . .These sails should give her a stability at sea, which the majority of our Mediterranean yachts sadly require. With so many interesting ports at easy distances the one from the other, the whole way between Gibraltar and Constantinople, there can be no reason for going at a speed exceeding ten knots, which speed could easily be obtained under steam and sail. The dislike to going afloat would thus be much lessened in the minds of those who may not be good sailors, their comfort also would be enormously increased, and providing that time is not of overwhelming importance, I am certain that owners at the end of their cruise, will feel more satisfied with yachts such as I have described, than they could be with any greyhound-built vessel, of which such numbers are now to be seen in the Mediterranean.
>
> . . .As to the size of the vessel, she should certainly not be less than 150 tons. As to how large she should be, must, of course, depend upon the means at the disposal of the owner, and the purposes for which he requires her.

In the Edwardian era more yachts began to make the voyage to the Mediterranean and although many of these were still in the category of little ships, there were numbers of smaller yachts under twenty tons as well. Many of the larger yachts of this era are still around, cared for by loving owners with lots of money or earning their keep as luxury charter yachts. In between the wars it was popular to combine a shooting and yachting expedition, woodcock and deer in Albania, wildfowl in Greece, boar in Turkey, but the Earl of Cavan was able to advise that 'Lions cannot now be found within a day's rail of any yacht anchorage in North Africa' and 'they will be unusually lucky if they return with one specimen'.

After the Second World War an increasing number of small yachts began to cruise the Mediterranean. Small yachts had been shown to be capable of extended voyages with the exploits of Humphrey Barton in *Vertue XXVI* and Adlard Coles in *Cohoe*. The Mediterranean had its own unsung heroes with the voyages of A. G. H. Macpherson in *Driac II* before the war and the more relaxed cruises of Ernle Bradford in his Dutch botter *Mother Goose* after the war. Right up until the Sixties a voyage to the Mediterranean was an adventure equal to a voyage to the South Seas or the Caribbean, not in distance and days at sea, but in the sense of an adventure that offered excitement and the unknown. The western Mediterranean was barely known and the eastern Mediterranean little visited at all.

In the late Sixties and into the Seventies the number of charter boats began to gradually increase. At first most of these were yachts, large and small, with a skipper and crew, but smaller boats for adventurous bareboat charter also began to make an appearance. In the 1970s the Yacht Cruising Association put the first flotilla yachts in Greece. The concept of flotilla sailing was an immediate success and flotilla holidays spread to other parts of Greece, Yugoslavia, Turkey, Italy, France, Spain and eventually back to England from whence the idea had originated. More and more private yachts began to cruise around the Mediterranean and in a sense it has become the playground of northern Europe.

It is easy to get the impression that the Mediterranean is full to the brim with yachts, both charter and private. It is not. In some areas you will sail for days without seeing another yacht and far from feeling claustrophobic, you will begin to look around for another yacht for company and to swap experiences with over a drink or two. Sail out of high season and you have the Mediterranean virtually to yourself. Around the highly populated areas and popular charter spots you will see large numbers of yachts, but get away from them and the indented coast and large numbers of islands provide a sanctuary for those who want to explore and discover a deserted cove or two.

2.6 Guidebooks

Yachting pilot books and guides often contain a large amount of information unrelated to finding and getting into harbours or anchorages: information about the history and customs of a place, about its character and 'feel', the local industry and agriculture, cuisine, the sort of things that might attract one there in preference to another place or that might be interesting anyway. If such books don't, they should; however any such peripheral information must be squeezed in with the essential navigation and pilotage data, and some tend to reflect the authors' tastes. Most of us want a more detailed account of a country or place. Guide books offering such information exist for all of the Mediterranean countries, but like all books some are to be savoured while some are just plain bad at the job they purport to do.

For solid background information on things historical and archaeological the Blue Guides from A & C Black provide reams of information though some of it can be a bit stodgy. Footprint Guides are expanding their coverage of Mediterranean countries and cities but at present only do Spain and Turkey. Others are planned in the near future and these guides are hard to beat for dependable all-round information. The Rough Guides have moved away from their backpacking origins and now have more information on things to do and see. They also have some of the best information on getting around, local sights and sounds and eating out. The old Collins Companion Guides are now being updated and republished. Each of these was written by well-travelled writers in the respective countries and some of them are outstanding on the history and geography of an area. Apart from these series of books, there are often one-off guides that provide some of the best information on a particular country and its people. For these you will have to do a little research, but the sort of books I am thinking of are Patrick Leigh Fermor's books on Greece, Lord Kinross on Turkey, and Norman Lewis on Italy. These are not guidebooks as such, but they often give an insight into a country and its culture that the guide book cannot. As well as writers in this century, it can be interesting to read classic accounts by 19th century travellers in the Mediterranean. Many of these are being reissued, and apart from describing a place as it was a hundred or so years ago, a lot of these books are amusing and erudite and still a pleasure to read. Foremost among these is Kinglake's *Eothen*, Curzon's *Visit to the Monasteries in the Levant*, and Morritt's *A Grand Tour*.

There are a number of classic accounts of sailing in the Mediterranean. Ernle Bradford cruised around after the Second World War and wrote a number of books including *Ulysses Found*, an account of the geographical places that can still be identified as those described in Homer. Immediately after the war George Millar sailed through the French canals and on to Greece, and in *Isabel and the Sea* he describes the terrible damage inflicted on the Mediterranean countries during the war. More recently, Tim Severin constructed a replica of a Homeric scouting galley and retraced the path of Jason and the Argonauts in search of the golden fleece and recently the voyage of Ulysses on his way home from the Trojan War.

In the end, the sort of guidebooks you get will reflect your interests and the amount of time you are going to stay in a country. 'The only useful guidebook', Aldous Huxley was fond of saying, 'will be the one which he himself has written', but given that few of us have the ability or the inclination to do this, we must be content with criticising those that already exist. The longer you are in a country and the more interested you become in it, inevitably the more books you will accumulate on its different facets. One of the enduring problems I have on my boat is finding room for all the books I like to have around me, old friends and new finds; and the more familiar one becomes with all the sources of information on a place, the easier it is to flip through a new guidebook and dismiss it – or avidly pull out your wallet to buy a copy.

There are still places where you can get off the beaten track. Agothonisi in Greece

3. Yachtsman's seven-language dictionary

English	Spanish	French	Italian	Greek	Turkish	German
3.1 DIRECTIONS						
East	Este	Est	Est	Anatolokos	Doğu	Ost
North	Norte	Nord	Nord	Vorios	Kuzey	Nord
South	Sur	Sud	Sud	Notios	Güney	Süd
West	Oeste	Ouest	Ovest	Dhitikos	Bati	West
3.2 NAVIGATION						
Ahead	Avante	En avant	Avanti	Proso	Ileri	Voraus
Astern	Atrás	En arrière	Indietro	Anapoda	Tornistan	Zurück
Binoculars	Gemelos, prismáticos	Jumelles	Binocoli	Kialia	Dürbün	Fernglas, Doppelglas
Call sign	Señal de llamada	Indicatif	Nominativo di chiamata		Çağri işareti	Rufzeichen
Chart	Carta náutica	Carte marine	Carta	Naftikos hartis	Deniz haritasi	Seekarten
Chart table	Mesa de cartas	Table à cartes	Tavolo da carteggio		Harita masasi	Kartentisch
Compass	Compas, aguja naútica	Compas	Bussola	Pixida	Pusula	Kompaß
Course	Rumbo	Cap, route	Rotta	Poria	Rota	Kurs
Current	Corriente	Courant	Corrente	Revma	Akinti	Strom
Degree	Grado	Degré	Grado	Mira	Derece	Grad
Depth	Fondo, profundidad	Profondeur	Profondità	Vathos	Derinlik	Tiefe
Deviation	Desvio	Déviation	Deviazione	Parectopi	Deviyasyon, Arzi sapma	Deviation
Dividers	Compas de puntas	Pointes sèches	Compasso a punte fisse	Diavitis	Pergel	Kartenzirkel
Echo sounder	Sonda acústica	Echo sondeur	Scandalaglio ultra-sonoro	Vythometro	Iskandil	Echolot
Frequency	Frecuencia	Fréquence	Frequenza	Synotita	Frekans	Frequenz
Hand bearing compass	Aguja de marcar	Compas de relèvement	Bussoletta portatile per rilevamenti		Kerteriz pusulasi	Handpeilkompaß
Latitude	Latitud	Latitude	Latitudine	Yeografico platos	Enlem	Breite
Leading line	Enfilación	Alignement	Allineamento	Eftigramissi	Geçiş hatti	Leitlinie
Lights	Luces	Feux	Segnalamente luminoso	Fota	Fenerler	Leuchtfeuer
List of lights	Cuaderno de faros	Livre des phares	Elenco fari		Fenerler el kitabi	Leuchtfeuerver-zeichnis
Patent log	Cordera de patente	Loch enregistreur	Solcometro brevettato	Dromometro	Paraketa	Patentlog
Longitude	Longitud	Longitude	Longitudine	Yeografico mikos	Boylam	Länge
Nautical almanac	Almanaque náutico	Almanach nautique	Effemeridi nautiche	Naftico almanac	Notik almanak	Nautischer Almanach
Mile	Milla	Mille	Miglio	Milion	Deniz mili	Meile
Operating time	Hora de servicio	Heures d'émissions	Orario di lavoro	Hronos liturgias	Servis saati	Sendezeit
Parallel ruler	Regla de paralelas	Règles parallèles	Righello per parallelo	Diparallios	Paralel cetvel	Parallellineal
Pilotage instructions	Derrotero	Instructions Nautiques	Portolano	Pilotos	Deniz el kitabi	Seehandbuch
Port	Babor	Bâbord	Sinistra	Aristera	Iskele	Backbord
Protractor	Transportador	Rapporteur	Goniometro	Mirognomonio	Açiölçer	Winkelmesser
Radiobeacon	Radiofaro	Radiophare	Radiofaro	Radiofaros	Radyo bikin	Funkfeuer
Radio direction finder	Radio-goniometro	Radiogoniomètre	Radiogonometro	Radiogoniometro	Radyogonyometre	Funkpeiler
Radio receiver	Receptor de radio	Poste récepteur	Radioricevitore	Radiofono	Radyo alicisi	Empfangsgerät
Radio station	Estación de radio difusión	Station d'émission	Stazione radio trasmittente	Radiofonikos stathmos	Radyo vericisi	Rundfunksender
Radio telephone	Radio teléfono	Radio-téléphone	Radiotelefono	Radiotilephono	Radyotelefon	Sprechfunkgerät
Sextant	Sextante	Sextant	Sestante	Exandas	Sekstant	Sextant
Starboard	Estribor	Tribord	Dritta	Dexia	Sancak	Steuerbord
Tide	Marea	Marée	Marea	Palirria	Gelgit, med ve cezir	Die Gezeiten
Variation	Variación	Déclinaison	Declinazione	Apodisi	Varyasyon, Tabii sapma	Missweisung
Wind abeam	Viento de través	Vent de travers	Vento a mezza nave o al traverso	Plevzikos anemos	Apaz rüzgar	Halber Wind
3.3 CHART TERMS						
Anchorage	Fondeadero	Mouillage	Ancoraggio	Angirovolion	Demiryeri	Ankerplatz
Bay	Bahia	Baie	Baia	Ormos	Körfez	Bucht
Beach	Playa	Plage	Spiaggia	Paralia	Kumsal	Strand
Beacon	Baliza	Balise	Meda	Simadura	Nişan	Bake
Big	Grande	Grand	Grande	Megalos	Büyük	Groß
Bight, cove, creek	Cala, caleta	Anse, baie	Cala, insenatura	Angali	Bük, Koy	Bucht
Bridge	Puente	Pont	Ponte	Yefira	Köprü	Brücke
Buoy	Boya	Bouée	Boa	Simandir	Şamandira	Tonne
Cape	Cabo	Cap	Capo	Miti, pounda	Burun	Kap
Castle, fort	Castillo	Château	Castello	Kastron	Hisar	Schloß
Channel	Canal	Chenal	Canale	Avlax	Yol	Fahrwasser
Church	Iglesia	Eglise	Chiesa	Moni	Kilise	Kirche
City	Ciudad	Ville	Città	Polis	Şehir	Stadt
Cliff	Acantilado	Falaise	Scogliera	Gremmos	Sarp	Steil
Deep	Profundo, hondo	Profond	Profondo	Vathi	Derin	Tief
Drinking water	Agua potable	Eau potable	Acqua potabile	Nero	Su	Trinkwasser
Flag	Bandera	Pavillon	Bandiera	Simea	Sancak	Flagge
Forest	Bosque	Forêt	Foresta	Dasos	Orman	Wald
Gulf	Golfo	Golfe	Golfo	Kolpos	Körfez	Golf

English	Spanish	French	Italian	Greek	Turkish	German
Harbour, port	Puerto, darsena de yates	Port, bassin pour yachts	Porto, porticciolo per yachts	Porto, skala Limani	Liman	Hafen
Headland	Promontorio	Promontoire	Promontorio	Akrotirion	Burun	Vorgebirge
Hill	Colina	Colline	Collina	Lofos	Tepe	Hügel
Island	Isla	Ile	Isola	Nisos, nisia	Ada(si), Adalar(i)	Insel
Lake	Lago, laguna	Bras de mer, lac	Lago	Limni	Göl	See, Binnensee
Lighthouse	Faro, fanal	Phare	Faro	Faros	Deniz feneri, Fener	Leuchtturm
Marsh	Marisma	Marais, marécage	Pantano, acquitrino	Limni	Balçik	Sumpf
Mole	Muelle	Môle	Molo	Molos	Mendirek, Set	Mole
Mountain	Monte	Montagne, mont	Montagna	Oros	Dağ	Berg
Mouth	Desembocadura	Embouchure	Bocca, foce	Bucca	Ağiz	Mündung
Mud	Fango	Vase	Fango	Laspi	Çamur, Balçik	Schlick
Overfalls	Escarceos	Remous	Frangenti di marea	Yfalos	Girdap, Anafor	Stromkabbelung
Peninsula	Península	Péninsule	Penisola	Khersonisos	Yarimada(si)	Halbinsel
Quay	Muelle	Quai	Banchina	Skala	Iskele	Kai
Reef	Arrecife	Récif	Scogliera	Skopelos	Döküntü, kaya(si)	Riff
River	Rio	Rivière, fleuve	Fiume	Potamos	Nehir, nehri	Fluß, Strom
Rocks	Rocas	Rochers	Scogli	Petra, vrakhos	Kaya, Kaya(si)	Klippe
Sandspit	Banco de arena, bajio	Banc de sable	Secca		Topuk	
Sandbank						
Sea	Mar	Mer	Mare	Pelago, thalassas	Deniz	See, Meer
Shoal	Bajo	Haut-fond	Basso fondale, secca	Avathi	Siğlik	Untiefe
Small	Pequeño	Petit	Piccolo	Mikros	Küçük	Klein
Tower	Torre	Tour	Torre	Pirgos	Kule	Turm
Strait	Estrecho	Détroit	Stretto, bocche	Stena	Boğaz	Meerenge
Village	Pueblo	Village	Villaggio	Kluara (Chora)	Köy(ü)	Dorf
Wind	Viento	Vent	Vento	Anemos	Rüzgar	Wind

3.4 LIGHT CHARACTERISTICS

English	Spanish	French	Italian	Greek	Turkish	German
F.	F.	Fixe	Fissa		Sabit	F.
Oc.	Oc.	Occ.	Int.		Hüsuflu	Ubr.
Iso	Iso./Isof	Iso	–		Izofaz	Glt.
Fl	D.	É	Lam.		Çakarli	Blz/Glk
Q	Ct.	Scint	Sc.		Seri	Fkl.
IQ	Gp.Ct.	Scint.dis	Sc.Int		Kesintili seri	Fkl.unt.
Al	Alt	Alt.	Alt.		Değiştiren	Wchs.
Oc(..)	Gp.Oc. Gr.Oc.	...Occ.	Int.(..)		Hüsuflu (...)	Urb.(...)Urb.Grp.
Fl(..)	Gp.D.	...É	Lam.(..)		Çakarli(...)	Blz.(...)/Blk.(...) Blz.Grp../Blk.Grp.
Mo	Mo	–	–		Mors Kod	Mo
FFl	F.D.	Fixe É	F.lam.		Sabit çakarli	F.& Blz.Mi.
FFl(..)	F.Gp. D./Gp.Dyf	Fixe...É	F.lam.(..)		Sabit çakarli(...)	F.& Blz.(...)Mi.

3.5 IN HARBOUR

English	Spanish	French	Italian	Greek	Turkish	German
Anchoring prohibited Ankern	Fondeadero prohibido	Défense de mouiller	Divieto d'ancoraggio	Apagorevete i agyrvolia	yasaktir	Demirlemek verboten
Customs office	Aduana	Bureau de douane	Ufficio doganale	Telonio	Gümrük Müdürlüğü	Zollamt
Harbour master	Capitán de puerto	Capitaine de port	Capitano del porto	Limenarchis	Liman Başkani	Hafenkapitän
Harbour master's office	Comandancia , capitanía de puerto	Bureau du capitaine de port	Capitaneria di porto	Grafio limenarchi	Liman Başkanliği	Büro des Hafenkapitäns
Immigration officer	Official de imigración	Agent du service de l'immigration	Controllo passaporti	Axiomaticos metanastefsis	Pasaport polisi	Beamter der Passkontrolle
Mooring place	Amarradero	Point d'accostage	Posto d'ormeggio	Destres	Iskele	Festmacheplatz
Prohibited area	Zona prohibida	Zone interdite	Zona vietata	Apagorevmeni periohi	Yasak Bölge	Verbotenes Gebiet

3.6 SHIP'S PAPERS

English	Spanish	French	Italian	Greek	Turkish	German
Certificate of registry	Patente de navegación	Acte de francisation	Certificato di classificazione	Niologio	Ruhsat belgesi	Registrierungs-Zertifikat
Customs clearance	Despacho de aduana	Dédouanement	Pratica di sdoganamento	Teloniakes diatyposis	Gümrük işlemi	Zollabfertigung
Insurance certificate	Póliza de seguro	Certificat d'assurance	Certificato d'assicurazione	Asfalia	Sigorta poliçesi	Versicherungs-police
Passport	Passaporte	Passeport	Passaporto	Diavatirio	Pasaport	Reisepaß
Ship's log	Cuaderno de bitácoro	Livre de bord	Giornale di chiesuola	Imerologio pliou	Gemi jurnali	Schiffstagebuch, Logbuch

3.7 WEATHER TERMS

English	Spanish	French	Italian	Greek	Turkish	German
Anticyclone, high	Anticiclón, alta	Anticylone, haut	Anticiclone	Anticyclonas, ypsilo	Yüksek basinç	Hoch
Area	Región	Région, zone	Regione, zona	Periohi	Alan(i)	Gebiet
Changeable	Variable	Variable	Variabile	Metarlitos	Değişken	Wechselhaft
Deepen	Intensificación	Se creuser	Approfondirsi	Vathy	Derinleşen	Sich vertiefen
Depression, low	Depresión	Dépression, bas	Depressione	Varometrico hamilo	Alçak basinç	Depression, Tief
Fine	Tranquilo, despejado	Beau temps	Bello	Ethrios	Açik	Heiter, schön
Front, cold	Frente frío	Front froid	Fronte freddo	Psihro metopo	Soğuk cephe	Kaltfront
Front, warm	Frente calido	Front chaud	Fronte caldo	Thermo metopo	Sicak cephe	Warmfront
High-pressure area	Zona de alta presión	Zone de haute pression	Area di alta pressione	Periohi ypsilon pieseon	Yüksek basinç alani	Hochdruckgebiet
Low-pressure area	Zona de baja presión	Zone de basse pression	Area di bassa pressione	Periohi haxilon pieseon	Alçak basinç alani	Tiefdruckgebiet
Occlusion	Oclusión	Occlusion	Occlusione	Sísfixi	Kapali cephe, Oklüzyon	Okklusion
Quickly	Rápidamente	Rapidement	Rapidamente	Grigora	Hizli, Hizla	Schnell, rasch
Ridge	Dorsal, cresta	Crête	Cresta	Korifi	Sirt	Rücken
Rise/Drop	Subida/Caída	Hausse/Chute	Salita/discesa	Anerhete/Katerhete	Yükselme	Zunahme/Sturz

English	Spanish	French	Italian	Greek	Turkish	German
Settled	Sostenido, asentado	Temps établi, stable	Stabile	Ametarlitos	Istikrarlï	Bestandig
Slowly	Lentamente	Lentement	Lentamente	Arga	Yavaş	Langsam
Spreading	Extendiendo	S'étalant, s'étentant	Allargantesi, que	Diasparta	Yayilan, yayilmakta si sparge	Sich ausbreitend
Stationary	Estacionario	Stationnaire	Stazionario	Stasimo	Sabit	Stationär
Steady	Fijo, constante	Stable	Costante	Stathero	Devamli	Gleichbleibend
To Rise/Fall	Subir/Bajar	Monter/Baisser	Salire/discendere	Sikono/ Ripto	Düşme	Steigen/fallen
Temperature	Temperatura	Température	Temperatura	Thermocrassia	Isi	Temperatur
Trough	Vaguada	Creux	Saccatura di bassa pressione	Kilia	Çanak	Trog, Ausläufer
Velocity	Velocidad	Vitesse	Velocità	Tahitita	Hiz	Geschwindigkeit
Weather forecast	Previsión meteorológica	Prévisions météo	Previsioni meteo	Provlepsi kerou	Hava tahmini	Wettervor- hersage

SKY

English	Spanish	French	Italian	Greek	Turkish	German
Clear sky	Claro, despejado	Pur, clair, dégagé	Cielo chiaro, sereno	Ethrios	Açik gökyüzü	Wolkenlos, klarer Himmel
Cloudy	Nubloso	Nuageux	Nuvoloso	Synefiasmenos	Bulutlu	Bewölkt, wolkig
High cloud	Nubes altas	Nuages hauts, élevés	Nubi alte	Ypsili synefia	Yüksek bulut	Hohe Wolken
Low cloud	Nubes bajas	Nuages bas	Nubi basse	Hamili synefia	Alçak bulut	Niedrige Wolken
Overcast	Cubierto	Couvert	Coperto	Katholiki synefia	Kapali	Bedeckt

BEAUFORT SCALE

English	Spanish	French	Italian	Greek	Turkish	German
Calm	Calma	Calme	Calma	Apnia	Sakin	Windstille
Fresh breeze	Fresquito	Bonne brise	Vento teso	Labros	Frişka rüzgar	Frische Brise
Gale	Duro	Coup de vent	Burrasca	Thyelodis	Firtina	Stürmischer Wind
Gentle breeze	Flojo	Petite brise	Brezza tesa	Leptos	Hafif rüzgar	Schwache Brise
Hurricane	Huracán	Ouragan	Uragano	Typhonas	Tayfun, Kasirga	Orkan
Light air	Ventolina	Très légère brise	Bava di vento	Ypopneon	Hafif esinti	Leiser Zug
Light breeze	Flojito	Légère brise	Brezza leggera	Asthenis	Çok hafif rüzgar	Leichte Brise
Moderate breeze	Bonancible	Jolie brise	Vento moderato	Metrios	Mutedil rüzgar	Mäßige Brise
Near gale	Frescachón	Grand frais	Vento forte	Poly dynatos	Firtinaya yakin rüzgar	Steifer Wind
Storm	Temporal	Tempête	Tempesta	Dynati thyela	Çok şiddetli firtina	Schwerer Sturm
Strong breeze	Fresco	Vent frais	Vento fresco	Dynatos anemos	Kuvvetli rüzgar	Starker Wind
Strong gale	Muy duro	Fort coup de vent	Burrasca forte	Thyela	Şiddetli firtina	Sturm
Violent storm	Borrasca	Violente tempête	Tempesta violenta	Sfothri thyela	Aşiri şiddetli firtina	Orkanartiger Sturm

VISIBILITY

English	Spanish	French	Italian	Greek	Turkish	German
Fog	Niebla	Brouillard	Nebbia	Omihli	Sis	Nebel
Good	Buena	Bonne	Buona	Kali	Iyi	Gut
Haze	Calima	Brume de beau temps, brume sèche	Foschia	Xiri Ahlis	Hafif puslu	Dunst
Mist	Neblina	Brume légère, mouillée	Caligine	Ygri Ahlis	Pus	Feuchter Dunst, diesig
Moderate	Regular	Médiocre, réduite	Discreta	Metria	Orta	Mittel
Poor	Mala	Mauvaise	Cattiva	Periorismeni	Kötü	Schlecht

WIND

English	Spanish	French	Italian	Greek	Turkish	German
Back	Rola contra las manillas del reloj	Adonner (dans le sens contraire des éguilles d'une montre)	Girare del vento in senso antiorario	Trofi	Saat yelkovaninin tersine dirisa etmek	Zurückdrehen, krimpen
Decreasing, Moderating	Disminuyendo	Décroissant	Che cala, che diminuisce	Metriazete	Gerilemek	Abnehmend
Drop, abate	Disminuir	Tomber, diminuer	Caduta, attenuazione de force	Kopazi	Mayna etmek	Nachlassen
Gust	Racha	Rafale	Raffica	Ripi	Sağnak	Windstoß
Increasing, freshening	Aumentando	Fraîchissant	In aumento, che aumenta	Freskari	Sertlemek	Zunehmend
Land breeze	Terral	Brise de terre	Brezza di terra	Apogia Avra	Gece rüzgari	Ablandige Brise, Landbrise
Prevailing wind	Viento dominante	Vent dominant	Vento predominante	Epikratun Anemos	Hakim rüzgar	Vorherrschender Wind
Sea breeze	Brisa de mar, virazón	Brise de mer	Brezza di mare	Thalassia Avra	Imbat	Seebrise
Squall	Turbonada	Grain	Groppo	Lelapa	Bora	Bö
Veer	Rola con las manillas del reloj	Virer au...(dans le sans des éguilles d'une montre)	Girare del vento in senso orario	Trofi	Saat yelkovani yönünde dirisa etmek	Rechtsdrehen, ausschießen

SEA

English	Spanish	French	Italian	Greek	Turkish	German
Breaking seas	Rompientes	Lames déferlantes	Frangenti	Trikimiodis	Çatlak, Kirilan dalga	Brechende Seen
Calm	Calma	Plate, calme	Calmo	Iremi	Sakin	Glatt, ruhig
Ripples	Mar rizada	Vaguelettes, rides	Ondulato, increspato	Ritida	Dalgacik	Gekräuselt
Rough sea	Picada	Grosse mer, mer agitée	Mare molto agitato	Taragmeni	Kaba dalga	Große See
Short	Mar corta	Lames courtes	Mare corto	Vrahia	Kisa	Kurz
Steep	Mar gruesa	Mer creuse	Onde alte		Dik	Steil
Swell	Mar de leva, de fondo	Houle	Mare morto o lungo	Apothalassia	Soluğan, Ölü deniz	Dünung
Trough	Seno	Creux	Gola, Solco	Kilia	Dalga çukuru	Wellental
Waves	Olas	Vagues, ondes, lames	Onde	Kymata	Dalga	Wellen, Seen

English	Spanish	French	Italian	Greek	Turkish	German
WEATHER CONDITIONS						
Dry	Seco	Sec	Secco	Xyros	Kuru	Trocken
Hail	Granizada	Grêle	Grandine	Halazi	Dolu	Hagel
Rain	Lluvia	Pluie	Pioggia	Vrohi	Yağmur	Regen
Shower	Aguacero	Averse	Rovescio, acquazzone	Neropondi	Sağnak	Schauer
Sleet	Aguanieve	Neige fondue	Pioggia ghiacciata	Hiononero	Karla karişik yağmur	Schneeregen
Snow	Nieve	Neige	Neve	Hioni	Kar	Schnee
Thunderstorm	Tempestad, borrasca	Orage	Temporale	Kategida	Bora	Gewitter
Wet	Húmedo	Humide	Umido	Ygros	Islak	Naß
3.8 BOAT TYPES						
Bermudian ketch	Queche bermudo	Ketch bermudien	Ketch a vela Marconi		Keç	Ketsch
Bermudian sloop	Balandro de Bermudas	Sloop bermudien	Sloop a vela Marconi		Slup	Slup
Bermudian yawl	Balandro de baticulo	Yawl bermudien	Yawl a vela Marconi		Yol	Yawl
Cruiser	Yate crucero	Bateau de croisière	Barca da crociera	Cruiseroplio	Gezi teknesi	Fahrtenyacht
Dinghy	Bote, chinchorro	Canot, bateau de sauvetage	Dinghy	Fuskoti varka	Dingi, servis botu	Dingi, Beiboot
Fishing boat	Barca de pesca	Bateau de pêche	Barca da pesca	Psarathiko	Balikçi teknesi	Fisherboot
Gaff cutter	Cachemarin	Cotre franc, aurique	Cutter con randa e picco		Randa kotra	Gaffelkutter
Launch	Lancha	Vedette	Lancia	Larncha	Işkampavya, servis botu	Barkasse
Life boat	Bote salvavidas	Canot, bateau de sauvetage	Scialuppa di salvataggio	Sossivios lemvos	Filika	Rettungsboot
Masthead cutter	Balandra de mastelero	Cotre en tête de mât	Cutter con fiocco in testa d'albero		Markoni kotra	Kutter mit Hochtakelung
Merchant vessel	Buque mercante	Navire marchand	Nave mercantile	Eborrico scafos	Ticaret gemisi	Handelsschiff
Motor cruiser	Motora	Croiseur à moteur	Barca a motore		Motoryat	Motorkreuzer
Motor sailer	Moto-velero	Bateau mixte	Veliere a motore	Istorforo me mechani	Motorlu ve yelkenli yat	Motorsegler
Ocean racer	Yate de regatas océanica	Bateau de course, de croisière	Barca da regata oceanica	Aniktis thallasas	Açikdeniz yariş teknesi	Hochseerenn-yacht
Pilot boat	Bote del práctico	Bateau pilote	Pilotina, barca del pilota	Pilotina	Pilot teknesi	Lotsenboot
Staysail schooner	Goleta a la americana	Goélette à voile d'étai	Shooner a vele di taglio		Velena uskuna	Stagsegel-schoner
Tanker	Petrolero	Bateau citerne	La nave cisterna	Dexamenoplio	Tanker	Tanker, Tankschiff
Tug	Remolcador	Remorqueur	Rimorchiatore	Rymulko	Romörkör	Schlepper
Yacht	Yate	Yacht	Yacht	Thalamigos	Yat	Yacht
3.9 SAILS AND RIGS						
Batten pocket	Bolsa del sable	Etui ou gaine de latte	Guaina per stecca	Jepi	Balen cebi	Lattentasche
Bolt, rope	Relinga	Ralingue	Gratile		Gradin halati	Liektau
Boom	Botavara	Bôme	Boma		Bumba, maça	Baum
Bottle screw, turnbuckle	Tensor	Ridoir	Arridatoio, tendisartie	Matsa entatiras	Liftin uskur	Wantenspanner
Chain plate	Cadenote	Cadène	Landa	Kadena portousi	Larmo demiri	Rüsteisen, Pütting
Clew	Puño de escota	Point d'écoute	Bugna		Iskota yakasi	Schothorn
Collar	Encapilladura	Jupe	Collare		Direk çemberi	Mastkragen
Cringle	Garrucho de cabo	Anneau, patte	Brancarella		Matafiyon	Legel
Crosstrees	Crucetas	Barres de flèche	Crocette basse	Stavros	Gurcatalar	Saling
Crutch, gallows	Posa botavara	Support de bôme, portique	Sostegno boma, forcola, forcaccia		Makas	Baumbock, Baumstütze
Diamonds	Losange	Losanges	Strallinggaggi			Diamantwanten
Downhaul	Cargadera	Hale-bas	Carica-basso		Gargari halati	Halsstreckertalje
Fisherman staysail	Vela alta de estay	Voile d'étai de flèche	Vela di strallo 'Fisherman'		Mizan velenasi	Besanstagsegel
Foot	Pujamen	Bordure	Base o piede	Podia	Altabaşo yakasi	Unterliek
Fore and aft sail	Vela cuchillo	Voile longitudinale	Vela di taglio		Sübye arma	Schratsegel
Forestay, jib stay	Estay de proa	Etai avant ou de trinquette, draille	Stallo di prora		Baş istiralya	Vorstag, Fockstag
Genoa	Génova	Génois	Genova	Flokos No1	Cenova	Genua, Kreuzballon
Genoa staysail	Foque balón	Foc ballon	Trinchettina		Balon trinket	Raumballon
Gunter	Vela de cortina, guaira	Houari	Vela alla portoghese		Sürme pena	Huari, Steilgaffel-takelung
Halyard	Driza	Drisse	Drizza	Mantari	Mandar, Kandilisa	Fall
Head	Puño de driza	Point de drisse	Antennale		Pik yakasi	Kopf
Headboard	Tabla de gratil	Planche de tête	Tavoletta		Pik takviyesi	Kopfbrett
Headsail	Foque, vela de proa	Voile d'avant	Vela di prora		Flok	Vorsegel
Horse	Pie de gallo	Barre d'écoute	Barra o ferroguida di scotta		Iskota arabasi	Leitwagen
Hounds	Cacholas de un palo	Jottereaux, capelage	Intelaiature di supporto		Direk mauna yataklari	Mastbacken
Jib	Foque	Foc	Fiocco	Ergathis	Flok	Klüver
Jumper stay	Estay de boza	Etai de guignol	Stallinggaggi		Karanfil	Jumpstag
Jumper struts	Contrete	Guignol	Crocette alte		Karanfil gurcatasi	Jumpstagspreize
Kicking strap, vang	Trapa	Hale-bas de bôme	Ostino, ritenuta	Kratitiris	Bumba kasari	Baumniederholer

English	Spanish	French	Italian	Greek	Turkish	German
Leech, leechline	Baluma, ánima de chute	Chute, hale-bas	Balumina e tirante della balumina	Krifo	Güngörmez yakasi	Achterliek Regulierleine
Luff	Gratil	Guindant, envergure	Lato d'inferitura	Granti	Orsa yakasi	Vorliek
Luff wire	Relinga de envergue	Ralingue d'acier	Tirante della ralinga	Tiranta stogranti	Orsa teli	Drahtvorliek
Lugsail	Vela cangreja, al tercio	Voile à bourcet, au tiers	Vela al quarto o al terzo		Kavançali seren yelkeni	Luggersegel
Main staysail	Vela de estay mayor	Grand-voile d'étai	Strallo di maestra		Grandi velenasi	Großstagsegel
Mainsail	Vela mayor	Grand-voile	Vela maestra, randa	Maistra	Ana yelken	Großsegel
Mast	Palo	Mât	Albero	Katarti	Direk	Mast
Mast hoop	Zuncho	Cercle de mât	Canestrello		Direk çemberi	Mastring, Legel
Mizzen	Mesana	Artimon, tape-cul	Mezzana		Mizan	Treiber
Mizzen staysail	Entrepalos	Foc ou voile d'étai d'artimon	Vela di strallo di mezzana		Mizan velenasi	Besanstagsegel
Outhaul	Envergue de puño	Hale-dehors, étarqueur	Fuetto		Abli	Ausholer
Partners	Fogonadura	Etambrai	Mastra d'albero		Direk braketi	Mastfischung
Peak	Pico	Pic, empointure	Angolo di penna		Cunda, pik	Piek
Preventer backstay	Poparrás	Pataras, étai arrière	Stallo di poppa		Kiç istiralya	Achterstag
Ratlines	Flechadura, flechates	Enfléchure	Griselle		Iskalarya	Webeleine
Reef point	Tomadores de rizo	Garcette	Matafione di terzaruolo	Mouda	Camadan kalçetesi	Reffbändsel
Roach	Alunamiento	Rond, arrondi	Lunata		Sehim	Rundung des Achterlieks
Sheet	Escota	Ecoute	Scotta	Scotta	Iskota	Schot
Shroud	Obenque	Hauban	Sartia	Csartia	Çarmih	Want
Spinnaker	Espinaquer	Spinnaker	Spinnaker	Baloni	Balon, Spinaker	Spinnaker
Spitfire, storm jib	Foque de capa	Tourmentin	Fiocco di cappa	Flokos thielis	Firtina floku	Stormfok
Spritsail	Vela tarquina, abaníco	Livarde	Vela a tarchia		Gönderli yelken	Sprietsegel
Square sail	Vela cuadra, redonda	Voile carrée	Vela quadra	Tetagono pani	Kabasorta arma	Rahsegel
Staysail	Vela de estay	Trinquette	Vela di taglio, vela di strallo	Tronketo	Velena, trinket	Stagsegel
Step and heel	Carlinga y coz o mecha	Emplanture et pied	Scassa e piede	Skantza	Direk iskaçasi	Mastspur und Mastfuß
Tabling	Vaina	Doublage, gaine	Vaina		Yaka astari	Doppelung
Tack	Puño de armura	Point d'armure	Angolo di mura	Podi	Karula yakasi	Hals
Throat	Puño de driza	Gorge	Gola		Çatal yakasi	Klau
Topping lift	Amantillo	Balancine	Mantiglio	Balancini	Balansina	Dirk
Topsail	Escandalosa	Flèche	Controranda		Gabya yelkeni	Toppsegel
Truck	Tope	Pomme	Formaggetta		Direk kapellasi	Masttopp
Trysail	Vela de capa	Voile de cape	Vela di cappa		Firtina yelkeni	Stormzeil
Wishbone staysail	Vela de pico vacio	Wishbone	Vela di strallo wishbone		Çatal bumbali velena	Wishbone-stagsegel
Yankee	Trinquetilla	Yankee	Fiocco		Yenki flok	Yankee-Klüver

3.10 PARTS OF A BOAT

English	Spanish	French	Italian	Greek	Turkish	German
Beam	Bao	Barrot	Baglio	Platos	Kemere	Balken
Bilges	Sentina	Bouchain, fonds	Sentina	Sentina	Sintine	Bilge
Bilges	Cuñas	Cales	Cunei	Kitos	Sintine	Bilge
Bottom	Fondo, carena	Carène, oeuvres vives	Carena, opera viva	Yfala	Karina	Unterwas-serschiff
Bow	Proa	Etrave, avant	Prora	Maska	Prova	Bug, vorn
Bulkhead	Mampara	Cloison	Paratia	Bulmes	Perde	Schott
Bulwark	Borda, regala	Pavois	Parapetto	Parapetto	Parampet	Schanzkleid
Bunk, berth	Litera	Couchette	Cuccetta	Cuketta	Ranza	Koje
Cabin	Camarote	Cabine	Cabina, locale	Cabina	Kamara	Kajüte
Cabin sole	Plan de cámara	Plancher	Piano di calpestio		Farşlar	Bodenbrett
Chain locker	Pañol de cadena	Puits à chaîne	Pozzo delle catene	Freatioalision	Zincirlik	Kettenkasten
Cockpit	Bañera	Cockpit	Pozzetto		Havuzluk	Plicht
Deck	Cubierta	Pont	Ponte	Katastroma	Güverte	Deck
Draught	Calado	Tirant d'eau	Pescaggio	Vithisma	Draft, su kesimi	Tiefgang
Fairlead	Galápago, guía	Chaumard	Passacavo a bocca di rancio	Tomodigos	Kurt ağizi	Lippe, Klüse
Fender	Defensa	Défense	Parabordo, paglietto	Baloni	Usturmaça	Fender
Floor	Varenga	Varangue	Madiere	Dapedo	Döşek	Bodenwrange
Foc'sle	Castillo proa	Poste avant	Castello di prora	Kabuni	Başalti	Vorschiff
Hatch	Escotilla	Ecoutille	Boccaporto	Buccaporta	Kaporta	Luk
Hull	Casco	Coque	Scafo	Scafos	Karina	Rumpf
Keel	Quilla	Quille	Chiglia	Karena	Omurga	Kiel
Keelson	Sobrequilla	Carlingue	Paramezzale	Sotropi	Kontraomurga	Kielschwein
Lavatory, head	WC, sanitario	Toilettes	Locale igienico, WC	Tualetta	Tuvalet	Toilette
Length overall	Eslora total	Longueur hors-tout	Lunghezza fuori tutto	Megisto mikos	Tam boy	Länge über alles
Lifeline	Pasamano	Filière	Battagliola	Hizagogos	Vardavela teli	Rettungsleine, Reling
Planking	Tablazón del casco	Bordage	Fasciame	Petsoma	Kaplama, mader	Beplankung
Propeller, screw	Hélice	Hélice	Elica	Propela	Uskur, pervane	Propeller, Schraube
Pulpit	Púlpito	Balcon avant	Pulpito		Pulpit, baş korkuluk	Bugkorb
Pushpit	Púlpito de popa	Balcon arrière	Pulpito poppiero		Puşpit, kiç korkuluk	Heckkorb
Rudder	Timón	Gouvernail, safran	Timone	Timoni	Dümen	Ruder
Spinnaker boom	Tangón del espinaquer	Tangon de spi	Asta dello spinnaker, tangone		Balon gönderi	Spinnakerbaum
Stanchion	Candelero	Chandelier	Candelieri	Pundelli	Puntel	Stütze
Stern	Popa	Poupe, arrière	Poppa	Piymni	Kiç	Heck

English	Spanish	French	Italian	Greek	Turkish	German
Sternpost	Codaste	Etambot	Dritto di poppa	Podostima	Kiç bodoslama	Achtersteven
Tiller	Caña	Barre	Barra del timone	Lagudera	Yeke	Pinne
Transom stern	Popa de yugo	Arrière à tableau	Poppa a specchio		Ayna	Spiegelheck
Waterline, boot topping	Linea de flotación	Ligne de flottaison	Linea di galleggiamento	Issalos	Filato	Wasserlinie
Wheel	Rueda del timón	Roue	Ruota del timone	Timoni	Dümen simidi	Rad

3.11 BOAT EQUIPMENT

English	Spanish	French	Italian	Greek	Turkish	German
Anchor	Ancla	Ancre	Anchora	Agira	Çapa demiri	Anker
Anchor warp	Amarra del ancla	Aussière, câblot	Cavo di tonneggio	Skiniagyras	Demir trosasi	Ankertrosse
Anti-fouling paint	Pintura de patente, anti-incrustante	Peinture antisalissante, antifouling	Pittura sottomarina, antincrostazione	Moravia	Zehirli boya	Anwuchsverhütende Farbe
Bilge pump	Pompa di sentina	Pompe de cale	Bombas de achique	Adlia Sentinas	Sintine pompasi	Lenzpumpe
Block	Motón	Poulie	Bozzello	Maccaras	Makara	Block
Blown fuse	Fusible fundido	Fusible fondu, plomb sauté	Valvola bruciata, saltata	Ilectriki Asfalia	Yanik sigorta, Atik sigorta	Durchgebrannte Sicherung
Boat topping	Pintura de la flotación	Bande de flotaison	Pittura protettiva	Ifalochroma	Filato	Wasserpaß-Farbe
CQR, or plough anchor	CQR, arado	CQR, ou ancre charrue	CQR		Pulluk demir, CQR demir	Pflugscharanker
Chain, cable	Cadena, cable de ancla	Chaîne, cable d'ancre	Catena, cavo, gomena	Kadena	Demir zinciri	Ankerkette
Cleat	Cornamusa	Taquet	Galloccia	Destra	Koç boynuzu	Klampe
Current	Corriente	Courant	Corrente	Revma	Akinti	Strom
Danforth	Danforth	Ancre à bascule	Danforth		Danforth demir	Danforthanker
Distress flares	Bengala	Feux de détresse, fusées	Fuochi per segnalazioni pericoli	Fortovolides kinidina	Işaret fişeği	Notsignalfeuer
Electric lighting	Alumbrado electrico	Eclairage électrique	Illuminazione elettrica	Ilectrikos fotismos	Elektrikli aydinlatma	Elektrische Beleuchtung
Enamel paint	Pintura de esmalte	Peinture lacquée	Pittura a smalto	Ladoboyia	Sentetik boya	Glanzanstrich
Fire extinguisher	Extintor	Extincteur d'incendie	Estintore	Pyrosvestiras	Yangin söndürücü	Feuerlöscher
Fisherman's anchor	Ancla de cepo	Ancre à jas	Ancora		Admiralti demir, Balikçi demiri	Stockanker
Gas stove	Cocina de gaz	Réchaud à gaz	Fornello a gaz	Furnos igraeriu	Likid gazli ocak	Propangaskocher, Gasherd
Horseshoe lifebuoy	Salvavidas abierto (de herradura)	Bouée en fer à cheval, bouée de sauvetage	Salvagente a ferro di cavallo	Imicyclio sosivio	Nal tipi can simidi	Rettungsweste U-förmig mit Licht
Inflatable life raft	Balsa neumática	Canot pneumatique	Zattera di salvataggio gonfiabile	Fuskoti sosivios shedia	Şişme can sali	Aufblasbare Rettungsinsel
Jam cleat	Barbeta	Taquet coinceur, coinceur d'écoute	Strozzacavi		Cem kilit	Curryklemme, Schotklemme
Jubilee clip	Abrazadera	Collier de serrage	Fascetta a vite		Hortum kelepçesi	Schlauchschelle
Life jacket	Chalecos salvavidas	Gilet de sauvetage	Salvagente a giachetta	Sosivios jaketta	Can yeleği	Schwimmweste
Methylated spirits	Alcohol desnaturalizado	Alcool à brûler	Alcool denaturado		Mavi ispirto	Brennspiritus
Navigation lights	Luz de navegación, luz de situación	Feux de navigation, de route, de position	Fanali di via	Fota Nafsiploias	Seyir fenerleri	Positionslaternen, Seitenlaternen
Oar	Remo	Rame	Remo	Kupi	Kürekler	Riemen
Paint brush	Brocha	Pinceau	Pennello, pennellesse	Pinello	Boya firçasi	Pinsel
Painting	Pintado	Peinture	Pitturare	Hromatisma	Boya	Anstrich
Pressure stove	Cocina de petróleo	Réchaud à pétrole	Fornello a pressione		Pürmüz ocaği	Petroleumkocher
Primer	Imprimación	Couche d'impression	Prima mano	Astari	Astar boya	Grundanstrich
Safety harness	Cinturón de seguridad	Harnais	Cintura di sicurezza	Exartimata asfalias	Emniyet kemeri	Sicherheitsgurt
Sandpaper	Papel de lija	Papier de verre	Cartavetro	Yaloharto	Zimpara kağidi	Sandpapier
Sea anchor	Ancla flotante	Ancre flottante	Ancora galleggiante		Deniz demiri	Seeanker, Treibanker
Seacock	Llave de paso	Vanne	Valvola di arresto	Crounos	Kilistin	Seeventil
Shackle and pin	Grillete y pasador o perno	Manille et vis, manille et clavette	Maniglione e perno	Naftiko klithi me piro	Kilit ve harbisi	Schäkel und Bolzen
Sheave	Roldana	Réa	Puleggia	Raulo	Makara dili	Scheibe
Short circuit	Corto circuito	Court-circuit	Corto circuito	Vrahikykloma	Kisa devre	Kurzschluß
Switch	Interruptor	Commutateur	Interruttore	Diakoptis	Anahtar, sviç	Schalter
Undercoat	Primera mano de pintura	Sous-couche	Mano di fondo	Ypostroma	Astar boya	Vorstreichfarbe
Varnish	Barniz	Vernis	Vernice	Verniki	Vernik	Lack
Voltage	Voltaje	Voltage, tension	Voltaggio	Volt	Gerilim, Voltaj	Spannung
Winch	Winche, chigre	Winch, treuil	Verricello	Vidgi	Vinç, Irgat	Winde, Winsch
Winch handle	Palanca del winche	Levier	Manovella	Manirella	Vinç kolu	Kurbel
Windlass, capstan	Molinete, chigre, cabrestante	Guindeau, cabestan	Argano a salpare, argano	Ergatis vidgi	Dik irgat	Ankerwinde, Ankerspill
Wiring	Instalación	Cablage électrique	Cavi	Klodiosoi	Tenvirat	Leitung

3.12 BOAT ENGINE

English	Spanish	French	Italian	Greek	Turkish	German
Atomiser, injector	Inyector	Injecteur	Iniettore	Beck	Enjektör	Einspritzdüse
Battery	Batería	Batterie	Batteria	Batteria	Akü, batarya	Batterie

English	Spanish	French	Italian	Greek	Turkish	German
Bolt	Perno	Boulon	Boulone	Vida bouloni	Saplama	Bolzen
Clutch	Embrague	Embrayage	Frizione		Debreyaj, Kavrama	Kupplung
Cylinder head	Culata	Culasse	Testata (dei cilindri)	Kefali mihanis	Silindir kapaği	Zylinderkopf
Diesel engine	Motor diesel	Moteur diesel	Motore diesel	Mihani diesel	Dizel motoru	Dieselmotor
Diesel fuel pump	Bomba de inyección	Pompe d'injection	Pompa d'iniezione	Adlia petreleu	Enjektör pompasi	Einspritzpumpe
Distilled water	Agua destilada	Eau distillée	Acqua distillata	Apostagmeno nero	Ari su	Destilliertes Wasser
Drive belt	Correa	Courroie de transmission	Cinghia	Imanda	V-kayişi	Treibriemen
Fuel filter	Filtro de combustible	Filtre à combustible	Filtro del combustibile	Filtro venzinis/ petreleu	Yakit filtresi	Treibstoffilter
Fuel tank	Tanque de combustible	Reservoir à combustible	Serbatoio del combustibile	Reservior	Yakit tanki	Kraftstofftank
Gearbox	Caja de cambio	Bôite de vitesse, inverseur	Cambio	Kinitio tahititon	Şanziman	Getriebekasten
Generator	Dinamo	Dynamo	Generatore	Yenitria	Jeneratör, Dinamo	Lichtmaschine
Grease	Grasa	Graisse	Grasso	Grasso	Gres yaği	Fett
Hose	Manga	Tuyau	Tubo	Lastihenios Solinas	Hortum	Schlauch
Hydraulic fluid	Aceite hidráulico	Liquide hydraulique	Liquido idraulico	Ydrarliko ygro	Hidrolik yaği	Hydraulisches Öl
Nut	Tuerca	Ecrou	Dado	Paximadi	Somun	Mutter
Oil	Aceite	Huile	Olio	Ladi mihanis	Yağ	Öl
Petrol engine	Motor de gasolina	Moteur à essence	Motore a benzina	Venzinomihani	Benzin motörü	Benzinmotor, Otto-Motor
Propeller	Hélice	Hélice	Elica	Propella	Pervane, uskur	Schraube
Propeller shaft	Arbol de la hélice	Arbre d'hélice	Albero dell'elica		Pervane mili	Schraubenwelle
Starter motor	Motor de arranque	Démarreur	Motorino d'avviamento	Miza	Marş motoru	Anlasser
Water pump	Bomba de agua	Pompe à eau	Pompa dell'acqua	Adlia nero	Su pompasi	Wasser-pumpe

3.13 TOOLS

English	Spanish	French	Italian	Greek	Turkish	German
Adjustable spanner	Llave adjustable	Clé anglaise	Chiave regolabile	Gallico klidi	Ayarli anahtar, kurbağacik anahtar	Schrauben- schlüssel
File	Lima	Lime	Lima	Lima	Eğe	Feile
Hacksaw	Sierra para metal	Scie à métaux	Sega per metallo	Sidiro priono	Lama testere	Mettallsäge
Hammer	Martillo	Marteau	Martello	Sfiri	Çekiç	Hammer
Pliers	Alicates	Pinces	Pinze	Pensa	Pense	Zange
Saw	Sierra	Scie	Sega	Prioni	Testere	Säge
Screwdriver	Destornillador	Tournevis	Cacciavite	Katsavidi	Tornavida	Schraubenzieher
Spanner	Llave para tuercas	Clé	Chiave	Klidi	Anahtar	Engländer

3.14 METALS

English	Spanish	French	Italian	Greek	Turkish	German
Aluminium	Aluminio	Aluminium	Alluminio	Aluminio	Alüminyum	Aluminium
Brass	Latón	Laiton	Ottone	Brudios	Sari, Pirinç	Messing
Bronze	Bronce	Bronze	Bronzo		Bronz	Bronze
Copper	Cobre	Cuivre	Rame	Halkos	Bakir	Kupfer
Galvanised iron	Hierro galvanizado	Fer galvanisé	Ferro galvanizzato	Galvanismeno	Galvaniz demir	Verzinktes Eisen
Iron	Hierro	Fer	Ferro	Sidero	Demir	Eisen
Lead	Plomo	Plomb	Piombo	Molyvi	Kurşun	Blei
Stainless steel	Acero inoxidable	Acier inoxidable	Acciaio inossidabile	Anoxidoto	Kromnikel çelik, Paslanmaz çelik	Rostfreier Stahl
Steel	Acero	Acier	Acciaio	Atsali	Çelik	Stahl

3.15 MATERIALS

English	Spanish	French	Italian	Greek	Turkish	German
Cotton	Algodón	Coton	Cotone	Vamvaki	Pamuk	Baumwolle
Fibreglass	Fibra de vidrio	Fibre de verre	Lana di vetro	Yalovamvakas	Fiberglas, cam elyafi	Glasfaser
Leather	Cuero	Cuir	Cuojo	Derma	Deri, kösele	Leder
Nylon	Nilon	Nylon	Nylon	Nylon	Naylon	Nylon, Perlon
Plastic	Plástico	Plastique	Plastica	Plastico	Plastik	Kunststoff
Polyester	Poliester	Polyester	Poliestere	Polyester	Polyester	Polyester
Resin	Resina	Résine	Resina	Ritini	Reçine	Harz

3.16 TIMBER

English	Spanish	French	Italian	Greek	Turkish	German
Dry rot	Hongo de madera	Pourriture sèche	Carie secca	Scorofogomia	Kuru ortamda çürüme	Trockenfäule
Laminated	Laminado	Contré, laminé	Laminato		Lamine	Laminiert
Mahogany	Caoba	Acajou	Mogano	Maoni	Maun	Mahagoni
Oak	Roble	Chêne	Quercia	Velanidia	Meşe	Eiche
Pitch pine	Pino	Pitchpin	Pitch pine	Pitch pain	Piçpayn, Çirali çam	Pitchpine
Rot	Putrición	Pourriture	Marcito, cariato	Sapio	Çürüme	Fäulnis
Teak	Teca	Teck	Tek	Tik	Tik	Teak

3.17 FASTENINGS

English	Spanish	French	Italian	Greek	Turkish	German
Bolt	Perno	Boulon	Bullone	Bulloni	Saplama	Bolzen
Metal dowel	Espiga de metal	Goujon	Caviglia di ferro	Karfi	Metal dübel	Metalldübel
Nail	Clavo	Clou	Chiodo	Vida	Çivi	Nagel
Rivet	Remache	Rivet	Chiodo	Pritsini	Perçin	Niete
Screw	Tornillo	Vis	Vite		Vida	Schraube
Weld	Soldar	Souder	Saldare	Ilectro colisi	Kaynak	Schweißen

3.18 FIRST AID

English	Spanish	French	Italian	Greek	Turkish	German
Anti-seasickness pills	Pildoras contra el mareo	Remède contre le mal de mer	Pillole contro il mal di mare	Diskia naftias	Deniz tutmasina karşi ilaç	Antiseekrank- heitsmittel
Antiseptic cream	Pomada antiséptica	Onguent	Antisettico antiseptique	Antisiptiki crema	Antiseptik krem	Antiseptiche Salbe
Apirin tablets	Pastillas de aspirina	Aspirine	Aspirina	Aspirines	Aspirin	Aspirintabletten
Bandage	Venda	Bandage	Benda	Epidesmos	Bandaj	Binde
Disinfectant	Desinfectante	Désinfectant	Desinfectante	Aploimadico	Dezenfektan	Desinfektion-

English	Spanish	French	Italian	Greek	Turkish	German
Indigestion tablets	Pastilla laxantes	Pillules contre l'indigestion	Pillole contro l'indigestione	Diskia dispepsias	Hazimsizlik ilaci	Tabletten gegen Darmstörungen smittel
Sticking plaster	Esparadrapo	Pansement adhésif	Cerotto	Tsirota	Flaster	Heftplaster
Thermometer	Termómetro	Thermomètre	Termometro	Thermometro	Termometre	Thermometer
Wound dressing	Botiquin para heridas	Pansement stérilisé	Fascie per ferite		Pansuman	Verbandzeug

3.19 ASHORE

English	Spanish	French	Italian	Greek	Turkish	German
Baker	Panadero	Boulanger	Fornaio	Fournos	Firin	Bäcker
Bank	Banco	Banque	Banca	Trapeza	Banka	Bank
Beef	Carne de vaca (biftec)	Boeuf	Manzo	Moshari	Siğir eti	Rindfleisch
Beer	Cerveza	Bière	Birra	Bira	Bira	Bier
Biscuits	Galletas	Biscuits	Biscotti	Biscota	Bisküvi	Kekse, Gebäck
Bread	Pan	Pain	Pane	Psomi	Ekmek	Brot
Bus	Autobús	Autobus	Autobus	Leoforio	Otobüs	Bus
Butcher	Carnicero	Boucher	Macellaio	Hasapis	Kasap	Metzger
Butter	Mantequilla	Beurre	Burro	Voutrio	Tereyağ	Butter
Cheese	Queso	Fromage	Formaggio	Tyri	Peynir	Käse
Chemist	Farmaciá	Pharmacie	Farmacia	Farmakio	Eczane	Apotheke
Chicken	Pollo	Poulet	Pollo	Kotopoulo	Tavuk	Hühnchen
Coffee	Café	Café	Caffè	Cafes	Kahve	Kaffee
Dentist	Dentista	Dentiste	Dentista	Othondoyatros	Dişçi	Zahnarzt
Detergent	Detergente	Détergent	Detergente	Aporipandico	Deterjan	Waschmittel
Doctor	Medico	Médecin	Dottore	Yatros	Doktor	Arzt
Drinking water	Agua potable	Eau potable	Acqua potabile	Posimo nero	Içme suyu	Trinkwasser
Eggs	Huevos	Oeufs	Uova	Avga	Yumurta	Eier
Fish	Pescado	Poisson	Pesce	Psari	Balik	Fisch
Flour	Harina	Farine	Farina	Alevri	Un	Mehl
Fruit	Frutas	Fruits	Frutta	Fruta	Meyva	Obst
Garage	Garage	Garage	Garage		Garaj, Otogar	Autowerkstatt
Greengrocer	Verdulero	Marchand de légumes	Verduraio	Manavis	Manav	Gemüsehändler
Grocer	Tendero de comestibles	Epicier	Salumiere, droghiere	Pandopolis	Bakkal, Market	Krämer
Ham	Jamón	Jambon	Prociutto	Jambon	Jambon	Schinken
Honey	Miel	Miel	Miele	Meli	Bal	Honig
Hospital	Hospital	Hôpital	Ospedale	Nosokomio	Hastane	Krankenhaus
Jam	Mermelada	Confiture	Marmelatta	Marmelada	Marmelat, Reçel	Marmelade
Lamb	Carne de cordero	Agneau	Agnello	Arni	Koyun eti	Lammfleisch
Market	Mercado	Marché	Mercato	Agora	Market, Pazar	Markt
Meat	Carne	Viande	Carne	Creas	Et	Fleisch
Milk	Leche	Lait	Latte	Gala	Süt	Milch
Newspapers	Periódicos	Journaux	Giornali	Efimeriida	Gazete	Zeitungen
Oil	Aceite	Huile	Olio	Ladi	Yağ	öl
Pepper	Pimienta	Poivre	Pepe	Piperi	Karabiber	Pfeffer
Pork	Carne de cerdo	Porc	Carne di maiale	Hirino	Domuz eti	Schweinefleisch
Post office	Correo	Poste	Ufficio postale	Tahithromio	Postane	Postamt
Railway station	Estación de ferrocarril	Gare	Stazione ferrovia	Stathmos trenou	Tren istasyonu	Bahnhof
Rice	Arroz	Riz	Riso	Ryzi	Pirinç	Reis
Sailmaker	Velero	Voilier	Veleria	Kateskevastis panion	Yelkenci	Segelmacher
Salt	Sal	Sel	Sale	Alati	Tuz	Salz
Sausages	Embutidos	Saucisses	Salsiccie	Lucanico	Sosis	Würstchen
Stamps	Sellos	Timbres	Francobolli	Grammatosima	Pul	Briefmarken
Sugar	Azúcar	Sucre	Zucchero	Zahari	Şeker	Zucker
Supermarket	Supermercado	Supermarché	Supermercato	Supermarket	Süpermarket	Supermarkt
Tea	Té	Thé	Té	Tsai	Çay	Tee
Veal	Carne de ternera	Veau	Carne di vitello	Moshari	Dana eti	Kalbfleisch
Vegetables	Legumbres, verduras	Légumes	Verdure	Lahanika	Sebze	Gemüse
Wine	Vino	Vin	Vino	Krasi	Şarap	Wein
Yacht chandler	Almacén de efectos	Fournisseur de navales	Rifornitore di marine	Promithies marina	Yat levazimatçisi	Yachtausrüster

English	Spanish	French	Italian	Greek	Turkish	German
3.20 COLOURS						
Black	Negro	Noir	Nero	Mavros	Kara, Siyah	Schwarz
Blue	Azul	Bleu	Azzure	Galazios	Gök, mavi	Blau
Green	Verde	Vert	Verde	Prassinos	Yeşil	Grün
Red	Rojo	Rouge	Rosso	Kokkinos	Kirmizi, kizil	Rot
White	Blanco	Blanc	Bianco	Levkos	Ak, beyaz	Weiß
Yellow	Amarillo	Jaune	Giallo	Kitrinos	Sari	Gelb
3.21 NUMBERS						
One	Uno	Un	Uno	Ena	Bir	Eins
Two	Dos	Deux	Due	Dyo	İki	Zwei
Three	Tres	Trois	Tre	Tria	Üç	Drei
Four	Cuatro	Quatre	Quattro	Tessera	Dört	Vier
Five	Cinco	Cinq	Cinque	Pente	Beş	Fünf
Six	Seis	Six	Sei	Exi	Alti	Sechs
Seven	Siete	Sept	Sette	Epta	Yedi	Sieben
Eight	Ocho	Huit	Otto	Octo	Sekiz	Acht
Nine	Nueve	Neuf	Nove	Enia	Dokuz	Neun
Ten	Diez	Dix	Dieci	Decca	On	Zehn
Eleven	Once	Onze	Undici	Endeca	Onbir	Elf
Twelve	Doce	Douze	Dodici	Dodecca	Oniki	Zwölf
Thirteen	Trece	Treize	Tredici	Deccatria	Onüç	Dreizehn
Fourteen	Catorce	Quatorze	Quatordici	Deccatessera	Ondört	Vierzehn
Fifteen	Quince	Quinze	Quindici	Deccapente	Onbeş	Fünfzehn
Sixteen	Dieciséis	Seize	Sedici	Deccaexi	Onalti	Sechzehn
Seventeen	Diecesiete	Dix-sept	Diciasette	Deccaepta	Onyedi	Siebzehn
Eighteen	Dieciocho	Dix-huit	Diciotto	Deccaocto	Onsekiz	Achtzehn
Nineteen	Diecinueve	Dix-neuf	Diciannove	Deccaenia	Ondokuz	Neunzehn
Twenty	Veinte	Vingt	Venti	Ikosi	Yirmi	Zwanzig
Thirty	Treinta	Trente	Trenta	Trianta	Otuz	Dreißig
Forty	Cuarenta	Quarante	Quaranta	Seranta	Kirk	Vierzig
Fifty	Cincuenta	Cinquante	Cinquanta	Peninta	Elli	Fünfzig
Sixty	Sesenta	Soixante	Sessanta	Exinda	Altmiş	Sechzig
Seventy	Setenta	Soixante-dix	Settanta	Evdominda	Yetmiş	Siebzig
Eighty	Ochenta	Quatre-vingt	Ottanta	Ogdonda	Seksen	Achtzig
Ninety	Noventa	Quatre-vingt-dix	Novanta	Eneninda	Doksan	Neunzig
One hundred	Cien	Cent	Ciento	Ecato	Yüz	Einhundert
Thousand	Mil	Mille	Mille	Hilia	Bin	Tausend

3.22 ARABIC NUMERALS

1	١	10	١٠
2	٢	20	٢٠
3	٣	30	٣٠
4	٤	40	٤٠
5	٥	50	٥٠
6	٦	100	١٠٠
7	٧	200	٢٠٠
8	٨	1000	١٠٠٠
9	٩		

4. Yacht and equipment

4.1 Equipment

Electricity

In all marinas and some other harbours it is possible to plug into mains electricity on the pontoon or quay. Most marinas include electricity in the berthing charge so it is worthwhile being equipped to take advantage of it. Unfortunately this will mean a variety of connectors to plug into whatever socket a marina is using, and it is really a matter of adapting what you have in the best way possible. Most connections are 220V 50Hz, but some marinas also have 330V. In some of the municipal harbours where electricity and water 'boxes' have been installed, the connections can be potentially dangerous and the supply is prone to surges. Turn off any sensitive equipment on board or it may be damaged by the irregular nature of the supply.

When you are away from all-singing-all-dancing marinas you will have to rely on generating the stuff yourself. In any anchorages and in some harbours, especially in the eastern Mediterranean, you must be pretty well self-sufficient for electricity on board; that means totting up your consumption and fitting batteries with sufficient capacity and the means to charge them. Most yachts opt for solar panels or wind generators to top up the charging from the engine alternator. In addition it is worthwhile fitting a 'smart' regulator to the alternator in place of the standard regulators supplied by the manufacturers. It may also be possible to fit an additional or larger alternator to an engine, depending on the relative size of the engine to the boat.

If at all possible don't rely an running a generator to top up batteries and run equipment. While a quiet generator that doesn't annoy anyone is OK in a crowded anchorage, there is nothing more irritating than to be near a boat with its generator running in what would be an otherwise tranquil anchorage. It can also be annoying in a marina.

Ventilation

Yachts built for northern climates will have inadequate ventilation for the hot Mediterranean. Extra skylights and vents and additional insulation can help solve the problem. Yachts with deckhouses and motorboats with large expanses of glass should have covers, normally in white canvas, made up to cover the windows when the sun is out or you will get a 'greenhouse effect' down below. A wind-scoop to funnel air down the front or saloon hatches makes a big difference to life below; several commercially produced scoops are on the market, or get your own made up.

Awnings

A good sun awning is an essential piece of boat equipment. Much of your time will be spent in the cockpit so the awning should be designed to be a comfortable height above the cockpit seats and should have side curtains for when the sun is low in the evening. Make the awnings from dark-coloured canvas as light materials cause a glare and nylon and Terylene materials flap and crack in the slightest breeze.

A permanent awning rigged over the cockpit along the lines of the bimini common in the Caribbean keeps you cool not only in harbour, but when sailing or motoring as well. When sailing you can, if you so desire, fold the bimini back for a clearer view of the sails.

Some skippers worry about the bimini being up in strong winds, but most people, myself included, have only found it necessary to fold them away when the wind gets above 35 knots or so. In fact, on *Tetra* the bimini stayed up for the entirety of the trip to SE Asia and back, and on *seven tenths* the only time the bimini was removed was when Hurricane George threatened. Otherwise it stayed up for two transatlantics and several Caribbean Mediterranean circuits.

Refrigerators

For those who can't do without cold drinks, a refrigerator is an essential piece of equipment. If it is going to draw power from your batteries it may be necessary to install an additional battery and revise your charging methods - a refrigerator is estimated to use around 50-60 per cent of total power consumption on most yachts. Smaller yachts without auxiliary generators usually fit a solar panel or two or a wind-powered generator to supply the much-needed amps to avoid that dull 'thunk' in the morning when you try to start the engine on flat batteries.

The heat-absorption and thermo-electric types do not work well in the high ambient temperatures of the Mediterranean. The type having a compressor working off the batteries (high current drain) or off the engine work the best. Install a holding plate and get a top-opening refrigerator so that the cold air does not fall out every time it is opened. As a general rule, most refrigerators do not have adequate insulation – 10cm (4in) should be the minimum.

And don't forget that ice is available in most harbours, so the humble icebox can be used with the advantage that it costs virtually nothing and never breaks down.

Showers

A shower is useful inside a yacht, but it is perhaps most useful if it can be used outside on deck or in the cockpit to wash off after swimming in the salty Mediterranean. Large water tanks or even a separate water tank may be required. Many modem craft have a shower installed on the aft swimming platform and this makes a lot of sense. Most 'sunshower' outfits, simply a black bag with a hose and shower rose attached, also work well, though the water inside can get too hot if the bag is left in the sun for long at the height of summer.

In the summer it can get very hot, and you don't always want to go for a swim or deplete the water tanks by having a full shower. A useful way of cooling off is to buy a spray bottle (the sort used for indoor plants will do) and spray a fine mist of water over the face, neck, arms and legs, indeed any exposed bit of the anatomy. This will cool you off surprisingly well with a

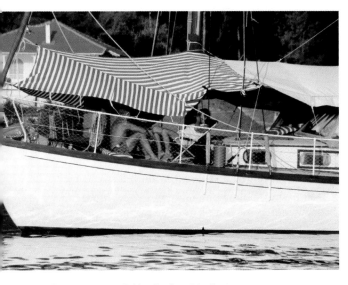

Awnings are essential in the hot Mediterranean summer – though they don't need to be quite as elaborate as this

A wind-sock will funnel a gentle breeze below and keep things ventilated

A permanent bimini and canvas hatch covers will keep things cool below at sea and in harbour

A winter cover will keep the boat clean through the lay-up months in the winter

minimum of water consumption. It may sound silly, but try it and you will be pleasantly cooled.

Holding tanks

Holding tanks are not yet required by law for private yachts visiting the Mediterranean, despite all the rumours that fly around cruising forums. What can happen is that you can be fined for pumping out a toilet ('black water') in a harbour or in an enclosed bay, and I for one go along with this 100% as I have no desire to watch toilet contents being pumped out, or swim around someone else's sewage outlet. It is likely that a requirement for holding tacks will be made law at some time in the future.

Any holding tank installation must be able to pump out at sea (the requirement is theoretically 3 miles offshore) as few marinas and no harbours have pump-out facilities ashore. Every yacht should endeavour to do its bit to keep harbours and anchorages free of faeces and either use toilets ashore or utilise the holding tank on board. If you are not going 3 miles offshore then 1 would suggest that 2 miles offshore is better than in the harbour or anchorage.

The installation must be installed with odour-free hose, a good-sized vent/breather and preferably a vent filter, of which there are several available on the market. The combination of these three ingredients will keep holding tank smells at bay, assuming the rest of the installation is professionally fitted and a stainless steel (or preferably polypropylene) tank is used. The holding tank in my boat is installed in the heads and the toilet pumps through it all the time. To use the holding tank the toilet outlet seacock is closed. To empty the holding tank the outlet is opened and gravity and a bit of pumping do the rest.

4.2 Diesel Engines

A reliable engine is necessary for motoring through the inevitable calms a yacht will encounter, and on other occasions to motor against the strong winds and short seas of the Mediterranean to get into harbour. A petrol engine can be dangerous as in the high summer temperatures petrol vaporises easily and the risk of fire, or an explosion, is greater than in more northern latitudes. This risk applies equally to outboards, whether for the tender or as a backup on a motorboat, and it pays to think carefully about ventilation and petrol stowage. I have witnessed several explosions fuelled by petrol and the results have not been pretty.

If you are installing a new engine try to purchase one for which it will be easy to find spares in the Mediterranean. A less well-known make may be cheaper for the initial purchase, but can lead to trouble if you have to continually get spares sent out to wherever you are in the Mediterranean and if the local mechanics have little or no knowledge of your engine. It is all very well getting a marinised diesel block that is common, but it is usually the marinised add-ons that cause the trouble and they may be made only in the country of origin. Getting hold of a service and spares manual is also worth the effort. Although not exhaustive, spares for the following list of common marques can usually be found without too much bother: Volvo Penta, marinised Fords, Perkins,

Yanmar, Mercedes, Caterpillar, MAN, and marinised GM diesels.

Engine checks

Before starting check:
1. Battery switch is on engine battery or reserve (non-domestic battery).
2. Oil level.
3. Fresh water coolant level.
4. Raw water cooling inlet is open.

Immediately after starting check:
1. Oil pressure gauge or oil pressure warning light.
2. Raw water is coming out of exhaust (unless a dry exhaust system).

Every week check:
1. Pulley belt tension. Normally belt should depress 14mm (0·5") at slackest but check with manual.
2. Raw water inlet strainer.
3. Gear-box oil.
4. Inspect fuel filter. If there is water/contamination in the bowl then run off until clean fuel comes through.

Rough guide to engine troubleshooting

Engine won't turn over
Batteries low or flat
- check battery switch is on.
- check battery switch is on engine battery or reserve battery.
- check voltmeter or battery condition meter or check specific gravity of electrolyte with hygrometer. Turn a light(s) on and when you try to start the engine if the light(s) dims the battery is low.

Starter motor problem
- ignition circuit faulty. Bridge the battery and switch terminals on the starter motor – if the engine cranks there is a problem in the ignition circuit. Check for loose wires or connections.
- solenoid sticking (doesn't click). Tap solenoid gently with a small screwdriver head. Don't hit it hard as modern solenoids have delicate electronic circuitry.
- starter motor sticking (solenoid makes a solid click but starter motor doesn't turn). Try tapping starter motor case gently with a small wrench. Note engine may be seized so be gentle.
- starter motor defective.

Engine seized
- try to turn a small motor by hand either with engine starting handle or by pulley belts. If it doesn't turn over it is seized. For large engines try lifting decompression levers and turning over. In any case of a seized engine seek help. Engine may be heat-seized, may have a major mechanical failure, or may have water in the cylinders.

Engine turns but doesn't start
Engine turns slowly
- batteries low. Turn a light(s) on and if it dims when you try to start the engine the batteries are low. Check battery switch is on the engine battery or reserve battery. Recharge batteries.

- engine cold (unlikely in the Mediterranean in the summer). Follow glow plug procedure if fitted.

Fuel starvation
- check throttle lever is half or more engaged. check fuel level in tank. Check fuel tap is open.
- visually check fuel lines and connections for a leak.
- check for 'diesel bug' in the tank and fuel filter (system must be totally purged of fuel if 'diesel bug' is evident in any quantity).
- loosen injector connection nut and turn engine. If no fuel spurts out check fuel line, filter(s), and tank for obstructions. Bleed engine.

Air starvation
- check air supply is unobstructed. Often there are ducts in a cockpit locker or elsewhere that may have been accidentally covered.
- check air filter. Clean if necessary.

Engine runs but is underpowered

Check
Fuel
- check fuel lines visually. Check for 'diesel bug' or water in the fuel filter. Clean fuel supply and bleed.
- if there is white smoke there may be water in the fuel.

Air
- check air supply is unobstructed and air filter is clean.

Propeller fouled
- check propeller is unobstructed. Plastic or rope may be fouling the propeller. A bread knife or other knife with a serrated edge is good for cutting away rope or plastic. Engine must be turned off; ensure no-one goes anywhere near the ignition key.

Mechanical defect
- if there is excessive white smoke the head gasket may be blown.
- if there is excessive blue smoke the piston rings may be worn or stuck or the valves and guides may be worn or stuck. Major mechanical repairs will be necessary to remedy the fault.
- if there is excessive black smoke under normal loads the injectors, high pressure fuel pump, or timing may need attention. Try bleeding in case one injector is out. Otherwise consult for more specialised attention. Injectors and high pressure pumps are finely tuned pieces of equipment.

Old engines
- turn off auxiliary equipment: refrigerator/radar/lights/radio to take any alternator or mechanical compressor loads off the engine.

Engine runs but overheats
If water is not coming out of exhaust
- check water inlet. Is the sea-cock open? Is the hose to the water pump intact? Is the inlet water strainer clear of obstructions?
- is the water inlet blocked on the outside? Plastic or weed can easily be sucked onto the inlet and block it.
- water pump. Check impeller. Check pulley if applicable. Check for other mechanical defect.

Fresh water coolant
- check coolant level.
- check fresh water system plumbing for defects.

Bleeding a diesel
Some engines are self-bleeding and after turning over the engine for a bit the fuel system will bleed itself. Some are not. Check manufacturer's handbook for advice.
- quick bleed (never recommended but we all do it, though it doesn't always work). Ensure throttle lever is engaged. Back off injector nut (on fuel supply line) while turning the engine over by hand or on the starter motor until only fuel comes out (no air bubbles). Tighten nut while still turning engine over. On a four cylinder you may get away with doing only two injectors. Do a full bleed later.
- full bleed. In order bleed the low pressure fuel pump, high pressure fuel pump, and each injector in turn until only fuel comes out. Try not to spill diesel everywhere by putting rag waste under connections and in the engine bilge.

Smoke signals
White smoke may mean
1. Water in the fuel.
2. Blown head gasket.
3. Air in fuel.

Black smoke may mean
1. Improper injection, timing, or high pressure fuel pump settings.
2. Overload. It is common for a bit of black smoke on start-up but once warm the engine should be backed off from excessive revs which produce black smoke.
3. Air starvation or filter/turbocharger problems.

Blue smoke may mean
1. Mechanical defect, commonly worn or stuck piston rings and/or valves and guides.
2. Too much oil in crankcase. Check oil level.

Suggested minimum engine tool kit
Complete socket set, metric or imperial depending on your engine.
Set of open-ended or ring spanners, metric or imperial.
Large adjustable spanner (big enough for the propeller nut and sea-cocks).
Medium and small adjustable spanners.
Medium and large mole-grips.
Medium pipe wrench.
Set of Allen keys.
Set of normal and Phillips screwdrivers.
Pliers – normal and needlenose.
Ball-peen hammer.
Set of feeler gauges, metric or imperial.
Brass bristle wire brush.

Suggested minimum engine supplies
Engine oil.
Gearbox oil.
Appropriate greases.
WD40 or equivalent.
Insulation tape and self-amalgamating rubber tape.
PTFE tape.
Selection of stainless steel jubilee clips.

Silicone sealant.
Petroleum jelly.
Gasket goo (for emergency gasket repairs).

Suggested minimum engine spares

Oil filter.
Fuel filters.
Top-end gasket set (or at least a head gasket).
Several impellers for raw water cooling pump.
Pulley belts as required for engine.
Injector sealing washers.
O-ring kit (as required).
Spare engine key.
More extensive engine spares kit – add:
Spare injector or nozzle.
Injector liner and washers.
Water pump spares kit.
Lift pump diaphragm.
Thermostat.

Winter lay-up engine check-list

1. Run the engine to operating temperature. Drain or pump out the engine oil. Refill with fresh oil.
2. Drain the raw water cooling system. Flush through with freshwater. The easiest way to do this is usually to stick a hose in the water inlet or remove the inlet pipe and stick it in a bucket which is refilled by the hose. Run in 50–50 water-antifreeze mixture at the end to coat waterways. Drain system including low spots. Plug the water inlet with oily rag.
3. Drain freshwater cooling system and replace with water-antifreeze mixture as per handbook.
4. Drain water-trap box in exhaust. Plug exhaust with oily rag.
5. Remove and grease waterpump impeller with petroleum jelly.
6. Check any anticorrosive zincs and replace if necessary.
7. Clean fuel filters and drain water out if necessary.
8. Grease any appropriate points, not forgetting the Morse controls.
9. Spray WD40 or oil into inlet manifold and turn engine slowly (without starting) to coat cylinder walls.
10. Turn engine to compression stroke.
11. Fill fuel tank to avoid condensation.
12. Wipe engine with an oily rag or a mixture of petroleum jelly dissolved in petrol or spray with WD40, to avoid external corrosion.
13. Clean engine compartment. Be careful not to leave oil and diesel in the engine bilge.
14. A custom-made winter cover for the deck or the whole boat will repay the investment by keeping the sun and dust off the boat while it is laid up. In many yards there can be a fair bit of dust blowing around and when it settles and then it rains, the result is later baked by the sun to a red-clay finish. The cover will also prevent UV damage to fittings and brightwork.

4.3 Electrics

Basic definitions and formulae

Current The rate at which an electrical charge moves or the flow rate of an electrical charge. Measured in amps (*amperes*). Abbreviation **I**.

Voltage (or Voltage potential). The force which moves an electrical flow. There must be a Potential Difference between two points for a flow. Abbreviation **V**.

Watt The rate of energy consumption. Technically 1 Watt = 1 Joule/sec. 746 Watts = 1 horsepower. Watts = Volts x Amps (W = V x I). Abbreviation **W**.

Resistance The resistance to a current. Measured in Ohms and governed by Ohm's Law. Resistance = Volts / Amps (R = **V/I**). Abbreviation **R**.

The water analogy Visualise a river. The current is the rate at which water passes you on the bank. The voltage is the pressure (say a reservoir further up) pushing the water down. The Watt is a waterwheel turning at *xyz* revolutions. The resistance is any obstruction in the river impeding the flow. But remember electricity is not water and this is an analogy.

Amp-Hours Current multiplied by the time it flows. Commonly used to describe battery storage and current consumption. An 80 Amp-hour battery will, in theory, provide one amp for 80 hours. In practice no battery should ever be completely discharged. Rule of thumb: deep cycle batteries can be 50% discharged before recharging.

Typical power consumption figures
(12 Volts, ranked in order of consumption)

	Amps	Duration		Amp hours
Anchor winch	75–300	10 min	=	12·5 to 50
SSB transmit	25–30	15 min	=	6·25 to 7·5
Autopilot	1–15	6 hours	=	6 to 90
Spotlight	8–12	15 min	=	2 to 3
Refrigerator	4–10	6 hours	=	24 to 60
Spreader lights	4–10	15 min	=	1 to 2·5
Radar	2·5–10	3 hours	=	7·5 to 30
VHF transmit	5–6	20 min	=	1·6 to 2
Bilge pump	3–6	20 min	=	1 to 2
Navigation lights	5	8 hours	=	40
Freshwater pump	3–6	1 hour	=	3 to 6
Tri-colour	3–5	8 hours	=	24 to 40
Cabin light	1–4	4 hours	=	4 to 16
SSB receiver	1–2	1 hour	=	1 to 2
Fluorescent light	1–2	4 hours	=	4 to 8
VHF receiver	0·5–1·5	4 hours	=	2 to 6
GPS	0·2–1	6 hours	=	1·2 to 6
Anchor light	1	8 hours	=	8
CD player	1	2 hours	=	2
Depth sounder	0·1–0·5	2 hours	=	0·2 to 1
Instruments	0·1–0·2	6 hours	=	0·6 to 1·2

Battery charge

Full charge	12·6 volts
50% charge	2·2 volts
0% charge	11·7 volts

Specific gravity (Temperature sensitive)

At 15°C (60°F)	Full charge	=	1·273
	50% charge	=	1·163
	0% charge	=	1–128

Most yachts opt for a solar panel or a wind generator to top up the batteries – or both. Just make sure your wind generator is not of the irritating noisy variety which make a Force 4 sound like a whole gale

Electrical symbols

+ +	Lines crossing without connection
+ +	Lines crossing with connections
—⋀⋀—	Resistance
—⊡—	Variable resistor
—⊣⊢—	Capacitor
—▶—	Diode
—⌐⌐	Switch
—⌒⌒—	Fuse
—⋀—	Circuit breaker
⊒⊒⊒	Transformer, non-isolating
⌒⌒⌒	Coil (winding)
⌐⌐⌐⌐	Instrument case, grounded

Suggested basic electrical toolkit

Multimeter (basic model adequate)
12 volt test lamp
Small screwdriver, normal and Phillips head.
Needlenose pliers
Normal pliers

Crimper tool and selection of terminals and connectors
12 volt soldering iron
Solder (rosin core)
Solder paste (non acid flux)
Hygrometer
Insulation tape

Basic spares kit

Fuses (a range of sizes and ratings)
Light bulbs (for all the different types on board)
Assorted lengths of wire for get-you-home repairs.

4.4 Sail care

All sails should be protected from ultraviolet (UV) radiation when not in use. UV radiation is the principal cause of sailcloth degradation in the Mediterranean.

1. Bag hanked on foresails when not in use or arrange a long pouch on the guard rails if sails are left on deck when sailing.
2. Always cover the mainsail with a sailcover when it is not in use. If you have a conventional main then it is worthwhile investing in a cover permanently attached to the boom and held in place with lazyjacks which will guide the main down into it. These self-stowing affairs go under different names ('easy-stow', 'pack-away', etc.) and can be ordered from a sailmaker for retrofitting if necessary. Apart from letting you drop the main quickly and easily, the fact that the cover is permanently in place and easy to use encourages laid-back crew and skippers to cover the mainsail up and prevent UV damage.
3. Roller reefing headsails have a sacrificial strip sewn on the foot and leach to cover the sail proper when it is furled.
4. Roller reefing mainsails have a sacrificial strip sewn on the tack which normally projects when it is furled. Roller reefing mainsails on a reefing mechanism standing proud of the mast should have a sacrificial strip on the foot and leach as per roller reefing headsails.

Cleaning Sails

All sails should be thoroughly washed before being put away for the winter. Sails should be washed with a soapy mixture using ordinary washing-up detergent. Never use soap powder used for washing clothes. Leave the sail to soak overnight if desired and scrub out any dirty patches with a medium bristle scrubbing brush. Inflatable dinghies cleaned and rinsed out with fresh water can be usefully used for soaking sails. After soaking and scrubbing rinse a sail thoroughly with fresh water and hang up to dry.

Stains

1. *Oil and grease* Try a domestic cleaner based on carbon tetrachloride, a hand-cleaner like *Swarfega*, or a proprietary sail-cleaner. Do not use solvents on nylon. Do not use biological washing powders. Thoroughly rinse the area with fresh water afterwards.
2. *Mildew* Soak the affected area in a bleach mixture (1 part bleach to 10 parts water) for a short time. Scrub the affected area. Thoroughly rinse with fresh water.

Do not use bleach on nylon.

3. *Rust* Use a moderate mixture of oxalic acid (1 part oxalic acid to 20 parts water and leave to soak for an hour or so. Thoroughly rinse with fresh water.

4. *Blood* Use a moderate mixture of oxalic acid as above.
   Note Thoroughly wash your own hands after using oxalic acid. It is a poison. It is commonly available as a white crystalline powder from many chemists.

5. *Paint* Use a thinner such as white spirits or similar. Do not use specialised solvents for synthetic paints such as epoxies and polyurathenes. Do not use on nylon sails. Thoroughly rinse with fresh water.

Folding Sails

Sails and sailbags must be thoroughly dry or mildew will grow – even on synthetic sails! Sails should always be rolled loosely and not folded tightly. Flake a sail loosely along the luff in zig-zags and then roll loosely from luff to clew.

Repairs

1. *Sail tape* Quick repairs can be made with sticky sail tape applied over a rip or hole and firmly pressed on. It is surprisingly durable if properly applied to a clean dry area. Apply a round patch rather than a square patch so there are not corners to catch and lift.

2. *Herringbone stitch* Used for tears. Do not apply too much pressure, just enough to bring the edge of the tear together.

3. *Seams* The best policy is to follow the original holes. This will reproduce only half of the machine stitch (it is possible but tedious to go over the seam again to do the other half) but is usually strong enough until it can be looked at by a sailmaker.

4. *Slides* Sew a length of tape to the slide and then pass the tape twice around through the eye of the sail and the slide, then sew the end through all the thicknesses of tape. Most slides are now held on by plastic 'pop' shackles and it is easier and no more expensive to carry these as well as a few spare slides.

Seam

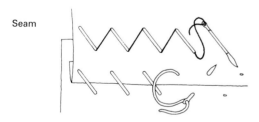

Tear

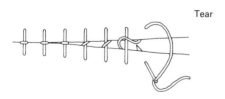

Headsail reefing checklist

(Reproduced courtesy of Rotostay UK)

As part of your maintenance schedule check out these five potential trouble spots. Your headsail reefing system not only rolls up your genoa but also holds up your mast. It is therefore important that you give it a thorough inspection at regular intervals.

Loose joining links

The sections of your aluminium luff foil will be joined together with internal sleeves or links. These links are fastened in position by a variety of different methods depending on the make of your system; screws, rivets, pins, glue, spring clips and buttons. Check each joint carefully for loose fastenings as a protruding screw or rivet head could jam on the halyard swivel and prevent it from passing. If the link is too loose then the luff grooves can become out of alignment and cut or shred the sail's bolt rope and luff as you try to hoist it.

Halyard wrap

This is probably one of the most common causes of trouble with headsail reefing systems. The genoa halyard gets carried around with the luff foil and halyard swivel and wraps itself around the luff foil. As the halyard wrap becomes tighter it will stop the system from rotating. If unaware of the situation the crew may think that the reefing system is just stiff and resort to using a winch on either the reefing line or sheets depending on which way the sail is being rolled. This could be potentially disastrous. The halyard could snap, the joining links or foil could become twisted, or the forestay could become stranded and break. Therefore make it a rule: if the system feels unduly stiff when either setting or furling the sail, you first look aloft and check for wrap before using a winch.

Wrap most commonly occurs on installations where the halyard runs from its sheave to the halyard swivel parallel with the luff foil. The halyard has little or no mechanical advantage to resist the turning moment from the halyard swivel and therefore twists around with the revolving luff foil, if however, the halyard is pulled back 12° to 17° away from the foil to the mast the problem is solved. Most systems do now provide a sheave or fairlead plate for riveting to the mast, whilst *Profurl* and *Plastimo* have their own anti-wrap devices fitted above the luff foil. Whatever system you have do check that there is some anti-wrap device fitted and that it works.

Drum and halyard swivels

Always check these out before fitting the sail back to the system. Firstly try the system for free rotation by simply pulling out the reefing line and then rolling it back the other way by hand. Then last a short strop (1·5m) between the drum and the halyard swivel, shackle the halyard to the swivel and tension it up as though the rope strop was a sail. You can now feel the halyard swivel for free rotation under load and without going up the mast. The drum bearings and tack swivel (if fitted) will also now be under load so check them out again. Refer to your system's service manual if any of the swivels feel stiff.

Forestay and toggles

Inside the luff foil of virtually all makes of reefing gear is the forestay wire; out of sight but, please, not out of mind. This forestay is not only a structural part of the standing rigging supporting the mast, but also forms the centre 'spindle' around which the foil rotates. There is therefore a frictional load between foil and stay which is normally minimised by means of plastic rollers or bearings fitted at intervals up the inside of the luff foil. However, if the bearings slip or become tight the forestay could experience a twisting moment which in extreme cases can result in the forestay stranding or opening out at the terminal ends. It is therefore important to inspect at least the top end of the forestay wire directly below the terminal every season. You could reasonably expect the forestay to last seven or eight seasons, depending on usage of the reefing gear, after which you should consider replacing it or at least inspecting its whole length. Deck toggles, link plates and bottle screws fitted below the reefing drum should also be checked thoroughly for bends and cracks as reefing systems tend to exert a fair degree of lateral leverage not experienced with ordinary forestays. It is therefore imperative that every installation has a proper toggle giving both athwartships and fore/aft movement fitted at both the mast and deck/stemhead fittings.

Reefing Line

Pull all the reefing line off the drum and inspect carefully for wear and chafe. Never 'end to end' a reefing line . . . if it is worn replace it. Check the deck fairleads, stanchion and turning blocks for sharp edges. Too many blocks can increase the frictional load on the reefing line dramatically, making the system feel unnecessarily stiff. Four fairleads should be quite sufficient for a 35ft yacht.

If you need technical advice for your particular system then do call an expert:

Furlex (Seldon Masts Ltd) ☎ 01489 484000
Harken UK Ltd ☎ 01590 689122
email enquiries@harken.co.uk
Hood Yacht Spars Ltd ☎ 01621 782821
email HoodSparUK@aol.com
Plastimo (UK) Ltd ☎ 02380 262211
email sales@plastimo.co.ukΔ40
Profurl (IMP) ☎ 01763 241300
email info@profurl
email sales@improducts.co.uk
Rotomarine Ltd ☎ 02392 583633

4.5 Gas

Butane and Propane guidelines

Most gas appliances will run on either butane or propane.

Propane is stored at approximately 3 times the pressure of butane. A BUTANE BOTTLE MUST NEVER BE FILLED WITH PROPANE. If this happens the butane bottle will vent gas or it may split the steel cylinder. Either could be catastrophic.

In the Mediterranean climate a bottle should not be filled to more than 70% full or it may vent or split a cylinder.

For practical advice on the do's and don'ts of gas I recommend a copy of Calor Gas' *Notes for Blue Water Yachtsmen* which can be obtained from: Calor Gas Ltd, Appleton Park, Slough SL3 9JG, United Kingdom www.calormarineshop.co.uk

4.6 Knots

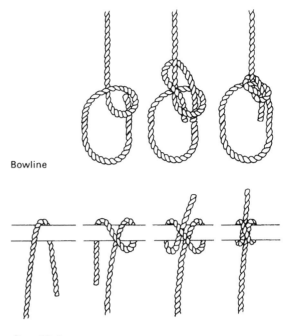

Bowline

Clove Hitch

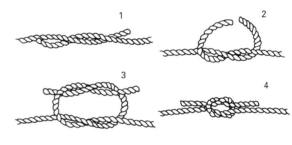

Reef Knot

Fisherman's Bend

Sheet Bend

Figure of eight and double figure of eight

Round turn and two half hitches

Vertical cleating lines and securing excess to the cleat

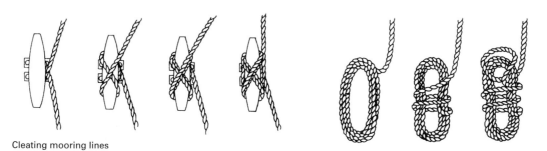

Cleating mooring lines

Coiling ropes

4.7 Conversions

S.I. - BRITISH UNITS
* Indicates a conversion factor which is exact.

	British units to S.I		S.I. units to British	
LENGTH				
millimetre (mm)	1 in	= 25·4 mm*	1 mm	= 0·039 370in
centimetre (cm)	1 in	= 2.54 cm*	1 m	= 3·280 83ft
metre (m)	1 yd	= 0·9144 m*	1 m	= 1·093 61yd
kilometre (km)	1 N Mile	= 1.852 km	1km	= 0·539 N Mile (approx)
kilometre (km)	1 mile	= 1·609 34 km	1 km	= 0·621 371 Mile
OTHER COMMON CONVERSIONS				
Nautical Mile	1 N Mile	= 1.151 M	1M	= 0·868 N Mile (approx)
Yard (Yd)	1 Mile	= 1760 Yds	1 N Mile	= 2000 Yds (approx)
Cable	1 Cable	= 200 Yds	1 N Mile	= 10 Cables (approx)
Fathom	1 Fathom	= 1.8288m*	1 Fathom	= 2 yards (6 feet)
AREA				
square millimetre (mm^2)	1 in^2	= 645·16 mm^2*	1 mm^2	= 0·001 550 in^2
square centimetre (cm^2)	1 ft^2	= 0·092 903 m^2	1 m^2	= 10·7639 ft^2
square metre (m^2)	1 yd^2	= 0·836 127 m^2	1 m^2	= 1·195 99 yd^2
square kilometre (km^2)	1 acre	= 4046·86 m^2		
hectare (ha) = 10000m^2	1 acre	= 0·404 686 ha	1 ha	= 2·471 05 acre
VOLUME				
cubic millimetre (mm^3)	1 in^3	= 16387·1 mm^3	1 mm^3	= 0·000 061 0237 in^3
cubic centimetre (cm^3)	1 ft^3	= 0·028 3168 m^3	1 m^3	= 35·3147 ft^3
cubic metre (m^3)	1 yd^3	= 0·764 555 m^3	1 m^3	= 1·307 95 yd^3
litre (l) = 0·001m^3	1 gal	= 0·004 546 09 m^3	1 m^3	= 219·969 gal
	1 pint	= 0·568 26 1 litre	1 litre	= 1·759 75 pint
	1 gal	= 4·546 09 litre	1 litre	= 0·219 969 gal
	1 gal	= 1·2 US gal	1 litre	= 0·26 US gal
	1 freight ton (40ft^3)	= 1·1327 m^3		
MASS				
gramme (g)	1 oz (avdp)	= 28·3495 g	1 g	= 0·035 274 oz (avdp)
kilogramme (kg)	1 lb	= 0·453 592 37 kg*	1 kg	= 2·204 62 lb
	1 cwt	= 50·8023 kg	1t (tonne)	= 0·984 207 ton
tonne (t) = 1000 kg	1 ton	= 1016·05 kg	1t (tonne)	= 2204·62 lb
	1 ton	= 1·016 05t (tonne)		
DENSITY				
kilogramme/cubic metre (kg/m^3)	1 lb/ft^3	= 16·0185 kg/m^3	1 kg/m^3	= 0·062 428 lb/ft^3
gramme/cubic centimetre (g/cm^3)	1 lb/in^3	= 27·6799 g/cm^3	1 g/cm^3	=0·036 127 lb/in^3
tonne/cubic metre (t/m^3)	1 ton/yd^3	= 1·328 94 t/m^3	1 t/m^3	=0·752 479 ton/yd^3
FORCE				
newton (N)	1 tonf	= 9·964 02 kN	1 kN	= 0·100 361 tonf
kilonewton (kN)	1 lbf	= 4·448 22 N	1 N	= 0·224 809 lbf
meganewton (MN)	1 poundal	= 0·138 255 N	1 N	= 7·233 01 poundal
VELOCITY				
metre/second (m/s)	1 in/s	= 25·4 mm/s*	1 mm/s	= 0·039 3701 in/s
kilometre/second (km/s)	1 ft/min	= 5·08 mm/s	1 mm/s	= 0·196 85 ft/min
knot International = 1,852·0 m/h	1 ft/s	= 0·30348 m/s*	1 m/s	= 3·280 84 ft/s
	1 mph	= 0·447 040 m/s	1 km/h	= 2·236 94 m/s
	1 mph	= 1·609 34 km/h	1 km/h	= 0·621 371 mph
	1 knot (British)	= 1·000 64 knot (inter)	1 knot (inter)	= 0·999 36 knot (British)
	1 knot	= 1·152 mph		
	1 knot	= 1·85 km/h		
VOLUME FLOW RATE				
cubic metres/second (m^3/s)	1 ft^3/s	= 0·028 3168 m^3/s	1 m^3/s	= 35·3147 ft^3/s
cubic metres/hour (m^3/h)	1 gal/h	= 0·004 546 09 m^3/h	1 m^3/h	= 219·969 gal/h
litres/hour (1/h)	1 gal/h	= 4·456 09 l/h	1 l/h	= 0·219 969 gal/h
litres/second (l/s)	1 gal/min	= 0·272 765 m^3/h	1 m^3/h	= 3·666 16 gal/min
	1 gal/min	= 0·075 768 2 l/s	1 l/s	= 13·1981 gal/min
ENERGY				
joule (J)	1 kWh	= 3·6 MJ*	1 MJ	= 0·277 778 kWh
kilojoule (kJ)	1 ftlbf	= 1·355 82 J	1 J	= 0·737 562 ftlbf
megajoule (MJ)	1 ftpdl	= 0·042 1401 J	1 J	= 23·7304 ftpdl
	1 therm	= 105·506 MJ	1 MJ	= 0·009 478 13 therm
	1 Btu	= 1·055 06 kJ	1 kJ	= 0·947 813 Btu
POWER				
watt (W)	1 hp	= 745·700 W	1W	= 0·001 341 02 hp
kilowatt (kW)	1 ftlbf/s	= 1·355 82 W	1W	= 0·737 561 ftlbf/s
megawatt (MW)				

TORQUE CONVERSION
1 lb ft = 1·356 Newton metres (Nm)
1 Nm = 0·737 lb ft

TEMPERATURE CONVERSION

Centigrade to Fahrenheit: $\dfrac{C \times 9 + 32}{5} = F$

Fahrenheit to Centigrade: $\dfrac{(F - 32) \times 5}{9} = C$

0°C = 32°F
0°F = −17·8°C

ELECTRICITY CABLES { CAPACITY

Current rating (Amps)	Cable
5	1/·044 or 3/·029
10	1/·064 or 3/·036
15	7/·029
24	7/·036
31	7/·044
37	7/·052
46	7/·064
53	19/·044
64	19/·052
83	19/·064
118	19/·083

GALVANIC CORROSION

Anodic — *Corroded end*

Metal	Approx. Voltage
Magnesium alloy	−1·6
Galvanised iron	−1.05
Zinc	−1·03
Aluminium 3003	−0·94
Cadmium	−0·80
Aluminium	−0·75
Carbon steel	−0·61
Grey iron	−0·61
Lead	−0·55
Type 304 stainless steel (active)	−0·53
Copper	−0·36
Admiralty brass	−0·29
Manganese bronze	−0·27
70/30 Copper-nickel	−0·25
Nickel 200	−0·20
Silicon bronze	−0·18
Type 316 stainless steel (active)	−0·18
INCONEL (Inco registered trademark) alloy 600	−0·17
Titanium	−0·15
Silver	−0·13
Type 304 stainless steel (passive)	−0·08
MONEL (Inco registered trademark)	−0·08
Type 316 stainless steel (passive)	−0·05

Increasing nobility (left margin)

Cathodic — *Protected end*

To prevent corrosion in the presence of seawater the voltage difference between two dissimilar metals should not exceed 0·20 Volts. The *less* noble metal corrodes away fastest.

4.8 Rope sizes and strengths

Reproduced courtesy of Marlow Ropes Ltd

SIZES & STRENGTHS

Strength = average breaking load

SD3 Racing (Spectra/Dyneema) Improved strengths

Dia. mm	1}5	2	3	4	5	6
Strength kg	12	163	244	590	989	1506
Dia. mm	8	10	12	14	16	18
Strength kg	2994	4139	5738	7984	9979	12973
Dia. mm	20	22	24			
Strength kg	14062	17237	20412			

SD3 Cruising (Spectra/Dyneema)

Dia. mm	8	10	12	14
Strength kg	1506	3067	4070	5562

Dyneemar Lite

Dia. mm	6	8
Strength kg	590	989

Tapered SD3

Dia. mm	6	9
Strength kg	590	1506

KT3 100% Aramid core

Dia. mm	3}5	4}5	5}5	6	8	10
Strength kg	480	630	830	1480	3180	4510
Dia. mm	12	14	16			
Strength kg	6810	10000	11470			

Marlowbraid polyester

Dia. mm	6	8	9	10	12	14
Strength kg	1070	1820	2250	3190	4320	5970
Dia. mm	16	18	20			
Strength kg	7840	9040	10190			

16-plait matt polyester

Dia. mm	8	9	10	12	14	16
Strength kg	1490	1970	2890	3770	5130	6700
Dia. mm	18					
Strength kg	8410					

Doublebraid

Dia. mm	6	8	9	10	12	14
Strength kg	900	1590	1810	2210	3180	4330
Dia. mm	16	18	20	22	24	26
Strength kg	5660	7160	8840	10690	12720	14930

8-plait pre-stretched polyester

Dia. mm	4	5	6	7	8
Strength kg	380	600	790	890	1400

Hi-Brites

Dia. mm	2	3	4	5	6
Strength kg	55	125	230	350	500

8-plait standard polyester

Dia. mm	1	1}5	2	3
Strength kg	35	90	130	210

8-plait low stretch matt polyester

Dia. mm	4	5	6	8	9	10
Strength kg	270	350	540	930	1040	1210

8-plait Marstron multifilament polypropylene

Dia. mm	5	6	8	9	10
Strength kg	370	460	710	1040	1310

3-strand pre-stretched polyester

Dia. mm	3	4	5	6	7	8
Strength kg	340	620	740	1100	1450	1830
Dia. mm	9	10	12	14		
Strength kg	2310	2800	3550	5250		

3-strand standard polyester

Dia. mm	4	6	8	10	12	14
Strength kg	420	760	1420	2360	3200	3930
Dia. mm	16	18	20	24	28	32
Strength kg	5090	7100	7770	11210	14640	18840

3-strand nylon

Dia. mm	8	10	12	14	16	18
Strength kg	1910	2710	3750	5100	6640	7920
Dia. mm	20	24	28	32		
Strength kg	9790	14260	18640	22600		

Multiplait nylon

Dia. mm	10	12	14	16	18	20
Strength kg	2770	3800	4670	6640	7270	9890
Dia. mm	24	28	32			
Strength kg	14370	18550	23930			

Dock Line

Dia. mm	12	14	16
Strength kg	4048	5510	7197

3-strand Nelson spunstaple polypropylene

Dia. mm	6	8	10	12	14	16
Strength kg	670	1210	1760	2410	3250	4200
Dia. mm	18	20	24	28	32	
Strength kg	4840	6210	8430	10800	13600	

3-strand Marstron

Dia. mm	6	7	8	9	10	12
Strength kg	400	620	800	980	1230	1270
Dia. mm	14	16				
Strength kg	2210	3053				

3-strand Hardyhemp polypropylene

Dia. mm	6	8	10	12	14	16
Strength kg	390	640	1030	1470	2020	2870
Dia. mm	18	20	24			
Strength kg	3330	4470	5940			

3-strand blue Sturdee polypropylene

Dia. mm	4	6	8	10	12	14
Strength kg	430	580	1230	1660	2580	3390

Keel boats Sheet sand halyards size selector
Chart shows usual sail area in square feet for a given boat length in metres. If your boat is rigged with larger sails, use the rope size indicated for the sail area.

Overall yacht length m	6-8	9	10	11	12	14	16	18
Approx. sail area sq.ft								
Main	90	144	171	198	252	405	540	720
Genoa/Jib	100	180	270	360	450	630	765	900
Spinnaker	405	495	585	765	990	1260	1620	1980
Sheet size mm dia.								
Main	8	8	8	10	12	12	14	16
Genoa/Jib	10	10	12	12	14	14	16	16
Spinnaker	8	10	10	10	12	12	12	14
Spinnaker/Guy	10	10	12	12	12	14	14	16

Suggested sheet ropes: Marlowbraid, 16-plait matt, KT3/SD3 Racing.

Halyard size mm dia.								
Main	8	10	10	10	12	12	12	14
Genoa/Jib	8	10	10	12	12	12	14	16
Spinnaker	8	8	19	10	12	12	12	14

Suggested halyard ropes: Marlowbraid, KT3 SD3 Racing or super pre-stretched polyester
Remember for KT3/SD3 Racing sheets or halyards you can go down a size.

Mooring ropes mm dia.								
Displacement (approx) tonne	2	4	5	6}5	8	11	12	20
Polyester/Nylon	8-10	12	12	14	14	16	18	24
Polypropylene (Nelson)	10-12	14	16	18	20	20	24	14

Suggested mooring ropes: 3-strand standard polyester, Multiplait nylon, or 3-strand nylon.

Anchor warps, painter lines								
Nylon	12	14	16	16	18	20	20	24
Polyester	14	16	18	18	20	24	24	24
Nylon (Kedge)	8	8	8	10	10	12	12	12

Suggested ropes: Multiplait nylon, 3-strand nylon

Anchors and chains								
Bruce	5	7}5	10	10	15	20	20	30
Danforth & CQR	8	14	14	14	19	25	25	34
Chain	8	8	10	10	10	12	12	12

Bruce, Danforth and CQR anchor on kg. Other sizes are diameter in mm

Dinghies

	Halyards KT3 SD3 Racing Marlowbraid Pre-stretched	Sheets 8-plait matt 16-plait matt 8-plait Marstron	Colour code
Sizes are diameter in mm			
Main	6	8 or 10	White
Jib	6	8 or 10	Blue
Spinnaker	6	6	Red

Control lines 5 or 6mm LS 8-plait matt, where very low stretch required use KT3/Spectra.
Note When using Marlow KT3/SD3 Racing you can go down a size

5. Anchoring and berthing

5.1 Anchors

Bruce Plough type from a design originally used to hold oil platforms in place. One piece drop-forged. Holds well on a short scope. Can have difficulty getting through weed and at times can pick up conveniently sized rocks in the three flukes.

Manufacturer's recommended anchor weights

Boat length (m)	Chain diameter (mm)	Anchor weight (kg)
7	6	2
8·5	6	5
12	10	7·5
14	10	10
17·4	13	15
22	16	20
27·5	19	30

In practice most people have found the anchor weights should be adjusted by a factor of two i.e. a 8·5m boat should have a 10kg and a 12m boat a 15kg anchor.

CQR The original plough anchor. CQR equates to 'secure'. Two piece with a swivelling plough on a stock. Probably the most common bower anchor. Imitation plough-type anchors do not usually have the weighted tip of the CQR, which makes them more difficult to dig in.

Manufacturer's recommended anchor weights

Boat length (m)	Chain diameter (mm)	Anchor weight (kg)
6·5	6	6·8 (1·5lbs)
8	6	9 (20lbs)
9	8	11·3 (25lbs)
11	10	15·8 (35lbs)
13	10	20·4 (45lbs)
16·5	13	34 (75lbs)

Delta A new anchor that looks similar to a CQR but has no moving parts. One piece drop-forged. It has a weighted tip and is designed to turn itself to a holding position the right way up however it lands.

Manufacturer's recommended anchor weights (For a cruiser-racer sailing yacht. Other craft may need to adjust the anchor weight slightly.)

Boat length (m)	Chain diameter (mm)	Anchor weight (kg)
6·8	6	4
9	6	6
12	8	10
15·5	8	16
19	10	25
23	10	40

Bügelanker A one-piece spade-like anchor that Germans swear by. It has been around long enough to gain a good reputation and appears to get through weed well.

Spade A new anchor that, like the Bügelanker, relies on a 'shovel' or 'spade' type shape to give good holding power – though at a substantial price increment. Gives good holding power once in but can have difficulty getting through weed.

Fisherman Old fashioned but still with its uses. Holds well in thick weed and soft mud. Clumsy for most boats to use as a main anchor and easily fouled by the rode if the boat turns with wind or current. An excellent anchor in difficult holding and when taking a long line ashore. There are now excellent variations where the flukes fold so that the anchor can be easily packed away.

Recommended anchor weights
In general the old rule of one pound of anchor for every foot of boat applies for the Fisherman. Thus:

Boat length (ft)	Boat length (m)	Anchor weight (lb)	Anchor weight (kg)
25	7·5	25	11·4
35	10·5	35	15·9
45	13·5	45	20·5
55	16·5	55	25

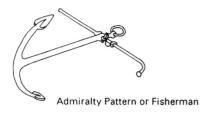

Admiralty Pattern or Fisherman

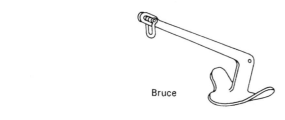

Bruce

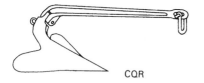

CQR

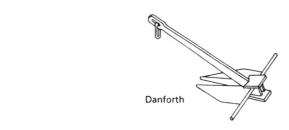

Danforth

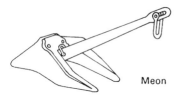

Meon

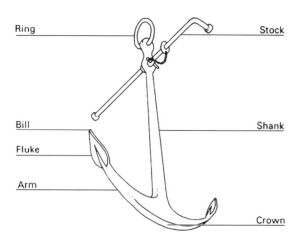

Ring Stock

Bill Shank

Fluke

Arm

Crown

Official recommendations are around 10% over this depending on the size of chain.

Danforth Originally designed in the USA by R. Danforth but now widely imitated. It is essential that it is of strong construction as it is easy to bend the shank or flukes of weakly constructed imitations. Good kedge anchor which holds well in mud. Can be fouled by the rode if used as a main anchor.

In general anchor weights are less than for the fisherman and plough types, at around 30% less depending on the weight and length of chain used. If used as a main anchor equivalent weights of the CQR are recommended or a maximum of or 10% less.

Thus (for use as a kedge with minimal chain)

Boat length (m)	Anchor weight (kg)
6	8
11	10·5
13	13·5
15	18

Brittany Similar to the Danforth but with sharpened flukes and a narrow crown designed to get it to dig in quickly. Characteristics much as for the Danforth.

Fortress Of the Danforth family but constructed of aluminium with longer and appreciably sharper flukes. It defies the long held notion that an anchor should be of heavy steel construction and in practice works surprisingly well in sand and mud. Good at getting through weed. An excellent kedge or storm anchor. Its use as a main anchor is restricted by the possibility of fouling it with the anchor rode when swinging over it.

When going bow-to it is useful to have the kedge anchor permanently on the pushpit. It doesn't have to be a flash arrangement, just a bucket and a couple of stretchies will do.

Manufacturer's recommended weights

Boat length (ft/m)	Weight (lbs/kg)	Model no.
16/4·9	4/1·8	FX-7
28/8·6	6/2·7	FX-11
33/10·1	7/3·2	FX-16
39/12	14/6·4	FX-23
46/14	19/8·6	FX-37
53/16	31/14·1	FX-55

If used as a second bower anchor or main kedge the weight and model number should be moved up one.

Grapnel Recommended by some but really only practical as an anchor for a yacht tender.

5.2 Anchor chain/rope recommendations

For chain of the appropriate size the old rule to allow a scope of at least 3 times the depth of water is a useful working rule. If there is some sea entering an anchorage or strong gusts of wind you will need more scope. For 50/50 chain and rope a minimum scope of 4–5 times the depth of water must be allowed. For anchor warps 3-strand or 8-strand nylon is normally recommended, although there are also patent lines with a lead core that can be used. There are so many variables at work here (type of craft from light planing to heavy displacement, type of holding, type of anchor, shelter from seas) that hard and fast rules no longer apply.

Recommended chain and rope sizes

Boat length (m)	Chain diameter (mm)	Rope diameter (mm) using Nylon 3-plait
8	6–8	12
10	8–10	16
12	10	18
14	12	20
16	12	20

5.3 Anchoring problems

Anchoring in the Mediterranean presents two principal difficulties.

1. Difficult holding ground. Apart from common problems encountered elsewhere such as rocky bottoms or very soft mud, the principal problem is thick weed on the bottom which stops the anchor getting through to the bottom proper. The eel-grasses *Zostera marina* and *Cymodocea nodosa* are the two main species found. Either an anchor will have difficulty penetrating the weed or it will pick up a clump of weed on the flukes or point of plough types which blunt the ability of the anchor to get to the bottom. If an anchor gets a clump of weed on the bottom it must usually be raised to clear it and then you try again.

2. Depths. In many parts of the Mediterranean a yacht must anchor in depths of 10m or more. Many anchorages do not slope evenly up to the shore but rise up abruptly from 10–15m. These considerable depths account for the common practice of chain-rope combinations to make anchor handling easy.

5.4 Anchoring techniques

Many of the problems concerning anchoring in the Mediterranean are problems of technique. In general the following applies:

1. There is never a need to rush over anchoring. Have everything ready and spend some time looking at how other craft in the anchorage are lying.

2. Select a spot where you can swing free of other craft and try to select a sandy spot to let the anchor down onto (it is usually possible to see the bottom to 10m).

3. Let the anchor down onto the bottom and then reverse slowly back or let the yacht drift back with the wind, paying out the chain and rope as you go. DO NOT LET THE CHAIN AND ROPE PILE UP IN A HEAP ON THE BOTTOM.

4. When adequate scope has been let out reverse slowly back until the anchor bites. Then increase engine revs to a third or half to dig the anchor in.

5. If the anchor does not dig in then be prepared to do it again. Never worry about the audience watching. An anchor securely in means a good night's sleep.

6. In many parts of the Mediterranean where the sea bottom drops off quickly and winds are from a constant direction in the summer it is common practice to anchor and take a long line ashore to a tree or rock. Where winds are constant the rope ashore normally 'anchors' the boat against the off-shore wind. It is important when carrying out this manoeuvre to have the yacht tender ready with

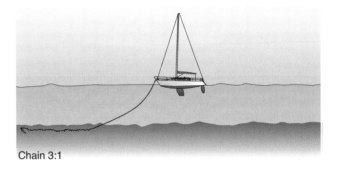

Chain 3:1

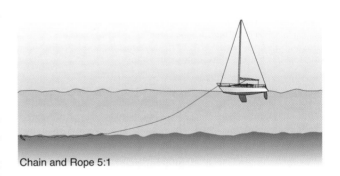

Chain and Rope 5:1

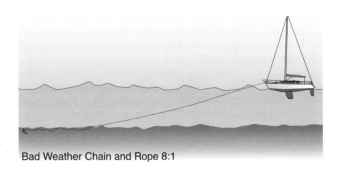

Bad Weather Chain and Rope 8:1

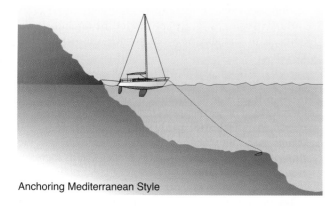

Anchoring Mediterranean Style

It is common practice in many parts of the Mediterranean to anchor with a long line ashore. The consistency of the prevailing winds makes this perfectly feasible and in tight anchorages means more boats can fit in

adequate warp flaked out and ready to run ashore. Have someone in the dinghy who can row or handle the outboard competently while laying out the line ashore.

5.5 Fouled anchors

Trip-lines There are relatively few anchorages where a tripline is recommended so most yachts do not use them. For everyday anchoring trip-lines can cause problems. They frequently foul the anchor rode proper when being deployed. They must be adequately buoyed so they are visible to other craft manoeuvring nearby. The line must not float on the surface to foul propellers. The line must not be too short or the buoy can lift the anchor off the bottom.

Opposite pull If an anchor is fouled under a rock or obstruction it may be possible to free it by leaving some chain/rope slack and motoring slowly to the opposite point to where you were lying and pulling on the anchor. Do not use too much horsepower but pull gently before raising the revs to about half. With some anchors, notably the Danforth types, it is easy to bend and distort the shank and flukes if too much force is used.

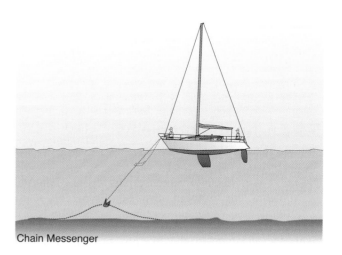

Chain Messenger

Fouled Anchor

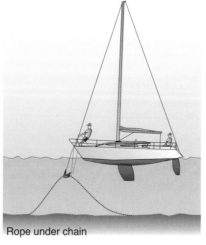

Rope under chain

Chain necklace It is useful to have a chain or lead ball necklace to which is attached a trip-line. Work the necklace down the anchor chain/rope until it gets to the anchor. Then use the tripline to pull in the opposite direction to which you were lying.

Diving If you cannot free-dive then there will probably be others around who can free-dive to at least 4–5m. Some young fit types can easily go down 10m. When manually trying to free an anchor on the bottom extreme care is needed not to be trapped by heavy chain. For deeper work there is little alternative but to engage a diver with tanks, or in extremes, abandon the anchor.

5.6 Berthing Mediterranean-style

For the most part berthing is stern or bows-to in the Mediterranean. In some harbours yachts berth alongside, mostly commercial or fishing harbours little frequented by yachts, where an anchor line would obstruct passage in the harbour, or where a current makes going stern or bows-to difficult.

There are advantages to going stern or bows-to:

- A yacht can leave comparatively easily from a berth. When alongside there may be three or four yachts outside making it a difficult process to leave.
- **Privacy** When alongside there will always be people walking over the decks if you are on the inside of any boats. When bows-to there is increased privacy from the gaze of onlookers on the quay.
- **Safety** If there is a surge in a harbour a yacht will not be squashed and scratched on the quay and yachts on the inside will not have unfair loads put on their hulls and mooring lines from boats on the outside. When stern or bows-to it is possible to ease off the line ashore and pull yourself off the quay a short distance if there is a surge in a harbour.
- **Vermin** Going stern or bows-to makes it less likely that cockroaches and rats can get on board.

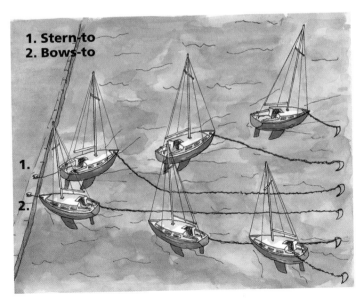

1. Stern-to
2. Bows-to

5.7 Stern or bows-to

It is now common for small to medium sized yachts (up to 13·5m) to go bows-to rather than stern-to. Even quite large yachts (up to 16m depending on displacement) will sometimes go bows-to if adequately equipped.

There are advantages:

- It is easier to manoeuvre a yacht going forwards rather than in reverse, especially if there is a cross-wind.
- There is a gain in privacy for aft cockpit boats.
- In some harbours where rubble extends underwater it is possible to get close to the quay whereas with a deep rudder aft this may be difficult or the rudder may be damaged.

There are some disadvantages:

- In an emergency it can be difficult to leave quickly and efficiently compared to those who are stern-to and can just motor out forward.
- Most anchor hauling must be done manually whereas leaving a berth when stern-to is easy with a manual or electric anchor winch.
- Unless efficiently organised it can be a bother getting the anchor and line out of a locker. Most yachts have a stern anchor permanently mounted and ready to go on the stern.
- If any chop is pushed across a harbour it will tend to push against the stern and may push a yacht onto the quay. When a yacht presents its bows to any chop there is much less resistance.

Going stern or bows-to

1. Have everything ready and in place before entering a harbour, or make it ready in the harbour if it is large enough to do so inside the shelter of a breakwater. Put fenders out on either side. Have mooring lines flaked, cleated off at one end, and led free through pulpit or pushpit. Have a spare long line coiled and ready to throw should it be needed. Make sure the anchor, chain and/or rope is ready to run.
2. Take your time picking a berth and note the position of the anchor lines from the other yachts already berthed. Note any anchor lines lying at skewed angles across any berth you have chosen.
3. Do not be tempted to lay your anchor line at an angle to account for cross-winds in a berth. If your anchor cannot hold you straight in a cross-wind then your anchor and chain is too small for the job. If you are going bows-to then think about going stern-to if the main bower anchor is heavier and on chain. If you lay your anchor at an angle across other yachts' anchors expect no sympathy when they haul your anchor up and your yacht bounces on the quay. Worse still, you may uproot another yacht's anchor, causing it to lie against the yacht next to it which lies against the next yacht and so starts a domino reaction, causing chaos and making it necessary for a number of yachts to re-lay their anchors. You will not be popular.
4. **Bows-to** Aim to drop your anchor about 4 boat lengths off the quay and slowly coast into a berth. Feed the anchor line out around a winch (one turn only) and use the anchor line to slow the yacht

Berthing bows-to is easier for smaller yachts and has the advantage of privacy from onlookers on the quay

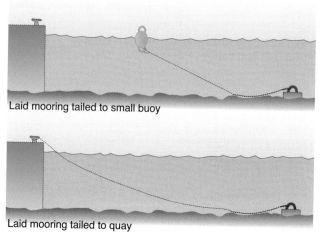

Laid mooring tailed to small buoy

Laid mooring tailed to quay

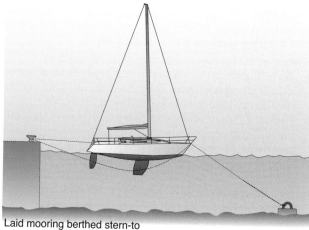

Laid mooring berthed stern-to

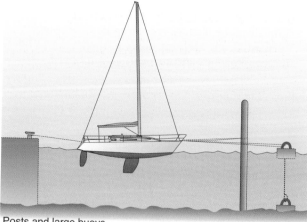

Posts and large buoys

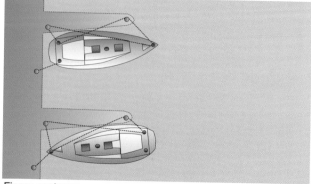

Finger pontoons

closer to the quay. Do not motor at speed into a berth as reverse is notoriously unreliable for stopping a yacht quickly. When the mooring lines are made off tighten the stern anchor. The most common mistake is to drop the anchor too short when there will be insufficient scope for it to bite.

5. **Stern-to** Aim to drop your anchor about 4 boat lengths off and ensure the chain runs freely. If the chain snatches the bows will be pulled off course making the helmsman's job a nightmare. The chain should be taken up gently when the stern is half a boats length off the quay. The boat can easily be brought up by a burst of forward. Only when the stern lines are made off should the anchor be tightened. The most common mistake is to keep the anchor chain taut, which will only keep pulling the boat off the proper course astern. Most yachts do not go astern with any ease and once a yacht is going astern keep the way on – standing on the 'wrong' side of the wheel helps the helmsman.

Going stern or bows-to takes a bit of practice at first, but with care and preparation it is not the hardship it is sometimes made out to be

5.8 Fouled anchors (berthing)

In many harbours your anchor will be fouled either by the incompetence of other yacht handlers, or because the harbour is just so crowded that a fouled anchor is inevitable. Care is needed when clearing a fouled anchor. The following procedure should be used:

1. Haul up the offending chain or anchor so it is just below or at the surface. If no electric winch is available or the winch cannot cope, assistance can be provided by tying a line to the chain and leading the end to a primary winch.
2. Cleat off the end of a line and lead it under the offending chain or anchor and back to the cleat.
3. Release your own anchor and work it free of the other chain or anchor. You may need to do this from the yacht tender.
4. Release the end of the line standing well clear – there is a lot of weight on it and the bitter end can be dangerous as it whips off the cleat.

5.9 Marina berths

Most marinas have laid moorings, posts, or finger pontoons for a yacht to go stern or bows-to. An anchor should not be used. The exception is for very large yachts for which there are no suitable laid moorings. Marina berths are normally one or a mixture of the following:

Anchor thief In some Mediterranean chandlers you can buy a shallow hook with an attachment for a tripping line. It has acquired the delightful name: the 'anchor thief'. Basically, once you have pulled the offending chain or rope of the fouled anchor to near the surface, then the anchor thief is lowered and hooked under it. Once you have cleared your own anchor and chain then the trip line on the back of the anchor thief is pulled to release the offending chain.

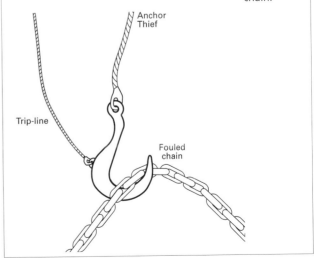

47

It takes muscle (and winch) power to get the offending anchor up and a line onto it

1. **Laid moorings tailed to the quay** The line to the quay is attached to a sinker, usually chain, which in turn is attached to a mooring block or heavy mooring chain running parallel to the quay. The line can be picked up with a boathook or picked up by the crew near the quay and led to the bow or stern (depending on whether going stern or bows-to) to be tied off. Sometimes you will get to the chain sinker and in this case the chain must be tied off. You are advised to wear gloves as the rope or chain may be covered in coral worm or barnacles which will cut bare flesh or may be covered in mud from the bottom. When leaving allow sufficient time for the sinker to pull the rope to the bottom when it is released. Do not untie the rope from the quay as when you go the bitter end will be pulled to the bottom by the sinker and marina staff will not be amused.

2. **Laid moorings tailed to a buoy** A variation on 1. In this case the rope is led to a small marker buoy which must be picked up. Use a boathook to pick up the marker buoy and attached mooring line and lead it to the bow or stern to be tied off. Care is needed when leaving not to get the line and buoy around the propeller.

3. **Posts** Normally used in Spain and France where the *tramontane* or *mistral* blows violently. Normally there is a post on either side of a berth and lines attached to the posts are taken to the bow or stern (depending on whether going stern or bows-to). In a few cases you will have to use your own lines, but this is rare.

4. **Finger pontoons** Nose in and tie up alongside the pontoon with springs to keep the boat off the quay. Finger pontoons are generally quite short so if you have an amidships cleat use it in preference to the bow or stern (outermost) cleat. Care is needed to position fenders correctly (most finger pontoons are quite low) and when jumping onto the pontoon as most will submerge at an alarming (for the bulky among us) rate into the water.

6. Marine Life

6.1 Marine life

When you first slip into the warm waters of the Mediterranean with a mask and snorkel, you will probably be disappointed: there is not the profusion of marine life you expected. Trailing a spinner behind the boat catches nothing for days. Is something wrong with the lure, or are there no fish? In the restaurants, you will be agog at the price of fish compared to anything else. You must surely mutter that you had thought this was a sea teeming with marine life, home of the *bouillabaisse*; where the ancient Greeks gambolled with dolphins and Roman writers expounded on the delights of the seafood in Mare Nostrum, the sea where Aristotle virtually invented marine biology and 2000 years later Jacques Cousteau popularised it. Where is it all?

The Mediterranean has never been rich in marine life. It is a sea that has been written about, studied, fished and sailed on for thousands of years. Its marine life has long been described and illustrated, and the peoples around the shores have been experimenting with fish recipes literally since Moses came down from the mountain, and probably longer. The Romans exalted in seafood and their descendants continue to produce fish dishes both novel and tasty. But that doesn't mean there is or ever has been much fish around, rather that it has always been prized. In the Pacific, Atlantic and Indian Oceans there is an abundance of fish, and the coral reefs of the Red Sea make the Mediterranean look like a desert, which in a way it is.

The much-vaunted blueness and clarity of the Mediterranean results from it being poor in plankton, the basis of the marine ecosystem. Plankton is scarcest in the eastern basin; the western basin is boosted by the inflow of less saline water and Atlantic plankton through the Straits of Gibraltar. Man as usual has managed to complicate the picture with the construction of the Aswan Dam in 1964. Formerly the Nile brought valuable nutrients into the eastern basin, and 20,000 tons of sardines were caught annually by Egyptian boats. Now the dam holds back the river water to fertilise the land and the catch has dropped to 1000 tons annually. The Egyptians get more crops but fewer sardines.

A second important reason for the paucity of marine life is the relatively small area of continental shelf. Below 200 metres there is not the wealth of marine life that lives in shallower waters, and in most of the Mediterranean the depths drop away quickly to more than this. Two exceptions are the northern half of the Adriatic and a shelf off the eastern coast of Tunisia, which are comparatively prolific. Below 300 metres the water in the Mediterranean is not as cold as the icy temperatures found in the Atlantic and Pacific but is a relatively warm 13°C. This might seem to favour marine life in the depths of the sea, but in fact it does not. The water at these depths is very salty as well as warm, and such water cannot hold very much dissolved oxygen: the result again means a scarcity of fish life compared to the oceans.

The Mediterranean's weak fish population has also been harvested for thousands of years. Until recently some of the fishing practices were not exactly helping conservation. In Greece and Turkey you may notice that a few of the older fishermen are minus a hand or an arm: it was probably lost dynamiting for fish, when the fuse was underestimated by a second or two and the dynamite exploded just before it was dropped into the sea. After the Second World War there were a lot of explosives around and it seemed an easier way to fish than setting nets or long-lines. Unfortunately a dynamite blast under the water kills everything in the immediate vicinity – in effect it totally destroys a small part of an ecosystem – though only some of the fish killed by the blast float up to the surface while the rest decompose on the bottom. Today, the biggest problem is not dynamite but small-mesh nets and amateurs spearfishing. Where the fisherman leaves off, the holiday diver with mask, snorkel and speargun has sufficient time on his hands to go after almost anything that moves, and frequently he does, bringing in undersized fish and lobster.

After this, you must now be wondering if there is anything at all in the way of marine life. There is, and on a boat you are close to it all and if you know where to look there is a good deal to see in the water. Ashore in the fish markets there are species not normally encountered outside the Mediterranean. If you get the chance, try some of the unusual fish dishes in the restaurants. Italian cooks have a flair for combining seafood with other ingredients to produce some of the best dishes in the Mediterranean. Before you go, arm yourself with a guide to the marine life such as the *Hamlyn Guide to the Flora and Fauna of the Mediterranean Sea* or Tegwyn Harris' *The Natural History of the Mediterranean*. If you are a seafood gourmet add Alan Davidson's *Mediterranean Seafood*. Although the following section looks at what exists where, there is simply not enough space here to classify and describe all the marine life you might come across.

6.2 Sand, rocks, mud and sea

Sandy shores

Holiday companies know how strong the allure of sandy beaches is, and brochures for the Mediterranean often show long, deserted sandy shores stretching into the distance. In fact there are not that many sandy beaches in the Mediterranean and holiday-makers looking for them would be better advised to head for the shores of the Atlantic or Indian Oceans. Sandy beaches need large waves rolling in and depositing the stuff on the shore. In the Mediterranean this mainly occurs along the North African coast, although small coves facing the prevailing wind may acquire a small sandy strip.

The sandy shore is a difficult habitat and there is really very little marine life to be found on it. The absence of any real tide in the Mediterranean

The clarity of the Mediterranean results from it being poor in plankton. In ecological terms it can be compared to semi-arid land regions like the steppes in Siberia

exacerbates the problem. In tidal waters the diurnal ebb and flow brings in food for shore-dwellers, but here this doesn't occur. There is no prolific intertidal zone.

A number of molluscs do inhabit sandy shores. Some are filter feeders sifting the water for microscopic food particles, while others are carnivores burrowing into the sand, often to attack their filter-feeding cousins. Of the latter, the most famous is the dye murex, *Bolinus brandaris*, the little spiral mollusc that Phoenicians, Greeks and Romans gathered in large quantities to prepare the royal purple dye denoting high rank. Such was the scale of the industry that at one time it was said that the beaches of the Levant and Greece were covered with piles of old murex shells.

Most sand dwellers are burrowers that escape from predators by living under the sand, or in turn hide there just buried to wait for food to come along. Many of the sand burrowers, the polychaete worms and molluscs, will not be seen unless you dig them up. In the case of the lesser and greater weevers, two related fish that burrow into the sand, this can be dangerous as they have venomous spines which they raise to protect themselves when threatened. Should you accidentally tread on one, the dorsal spine can inject poison which can cause a painful injury.

On many sandy shores the marine grasses, the same plants that can make it difficult to get an anchor into the bottom, create a jungle habitat for various animals. Numerous species of small fish, the small breams, saupe, blennies and the bogue (with the amusing generic name *Boops boops*), are common, and a patient fisherman can try to catch a breed of fish who appear to have absorbed the wisdom of Solomon when it comes to getting bait off hooks without getting caught. On some grassy bottoms the harmless and fascinating seahorse will be seen, an evolutionary dead-end that is probably endangered most by the new inhabitants of the sandy shore swimming around with mask and snorkel. More commonly the seahorse's cousin, the pipefish, will be seen snaking across the surface at dusk.

Rocky shores

It is around the rocky shores that the wealth of marine life in the Mediterranean is to be found. For the most part the coast is a rocky one where cliffs drop sheer into the sea and rocky promontories crumble gradually into it. Often the capes and headlands provide a spectacular cross-section of the tremendous metamorphic forces that buckled and compressed the land. Different types of rock – granite, sandstones, schist, basalt – are folded together at different angles within a short distance of one another. At sea level, waves have pounded and eroded the rock, forming clefts and caves and pillars of the harder rock, shapes fantastic and caves often spectacular such as the miles of caverns and grottoes at Diros in Greece. But below sea level, below the pounding of the waves, there is a stable habitat for marine life. The relatively small tidal range ensures the constant conditions of the sub-littoral world and here a wide variety of marine life flourishes.

The large brown seaweeds, the green species and the delicate red ones grow prolifically. Various sponges, sea anemones, worms and fixed filter feeders shelter in them, and crustaceans and small fish in turn live among the sponges and seaweeds. A number of weird and wonderful invertebrates inhabit this world. One of the common beasties is the sea hare, a greeny-brown flabby creature who moves around by slowly flapping its wings like a miniature manta ray. When disturbed it emits a deep purple dye into the water. Other related species belonging to the sea hares and sea slugs have exotic purple bodies with yellow spots, or white bodies with orange spots and long feathery tentacles, or red and yellow bodies and what appears to be a sea anemone on the back: this genus provide some of the weirdest and most colourful sights to be seen around a rocky coast.

At dusk the rocky shores get positively overpopulated as all manner of animals move into shallower waters looking for food. The octopus is commonly found near the surface and is easily caught. Like the monkey in the Asiatic monkey trap, which will not unclench its fist to let food go even when in danger of being caught, the octopus will not let go of what might be food on the end of a line until too late – usually when it has been hauled up and into the boat. Larger fish such as the grouper, morays, the larger breams, and rays also move into shallower waters at dusk. Small fishing boats, the *lampera* or *pêche-à-la-lumière* with bright gas lamps, potter around the shallow waters from dusk until midnight capitalising on this influx of fish.

One common but not very welcome inhabitant of the rocky shore is the sea urchin, the most common being the black sea urchin, *Arbacia lixula*. On some rocky shores there are literally thousands of the little beasts, and it is prudent and much less painful to wear an old pair of plimsoles if wandering or swimming around an infested area. The sea urchins can nibble their way into soft rock and will even collect pebbles on the outside to disguise themselves from predators. Another common inhabitant is the common limpet. The Italians eat them straight off the rocks: a sharp knife extracts them from the shell, a squeeze of lemon and straight down. A bottle of cold white wine assuages the salt and citric flavoured white flesh.

Rather less common than the humble limpet are lobsters and crayfish. Over the years these crustaceans have been netted and potted so persistently for restaurant tables that there are not many of them around anymore. One of the more unusual crustaceans you may be presented with in a restaurant, particularly in Turkey, is the flapjack lobster, a bizarre flattened and horny version of a lobster known as the *cigale* in France, but not to be turned down – it is every bit as good as lobster proper.

Estuaries

All of the estuaries in the Mediterranean are river deltas. The virtual absence of tides to carry silt away means that it is deposited at the river mouths to form deltas that continue to grow. The Camargue, the huge swampy wilderness around the Rhone, is just such a delta; similarly, the shores of the northern Adriatic around the Po. Nearby in the Black Sea the spectacular Danube delta covers over 4500 square kilometres and is estimated to grow 24 metres to seaward annually.

The major river deltas are difficult for human beings

to develop and consequently abound with wildlife. They are frequently the winter home for birds or a stopover for migrants on their way to or from North Africa. Marine life is found not so much in the swampy areas but in the region between the fresh water and the sea. The rich sediment brought down is food for numbers of marine dwellers not in abundance elsewhere. Scallops and cockles are commonly found, as well as the large, orange fan mussel: there are flatfish such as plaice, flounder and sole, and rays such as monkfish, thornback, stingray and skate. Less commonly the sturgeon, the wonderfully armoured fish that produces the little black eggs some of us pay large amounts of money for, is found in the brackish water of the estuaries in the eastern Mediterranean and the Black Sea. Your chances of catching one are slim, though, as fishing rights are strictly controlled and rigidly enforced.

The open sea

While sailing across the sea in a yacht you are closer to the water and more aware of things in and on it than when on a ship. From large ships the sea usually appears deserted; on a yacht you know this is not so.

Sea birds, particularly the shearwater and gulls, are a good clue to something going on. Dolphins and tuna create a great deal of mess when they are rounding up fish and feeding, leaving fish bits or even small fish for the sea birds to scavenge. If you see a number of sea birds wheeling and diving over the sea there is every chance that dolphins or tuna are feeding, unless some ship has recently passed and dumped a load of edible garbage into the sea.

Another commonly encountered large fish is the swordfish. In the early summer tuna and swordfish migrate into the Mediterranean to spawn, many going all the way up to the Black Sea. For some reason swordfish like to rest on the surface and a yacht under sail will surprise them. There is an explosion of water as this magnificent fish leaps into the air and a resounding smack as it falls back. This habit of basking on the surface is used to good advantage by commercial fishermen, particularly in Italy and Spain, who creep up on the creature enjoying its innocent pleasures and harpoon it. Boats with bowsprits twice the length of the boat and a mast just as high have evolved for just this purpose. The skipper at the top of the mast guides the boat towards the swordfish and the harpooner at the end of the bowsprit does his job before the swordfish even realises a boat is around.

Sharks always pop up in any conversation about the sea, and the simple answer for the Mediterranean is that nearly all the common species are found there including the great white, the hammerhead and the blue shark. Having said that, it is highly unlikely you will see one except if a fisherman brings it in. After ten years in the Mediterranean I have positively identified a shark in the water on only three occasions. Commonly dolphin or tuna are mistaken for shark. Even the tail of the innocuous sunfish (also called headfish) has been mistaken for the dorsal fin of a shark not until closer inspection is the owner of the 'fin' identified as a sunfish, probably the least deadly denizen of the deep.

What you will see are jellyfish of one variety or another. Most of these are species such as the dirty brown *Pelagia* or the cauliflower-like *Cotylorhiza tubercalata*. Occasionally you will see the beautiful silver-blue and red sail and purple body of the Portuguese man-o-war, with powerful stinging cells trailing up to 30 metres under it. Superficially similar is the By-The-Wind-Sailor, a smaller distant cousin except for the important difference that it does not have long trailing tentacles. Both species do not actually drift passively downwind with their sails, but angle them to progress on something approaching a broad reach. Apart from covering more ground (even in a light breeze a Portuguese man-o-war can cover 10 kilometres in a day), it is thought that the evolutionary value of this ability is to avoid all the other organisms and marine flotsam that drift downwind, something especially important for the Portuguese man-o-war which could otherwise get its tentacles tangled in floating debris.

One might think that jellyfish were more or less immune to predators, but in fact several animals prey on them. The sunfish quite happily gobbles them up sting and all. More unusual is the Nautilus, a delicate purple sea snail whose striking purple shell you may find washed up on the shore. It floats on a raft of slimy mucous bubbles and on coming into contact with a jellyfish immediately starts feeding on it. Another unlikely predator is the leathery turtle, which cruises around snapping up jellyfish and salps. The more common loggerhead turtle sticks to crustaceans and molluscs although it has a predilection now and then for grazing on sea urchins.

6.3 Dangerous marine animals

It is possible to give the impression that the sea is literally full of nasty creatures just waiting for the opportunity to inflict injury. Nothing could be less true. Caution is necessary because the sea does contain dangerous animals, and is itself dangerous to our mammalian lungs which are not happy when filled with seawater. But compared to the land with its bacterial and viral diseases, insects, rats, poisonous animals and plants, it is far less dangerous. And these natural dangers are nothing compared to the man-made dangers we continually expose ourselves to.

Sharks These sleek, effficient machines are the greatest fear of swimmers, yet the chances of seeing one, let alone being attacked are rare. Films like *Jaws* and its imitators have produced a phobia that is out of all proportion to the threat. Roger Caras succinctly sums up the danger in his *Dangerous to Man*: 'They kill nowhere near the number of people that snakes do, only a fraction as many as are killed by lightning, and fewer in ten years, worldwide, than die in motor accidents in the United States on a single Fourth of July or Labor Day weekend.'

Sharks do not habitually attack man, indeed they tend to shy away from such encounters. They are indeed dangerous and not to be underestimated or trusted, but they do not seek out man to attack him in the water. Most instances have been in murky water where the visibility was bad, and appear to be cases where the shark thought a man was some other kind of food. If you see a shark, it is of course silly to stay in the water: get out as quickly as possible but without panic. If you are spearfishing do not trail bleeding fish on a line and if a shark approaches let him have the fish while you depart quietly. A shark can smell blood from a quarter of a mile away and home in on it with unerring accuracy – to the shark, blood means food.

There are many suggestions on how to scare off a shark although no evidence that any of them work. A shark intent on getting to something is a primitive machine that is difficult and sometimes impossible to dissuade from its purpose. You can try shouting underwater, charging at the shark to call its bluff or releasing a sudden stream of bubbles. Always face it and if it comes too close hit it with an object, but not your hand. A shark's placoid scales are as sharp as its teeth and hitting or rubbing against it is likely to draw blood (yours), which is the last thing you want. Always your intention should be to exit from its environment into your own as quickly and quietly as possible.

Moray eels Two species inhabit the Mediterranean, *Muraena helena* being the most common; it has a brown body dappled with yellow and can grow to 11 metres in length. The moray is not aggressive and the danger comes from accidentally intruding on its home. It inhabits crevices in rocks, wrecks and amphorae, anchoring most of its body inside with the head and about a third of its length poking out looking for food. Should you not see the eel, or unintentionally molest it, it will bite you. It has a formidable array of teeth but the jaws are not large so the bite rarely does much damage. Any bite should be treated to stop secondary infection, which is likely to be more dangerous than the bite itself.

Swordfish Although there are reports of dinghies being run through and sunk by infuriated swordfish, there are no authenticated cases in the Mediterranean. In my experience of working on Italian swordfishing boats and seeing these creatures from a yacht, they appear to shy away from man and have a great deal more to fear from us than we do from them.

Octopus In hoary old tales of the sea the octopus is the eight-armed monster which upsets small boats and holds divers under the water until they drown. I can still see the malevolent beast, with beady evil eyes on a prospective dinner in the form of a pearl diver, in an illustration from a *Boy's Own Annual*. While there may have been accidental deaths of this kind, there are no authenticated records of an octopus drowning anyone. The only possible danger is if it should nip you with its small parrot-like beak. Some species inject a mild venom, which in the Mediterranean species is like a bad jellyfish sting. Normally the octopus is a shy, retiring animal intent on keeping out of the way of dangerous humans.

In the Mediterranean there are four species; the Common octopus, *Octopus vulgaris*, is the one most often seen. These interesting cephalopods are caught in thousands every year, for octopus grilled, deep-fried, charcoal grilled, with a vinaigrette, in soup, pickled with spices, in a casserole with cheese and tomatoes, and in many other different ways, is regarded quite rightly as good food. In some countries, Greece and Turkey in particular, there are restaurants serving nothing but octopus in a variety of tasty ways.

Stingrays It is estimated that the stingray causes more injuries to man than all of the other species of fish combined, though the injuries are all accidental in that the stingray is not aggressive but is reacting to being disturbed. The European variety *Daspatis pastinaca* is common in the Mediterranean, usually inhabiting shallow water where the majority of injuries inevitably occur. If the fish is disturbed it lashes upwards with its tail where there is a barbed spine and the venom apparatus. The venom produces a throbbing, sharp or shooting pain in the area of the wound and may cause nausea, vomiting, rapid heartbeat, but rarely death. The victim should seek immediate medical help and in the meantime soak the wound, invariably on the foot or the leg, in very hot water. Hot water is believed to break down the proteins in the venom and since there are no known antidotes to most of these neurotoxins, that is the best you can do. Take care to avoid secondary infections and get a tetanus booster because tetanus bacillus is sometimes injected into the wound along with venom. When walking in shallow water where stingrays are known to be, wear shoes, shuffle your feet along the bottom and take a stick to poke ahead of you.

Weeverfish Two of the members of the family *Trachinidae* are commonly found in the Mediterranean. They are comparatively small fish which are caught for food in many countries. Indeed the weever is known to the French as the *vive* or *grand vive* and is considered essential for a good *bouillabaisse*. The danger from these fish comes from the venom they can inject through their dorsal and opercular spines. Like the stingray they lie half-covered on the bottom and it is possible to accidentally step on one. Weevers can be aggressive in their territory but cannot come up and stab you with a spine. Care must be taken when they are netted in case you accidentally touch the spines.

The venom injected causes excruciating agony, although the story of a fisherman amputating his own finger to gain relief after being stabbed is probably apocryphal. The pain rapidly spreads to other parts of the body, commonly with nausea and vomiting. Rapid heartbeat and difficulty with breathing may also occur, but although several deaths have been reported none are authenticated. Bathe the wound in hot water and seek medical help as soon as possible.

Jellyfish Of all the animals described, those you are most likely to encounter are jellyfish. In certain years there can be a veritable plague of them and at such times, about every three or four years by my reckoning, it pays to choose your swimming spots carefully. The danger from jellyfish is from their stinging cells, which can cause anything from a mild itching sensation to the injection of a potent neurotoxin which in the case of the sea wasp can kill. Fortunately the sea wasp is rare in the Mediterranean.

All jellyfish sting, to immobilise their prey and protect themselves from predators, but the potency and amount of venom injected varies between species. They do not attack, but rather, as Roger Caras points out, sting anything they come into contact with 'they pulse and float along. . .waiting patiently to bump into something they can eat. They sting anything they encounter. . .to avoid the sting, man has only to avoid the bump. While he may be able to depend on the fear, quiet good nature, or the escape 'reflexes' of other potentially dangerous animals, he cannot do this with jellyfish. He must learn to keep out of the way.'

Aurelia aurita, the common jellyfish, has a saucer-shaped transparent body up to 10 cm across with four distinctive purple-violet crescents grouped around the centre. Four frilly mouth arms hang down from the body. It is not a vicious stinger; a light contact is like a nettle although prolonged contact can be more painful.

The compass jellyfish, *Chrysaora hysoscella*, also has a saucer-shaped transparent body with 16 characteristic radiating bands on top. Slender tentacles trail from the periphery and four mouth arms longer than the tentacles hang down from the centre. It is up to 30 cm across. As a stinger it is similar to the common jellyfish.

Pelagia noctiluca is a mushroom shaped jellyfish up to 10 cm across, and is light yellowbrown with 'warts' on top. Long trailing tentacles can inflict severe and painful stings.

Charybdea marsupialis or Mediterranean sea-wasp has a box-shaped transparent body up to 6 cm long with four tentacles up to 30 cm long. It can inflict severe and in some cases fatal stings. Luckily it is rarely encountered.

Rhizostoma pulmo has a dome-shaped body coloured blue-white-yellow and up to 90 cm across. Under the body are numerous mouth-arms fused into branches. Not known as a vicious stinger.

Cotylorhiza tubercalata is saucer shaped with an easily identified central dome up to 20 cm across. The mouth-arms and tentacles are a fused mass below the body with a few longer tentacles with frilly tips. It is a dirty brown-green in colour, the green colour coming from commensal algae growing on it. Not a vicious stinger.

Physalia physalis or Portuguese man-o-war. An elongated silver-blue float edged in magenta and purple, up to 30 cm long and 10 cm wide. It has a conspicuous transparent or light blue 'sail' held up by water pressure. Underneath the float is a community of different individuals: the Portuguese man-o-war is not one creature but many larval and adult forms somehow all working together as a single entity. Among its specialised organisms are some with very long stinging cells up to 30 metres long, capable of dealing painful and potentially very dangerous stings. These jellyfish should not be touched even when washed up on the beach and apparently dead.

There is no known antidote to jellyfish stings though there are a number of ways of obtaining relief. Dilute alkalis such as ammonium hydroxide, sodium bicarbonate or a freshly sliced onion applied to the wound have proved effective. Olive oil, sugar and ethyl alcohol or meths have been suggested. One tip which sounds promising is to use meat tenderiser, which apparently breaks down the protein base of the venom. If there are complications from a sting such as palpitations of the heart or breathlessness, medical help should be sought quickly.

When hauling up the anchor in an area infested with jellyfish be sure to wear gloves. The stinging tentacles, particularly of *Pelagia noctiluca* and the Portuguese man-o-war, often get caught up in anchor chain or rope and if you are pulling it up or flaking down with bare hands, you can easily be stung.

Sea urchins Take care not to get sea urchin spines in your feet when swimming or walking where they lie on the bottom. Some sea urchins have a mild venom, but the chief danger is from secondary infection when the spines break off in your feet. Wearing shoes is the best defence.

By-the-wind-sailor
Velella velella

Rhizostoma pulmo

Portuguese man-o'-war
Physalia physalis

Compass jellyfish
Chryassaora hysoscella

Pelagia noctiluca

6.4 Aide-memoire for yachtsmen to avoid polluting the sea

1. Do not throw non-biodegradable refuse over the side anywhere.
2. If within 3M of the coast do not throw biodegradable refuse over the side. Whole fruit and vegetables, cabbage and lettuce leaves, orange skins and the like do not decompose readily and are not readily eaten by scavengers such as gulls.
3. Bring non-biodegradable and relevant biodegradable refuse ashore for proper disposal.
4. Avoid spilling fuel or pumping out oily bilges within 5M of the coast. Many marinas have special disposal facilities for waste oil. Break down any diesel/oil in the bilge with a little detergent before pumping out offshore.
5. Avoid using a sea toilet without a holding tank in harbours and anchorages. In many places there are severe fines for pumping out toilets in harbour. Pump out holding tanks when at least 2-3M offshore. Do not use strong disinfectants in toilets as it harms marine life.
6. Avoid using strong detergents for washing up or cleaning the boat. In many places there are severe fines for pumping out excessive amounts of detergent in harbour.
7. Avoid using damaging cleaning chemicals on the hull and deck.
8. Avoid scrubbing the bottom in confined places where antifouling residue can damage marine life.
9. Use mild antifoulings and avoid those with tributyl tin (TBT) which is banned in some countries.
10. Do not empty solvents and paint residues into the sea or where they can leach into waterways.
11. Do not empty waste oil or diesel into or near the sea. Dispose of it in sealed cans in the rubbish or in the special receptacles provided in some marinas.
12. Ashore do not light fires where the surrounding vegetation could catch light or in strong winds. Always keep a bucket of water handy. In some countries it is prohibited to light fires in the summer months except in allocated places.
13. When snorkelling or diving with bottles do not disturb the marine life unduly by removing plants or animals.

Useful addresses

Greenpeace, Canonbury Villas, London N1 2PN ☎ 020 7865 8100 *email* info@ukgreenpeace.org www.greenpeace.org.uk

Friends of the Earth, 26-28 Underwood Street, London N1 7JG ☎ 020 7490 1555 *email* info@foe.co.uk www.foe.co.uk

Environmental Investigation Agency (EIA), ☎020 7354 7960 email info@eia-international.org www.eia-international.org

Worldwide Fund for Nature, Panda House, Weyside Park, Godalming, Surrey GU7 1XR ☎ 01483 426444 www.wwf-uk.org

British Trust for Ornithology, National Centre for Ornithology, The Nunnery, Thetford, Norfolk IP24 2PU ☎ 01842 750050 www.bto.org

World Meteorological Organisation, 7 bis Avenue de la Paix, CP2300 – 1211 Geneva 2, Switzerland ☎ +41 22 730 8111 www.wmo.ch

6.5 Common Mediterranean marine life

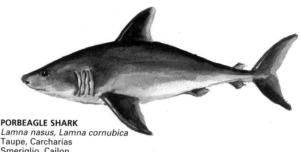

PORBEAGLE SHARK
Lamna nasus, Lamna cornubica
Taupe, Carcharías
Smeriglio, Cailon
Max length 400cm

DOGFISH
Scyliorhinus caniculus
Petite roussette, Skyláki,
Gattuccio, Pintarroja
Max length 75cm

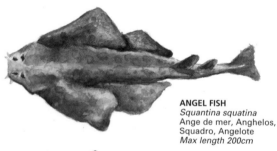

SARDINE
Sardina pilchardus
Sardine, Sardélla, Sardina, Sardina
Max length 20cm

ANGEL FISH
Squantina squatina
Ange de mer, Anghelos,
Squadro, Angelote
Max length 200cm

ANCHOVY
Engraulis encrasicolus
Anchois, Gávros, Acciuga,Boquerón
Max length 20cm

COMMON EEL
Anguilla anguilla
Anguille, Chéli, Anguilla, Anguila
Max length 150cm

MORAY EEL
Muraena helena
Murène, Smerna, Murena, Morena
Max length 150cm

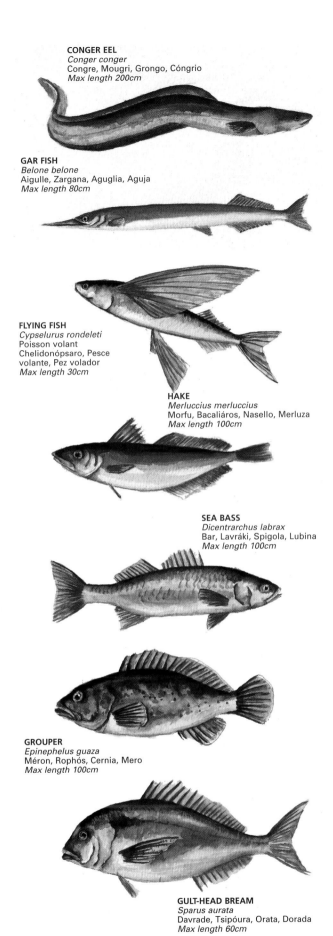

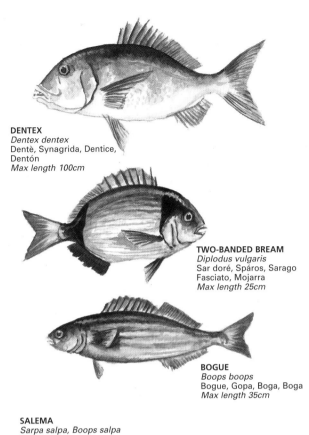

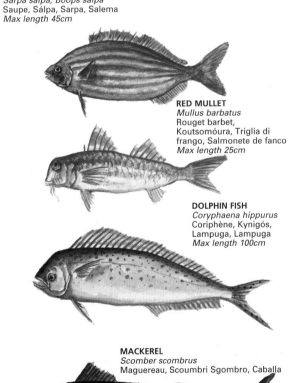

CONGER EEL
Conger conger
Congre, Mougri, Grongo, Cóngrio
Max length 200cm

GAR FISH
Belone belone
Aigulle, Zargana, Aguglia, Aguja
Max length 80cm

FLYING FISH
Cypselurus rondeleti
Poisson volant
Chelidonópsaro, Pesce
volante, Pez volador
Max length 30cm

HAKE
Merluccius merluccius
Morfu, Bacaliáros, Nasello, Merluza
Max length 100cm

SEA BASS
Dicentrarchus labrax
Bar, Lavráki, Spigola, Lubina
Max length 100cm

GROUPER
Epinephelus guaza
Méron, Rophós, Cernia, Mero
Max length 100cm

GULT-HEAD BREAM
Sparus aurata
Davrade, Tsipóura, Orata, Dorada
Max length 60cm

DENTEX
Dentex dentex
Dentè, Synagrida, Dentice,
Dentón
Max length 100cm

TWO-BANDED BREAM
Diplodus vulgaris
Sar doré, Spáros, Sarago
Fasciato, Mojarra
Max length 25cm

BOGUE
Boops boops
Bogue, Gopa, Boga, Boga
Max length 35cm

SALEMA
Sarpa salpa, Boops salpa
Saupe, Sálpa, Sarpa, Salema
Max length 45cm

RED MULLET
Mullus barbatus
Rouget barbet,
Koutsomóura, Triglia di
frango, Salmonete de fanco
Max length 25cm

DOLPHIN FISH
Coryphaena hippurus
Coriphène, Kynigós,
Lampuga, Lampuga
Max length 100cm

MACKEREL
Scomber scombrus
Maguereau, Scoumbri Sgombro, Caballa

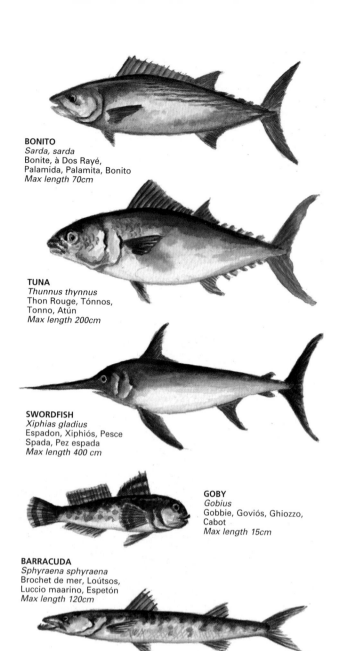

BONITO
Sarda, sarda
Bonite, à Dos Rayé,
Palamida, Palamita, Bonito
Max length 70cm

TUNA
Thunnus thynnus
Thon Rouge, Tónnos,
Tonno, Atún
Max length 200cm

SWORDFISH
Xiphias gladius
Espadon, Xiphiós, Pesce
Spada, Pez espada
Max length 400 cm

GOBY
Gobius
Gobbie, Goviós, Ghiozzo,
Cabot
Max length 15cm

BARRACUDA
Sphyraena sphyraena
Brochet de mer, Loútsos,
Luccio maarino, Espetón
Max length 120cm

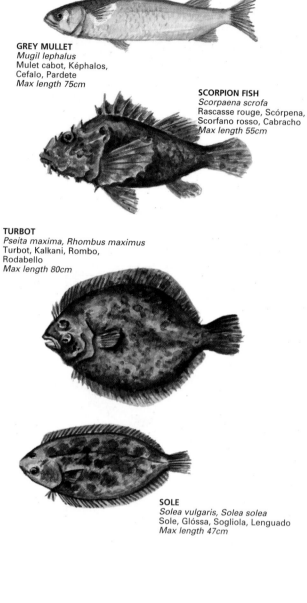

GREY MULLET
Mugil lephalus
Mulet cabot, Képhalos,
Cefalo, Pardete
Max length 75cm

SCORPION FISH
Scorpaena scrofa
Rascasse rouge, Scórpena,
Scorfano rosso, Cabracho
Max length 55cm

TURBOT
Pseita maxima, Rhombus maximus
Turbot, Kalkani, Rombo,
Rodabello
Max length 80cm

SOLE
Solea vulgaris, Solea solea
Sole, Glóssa, Sogliola, Lenguado
Max length 47cm

EUPHROSYNE DOLPHIN
Stenella coeruleoalba
Max length 2m

BOTTLE-NOSED DOLPHIN
Tursiops truncatus
Max length 3.6m

COMMON PORPOISE
Phocoena phocoena
Max length 1.8cm

COMMON DOLPHIN
Delphinus delphis
Max length 2.4m

RISSO'S DOLPHIN
Grampus griseus
Max length 4m

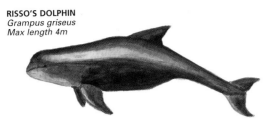

FLAT LOBSTER
Scyllarides latus
Grande cigale, Lyra
Magnosa, Cigarra
Max length 45cm

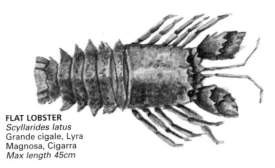

PILOT WHALE
Globicephala melaena
Max length 7.6m

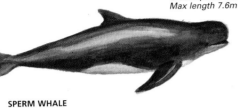

SPERM WHALE
Physeter catodon
Max length 18m

EDIBLE CRAB
Cancer pagurus
Tourteau, Siderokavoúras,
Granciporro, Buey
Max length 20cm

SPIDER CRAB
Maja squinado
Araignée, Kavouromána
Grancevola, Centolla
Max length 20cm

COMMON PRAWN
Palaemon serratus
Crevette Rose, Gardidaki,
Gamberello, Quisquilla

LOBSTER
Homarus gammarus
Homard, Astakós, Astice,
Bogavante
Max length 60cm

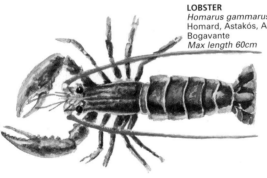

OCTOPUS
Octopus vulgaris
Pieuvre, Octapous, Polpo,
Polpo
Max length 300 cm

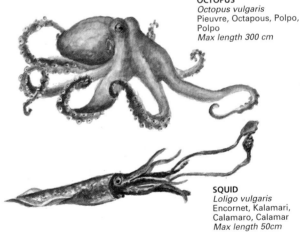

SQUID
Loligo vulgaris
Encornet, Kalamari,
Calamaro, Calamar
Max length 50cm

SPINY LOBSTER
Palinurus elephas
Langouste, Astakós,
Aragosta, Langosta
Max length 50cm

CUTTLEFISH
Sepia officinallis
Selche, Soupía, Seppia
Jibia
Max length 25cm

6. MARINE LIFE

57

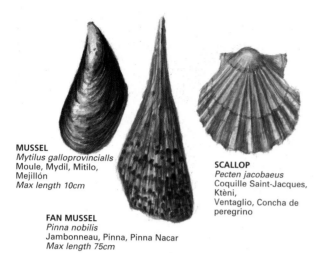

MUSSEL
Mytilus galloprovincialls
Moule, Mydil, Mitilo,
Mejillón
Max length 10cm

SCALLOP
Pecten jacobaeus
Coquille Saint-Jacques,
Ktèni,
Ventaglio, Concha de
peregrino

FAN MUSSEL
Pinna nobilis
Jambonneau, Pinna, Pinna Nacar
Max length 75cm

SEA URCHIN
Paracentrotus lividus
Oursin, Achinos, Riccio di
mar, Erizo de Mar
Max length 8cm

LIMPET
Patella caerulea
Patelle, Petalida, Patella,Lapa
Max length 5cm

OYSTER
Ostrea edulis
Huitre, Stridi, Ostrica, Ostra
Max length 12cm

ABALONE
Haliotis tuberculata
Ormeau, Ailótis, Orecchia
Marina, Oreja de Mar
Max length 10cm

Local names are in order:
French, Greek, Italian and Spanish

7. Basic First Aid

Compiled by Terence J. Carter (Thames Valley Medical and Rescue Unit)

7.1 First Aid box

The First Aid box must always be available and known to all on board; if you use anything from it replace it at once – your life may depend upon it.

Choose a good strong waterproof box, pack the items into polythene bags so that they stay dry and unsoiled.

Make sure that you can use the items in the First Aid box. DO NOT carry unnecessary items that will not be used – many commercial First Aid boxes contain items that are rarely used; stick to the list and you will not go wrong. The list has been made in the light of many years' experience in risk management and First Aid, on land and sea.

7 triangular bandages (slings and broad bandages)
6 packs of sterile gauze (dressings)
1 bag of cotton wool balls (wound cleaning)
1 roll of cotton wool (padding/general purpose)
10 packs of non-adherent (5cm x 5cm) dressings.
10 packs of non-adherent dressings (10cm x 10cm).
6 gauze bandages (5cm wide)
4 gauze bandages (7}5cm wide)
3 crepe bandages
4 compressed wound dressings (medium)
4 compressed wound dressings (large)
1 tube-gauze applicator (finger size)
1 roll tube-gauze finger dressing bandage
2 boxes assorted plasters for small cuts and wounds
3 sterile eye patches
1 eye bath
1 tube of antiseptic cream for general purposes/cuts and grazes
1 bottle antiseptic solution for cleaning wounds and instruments
1 bottle hydrogen peroxide for cleaning dirty wounds
sea sickness tablets (Stugeron by Jennsen)
Imodium capsules (diarrhoea treatment)
Paracetemol for pain
Aspirin for reducing fever
Indigestion tablets
1 digital thermometer
1 pair of sharp scissors
1 pair of blunt ended scissors
1 pair of splinter tweezers
1 pair of artery clamps
2 rolls of adhesive strapping
2 rolls of micropore tape; some people are allergic to zinc oxide tape
1 bottle of calamine lotion for sunburn/windburn
1 tube of 1% hydrocortisone cream for insect/fish stings
1 tub of bicarbonate of soda for insect/fish stings
2 packets of sterile strips for closing wounds (like sutures)
Consult local protocols for a suitable broad spectrum antibiotic, such as Ampicillin or Tetracycline, to be carried on long deep-sea trips only.

7.2 Shock

Shock is a depressed condition of the body arising from an insufficient supply of blood to the brain, resulting in oxygen deficiency. It accompanies injury, severe pain or sudden illness, and may vary in severity from a feeling of faintness to collapse or even death.

There are two types of shock:

- *True shock,* caused by loss of body fluids and blood.
- *Neurogenic shock,* caused by a nerve reaction.

The commonest, and therefore most important, cause of shock is loss of blood plasma which may occur with injury or disease.

The brain may be deprived of blood in two ways:

1. From a haemorrhage, when blood is irretrievably lost; though this is more often external and visible, it can also be from concealed or internal bleeding. Loss of plasma, as in burns, may produce similar a result. This loss is absolute, and if severe will have to be replaced by a blood or plasma transfusion (generally in hospital).
2. From nerve (neurogenic) shock, when much blood is pooled in internal organs and blood vessels and is therefore not available for general circulation. If sufficiently severe or prolonged, consciousness is lost (fainting). As recovery takes place, circulation improves and gradually becomes normal.

Other common and contributory factors are pain, exhaustion, stimulation of the sensory nerves of smell, sight and hearing, absorption of toxic substances from crushed muscles and burns and from bacterial infection or inflammation. Other causes are acute medical and surgical conditions, e.g. heart attack or perforated appendix.

Signs and symptoms of shock

Neurogenic shock This may vary from a slight feeling of faintness to a complete collapse. With slight degrees of shock there may be giddiness, pallor, nausea, cold clammy skin with a slow pulse at first, getting quicker before returning to normal.

True shock Where haemorrhage is the main cause these signs and symptoms are aggravated, depending on the degree of bleeding. The severity of true shock will depend on the rate and extent of blood loss, how long the shocked condition has lasted, the promptness of treatment.

General treatment of shock

- control the injury or cause.
- take the casualty away from the crowd, into the shade and fresh air. Beware of unnecessary movement as this could be just as harmful.
- Lay on back with head low and turned to one side and legs raised, this may be done by tilting the stretcher. If unconscious, use the recovery (D) position.
- loosen tight clothing about the neck, chest and waist.
- wrap casualty in a blanket – protect, but do not overheat.
- reassure the casualty and do not leave unattended. Let him or her smoke if he or she wishes, but only if injuries are minor.
- give nothing by mouth if the casualty is unconscious or suffering from head injury, internal or uncontrolled external bleeding, or if an operation may be necessary.
- in neurogenic shock, a cup of tea or coffee may be given during the recovery stage.
- do not apply heat or friction to the limbs, nor use a hot water bottle.

Remember, where there is a loss of blood a transfusion or even an operation may be necessary, therefore casualty evacuation becomes very urgent. Remember also:

- W Warmth
- R Rest, reassurance, relief of pain
- A Arrest bleeding
- F Fluids if safe. If in doubt – keep it out

7.3 Heart pain

Heart attack and cardiac arrest are the most common forms of heart pain that you will encounter.

Angina pectoris is the pain caused by the narrowing of the coronary arteries which supply the heart muscle, and which cannot cope with the demand made upon them by over-exertion e.g. running for a bus, or hauling halyards in a stiff wind. The attack will slow the person up and force him or her to rest.

Signs and symptoms

- severe pain in the chest, extending into one or both arms (usually the left) and jaw, maybe extending into the throat too.
- shortness of breath.
- signs and symptoms of shock.

Treatment

Let the patient rest in the most comfortable position and reassure him or her. If the patient has medication for this condition, assist him or her to take it – most known sufferers will always keep their medication with them. Once taken, the attack will quickly pass.

Heart attack *(Coronary thrombosis)*

This occurs when the heart is suddenly deprived of oxygen through the blood supply not getting to the heart muscle because a blood clot has blocked one or more of the coronary arteries.

Signs and symptoms

- crushing, vice-like pain in the centre of the chest, moving upwards down the left arm – can be mild or very severe.
- vice-like pain in the throat, unlike angina this pain will not go away with rest.
- attack may occur when patient is resting or doing any activity.
- patient is restless and feels he or she may die (feeling of impending doom).
- nausea and/or sickness.
- shortness of breath, rapid pulse, ashen skin.

Treatment

- sit the patient down in the upright position or W position (knees drawn up).
- if the patient is conscious give one aspirin to chew

EUROPEAN RESUSCITATION COUNCIL'S BASIC LIFE SUPPORT PROCEDURES

ALL PATIENTS

CHECK RESPONSIVENESS – Call and shake patient
NO RESPONSE – Call for help
OPEN AIRWAY – Head tilt – Chin lift or jaw thrust
CHECK BREATHING – Look, Listen and Feel

NO BREATHING

ADULT	CHILD	INFANT
CHECK FOR CIRCULATION carotid pulse for 5 seconds	GIVE 5 SLOW BREATHS mouth to mouth	GIVE 5 SLOW BREATHS mouth to mouth and nose
NO PULSE	CHECK FOR CIRCULATION carotid pulse for 5 seconds	CHECK FOR CIRCULATION Brachial pulse for 5 seconds
ACTIVATE EMERGENCY MEDICAL SERVICES	NO PULSE	NO PULSE OR RATE LESS THAN 60bpm
START CPR	START EXTERNAL CHEST COMPRESSIONS depth 3cm at 100bpm	START EXTERNAL CHEST COMPRESSIONS depth 2cm at 100bpm
2 SLOW BREATHS mouth to mouth and then 15 EXTERNAL COMPRESSIONS depth 4–5cm at 60 to 100bpm	1 BREATH then 5 EXTERNAL CHEST COMPRESSIONS*	1 BREATH then 5 EXTERNAL COMPRESSIONS
	ACTIVATE EMERGENCY MEDICAL SERVICES	ACTIVATE EMERGENCY MEDICAL SERVICES

Note If you are on your own and your casualty is an ADULT you must *activate the emergency medical services early and fast.*

With children and infants you must start CPR early. You may be able to take the child or infant with you to the telephone to call.
*May need 2:15 in child over 8 years.

---

slowly. He or she may collapse without warning. Be prepared to give CPR (Cardio-Pulmonary Resuscitation), observe the patient and record your observations every 10 minutes.

- if patient becomes unconscious, put in recovery position.
- radio for *URGENT* medical assistance. If you have oxygen on board give it.

Cardiac arrest

This is when the heart stops and the blood is not circulated to all the vital organs. If the brain is deprived of oxygen for more than 4 minutes the patient will suffer irreversible brain damage and die.

It can happen as a result of trauma, heart attack, suffocation, gassing, anaphylactic shock, drug overdose, hypothermia and severe blood loss.

Signs and symptoms

Absent pulse and breathing.

Treatment

See flow chart for adults, children and infants.

7.4 Choking

Choking will occur when food or other foreign bodies are trapped in the back of the throat.

Immediate action is required if the patient cannot breath and is gasping, or pointing to the throat, or the face, especially around the mouth or the lips, turns blue.

Encourage to cough. If no response, sweep the mouth and try to clear any debris. Bend him or her over and with the heel of the hand slap on the back 4 times – all the time encouraging to cough. If this does not dislodge the obstruction carry out the Heimlich method.

Heimlich method

- remove any debris or false teeth.
- encourage coughing.
- place your closed fist against the upper abdomen below the ribs, grasp your fist with right hand, press suddenly and sharply upwards with a thrusting action – do this 4/5 times fairly quickly; this should dislodge the obstruction by 'blowing it out like a cork from a bottle'.
- if the patient becomes unconscious lay him/her down, sit astride and do abdominal thrusts.
- turn head to one side, sit astride. Place your hands one on top of another, fingers pointing upwards, underneath the ribs on the upper abdomen. With a thrusting action sharply push and repeat 4 times, then turn the patient on his or her side and give 4 back blows. If this does not work try again to sweep the airway clear and commence rescue breathing.

In small children

Lay the child over your knee, commence the above using less force, and if the Heimlich method is required use one fist.

In babies

Hold baby upside down and slap the back with the flat of your hand. If Heimlich method is required use two fingers only. In all cases of airway obstruction be prepared to do CPR at any stage.

7.5 Fainting

A person may feel faint for various reasons, such a shock, witnessing an accident, hurting themselves, etc.

Treatment

- sit the patient down and put head between the knees. Apply a cold compress to the neck.
- lay the patient down, turn head to one side and raise the legs higher than the head. Apply cold compress to the head.
- reassure and talk to them.
- undo all tight clothing.

The patient will rapidly recover.

7.6 Epilepsy

This is a medical condition where there is disruption in the electrical impulses to the brain.
There are two types:

Minor Epilepsy

This attack may go unnoticed by the patient and those around, when it involves a loss of concentration. However the patient may show the following signs:

- temporary loss of memory.
- loss of concentration.
- possible odd behaviour and 'talking silly'.

Treatment

- do nothing except stay with the patient – never leave alone as this may precede a major attack.
- reassure the patient. Protect from any danger. If at sea take below.

Major Epilepsy

Most major attacks will just happen without any apparent warning to the observer.

The patient may have had a pre-warning or 'aura' which can manifest as a strange smell, odd sensations or change of mood.

Signs and symptoms

Most major fits follow a pattern and last no more than 5 minutes.

- Some patients cry out and fall to the ground unconscious and rigid.
- Breathing may stop, face turns red and the lips blue - this stage may last up to 30 seconds.
- Convulsions start when the muscles relax and the patient will jerk and thrash about uncontrollably. The patient may froth at the mouth (bloodstained if the tongue is bitten).
- There may be loss of both bladder and bowel control.
- The final stage is when all the muscles relax and breathing returns to normal – the patient may remain unconscious for several minutes – on regaining consciousness he or she may feel con-

fused, dazed or may behave oddly. Some patients fit several times, but this is very rare.

Treatment

- do not panic. If you have never seen a patient fit it can be very traumatic.
- move any fittings and furniture away from the patient.
- do not attempt to restrain, this will make him or her more violent.
- do not force the mouth open or try to put a hard object between the teeth (this is the quickest way to lose your fingers!).
- do not move the patient unless there is danger to his or her life. When the convulsions stop, place in the recovery position, ensure the airway is clear, and remain with the patient.
- do not attempt to wake. When the patient regains consciousness treat any injuries that may have been caused.

Radio for advice if the patient fits several times, or does not regain consciousness after 15 minutes.

7.7 Stroke

A stroke occurs when the blood supply carrying oxygen to the brain is cut off due to blockage or rupture of a blood vessel. The effect can be temporary or permanent, and may range from slight to severe.

The most common causes of stroke are: cerebral haemorrhage – a blood vessel ruptures; cerebral embolism – a clot forms in another part of the body and travels to the brain; cerebral thrombosis – a blockage occurs due to a blood clot and compression of a vessel.

This condition develops very suddenly and usually without warning.

Never discuss the patient's condition in front of him or her as stroke patients, even unconscious or apparently confused, can still understand.

Signs and symptoms

- sudden severe headache.
- confused state.
- progressive loss of consciousness.
- weakness or paralysis – may be confined to one side of the body, the patient may dribble, or have a drooping mouth and have slurred or impaired speech (may be mistaken for a drunk).
- loss of power to one or both limbs.
- loss of bladder and/or bowel control.

Treatment

- handle the patient gently, lay him or her down with head and shoulders raised, incline head to one side. Loosen all tight clothing. Support any paralysed limbs. Remove all dentures.
- if the patient becomes unconscious place in recovery position, preferably paralysed side down.
- place cold compress on skull and back of the neck. *Never* try to give a drink.
- keep warm but not over-warm as excessive heats speeds brain damage. *Never* leave the patient.
- radio for *urgent* medical assistance, stating you have a patient with a suspected stroke. Head for the nearest harbour.

AIR PASSAGES

If the unconscious casualty is lying on his back the tongue may fall backwards and block the air passage

If the neck is extended, the head pressed backwards and the lower jaw pushed upwards, the tongue moves forwards, thus opening the air passages

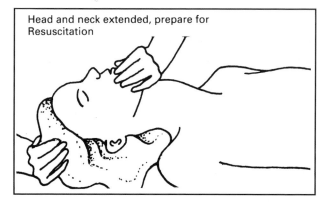

Head and neck extended, prepare for Resuscitation

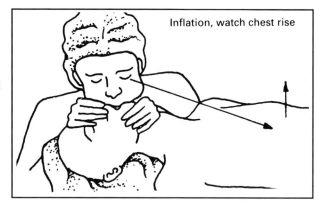

Inflation, watch chest rise

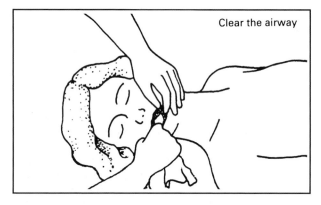

Clear the airway

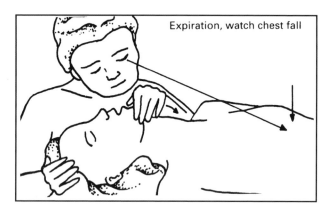

Expiration, watch chest fall

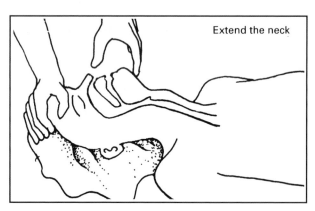

Extend the neck

RECOVERY POSITION

The technique mainly involves changes in the manipulation of the casualty's arms. The standard procedure is to tuck the nearest arm, palm up, into the casualty's side and then pull the furthest arm across their chest resting the hand on the shoulder.

The recommended routine is to pull the arm nearest to the rescuer put at right angles to the casualty's body with the elbow bent and the palm uppermost. The other arm is then placed across the chest as before but with the back of this hand held against the casualty's cheek.

The knee of the casualty's furthest leg is then pulled up and gripped just above the knee to pull them over into the correct position.

The rescuer's knees can be used to stabilise the casualty.

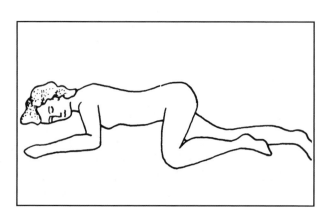

7.8 Unconsciousness

Unconsciousness is an abnormal state resulting from an interruption of the brain's normal activity.

Recognition
- look for any obvious signs of why patient is unconscius, e.g. identity bracelet, diabetic, needle marks, smell of alcohol, fallen masts or yards or swinging booms.
- diminished sweating (absence of sweating in most cases).
- hot, flushed, dry skin.
- full bounding pulse.

Treatment
- maintain an open and clear airway. Open the airway by lifting the chin and tilting the head. (The airway is in danger of being obstructed if the casualty is lying on his or her back, as the tongue can fall back into the back of the throat as the muscles that normally hold it correctly lose their control.) As there is no cough reflex, the saliva can choke the patient. Also, the stomach may regurgitate its contents into the throat, choking the patient.
- always carry out the following checks on any unconscious patient: record pulse rate, level of consciousness, breathing rate per minute, movement (see **AVPU** below)

```
A   Alert (eyes open)
V   responds to Voice
P   responds to Painful stimulus
U   Unresponsive, open to painful stimulus
```

- make a note of any changes, and check all levels every 10 minutes.
- write down all of the above information and inform the nearest medical facility of your findings by radio. Seek *urgent* assistance.
- never leave an unconscious person.
- never try to give a drink to an unconscious person
- be prepared to start CPR, see *7.3 Heart pain*.

Drunkenness

Any unconscious drunk is at risk from a blocked airway especially if the drunk is lying on his/her back on a bunk in a locked cabin, or collapsed on the jetty or wharf, as he/she will vomit and inhale, causing blockage of the air passages.

7.9 Wounds and bleeding

Blood and the circulation

Blood is made up of red and white blood cells and platelets suspended in a liquid called plasma. The functions of blood are to:
- carry nourishment round the body.
- carry oxygen to the tissues by means of the haemoglobin found in the red cells.
- remove waste products, such as carbon dioxide and urea, from the body tissues.
- carry hormones and antibodies around the body.
- assist in the defence of the body against infection, e.g. infected wounds or boils, when the white blood cells are required to engulf and destroy any invading bacteria.

The heart

The heart is a hollow muscular organ, about the size of a clenched fist, lying between the two lungs behind the sternum, protected by the rib cage, It acts as a pump, circulating blood around the body in the blood vessels.

Blood vessels

There are three main types of blood vessel:
- Arteries These are thick-walled, muscular tubes which carry blood away from the heart to the body tissues. Examples are the aorta and femoral artery. This blood is oxygenated.
- Veins These are thin-walled tubes which carry blood from the tissues to the heart. Examples are the inferior vena cava and the superior vena cava.
- Capillaries These are minute, thin tubes connecting the arteries and veins. In them occurs the exchange of oxygen and carbon dioxide, food and waste between the blood and the tissues.

Arteries carry blood containing oxygen, and veins carry blood which has had the oxygen extracted. The exceptions to this rule are the pulmonary artery which carries blood requiring oxygenation away to the lungs, and the pulmonary vein which carries blood containing oxygen to the heart.

The arteries and veins have non-return valves; this means the blood will flow in only one direction.

WOUNDS AND BLEEDING

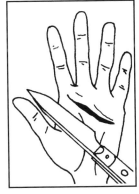

Incised or clean cut

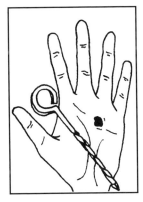

Pierced wound

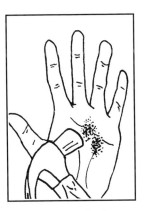

Contused or bruised

Punctured or stabbed

The pulse

Every time the heart beats it pumps into the arteries to expand as the blood passes through. The wave of expansion is called the pulse. The normal pulse rate of an adult is between 60 and 80 per minute. Children have a much higher pulse rate, ranging from 130 at birth to 80 at the age of 12. To take the pulse:

- place the tips of three fingers over the artery (radial, temporal or carotid).
- count the number of beats per minute, at the same time noting the strength and regularity of the beat.
- do not use your thumb to take the pulse.

The pulse rate is increased by:

exercise
fever
emotional stress
bleeding
dehydration
shock

The pulse rate is decreased in:

simple fainting
old age
sleep
casualties with head injuries
patients having drug therapies, e.g. morphine
highly trained athletes

Blood volume

The total quantity of blood circulating in the body of an average size adult is roughly ten or eleven pints. A good guide is one pint to every stone weight.

Wounds

A wound is an abnormal break in the tissues of the body, which may permit the escape of blood, externally or internally, and in either instance may allow the entrance of germs, causing infection. As in the case of external bleeding, internal haemorrhage may be either slight or severe.

Bleeding

Bleeding is also known as haemorrhage. Bleeding may be external and obvious, or internal and concealed.

External bleeding

Recognition

- in arterial bleeding, the blood spurts out of the wound in time with the heart beat
- in venous bleeding the blood wells out from the wound in an even flow.
- in capillary bleeding the blood oozes from the wound. This type of bleeding often stops without treatment.

Treatment

- reassure the casualty and lie him or her down to rest.
- provided that any injury will not be made worse, any injured limb which is bleeding should be raised as high as the comfort of the patient will allow. This reduces the flow of blood in the arteries and increases the drainage in the veins and so helps to reduce bleeding from the wound.
- place a dressing over the wound and apply pressure with the palm of the hand. A sterile dressing is best, but any piece of clean material will suffice if no sterile dressings are available. If the wound is large, make a pad of the dressing and press it into the wound at the point where the bleeding is worst.
- maintain pressure by the application of a firm bandage over the dressing(s) until the bleeding has stopped.
- if blood seeps through the first dressing, apply a second dressing on top of the first. Up to three dressings, one on top of the other, may be applied. They are not to be removed until the casualty arrives at the treatment centre.
- if these methods do not succeed it may be necessary to apply pressure to the appropriate pressure point.
- rest is vital. If the body is resting, the heart beats with less force and this reduces bleeding.

Internal bleeding

This type of bleeding usually occurs after the casualty has sustained a sharp blow to the abdomen or the back, a penetrating wound of the buttock, crush injury of the chest or subjection to blast.

Recognition

- history of what has occurred
- pallor
- cold, clammy skin
- rapid weak pulse
- restlessness and thirst
- dimness of vision

If the bleeding is within the abdomen there may be, additionally:
- vomiting
- blood in the faeces

If the bleeding is within the chest there may be, additionally:
- coughing
- distressed breathing

Treatment

- lie the casualty down at rest
- protect from the cold
- reassure him or her
- arrange early evacuation as urgent transfusion and surgery will be required
- if early evacuation is not possible, the casualty may be allowed a drink of water, unless there is abdominal injury

Note Internal bleeding may occur around the sites of fractures, particularly of large bones, e.g. the femur.

Natural arrest of bleeding

- retraction of the blood vessels – cleanly divided blood vessels tend to shrink closed and pull back into the tissue
- clotting of the blood

Tourniquets

Although the use of tourniquets is officially frowned upon I am including it because, as a sailor, you may find yourself many miles away from professional assistance and direct pressure may not be enough.

Though tourniquets are not used as a general rule, you need to be able to recognise and deal with them. As a sailor you may come across a situation where you are left little choice but to apply a tourniquet, e.g. if someone has had fingers torn off, therefore you need to understand the rules governing the application of a tourniquet.

A tourniquet can only be applied effectively in two places:

the upper arm
the thigh

The dangers associated with tourniquets are:
- they may actually increase bleeding
- they may damage main nerves and blood vessels
- they may cause gangrene in the affected limb.

Rules of use
- never use a tourniquet unless it is impossible to stop the bleeding by any other method.
- never cover a tourniquet with dressings or bandages.
- ensure that the casualty's forehead is clearly marked with a letter 'T' and the TIME the tourniquet was applied. It is possible that a tourniquet applied to a leg may be hidden by a stretcher blanket.
- A wrongly applied tourniquet can actually increase bleeding. Pressure which is insufficient to stop the flow of blood through the artery may nevertheless be sufficient to stop its return through the vein, with the result that external bleeding increases.
- if the tourniquet does not stop the bleeding, remove it.
- tourniquets must be released very slowly, to make sure there is not a sudden surge of blood to the wound, every 15 minutes. If the bleeding has stopped at this time remove the tourniquet altogether.
- ensure that the material used to make a tourniquet is broad enough not to cut into the skin.

7.10 Abdominal injuries

Abdominal injuries are usually the result of a direct blow or a penetrating wound of the abdominal wall, lower chest, groin or buttocks, but may arise from other causes.

Recognition

Any or all of the following points may indicate that an abdominal injury has occurred:
- a wound of the abdomen or lower chest
- a penetrating wound of the back, buttocks or groin
- history of a blow to the abdomen
- bruising of the abdominal wall
- history of subjection to blast injury
- pain in the abdomen
- tenderness in the abdomen (pain on pressure)
- vomiting, particularly of blood
- blood in the urine or faeces
- tense abdominal muscles
- symptoms and signs of internal bleeding

Treatment
- lay the casualty down on his or her back with knees drawn up and head and shoulders raised, or, alternatively, lay on side with knees drawn up. Raise the casualty's head and shoulders and support them with pillows.
- do *not* remove any foreign bodies protruding from or adhering to the wound.
- do *not* push any protruding organs back into place.

- completely cover the wounds with a wet field or other sterile dressing.
- do *not* give the casualty anything to eat or drink.

Evacuation
- evacuate the patient as a matter of urgency. Surgery will almost certainly be needed.
- position the casualty so that the wound does not gape open, this is usually done by laying him or her on back with knees drawn up and the head and shoulders raised, supported by pillow(s).

7.11 Chest injuries

(Penetrating (stab) wounds to the chest)
The main dangers from wounds to the chest are:
- damage to the heart
- damage to the lungs
- damage to the spleen

Any of these injuries can kill the casualty if not treated urgently with utmost care.

Recognition
- blueness of the lips and extremities may be present.
- a wound in the chest wall may allow direct access of air into the chest cavity. If so:
  i. during inspiration – the noise of air being sucked in may be heard.
  ii. on expiration – blood or bloodstained bubbles may be expelled from the wound.
- if the lung is injured, the casualty may also cough up bright red frothy blood.

Treatment

The aim of first aid is to seal the wound immediately and so prevent air entering the chest cavity.
- until the dressing can be applied, place the palm of the hand firmly over the wound.
- lay the casualty down with head and shoulders raised and the body inclined towards the injured side.
- plug the wound lightly with a dressing.
- cover the dressing with a thick layer of cotton wool.
- retain it firmly in position by strapping or a bandage.
- evacuate to hospital *urgently*.

7.12 Head injuries

Injuries to the head may cause wounds of the scalp and a fracture of the skull bones with or without damage to the underlying brain. If there has been damage or disturbance to the brain, consciousness may be clouded. Associated injuries to the spine, chest, abdomen or fractures to the limb bones may be present, especially if falling from a mast or yard.

Concussion

As the brain can move a little within the skull it can be shaken by a violent blow (like a jelly in a mould). This condition may and can usually does cause disturbance to the brain. Unconsciousness is always brief, followed by complete recovery.
Watch out for the following:
- dizziness and/or nausea.
- loss of memory of events at the time or immediately preceding the injury.
- headache.

Treatment

cold packs to the head.

- observation and AVPU, see *7.8 Unconsciousness*, even after apparent recovery.
- if condition gets worse radio for advice or seek nearest medical facility.
- if patient becomes irritable and unconscious place in recovery position.
- be prepared to do CPR, see *7.3 Heart pain*.

Skull fracture

The skull is designed to protect the brain and fractures of it are very dangerous. Suspect a skull fracture if there is:

- a wound on the head – germs can enter this and the brain, as above causing a major illness.
- straw coloured fluid tinged with blood coming from the nose, ears, or both.
- a soft area of depression in the scalp.
- wound or severe bruising behind the ears (battle signs).
- blood in the white of the eye, or bruising around the eyes (racoon eyes), or
- if skull is an unusual shape.

Treatment

- if patient is unconscious place in the recovery position. If patient is conscious lay him or her down with head and shoulders raised, support with pillows, cushions etc.
- if there is any of the described discharge coming from either ear, place on that side, so that the side is lower, and cover with a clean pad. *Do not plug the ear or nose.*
- look for other injuries and control any bleeding from the scalp.
- radio for *urgent* medical assistance.

Cerebral concussion

A very serious condition that will require *urgent* surgery. It is caused by pressure exerted on the brain from within the skull, by accumulation of blood or the brain swelling. It is often associated with a head injury or sports injury, e.g. boxing, and it may develop immediately or take several days to manifest.

As compression develops the following may occur:

- deterioration in the level of response.
- after a recent head injury the patient may appear to have made a full recovery, then starts to deteriorate with disorientation and confusion.
- severe headache.
- slow full pulse.
- noisy breathing, later becoming slow.
- unequal pupils.
- weakness or paralysis on one side of the face or body.
- a raised temperature, and a hot flushed face.

Treatment

- if unconscious place in recovery position. Place cold packs on neck and skull.
- if conscious, reassure and keep patient still. Place the cold packs as above.
- radio for URGENT medical assistance.

7.13 Stove-in chest

An increasingly common example is the 'steering wheel injury', caused when the driver of a motor vehicle is flung violently against the steering wheel. There may be a fracture of several ribs and of the breast bone, parts of which may be driven inwards possibly damaging the heart, lungs, liver or spleen, with the danger of internal bleeding. A severe compression injury may also cause this condition.

Recognition

- the casualty is severely distressed with difficult breathing.
- blueness of lips and extremities may be observed.
- the injured part of the chest wall will be seen to have lost its rigidity.
- paradoxical movement – instead of the chest moving normally with the remainder of the chest, it does the opposite; during inspiration it is sucked in, on expiration it is blown out.
- sufficient air does not enter the lungs and in consequence the blood cannot obtain enough oxygen.

Treatment

- loosen tight clothing – collar, tie, belt etc.
- place the casualty at rest, raise the head of stretcher to reduce pressure of the abdominal contents on diaphragm.
- immobilise the injured part of the chest wall by placing the arm with the elbow bent against it as a splint.
- secure by strapping or bandaging the arm to the chest.
- evacuate to hospital *urgently*.

7.14 Climatic illness (heat injuries)

Heat exhaustion

This is liable to occur when people work hard in the tropics. The condition causes circulatory failure due to the body's effort to lose heat rapidly (i.e. excessive sweating causes abnormal fluid and salt loss). Water deficiency heat exhaustion is more common than salt deficiency heat exhaustion.

Recognition

- headache, dizziness and nausea.
- cramps in the legs or abdomen.
- pale, clammy skin.
- weak pulse.
- normal, sub-normal or slightly raised oral temperature.
- casualty may be unconscious.

Treatment

- lie the casualty down at rest in a cool place.
- give frequent small drinks of salted water. The aim is to get as much water into the casualty as he or she will tolerate. Solutions can be made up by adding one crushed salt tablet to one pint of water or half a teaspoon of salt to a full water bottle.
- keep the casualty as cool as possible.
- take and record the oral temperatures every 15 minutes to see if it is rising. If it rises above 40°C

(104°F) casualty has heat stroke.

- evacuate the casualty as soon as possible.

Heat stroke (hyperpyrexia)

In this condition the heat regulating mechanism of the body breaks down. Heat stroke is a very serious condition and can be fatal.

Recognition

- disturbed or uncharacteristic behaviour, followed by delirium, partial loss of consciousness and coma.
- high oral temperature 40°C (104°F)
- fatigue, headache and irritability.
- nausea, vomiting and sometime diarrhoea.

Treatment

Reduce the casualty's temperature by whatever means available.

- lie the casualty down at once in the coolest place available.
- remove all clothing.
- sponge down with tepid water and fan body.
- take oral temperature every three or four minutes and continue to sponge and fan until temperature is below 39°C (102°F)..
- give frequent small drinks of cool water, as in treatment for heat exhaustion.

Evacuation

- a casualty with heat stroke must be evacuated urgently.
- take and record temperature every ten minutes during the journey.
- continue fanning and sponging the casualty while the temperature remains above 38°C (100°F).
- the mode of transport should be chosen with careful thought and consideration of the following:
  ventilation
  air flow
  internal temperature
  (for example, it may be wiser to use a Bedford 4-ton lorry than an ambulance.)
- do not allow the casualty to get cold during the journey.

Sunburn

This is caused by over-exposure to the rays of the sun. Normally the inexperienced tourist or water sports enthusiast is the first victim, thinking that the sun has the same strength in his northern home as in the Mediterranean. Sunburn can and does occur on dull and overcast days.

Recognition

- redness, the skin is lobster red.
- itchiness and tenderness.
- pain.
- blistering in severe cases.

Treatment

- place the casualty in the shade.
- cool the skin by spraying or sponging with cold water – this can be done in a shower or bath.
- give plenty of water to drink, or rehydration salts.
- paint the affected area with calamine lotion or yoghurt or after-sun preparation.

- if skin is extensively blistered do *not* prick blisters. Pack in wet dressing and seek medical advice.

Prevention of heat casualties

If proper precautions are taken, the risk of disability from heat is reduced. The main preventative measures are as follows:

Acclimatisation
New arrivals should have a programme of gradually increasing work and exercise for a period of two or three weeks.

Adequate fluids
Sweating means loss of considerable amounts of water in a day. This may be as high as 20 pints under extreme conditions. This fluid must be replaced. More water must be drunk than is necessary to quench thirst. A good rule is to drink 10 pints a day plus 1 pint for every hour of activity. *Do not* restrict water intake.

Adequate salt
Salt is lost from the body in sweat. In the tropics it may be necessary to increase the normal salt intake during the acclimatisation period. This can be in water (two crushed tablets or half a teaspoon of salt to a filled water bottle).

Suitable clothing
Loose, light clothing to allow good ventilation is required. It must be washed and changed frequently.

Enjoy the *sun*, but *be careful!*

And, remember to:

- *slip on a shirt*
- *slop on sunscreen*
- *slap on a hat.*

Hypothermia

If after recovery from the water the someone feels icy cold, he or she is probably suffering from hypothermia.

Take the temperature; if it has fallen below 33°C (95°F) the patient is suffering from hypothermia. The effects will vary from sea temperature to sea temperature as will the speed of the onset, and how fast the temperature falls.

Signs and symptoms

- shivering
- apathy and confusion
- may appear drunk
- lethargy
- may fall unconscious
- slow shallow breathing
- slow pulse
- ruddy complexion (caused by blood coming to the surface from the core)
- feels cold

Treatment

- remove all wet clothing at once.
- if conscious place in a warm bath 40°C (104°F) and rewarm rapidly.
- if no bath available place in a sleeping bag in warm dry clothing and a second person. (the body heat will add to the warming process).
- give high energy drinks and sweets or food. be prepared to carry out CPR, see *7.3 Heart pain.*

7.15 Fractures

A fracture is a cracked or broken bone. Where there is a history of force applied to a bone and the diagnosis is uncertain treat all such injuries as fractures.

Causes of fractures

1. Direct force, e.g. a kick or blow.
2. Indirect force which may break a bone at some distance from where the force is applied, such as a fall on the outstretched hand which may cause fracture of the collar bone.
3. Muscular contraction which may, for example, cause fracture of the knee cap.

Types of fracture

1. *Closed* or *simple*: when there is no wound leading down to the broken bone.
2. *Open* or *compound*: when there is a wound leading down to the broken bone, or when the fractured ends protrude through the skin thus allowing germs to gain access to the site of the fracture.
3. *Complicated*: when there is some other injury directly associated with the fracture, such as to an important blood vessel, the brain, nerves, lungs or when associated with a dislocation. A closed or open fracture can be complicated.

Signs and symptoms

- pain over the injured part.
- tenderness on gentle pressure.
- swelling and later bruising.
- loss of control and function.
- deformity of the limb, such as shortening or angularity (bend appearing in unusual position).
- irregularity of the bone may be felt.
- unnatural movement.

Treating fractures

- severe wounds and bleeding must be dealt with before continuing with treatment of fractures.
- treat the fracture where the casualty lies. The injured part must be secured, even if only in a temporary way, before the casualty is moved, unless life is immediately endangered.
- steady and support the injured part at once, and

maintain this control until such time as the fracture is completely secured. Support the fracture with suitable padded splints, ensuring that these do not obstruct the circulation by checking the pulse beyond the injury and keeping a careful watch for blueness or swelling. The bandages and splints should be loosened if these signs appear.

- treat the casualty for shock.
- evacuate the casualty according to priority.

Treatment of compound (open) fractures

In addition to the general treatment the fracture must also be treated as follows:

- never attempt to push back protruding bone ends.
- cover any wound with a sterile dressing and proceed with the first aid treatment as in a closed fracture.
- treat the casualty for shock.

Evacuation of a casualty with a fracture

Casualties with open fractures, complicated fractures or fractures of long bones must be evacuated urgently. Simple fractures are of low priority for evacuation providing the circulation is good.

Using bandages alone

Bandages should be applied sufficiently firmly to prevent movement, but not so tightly as to prevent the circulation of blood.

If the casualty is lying down, use a splint or similar object to pass the bandage under the trunk or lower limbs in the natural hollows of the neck, waist, knees and just above the heels. The bandages may then be worked gently into their correct position.

Using splints and bandages

Splints must be well padded and sufficiently long to immobilise the joint above and below the fracture. They may be improvised by using such aids as firmly folded newspaper, or well padded broom handles, over a piece of wood. Remember, all splints must be *well padded*.

Slings

Slings are used when it is necessary to support and afford protection to the upper limb. The arm sling is only effective when the casualty is sitting or standing.

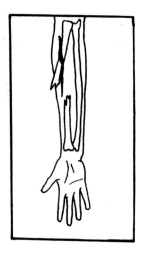 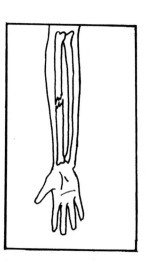 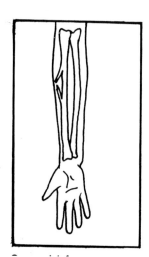 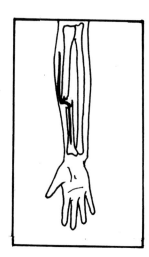

Dislocations

When the bones of a joint are forced out of their normal position, they are said to be dislocated. Tearing or stretching of the ligaments is always present. Dislocations may occur in combination with a fracture of one of the bones in the injured joint. This is called a fracture-dislocation.

Recognition

The signs are similar to those of a fracture but with a more marked deformity of the joint.

Treatment

- do not try to reduce the dislocation.
- put the injured part at rest in the most comfortable position. A splint may be useful for support.
- check the circulation at the extremities before and after treatment, and loosen splints and bandages when necessary.
- evacuate the casualty.
- dislocation should be reduced as early as possible after injury.

7.16 Spinal injuries

In spinal injuries the greatest risk is that the spinal cord may be damaged. The spinal cord is very delicate and if damaged the patient will suffer loss of power and sensation below the area injured.

Temporary loss can occur if the nerves are in some way pinched by a displaced disc or loose bone.

Seafarers on small boats or yachts are at risk from this type of injury, as are water skiers and bathers who dive in the wrong end of the pool. Many people are injured each year like these and many more are permanently damaged and paralysed by would be do-gooders who mishandle the spinal injury patient.

If you suspect a spinal injury has occurred carry out the following:

- reassure the casualty if conscious, tell him or her not to move, get a helper to hold the head by placing it in the neutral position by placing the hands over the ears, another holding the feet and apply *gentle* traction.
- make a stiff collar of rolled up newspapers about 4 inches deep and rolled in a triangular bandage – place this around the neck and tie in a reef knot (this will stabilise the cervical spine; some boats carry purpose-made cervical collars which are very good). Continue to hold the head/feet.
- pad around the head and shoulders of the casualty. Place broad bandages around the feet, legs, thighs and chest, strap or tape his/her head to the neck supporting pillows. *Do not* move unless in danger.
- get *urgent* assistance – stating 'spinal case'.
- In water-ski accidents where a skier comes off at speed, *always* apply a cervical collar until the patient has been seen and examined by a doctor, nearly all suffer from at least a whiplash injury. this collar *must* be put on before the skier leaves the water.
- in pool-side accidents the same applies; the collar must be applied in the pool where the water will assist keeping the patient buoyant. You can use a surfboard, wind-surfer or stretcher to float under the patient before carrying out spinal immobilising

procedure.
- be prepared to carry out CPR see *7.3 Heart pain* and if the patient goes unconscious put into the recovery position, but use two people to turn into this position, one always keeping the head in traction and still.

7.17 Burns and scalds

This is one of the worst things that can happen afloat. Burns and scalds can be caused by any number of sources plentiful on any boat, such as liquid gas (LPG), petrol, diesel fuel, hot engine exhausts, or even fat or cooking oil (especially dangerous if it catches fire). Other sources include, but are not limited to, strong acids and alkalis, high voltage electricity, lightning, and friction from a revolving wheel or a fast moving rope.

Although it may seem superfluous to say so, the first thing to do is to neutralise the source causing the burn or scald.

If fire is caused by bottled gas you must first turn off the gas at the main valve to prevent fire from being fed while you attempt to extinguish it using the appropriate fire extinguisher. When the fire is out, continue to cool the cylinder with running water, if it has been exposed to significant heat, until cool.

If fat or cooking oil catches fire, turn off the gas, cover the pan with a lid or damp cloth to starve the fire, and *do not lift* the cover to peep for ten minutes. *never* throw water onto a fat or oil fire as it will cause an explosion. If fire spreads onto the surrounding area use either Halon/CO_2/dry powder or foam extinguisher. Never use water based extinguisher on an electrical fire or you will become a casualty.

Whatever the cause of the burn or scald the injury to the skin is the same: the contents of the cells solidify and they die. The severity of the burn depends on the *depth* of the burn, the *area* of the burn, *age* of the patient and the *general condition* of the patient prior to the accident. Burns are classified as either *deep* or *superficial*, the former being injuries only to the outer layer of the skin, which will regenerate naturally.

Area of the burn

The larger the area of skin burned, the greater the loss of fluid from the damaged tissues. The lost fluid is mostly serum, but blood may be lost by coagulation in the damaged tissue. With larger burns the loss produces shock. Shock is the immediate danger, and urgent treatment is required to correct the fluid loss. As a rough guide, all burns of 18% or more of the body surface will require a transfusion.

Rule of nines

This is an estimation of the area of the burn:

a. the head and neck	9%
b. the front of the body	18%
c. the back of the body	18%
d. each arm	9%
e. each leg	18%
f. the perineum	1%

These figures should be used to estimate the area of the body burned, thus determining the severity of the burns.

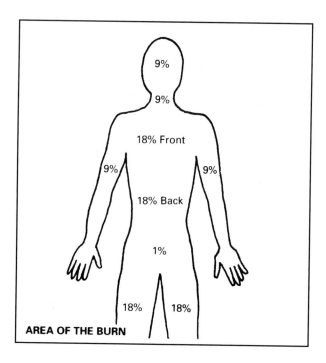

AREA OF THE BURN

Severity

Under 5%   not serious unless special areas involved
5% – 15%   serious, urgency depends on site
15% – 40% will require urgent medical attention
Over 40%   critically ill and may die.

Treatment for burns and scalds

- if water is available, the burned part should be immediately held under running water or immersed in cold water for at least ten minutes in order to disperse the heat left in burned tissues. This should be done within five minutes of the accident.
- cover the burned area with sterile or clean dressing.
- *burns of the face should be left exposed.*
- burns of the hands and feet may be covered with plastic bags with the open ends sealed at the wrist or ankle.
- put the patient at rest and, in the case of severe burns, lay him or her down.
- give fluids only if the casualty is not vomiting and is unlikely to reach hospital within two hours. Take the sodium chloride and sodium bicarbonate pack from your first aid kit, dissolve the contents in a water bottle and encourage the casualty to drink the contents slowly, and in sips. The patient may well need more than one bottle of this solution, particularly if evacuation is delayed and intravenous therapy is unavailable.
- treat for shock and reassure the casualty.
- evacuate the casualty.
- do not
  remove burnt clothing from the burn.
  apply ointments or lotions.
  prick blisters.

Though the treatment recommended above is basically correct, it has been discovered recently that a polythene film provides better protection to a burn than a dry dressing, due to the polythene's airtight characteristics. This method was used to its greatest advantage in the Falklands campaign and, as a result,

first aid kits are now issued with a roll of cling film. Care must be taken when using cling film in the area of the face or throat.

Commercial rehydration solutions, like those used for the treatment of diarrhoea, are excellent for the replacement of fluid lost in burns cases.

The Dutch are experimenting with the use of potato skins for the treatment of burns. Applied cold to the burn area, the potato skins help the healing process in second and third degree burns.

Chemical burns

This type of injury requires immediate treatment to prevent the condition becoming worse. In case of chemical injury:

- remove all contaminated clothing.
- wash the burn and surrounding area with large quantities of free running water to remove the chemical. Avoid contaminating unaffected areas.
- when the chemical has been removed, treat as a burn.
- pay particular attention to eyes, if contaminated.

Phosphorus burns

Phosphorus is often found in incendiary bombs and grenades. Though it is unlikely that a yachtsman will ever face an emergency involving phosphorus burns, good practice dictates that you be informed just in case.

Treatment for phosphorus burns is *urgent* and the person applying first aid must take care not to become a casualty himself. Treat as follows:

- immerse the area in water immediately and remove all contaminated clothing (add bicarbonate of soda to the water if possible).
- remove the phosphorus particles with forceps, or pliers, even a small stick, while they are under water. *Do not* use your fingers, and avoid burning yourself.
- apply a wet dressing to the burn and keep it wet with bicarbonate solution if possible.
- if there is not enough water to submerge the affected part, a wet cloth in polythene cover may help to suffocate the burning phosphorus.
- Evacuate these casualties urgently and ensure that the dressings are kept *soaking wet* throughout the journey.

7.18 Diabetic emergencies

Diabetics are usually aware of their condition and are usually well prepared for any emergency that may arise.

If, however, the diabetic has been overworking, under stress, drinking heavily, etc., his or her blood sugar level will be affected and the function of the brain will be impaired. This is known as hypoglycaemia.

Signs and symptoms

- weakness, fainting or hunger
- patient recognises he or she is having a *hypo* attack
- muscles tremors
- palpitations
- acting confused, strange or appears drunk (many diabetics have been arrested at this stage, suspected of being drunk)
- profuse sweating

- pale, cold clammy skin, shallow breathing
- level of response deteriorates
- bounding pulse
- breath smells of musty apples or cider

Treatment
- restore the blood level as quickly as possible by giving a strong sugary drink, chocolate, sugar lumps or other sugary foods.
- keep under observation and keep up the sugar intake until the patient is fully recovered.
- if the patient is unconscious open the airway, check the AVPU, see *7.8 Unconsciousness* and be prepared to resuscitate if required. At this stage the patient is very ill and requires *urgent* medical assistance.

Treatment
- Open the airway making sure there is no vomit blocking the air passages.
- Look for and treat other injuries.
- Place in recovery position and *do not* leave alone.
- Check the AVPU *(see above)* every 10 minutes.
- People laugh at drunks and drunks die as a result. Be prepared to resuscitate.

7.19 Weil's Disease (Leptospirosis)

This is caught through contact with water infected by animal urine. All those using waterways and river banks are at risk, since the disease can exist on wet vegetation and enters through cuts, grazes and the mucous membranes of the mouth, nose and eyes. Take the following simple precautions:
- cover any cuts or grazes with waterproof dressings before sailing.
- if skin injury occurs during contact with untreated water wash with clean water, treat with antiseptic and cover.
- avoid immersion and swallowing untreated water.
- after water activity, wash hands thoroughly (or shower if immersed) before eating, drinking or smoking.

First symptoms can be confused with 'flu, e.g. fever, pain in joints or muscles. If you develop these symptoms after spending time in or by water, tell your doctor immediately. Antibiotics are effective in the early stages of infection, but if left more serious problems develop.

7.20 Common poisons

A poison is any substance, whether liquid, solid or gas, which, when taken into the body in sufficient quantity, injures the body tissues and endangers life. Poisons are classified according to whether they are: *burning poisons (burn* the body tissues); *irritant poisons (irritate,* when swallowed, the stomach lining and digestive tract); *systemic poisons* (are taken either internally or externally and absorbed into the bloodstream to affect the various systems).

The route by which the poison is taken into the body also decides the extent of the injury and method of treatment. Poisons may be: *inhaled* (breathed into the lungs, taken up by the blood circulation and affect the nervous system); *absorbed* (taken in through the skin by contact or injection); *ingested* (swallowed).

General rules for the treatment of all types of poisoning
- if the casualty is conscious, quickly ask what has happened. He or she may lose consciousness at any time
- keep the airway clear
- if breathing has ceased, apply artificial respiration by the appropriate method
- keep the casualty warm, comfortable and at rest
- evacuate the casualty as a matter of urgency. If possible, go with him or her. If this is not possible, send a written message to the hospital describing what has happened
- place unconscious casualties in recovery position and evacuate them as a matter of urgency
- make sure that any empty containers and samples of vomit go with the casualty to the hospital

Inhaled poisons
Poisons are inhaled as a vapour or gas.
Examples of inhaled poisons are:
- carbon monoxide gas in the form of vehicle exhaust fumes, or from defective coal stoves
- petroleum fumes
- chemicals such as chlorine, phosgene and carbon tetrachloride
- sulphur dioxide and ammonia in refrigeration plant
- hydrogen sulphide which smells of rotten eggs and is found in areas where putrefied organic material occurs, e.g. sewers, drains, tunnels, caves

Recognition of poisoning by gases
- suspect gas poisoning when the casualty is found in a situation where gas poisoning may occur, e.g. in an enclosed space; or underneath a car with its engine still running
- the casualty may have respiratory distress, headache, dizziness, drowsiness and later become unconscious

Treatment
- avoid becoming a casualty yourself
- drag the injured person to pure air
- apply the general rules of treatment of poisoning

Poisons absorbed through the skin

Poisons may be taken in through the skin by:
- poisonous liquids falling on the skin which, if not quickly removed will be absorbed into the body. They may cause skin damage. Examples are petrol, organic phosphorus compounds (agricultural chemicals and blistering agents), phenol compounds.
- bites and stings from snakes, insects and marine animals.
- injection of drugs such as heroin and barbiturates.

Recognition of absorbed poisoning

Suspect when:
- the casualty is in a situation where contamination may occur, e.g. serving petrol, using certain weed killers, chemical agent attacks and the dispersal of weed killers and defoliating agents by aircraft.
- casualty complains of salivation, irritation of the nose, tightness of the chest, alteration of vision, headache. In serious contamination there will be respiratory distress, abdominal pain and vomiting
- there may be evidence of skin damage or injection blemishes.

Treatment

- move the casualty to safety
- remove any contaminated clothing
- remove surplus liquid from the skin without contaminating yourself and wash the affected area with if convulsions occur, protect the casualty from injury
- apply the general rules of treatment of poisoning

Swallowed poisons

Of the many poisonous substances which may be swallowed the following will often be encountered:
- infected food
- poisonous berries, plants and toadstools
- tablets which if taken in normal dosage are safe but when taken in excess are harmful e.g. aspirin, paracetamol tablets, sleeping tablets
- liquid chemicals taken either accidentally or intentionally; these are often grouped as acid or alkaline e.g. caustic soda, disinfectants, carbon tetrachloride, detergents and paraffin
- water and food contaminated by chemical agents, e.g. chemicals sprayed either as chemical agents or agricultural sprays, which fall onto uncovered water and food stocks
- Paraquat or Weedol, rat poison, arsenic

Recognition

Suspect poisoning when:
- person is unconscious or drowsy and/or lips and mouth are stained and burned, with an empty tablet or liquid container found nearby
- in a chemical defence situation, a chemical agent attack has taken place
- casualty complains of abdominal pains
- is retching and vomiting
- may have diarrhoea
- if he or she has swallowed drugs, may be drowsy

Treatment

- apply the general rules of treatment of poisoning
- if the casualty is conscious and there are signs of burning of the lips and mouth, do not induce vomiting but give one pint of water, milk or other non-irritating fluids such as barley water
- if the casualty is drowsy, try to keep him or her awake
- if the casualty is unconscious, place in the recovery position and evacuate urgently

7.21 Seasickness

Most people suffer at some time or other from seasickness, some more chronically and more often than others. I was recently seasick for the first time in ten years and though not incapacitated, it humbled me to think about the various remedies available, especially for those who are chronically afflicted. The following is a brief round-up of remedies.

Tablets A number of antihistamines are on the market: Avomine, Dramamine, Marzine RF, and Stugeron. Of these Stugeron is widely accepted as the most effective. They all cause drowsiness to some extent, though Stugeron to a lesser extent than others. These pills must be taken before setting sail, sometimes up to 4 hours before going to sea, their effect is minimal once someone begins to feel seasick. Other tablets such as Phenergan, Kwells, and Sereen contain hyoscine hydrobromide which has a sedative effect and leaves the sufferer drowsy.

Scopoderm disc A small elastoplast disc which is stuck behind the ear four hours before sailing. It contains hyoscine hydrobromide which is released slowly into the bloodstream and is said to reduce the sensitivity of the inner ear without causing undue drowsiness as it does in tablet form. The disc will work over two to three days and tests seem to indicate a good success rate. It is available only on prescription, cannot be used by young children, and for a minority does have some side effects such as minor drowsiness and one or two reports of mild hallucinations!

Homeopathic cures A number of homeopathic treatment are available: Nux Vomica 6, Coculus Indicus 6 and Ipecac 6 tablets. I have not tracked down any results from these. A number of old salts swear by natural remedies such as ginger, glucose and Vitamin B12. Ginger seems to be the favourite.

Sea bands Elasticated bands with a small plastic knob sewn into them can be purchased and when slipped over the wrist the knob is supposed to press on the nei-kuan pressure point, an acupuncture point that reduces nausea. The problem is hitting exactly the right point - something an acupuncturist spends years learning to do.

Generally Someone who is seasick should be kept warm, but should stay in the cockpit if possible. watching the horizon seems to have a curative effect, while down below, apart from the absence of a horizon, any odours, diesel, cooking food, will be enough to induce vomiting. When seasick try to eat something like dry bread or crackers, and drink plenty of water as vomiting causes dehydration. Someone who is mildly nauseous can be given something to do: operating a winch or even helming can reduce nausea. If you are regularly seasick at the onset of a voyage take the advice of a friend of mine who would eat only tinned pineapple because, he said, 'It tastes as good on the way up as on the way down'.

I have found Stugeron 15mgm, a white scored tablet made by Janssen, to be one of the best treatments for sea sickness, but remember to take them as prescribed, and take them *before* you sail. These tablets do not cause drowsiness, unlike some others on the market. You may also like to try using stem ginger which is a natural product and research indicates that it is very good.

In prolonged seasickness the patient will become dehydrated and must be encouraged to drink fluids.

7.22 Bee and wasp stings

These can be very painful and dangerous; some people have severe reactions to the poison or when stung in the throat or mouth.

Signs and symptoms

- sudden sharp pain
- swelling and redness around the sting

Treatment

- if a bee stings, remove the sting (a bee sting has a barb which it leaves in together with its sac)
- apply cold compress or ice
- apply solution of bicarbonate of soda, ammonia or hydrocortisone cream 1%

7.23 Jellyfish and other marine stings

Treatment

- reassure the patient
- act quickly before they activate more stinging cells. Pour alcohol or vinegar over the area to neutralise the poison, then make a paste of bicarbonate of soda and apply to the stung area; dust the area with meat tenderiser or talcum powder.
- if the marine creatures puncture the skin or leave spines i.e. sea eggs, put the limb or bathe the area in warm water as hot as the patient can bear for at least 10 minutes, then make a compress of olive oil and leave for 24 hours – the spines will then come out.

7.24 Snakebites

The severity of the bite will depend upon the species of snake. Most people die of panic or shock – not from the bite. Always try to kill and keep the snake for identification purposes.

Signs and symptoms

- puncture marks
- pain and swelling at the site
- nausea and vomiting
- in extreme cases laboured breathing
- disturbed vision
- general signs and symptoms of severe shock

Treatment

- do not cut the area or suck out the poison.
- place ice packs over the area
- wash the bite area with soap and water
- place broad bandages above and below the bite site, not too tight to cut off circulation – splint the limb if necessary
- arrange urgent removal to hospital, be prepared to carry out CPR, see *7.3 Heart pain.*

7.25 Sprains and strains

At sea many injuries to both muscles and ligaments occur due to slipping and falling on wet or heaving decks.

Signs and symptoms

- pain and tenderness around the joint increased by movement swelling
- bruising

Treatment

- rest the injured part
- immobilise
- cool with ice for at least ½ hour
- elevate the injured part

8. Safety and navigation schemes

8.1 SOLAS Regulations

The International Convention for the Safety of Life at Sea (SOLAS) Chapter V is concerned with Safety of Navigation, some of which applies to smaller vessels. From 1 July 2002 skippers of craft under 150 tons are required to conform to the following SOLAS V regulations. The regulations will almost certainly be applied in piecemeal fashion in the Mediterranean countries (if at all in some); nonetheless, you should be aware of them. See adjacent box for my précis of regulations.

- R19 A radar reflector (3 & 9 GHz) must be exhibited.
- R29 A table of life-saving signals must be available to the skipper/helmsman at all times.
- R31 Skippers must report to the coastguard on dangers to navigation including (R32) wrecks, winds of Force 10 or more and floating objects dangerous to navigation.
- R33 Vessels must respond to distress signals from another vessel.
- R34 Passage-planning is now mandatory. If a vessel involved in an incident can be shown not to have engaged in detailed passage-planning the skipper can be prosecuted. This is a very messy regulation and may involve having corrected charts and up-to-date pilotage instructions on board and keeping a ship's log.

8.2 Distress signals

Refer also to *10. Radio Services* for details on GMDSS, Radio Distress Call Procedure, Phonetic Alphabet and Morse Code.

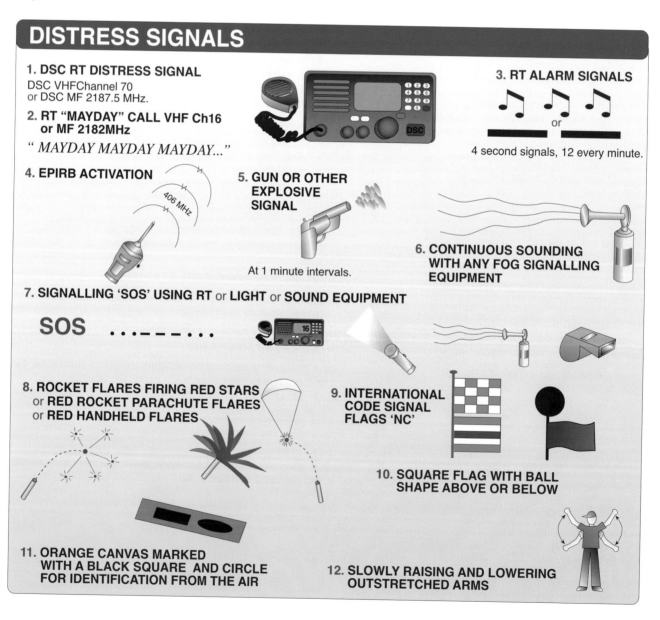

DISTRESS SIGNALS

1. DSC RT DISTRESS SIGNAL
DSC VHFChannel 70
or DSC MF 2187.5 MHz.

2. RT "MAYDAY" CALL VHF Ch16 or MF 2182MHz
" *MAYDAY MAYDAY MAYDAY...*"

3. RT ALARM SIGNALS
or
4 second signals, 12 every minute.

4. EPIRB ACTIVATION
406 MHz

5. GUN OR OTHER EXPLOSIVE SIGNAL
At 1 minute intervals.

6. CONTINUOUS SOUNDING WITH ANY FOG SIGNALLING EQUIPMENT

7. SIGNALLING 'SOS' USING RT or LIGHT or SOUND EQUIPMENT

SOS · · · — — — · · ·

8. ROCKET FLARES FIRING RED STARS or RED ROCKET PARACHUTE FLARES or RED HANDHELD FLARES

9. INTERNATIONAL CODE SIGNAL FLAGS 'NC'

10. SQUARE FLAG WITH BALL SHAPE ABOVE OR BELOW

11. ORANGE CANVAS MARKED WITH A BLACK SQUARE AND CIRCLE FOR IDENTIFICATION FROM THE AIR

12. SLOWLY RAISING AND LOWERING OUTSTRETCHED ARMS

LIFE-SAVING SIGNALS

SOLAS CHAPTER V REGULATION 29
To be used by Ships, Aircraft or Persons in Distress when communicating with life-saving stations, maritime rescue units and aircraft engaged in search and rescue operations.

Note: All Morse Code signals by light (below).

1. SEARCH AND RESCUE UNIT REPLIES

YOU HAVE BEEN SEEN, ASSISTANCE WILL BE GIVEN AS SOON AS POSSIBLE

Orange smoke flare

Three white star signals or three light and sound rockets fired at approximately 1 minute intervals

2. SURFACE TO AIR SIGNALS

MESSAGE	ICAO/IMO VISUAL SIGNALS	
REQUIRE ASSISTANCE	V · · · —	☒
REQUIRE MEDICAL ASSISTANCE	X — · · —	✚
NO or NEGATIVE	N — ·	▦
YES or AFFIRMATIVE	Y — · — —	▨
PROCEEDING IN THIS DIRECTION	↑	

Note: Use International Code of Signals by means of light or flags or by laying out the symbol on the deck or ground with items that have a high contrast background.

3. AIR TO SURFACE REPLIES

Note: Use signals most appropriate to prevailing conditions.

MESSAGE UNDERSTOOD

OR Drop a message. OR Rocking wings. Flashing landing or navigation lights on and off twice. OR   T — OR R · — ·

MESSAGE NOT UNDERSTOOD

Straight and level flight. ← - - - - - -   OR Circling.   OR   R · — ·   P · — — ·   T —

4. AIR TO SURFACE DIRECTION SIGNALS

SEQUENCE OF 3 MANOEUVRES MEANING PROCEED IN THIS DIRECTION

Circle vessel at least once.   Cross low, ahead of vessel rocking wings.   Overfly vessel and head in required direction.

YOUR ASSISTANCE IS NO LONGER REQUIRED

Cross low, astern of vessel rocking wings.

Note: As a non preferered alternative to rocking wings, varying engine tone or volume may be used.

5. SURFACE TO AIR REPLIES

MESSAGE UNDERSTOOD - I WILL COMPLY

Change course to required direction.   OR   T —   OR   Code & answering pendant "Close Up".

I AM UNABLE TO COMPLY

International flag "N".   OR   N — ·

6. SHORE TO SHIP SIGNALS

SAFE TO LAND HERE

Vertical waving of both arms, white flag, light or flare

OR   K — · —

LANDING HERE IS DANGEROUS ADDITIONAL SIGNALS MEAN SAFER LANDING IN DIRECTION INDICATED

OR

Horizontal waving white flag, light or flare. Putting one flare/ flag on ground and moving off with a second indicates direction of safer landing.

S · · ·   Landing here is dangerous.
R · — ·   Land to right of your current heading.
L · — · ·   Land to left of your current heading.

8.4 Signal flags

INTERNATIONAL CODE OF SIGNALS, MORSE CODE AND MEANINGS

Letter	Morse	Meaning	Letter	Morse	Meaning
A	.—	Diver down - keep well clear	N	—.	Negative / no
B	—...	Vessel carrying dangerous goods	O	———	Man overboard
C	—.—.	Affirmative/yes	P	.——.	Vessel leaving harbour / fishing boat: nets fouled
D	—..	Keep clear - vessel with restricted ability to manoeuvre	Q	——.—	Customs - I request free pratique
E	.	Altering course to starboard	R	.—.	I acknowledge your last signal / OK
F	..—.	Disabled vessel - communicate with me	S	...	Operating astern propulsion
G	——.	Pilot needed / fishing boat: hauling nets	T	—	Keep clear - pair trawling
H	....	Pilot on board	U	..—	Danger
I	..	Altering course to port	V	...—	Assistance needed
J	.———	Vessel is on fire - keep clear	W	.——	Medical assistance needed
K	—.—	I wish to communicate	X	—..—	Stop & watch for further signals
L	.—..	Stop your vessel immediately	Y	—.——	Vessel dragging anchor
M	——	I am stopped	Z	——..	Tug needed / fishing boats: shooting nets

8.5 IALA buoyage system A

In 1980 a conference, convened with the assistance of IMO and IHO, the lighthouse authorities and the representatives of international organisations concerned with aids to navigation agreed to adopt the rules of the new combined system of buoyage and gradually to introduce it throughout the world.

The system applies to all fixed floating marks, other than lighthouses, sectors of lights, leading lights and marks, lanbys, certain large light-floats and light-vessels. It serves to indicate:

- sides and centrelines of navigable channels
- navigable channels under fixed bridges
- natural dangers and other obstructions such as wrecks (which are described as 'New Dangers' when newly discovered and uncharted)
- areas in which navigation may be subject to regulation
- other features of importance to the mariner.

Marks

Five types of mark are provided by the IALA system A: Lateral, Cardinal, Isolated Danger, Safe Water and Special marks. They may be used in any combination.

Most lighted and unlighted beacons, other than leading marks, are included in the system. In general, beacon topmarks have the same shapes and colours as those used on buoys. (Because of the variety of beacon structures, the accompanying diagrams show mainly buoy shapes.)

Wrecks are marked in the same way as other dangers; no unique type of mark is reserved for them in the IALA System.

Colours

Red and green are reserved for Lateral marks, and yellow for Special marks. Black and yellow or black and red bands, or red and white stripes, are used for other types of marks as described later.

IALA system A implementation

Spain IALA System A implemented. There is some local variation in small fishing harbours.

France IALA System A implemented. There is some variation in shapes with much use made of pillar buoys and little use made of spherical buoys.

- wreck buoys may carry the word *Epave* in addition to *W*.

- mid-channel buoys have no topmark.
- transition mark has a double cross.
- buoys marking areas used for military practice carry the letters ZD.

Italy IALA System A implemented but with significant variations as follows.

Lateral system
- starboard hand buoys are black/black topmarks.

LA BUOYAGE SYSTEM A

Lateral marks

Port hand
All red
Topmark (if any): can
Light (if any): red

Starboard hand
All green
Topmark (if any): cone
Light (if any): green

Preferred channel to port
Green/red/green
Light (if any): Fl(2+1)G

Preferred channel to starboard
Red/green/red
Light (if any): Fl(2+1)R

Isolated danger marks
(stationed over a danger with navigable water around)
Black with red band
Topmark: 2 black balls
Light (if any): Fl(2) (white)

Special mark
Body shape optional, yellow
Topmark (if any): Yellow X
Light (if any): Fl.Y etc

Safe water marks
(mid-channel and landfall)
Red and white vertical stripes
Topmark (if any): red ball
Light (if any): Iso, Oc, LFl.10s or Mo(A) (white)

Cardinal marks

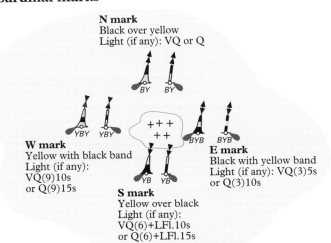

N mark
Black over yellow
Light (if any): VQ or Q

W mark
Yellow with black band
Light (if any):
VQ(9)10s
or Q(9)15s

E mark
Black with yellow band
Light (if any): VQ(3)5s
or Q(3)10s

S mark
Yellow over black
Light (if any):
VQ(6)+LFl.10s
or Q(6)+LFl.15s

International port traffic signals

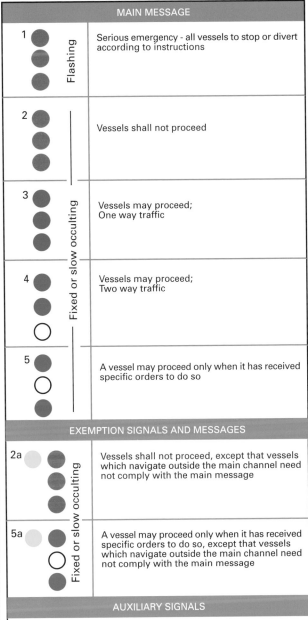

	MAIN MESSAGE	
1 (Flashing)	Serious emergency - all vessels to stop or divert according to instructions	
2 (Fixed or slow occulting)	Vessels shall not proceed	
3 (Fixed or slow occulting)	Vessels may proceed; One way traffic	
4 (Fixed or slow occulting)	Vessels may proceed; Two way traffic	
5 (Fixed or slow occulting)	A vessel may proceed only when it has received specific orders to do so	
EXEMPTION SIGNALS AND MESSAGES		
2a (Fixed or slow occulting)	Vessels shall not proceed, except that vessels which navigate outside the main channel need not comply with the main message	
5a (Fixed or slow occulting)	A vessel may proceed only when it has received specific orders to do so, except that vessels which navigate outside the main channel need not comply with the main message	
AUXILIARY SIGNALS		

Auxiliary signals can be added, as required, normally to the right of the column carrying the main message and normally utilising only white or yellow lights.

Such auxiliary signals could, for example, be added to message no. 5 to give information about the situation of traffic in the opposite direction, or to warn of a dredger operating in the channel

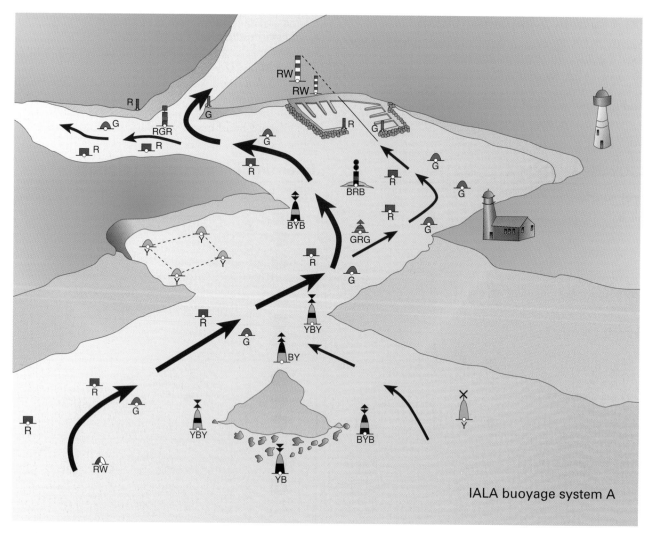

IALA buoyage system A

- middle ground, bifurcation or junction buoys are conical but painted as per the uniform system. Topmarks always have a sphere as the lower mark.
- mid-channel buoys are painted in diagonal stripes and if lit lights are usually isophase and usually red.
- fairway and transition buoys are not used.
- isolated danger marks are red and black bands with a red and black topmark. Usually lit with occulting white lights.

Cardinal system
- all buoys are conical.
- N quadrant is black and white stripes and black topmark.
- E quadrant is red and white chequers and red topmark.
- S quadrant is red and white stripes and red topmark.
- W quadrant is black and white chequers and black topmark.
- wreck buoys differ from the standard system but with the normal N/E/S/W quadrant topmarks.

Malta IALA System A implemented.
Slovenia/Croatia/Montenegro IALA System A largely implemented prior to the break-up of Yugoslavia. Current position unknown.

Albania Uniform System of Buoyage believed to be in use.

Greece IALA System A implemented. Much variation in small fishing harbours.

Turkey IALA System A implemented. Much variation in small fishing harbours and channels not used by large commercial vessels.

Cyprus IALA System A implemented. Some variation in small fishing harbours.

Syria IALA System A partially implemented.

Lebanon IALA System A partially implemented. Maintenance suspect.

Israel IALA System A implemented.

Egypt IALA System A implemented. Much variation in small harbours.

Libya IALA System A implemented.

Tunisia IALA System A partially implemented. Much local variation in small fishing harbours and some approach channels.

Algeria IALA System A partially implemented. Much local variation in small fishing harbours.

Morocco IALA System A partially implemented. Local variation in small fishing harbours.

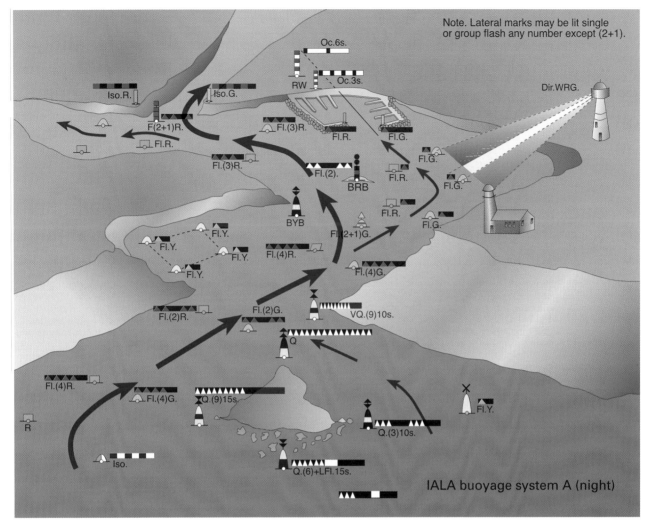

Note. Lateral marks may be lit single or group flash any number except (2+1).

IALA buoyage system A (night)

8.6 Traffic regulations

International Regulations for Preventing Collisions at Sea (1972)

PART A. GENERAL

Rule 1

Application

a. These Rules shall apply to all vessels upon the high seas and in all waters connected therewith navigable by seagoing vessels.

b. Nothing in these Rules shall interfere with the operation of special rules made by an appropriate authority for roadsteads, harbours, rivers, lakes or inland waterways connected with the high seas and navigable by seagoing vessels. Such special rules shall conform as closely as possible to these Rules.

c. Nothing in these Rules shall interfere with the operation of any special rules made by the Government of any State with respect to additional station or signal lights, shapes or whistle signals for ships of war and vessels proceeding under convoy, or with respect to additional station or signal lights or shapes for fishing vessels engaged in fishing as a fleet. These additional station or signal lights, shapes or whistle signals shall so far as possible, be such that they cannot be mistaken for any light, shape or signal authorised elsewhere under these Rules.

d. Traffic Separation Schemes may be adopted by the International Maritime Organisation for the purpose of these Rules.

e. Whenever the Government concerned shall have determined that a vessel of special construction or purpose cannot comply fully with the provisions of any of these Rules with respect to the number, position, range or arc of visibility of lights or shapes as well as to the disposition and characteristics of sound-signalling appliances, such

vessels shall comply with such other provisions in regard to the number, position, range or arc of visibility of lights or shapes, as well as to the disposition and characteristics of sound-signalling appliances, as her Government shall have determined to be the closest possible compliance with these Rules in respect of that vessel.

PART B. STEERING AND SAILING RULES

Section I. Conduct of vessels in any condition of visibility

Rule 4

Application

Rules in this Section apply in any condition of visibility.

Rule 5

Look-out

Every vessel shall at all times maintain a proper look-out by sight and hearing as well as by all available means appropriate in the prevailing circumstances and conditions so as to make a full appraisal of the situation and of the risk of collision.

Rule 6

Safe speed

Every vessel shall at all times proceed at a safe speed so that she can take proper and effective action to avoid collision and be stopped within a distance appropriate to the prevailing circumstances and conditions.

In determining a safe speed the following factors shall be among those taken into account:

a. By all vessels:

  i. The state of visibility;

  ii. the traffic density including concentrations of fishing vessels or any other vessels;

  iii. the manoeuvrability of the vessel with special reference to stopping distance and turning ability in the prevailing conditions;

iv. at night the presence of background light such as from shore lights or from back scatter of her own lights;

v. the state of wind, sea and current, and the proximity of navigational hazards;

vi. the draught in relation to the available depth of water.

b. Additionally, by vessels with operational radar:

i. the characteristics, efficiency and limitations of the radar equipment;

ii. any constraints imposed by the radar range scale in use;

iii. the effect on radar detection of the sea state, weather and other sources of interference;

iv the possibility that small vessels, ice and other floating objects may not be detected by radar at an adequate range;

v. the number, location and movement of vessels detected by radar;

vi. the more exact assessment of the visibility that may be possible when radar is used to determine the range of vessels or other objects in the vicinity.

Rule 7
Risk of collision

a. Every vessel shall use all available means appropriate to the prevailing circumstances and conditions to determine if risk of collision exists. If there is any doubt such risk shall be deemed to exist.

b. Proper use shall be made of radar equipment if fitted and operational, including long-range scanning to obtain early warning of risk of collision and radar plotting or equivalent systematic observation of detected objects.

c. Assumptions shall not be made on the basis of scanty radar information.

d. In determining if risk of collision exists the following considerations shall be among those taken into account:

i. such risk shall be deemed to exist if the compass bearing of an approaching vessel does not appreciably change;

iii. such risk may sometimes exist even when an appreciable bearing change is evident, particularly when approaching a very large vessel or a tow or when approaching a vessel at close range.

Rule 8
Action to avoid collision

a. Any action taken to avoid collision shall, if the circumstances of the case admit, be positive, made in ample time and with due regard to the observance of good seamanship.

b. Any alteration of course and/or speed to avoid collision shall, if the circumstances of the case admit, be large enough to be readily apparent to another vessel observing visually or by radar; a succession of small alterations of course and/or speed should be avoided.

c. If there is sufficient sea room, alteration of course alone may be the most effective action to avoid a close-quarters situation provided that it is made in good time, is substantial and does not result in another close-quarters situation.

d. Action taken to avoid collision with another vessel shall be such as to result in passing at a safe distance. The effectiveness of the action shall be carefully checked until the other vessel is finally past and clear.

e. If necessary to avoid collision or allow more time to assess the situation, a vessel shall slacken her speed or take all the way off by stopping or reversing her means of propulsion.

f. i. A vessel which, by any of these Rules, is required not to impede the passage or safe passage of another vessel shall, when required by the circumstances of the case, take early action to allow sufficient sea room for the safe passage of the other vessel.

ii. A vessel required not to impede the passage or safe passage of another vessel is not relieved of this obligation if approaching the other vessel so as to involve risk of collision and shall, when taking action, have full regard to the action which may be required by the Rules of this part.

iii. A vessel, the passage of which is not to be impeded, remains fully obliged to comply with the Rules of this part when the two vessels are approaching one another so as to involve risk of collision.

Rule 9
Narrow channels

a. A vessel proceeding along the course of a narrow channel or fairway shall keep as near to the outer limit of the channel or fairway which lies on her starboard side as is safe and practicable.

b. A vessel of less than 20m in length or a sailing vessel shall not impede the passage of a vessel which can safely navigate only within a narrow channel or fairway.

c. A vessel engaged in fishing shall not impede the passage of any other vessel navigating within a narrow channel or fairway.

d. A vessel shall not cross a narrow channel or fairway if such crossing impedes the passage of a vessel which can safely navigate only within such channel or fairway. The latter vessel may use the sound signal prescribed in Rule 34(d) if in doubt as to the intention of the crossing vessel.

e. i. In a narrow channel or fairway when overtaking can take place only if the vessel to be overtaken has to take action to permit safe passing, the vessel intending to overtake shall indicate her intention by sounding the appropriate signal prescribed in Rule 34(c)(i). The vessel to be overtaken shall, if in agreement, sound the appropriate signal prescribed in Rule 34(c)(ii) and take steps to permit safe passing. If in doubt she may sound the signals prescribed in Rule 34(d)

f. A vessel nearing a bend or an area of a narrow channel or fairway where other vessels may be obscured by an intervening obstruction shall navigate with particular alertness and caution and shall sound the appropriate signal prescribed in Rule 34(e).

g. Any vessel shall, if the circumstances of the case admit, avoid anchoring in a narrow channel.

Rule 10
Traffic separation schemes

a. This Rule applies to traffic separation schemes adopted by the International Maritime Organisation and does not relieve any vessel of her obligation under any other Rule.

b. A vessel using a traffic separation scheme shall:

i. proceed in the appropriate traffic lane in the general direction of traffic flow for that lane;

ii. so far as practicable keep clear of the traffic separation line or separation zone;

iii. normally join or leave a traffic lane at the termination of the lane, but when joining or leaving from either side shall do so at as small an angle to the general direction of traffic flow as practicable.

c. A vessel shall, so far as practicable, avoid crossing traffic lanes but if obliged to do so shall cross on a heading as nearly as practicable at right angles to the general direction of traffic flow.

d. Inshore traffic zones shall not normally be used by through traffic which can safely use the appropriate traffic lane within the adjacent traffic separation scheme. However, vessels of less than 20m in length and sailing vessels may under all circumstances use inshore traffic zones.

e. A vessel other than a crossing vessel or a vessel joining or leaving a lane shall not normally enter a separation zone or cross a separation line except:

i. in cases of emergency to avoid immediate danger;

ii. to engage in fishing within a separation zone.

f. A vessel navigating in areas near the terminations of traffic separation schemes shall do so with particular caution.

g. A vessel shall so far as practicable avoid anchoring in a traffic separation scheme or in areas near its terminations.

h. A vessel not using a traffic separation scheme shall avoid it by as wide a margin as is practicable.

i. A vessel engaged in fishing shall not impede the passage of any vessel following a traffic lane.

j. A vessel of less than 20m in length or a sailing vessel shall not impede the safe passage of a power-driven vessel following a traffic lane.

k. A vessel restricted in her ability to manoeuvre when engaged in an operation for the maintenance of safety of navigation in a traffic separation scheme is exempted from complying with this Rule to the extent necessary to carry out the operation.

l. A vessel restricted in her ability to manoeuvre when engaged in an operation for the lashing, servicing or picking up of a submarine cable, within a traffic separation scheme, is exempted from complying with this Rule to the extent necessary to carry out the operation.

Section II. Conduct of vessels in sight of one another
Rule 11
Application
Rules in this Section apply to vessels in sight of one another.
Rule 12
Sailing vessels
a. When two sailing vessels are approaching one another, so as to involve risk of collision, one of them shall keep out of the way of the other as follows:
  i.   when each has the wind on a different side, the vessel which has the wind on the port side shall keep out of the way of the other;
  ii. when both have the wind on the same side, the vessel which is to windward shall keep out of the way of the vessel which is to leeward;
  iii. if a vessel with the wind on the port side sees a vessel to windward and cannot determine with certainty whether the other vessel has the wind on the port or on the starboard side, she shall keep out of the way of the other.
b. For the purposes of this Rule the windward side shall be deemed to be the side opposite to that on which the mainsail is carried or, in the case of a square-rigged vessel, the side opposite to that on which the largest fore-and-aft sail is carried.

Rule 13
Overtaking
a. Notwithstanding anything contained in the Rules of Part B, Sections I and II any vessel overtaking any other shall keep out of the way of the vessel being overtaken.
b. A vessel shall be deemed to be overtaking when coming up with another vessel from a direction more than 22·5 degrees abaft her beam, that is, in such a position with reference to the vessel she is overtaking, that at night she would be able to see only the sternlight of that vessel but neither of her sidelights.
c. When a vessel is in any doubt as to whether she is overtaking another, she shall assume that this is the case and act accordingly.
d. Any subsequent alteration of the bearing between the two vessels shall not make the overtaking vessel a crossing vessel within the meaning of these Rules or relieve her of the duty of keeping clear of the overtaken vessel until she is finally past and clear.

Rule 14
Head-on situation
a. When two power-driven vessels are meeting on reciprocal or nearly reciprocal courses so as to involve risk of collision each shall alter her course to starboard so that each shall pass on the port side of the other.
b. Such a situation shall be deemed to exist when a vessel sees the other ahead or nearly ahead and by night she could see the masthead lights of the other in a line or nearly in a line and/or both sidelights and by day she observes the corresponding aspect of the other vessel.
c. When a vessel is in any doubt as to whether such a situation exists she shall assume that it does exist and act accordingly.

Rule 15
Crossing situation
When two power-driven vessels are crossing so as to involve risk of collision, the vessel which has the other on her own starboard side shall keep out of the way and shall, if the circumstances of the case admit, avoid crossing ahead of the other vessel.

Rule 16
Action by give-way vessel
Every vessel which is directed to keep out of the way of another vessel shall, so far as possible, take early and substantial action to keep well clear.

Rule 17
Action by stand-on vessel
a. i. Where one of two vessels is to keep out of the way the other shall keep her course and speed.
  ii. The latter vessel may however take action to avoid collision by her manoeuvre alone, as soon as it becomes apparent to her that the vessel required to keep out of the way is not taking appropriate action in compliance with these Rules.
b. When, from any cause, the vessel required to keep her course and speed finds herself so close that collision cannot be avoided by the action of the give-way vessel alone, she shall take such action as will best aid to avoid collision.
c. A power-driven vessel which takes action in a crossing situation in accordance with sub-paragraph (a)(ii) of this Rule to avoid collision with another power-driven vessel shall, if the circumstances of the case admit, not alter course to port for a vessel on her own port side.
d. This Rule does not relieve the give-way vessel of her obligation to keep out of the way.

Rule 18
Responsibilities between vessels
Except where Rules 9, 10 and 13 otherwise require:
a. A power-driven vessel underway shall keep out of the way of:
  i.   a vessel not under command;
  ii. a vessel restricted in her ability to manoeuvre;
  iii. a vessel engaged in fishing;
  iv. a sailing vessel
b. A sailing vessel underway shall keep out of the way of:
  i.   a vessel not under command;
  ii. a vessel restricted in her ability to manoeuvre;
  iii. a vessel engaged in fishing.
c. A vessel engaged in fishing when underway shall, so far as possible, keep out of the way of:
  i.   a vessel not under command;
  ii. a vessel restricted in her ability to manoeuvre.
d. i. Any vessel other than a vessel not under command or a vessel restricted in her ability to manoeuvre shall, if the circumstances of the case admit, avoid impeding the safe passage of a vessel constrained by her draught, exhibiting the signals in Rule 28;
  ii. A vessel constrained by her draught shall navigate with particular caution having full regard to her special condition.
e. A seaplane on the water shall, in general, keep well clear of all vessels and avoid impeding their navigation. In circumstances, however, where risk of collision exists, she shall comply with the Rules of this Part.

Section III. Conduct of vessels in restricted visibility
Rule 19
Conduct of vessels in restricted visibility
a. This Rule applies to vessels not in sight of one another when navigating in or near an area of restricted visibility.
b. Every vessel shall proceed at a safe speed adapted to the prevailing circumstances and conditions of restricted visibility. A power-driven vessel shall have her engines ready for immediate manoeuvre.
c. Every vessel shall have due regard to the prevailing circumstances and conditions of restricted visibility when complying with the Rules of Section I of this Part.
d. A vessel which detects by radar alone the presence of another vessel shall determine if a close-quarters situation is developing and/or risk of collision exists. If so, she shall take avoiding action in ample time, provided that when such action consists of an alteration of course, so far as possible the following shall be avoided:
  i.   an alteration of course to part for a vessel forward of the beam, other than for a vessel being overtaken;
  ii. an alteration of course towards a vessel abeam or abaft the beam.
e. Except where it has been determined that a risk of collision does not exist, every vessel which hears apparently forward of her beam the fog signal of another vessel, or which cannot avoid a close-quarters situation with another vessel forward of her beam, shall reduce her speed to the minimum at which she can be kept on her course. She shall if necessary take all her way off and in any event navigate with extreme caution until danger of collision is over.

1. Need of assistance

The following signals, used or exhibited either together or separately, indicate distress and need of assistance:

(a) a gun or other explosive signal fired at intervals of about a minute;

(b) a continuous sounding with any fog-signalling apparatus;

(c) rockets or shells, throwing red stars fired one at a time at short intervals;

(d) a signal made by radiotelegraphy or by any other signaling method consisting of the group · · · — — — · · · (SOS) in the Morse Code;

(e) a signal sent by radiotelephony consisting of the spoken word 'Mayday';

(f) the International Code Signal of distress indicated by N.C.;

(g) a signal consisting of a square flag having above or below it a ball or anything resembling a ball;

(h) flames on the vessel (as from a burning tar barrel, oil barrel, etc.);

(i) a rocket parachute flare or a hand flare showing a red light;

(j) a smoke signal giving off orange-coloured smoke;

(k) slowly and repeatedly raising and lowering arms outstretched to each side;

(l) the radiotelegraph alarm signal;

(m) the radiotelephone alarm signal;

(n) signals transmitted by emergency position-indicating radio beacons

(o) approved signals transmitted by radio-communications systems.

2. The use or exhibition of any of the foregoing signals except for the purpose of indicating distress and need of assistance and the use of other signals which may be confused with any of the above signals is prohbited.

3. Attention is drawn to the relevant sections of the International Code of Signals, the Merchant Ship Search and Rescue Manual and the following signals:

(a) a piece of orange-coloured canvas with either a black square and circle or other appropriate symbol (for identification from the air);

(b) a dye marker.

8.7 Traffic Separation Schemes

Within the Mediterranean the following Traffic Separation Schemes have been adopted by the International Maritime Organisation.

1. In the Strait of Gibraltar, 35°59'·1N, 5°25'·6W to 35°56'·3N, 5°45'·0W.
2. Off Cabo De Gato (Spain) 36°35'·0N 02°00'·0W.
3. Off Cabo De La Nao (Spain) 38°40'·0N 00°20'·0E.
4. Off Cani Island (Iles Cani, Tunisia), 37°31'·7N, 10°07'·6E.
5. Off Cape Bon (Cap Bon, Tunisia), 37°11'·7N, 11°06'·3E.
6. Saronic Gulf (Saronikós Kolpos, in the Approaches to Piraeus, Greece), 37°45'·1 N, 23°40'·9E.
7. Between Çanakkale Boğazi (The Dardanelles) and Istanbul Boğazi (The Bosphorus) including Marmara Denizi, 39°58'·00N, 25°57'·70E, 40°44'·81N, 27°38'·09E, 41°20'·23N, 29°11'·20E.

In addition, the Italian and Croatian governments have adopted the following traffic separation schemes which lie wholly within their territorial waters.

1. In Stretto di Messina, 38°14'·0N, 15°36'·6E (Government of Italy).
2. Approaches to Brindisi, 40°41'·0N, 18°00'·0E (Government of Italy).
3. Approaches to Chioggia, Malamocco and Venezia, 45°15'·50N, 12°31'·75E (Government of Italy).
4. Off Otok Palagruža, 42°16'·5N, 16°09'·5E (Government of Croatia).
5. In Vela Vrata, 45°07'·8N, 14°15'·8E (Government of Croatia).

Compliance with Rule 10 of the *International Regulations for Preventing Collision at Sea* is mandatory

for all vessels in or near to Traffic Separation Schemes adopted by the IMO, but this does not give any vessel a right of way over crossing vessels or relieve her of her obligations under the *Steering and Sailing Rules* if a situation arises in which risk of collision is deemed to exist.

When in the region of a traffic separation scheme:

1. Vessels will use the appropriate lane, keep clear of and avoid entering the separation zone, join or leave the traffic lane at the ends or, if this is not possible, then at a small angle.

2. Vessels of less than 20m and sailing vessels shall not impede the passage of power-driven vessels following a lane.

3. Vessels less than 20m and sailing vessels may use the inshore zones, though large numbers of small craft may be encountered in this region.

4. Traffic lanes must be crossed on a heading as nearly as practicable at right angles to the lane.

Traffic Separation Schemes established by governments within their territorial waters, are not always adopted by the IMO and the regulations governing their use, laid down by the government concerned, may modify the application of the *Steering and Sailing Rules* within these areas. On Admiralty charts, IMO and national traffic separation schemes are printed in the same format. This does not imply acceptance of the international validity of the national schemes but is only for the convenience of mariners.

8.8 Marine Reserves

In a number of Mediterranean countries, but principally Spain, France and Italy, marine reserves have been established. There is a rough conformity between the zones although specific regulations apply in the different countries. Zones are classified roughly as follows. There are three types of restricted zones. In some areas there is a fourth Zone D which seems to have a variable interpretation at a lower level than Zone C.

Zone A

1. It is prohibited to navigate or anchor in the designated area.
2. It is prohibited to fish in the area.
3. It is prohibited to pollute the area in any way including pumping bilge water or black and grey water.
4. It is prohibited to remove any plant and animal life and to interfere with the mineral strata of the area.
5. Bathing is restricted to designated areas.
6. The area is defined by four cardinal buoys at the cardinal limits of the designated area.

Zone B

1. It is prohibited to carry out any form of fishing.
2. Navigation and mooring are permitted although there may be specific restrictions at any one reserve.

Zone C

1. Commercial fishing is prohibited.
2. Sport fishing may be limited in some areas.

Note Speed restrictions can apply in Zone B and C areas. These vary by country and even within countries but are generally of the order of 3 to 5 knots.

8.9 Lights, shapes and sound signals

NAVIGATION SHAPES, LIGHTS AND SOUND SIGNALS

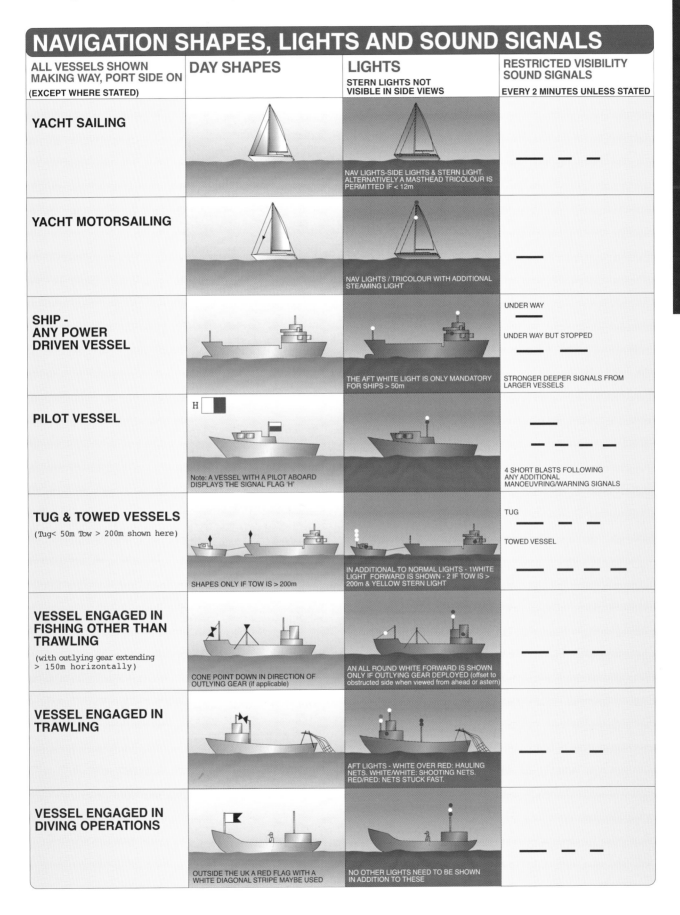

ALL VESSELS SHOWN MAKING WAY, PORT SIDE ON (EXCEPT WHERE STATED)	DAY SHAPES	LIGHTS STERN LIGHTS NOT VISIBLE IN SIDE VIEWS	RESTRICTED VISIBILITY SOUND SIGNALS EVERY 2 MINUTES UNLESS STATED
YACHT SAILING		NAV LIGHTS-SIDE LIGHTS & STERN LIGHT. ALTERNATIVELY A MASTHEAD TRICOLOUR IS PERMITTED IF < 12m	— – –
YACHT MOTORSAILING		NAV LIGHTS / TRICOLOUR WITH ADDITIONAL STEAMING LIGHT	—
SHIP - ANY POWER DRIVEN VESSEL		THE AFT WHITE LIGHT IS ONLY MANDATORY FOR SHIPS > 50m	UNDER WAY — UNDER WAY BUT STOPPED — — STRONGER DEEPER SIGNALS FROM LARGER VESSELS
PILOT VESSEL	H ▯ Note: A VESSEL WITH A PILOT ABOARD DISPLAYS THE SIGNAL FLAG 'H'		— – – — — – – — – – 4 SHORT BLASTS FOLLOWING ANY ADDITIONAL MANOEUVRING/WARNING SIGNALS
TUG & TOWED VESSELS (Tug< 50m Tow > 200m shown here)	SHAPES ONLY IF TOW IS > 200m	IN ADDITIONAL TO NORMAL LIGHTS - 1 WHITE LIGHT FORWARD IS SHOWN - 2 IF TOW IS > 200m & YELLOW STERN LIGHT	TUG — – – — TOWED VESSEL — – – –
VESSEL ENGAGED IN FISHING OTHER THAN TRAWLING (with outlying gear extending > 150m horizontally)	CONE POINT DOWN IN DIRECTION OF OUTLYING GEAR (if applicable)	AN ALL ROUND WHITE FORWARD IS SHOWN ONLY IF OUTLYING GEAR DEPLOYED (offset to obstructed side when viewed from ahead or astern)	— – –
VESSEL ENGAGED IN TRAWLING		AFT LIGHTS - WHITE OVER RED: HAULING NETS. WHITE/WHITE: SHOOTING NETS. RED/RED: NETS STUCK FAST.	— – –
VESSEL ENGAGED IN DIVING OPERATIONS	OUTSIDE THE UK A RED FLAG WITH A WHITE DIAGONAL STRIPE MAYBE USED	NO OTHER LIGHTS NEED TO BE SHOWN IN ADDITION TO THESE	— – –

RESTRICTION SIGNALS

ALL VESSELS SHOWN MAKING WAY, PORT SIDE ON (EXCEPT WHERE STATED)	DAY SHAPES	LIGHTS STERN LIGHTS NOT VISIBLE IN SIDE VIEWS	RESTRICTED VISIBILITY SOUND SIGNALS EVERY 2 MINUTES UNLESS STATED
VESSEL AT ANCHOR	ANY VESSEL, ANY SIZE	ADITIONAL LIGHT AFT IF > 50m	5 SECONDS EVERY MINUTE AND — — —
VESSEL AGROUND		ADDITIONAL LIGHT AFT IF > 50m	5 SECONDS EVERY MINUTE
VESSEL NOT UNDER COMMAND		NAV LIGHTS NOT TO BE SHOWN IF VESSEL IS NOT MAKING WAY	— — —
VESSEL RESTRICTED ABILITY TO MANOEUVRE	SHAPES OFTEN SHOWN BY TUGS	VESSEL < 50m	— — —
VESSEL RESTRICTED BY GEAR (eg dredging)	DIAMONDS (GREEN LIGHTS) SHOWN BY SIDE CLEAR TO PASS	RED LIGHTS (OR BALLS) SHOWN SIDE WITH OBSTRUCTIONS. VESSEL > 50m	— — —
VESSEL CONSTRAINED BY DRAUGHT		VESSEL > 50m	— — —

MANOEUVRING / WARNING SIGNALS

ALL SHIPS	—	— —	— — —	— — — —	— — — — — (— — — —)	— — — — —
	TURNING TO STARBOARD	TURNING TO PORT	OPERATING ASTERN PROPULSION	I AM UNSURE OF YOUR INTENTIONS/ KEEP CLEAR	I AM OVERTAKING ON YOUR PORT (OR STARBOARD) SIDE	I AGREE WITH YOUR INTENTION TO OVERTAKE

9. Navigation

Coastal navigation

9.1 The magnetic compass

A well designed compass should have:

- several short compass needles.
- a period of oscillation greater than the period of roll of the vessel.
- little friction at the pivot.
- the magnetic axis of the needles in line with the north and south points of the card.
- a card with a low centre of gravity.

Variation This is the angle between magnetic north and true north, named easterly if the compass card points to the east of true north and westerly if it points to the west. Places with the same variation lie on isogonals, the maximum variation of 180° being on the isogonal joining the magnetic pole to the geographic pole. In the Mediterranean the minimum variation of 0° occurs on the agonic line which (in 1995) lay to the east of Corsica and Sardinia.

Annual change in variation At any place there is a continuous slow change in the variation due to changes in the earth's magnetic field. This change is given on the chart and should be applied if large or if a number of years have elapsed since the chart was published. In the eastern Mediterranean the annual change is about 0°1'E increasing to about 0°5'E at the western end.

Deviation Deviation is caused by magnetic materials (steel, electric motors, generators, electric wiring, etc.) which deflect the compass from magnetic north and may have a maximum value of 180° if the compass is badly sited. It is named in a similar manner to variation; easterly if compass north lies to the east of magnetic north and westerly if compass north lies to the west of magnetic north. The deviation is not constant but changes with:

- the course being steered.
- changing the position of magnetic materials near the compass, such as a knife or UK 'copper' coinage minted after 1992 carried on the person, or switching on electrical equipment.
- the vessel's magnetism which changes slowly with time, being modified by on board vibration.

Compass error If magnetic courses or bearings are required, after drawing a true course on a chart, the simplest method is by applying the compass error to the true course or bearing. The compass error is the sum of the variation and the deviation, taking its name from the larger. When applying the resulting correction to your true chart course, use the mnemonic:

WEST IS BEST (ADD)
EAST IS LEAST (SUBTRACT)

For example
True course 294°; variation 3°W (from chart); Deviation 6°E (from deviation card for compass course 294°)
Error = 3°W + 6°E = 3°E
Magnetic course = 291° (Error is east therefore subtract the error)

The compass error can be checked by:

- transit bearings of suitably separated, charted fixed objects. Bearings etc. are not suitable.
- azimuths of the sun, stars, planets or moon, using either the A B C Tables or the formula given in the Astro Navigation section.
- azimuths of the stars using Imray's *Computed Star Azimuth Tables* (Latitude 40°N–60°N).
- table of azimuths of Polaris for use in the Mediterranean, in the celestial navigation section.
- table of bearings of the sun at visible or theoretical

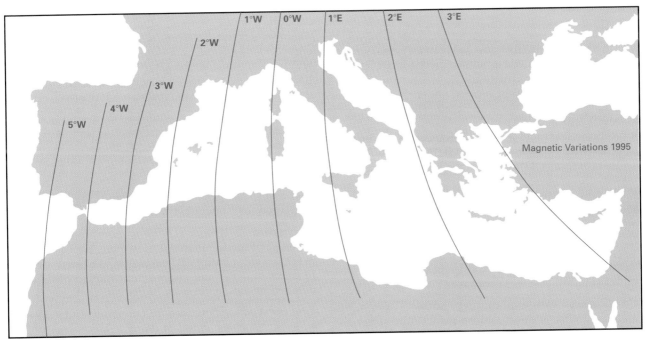

Magnetic Variations

sunrise or sunset in the celestial navigation section. (Other celestial bodies can also be used provided their dec is less than 23½°). The use of these tables is described in the *Astro Navigation* section.

Compass adjustment (The removal of the deviations of a compass by means of the fore & aft and athwartships correctors). When steering east then west, the fore & aft correctors are altered to remove the deviations found by comparing the true and compass bearings of a distant object or celestial body. The procedure is then repeated using the athwartship correctors when steering north then south. Before starting the adjustment:
- All magnetic materials should be in their sea-going positions.
- The ship should be upright.
- The positions of the correctors should be noted so that in the event of failure to re-adjust the compass satisfactorily the correctors can be returned to their original state.

Deviation card Swinging the ship to obtain a table of deviations should be carried out after adjusting the compass, after winter lay-up, or if large changes in the deviation are observed. The table is obtained by swinging through 360°, steadying on each 20° and comparing compass and true bearings. If electrical equipment causes changes in the deviations, then separate deviation cards should be compiled with the equipment switched on and off.

Hand bearing compass Because it is not used in the same position on board, its deviation cannot be obtained from a deviation card but should be found at the time of taking the bearings.

9.2 Charts and plans

Charts Most charts are drawn on the Mercator Projection ie latitude and longitude are straight lines drawn perpendicular to each other, and plans are often drawn on the Gnomonic Projection with parallels of latitude as curves and meridians converging towards the pole.
On charts:
- the natural scale (the ratio between an actual size on the earth and its size as shown on the chart) is only correct for the given latitude.
- chart reference datum is given under the chart title.
- heights of lights etc. are their elevations above MHWS or MHHW.
- vertical clearances are the clearances below bridges or overhead power cables at MHWS or MHHW.
- chart datum (CD) is usually the lowest astronomical tide.
- charted depths are given below the chart datum.
- drying heights are given above CD for rocks etc. which are exposed at low water.
- range of lights is the luminous range which depends on the light's intensity and ignores the elevation of the light and the observer's height of eye.
- bearings are true from seawards.

Cautionary and explanatory notes These notes under the chart title should be read before using the chart. They refer to:

- submarine exercising areas.
- military firing ranges.
- magnetic anomalies.
- oil and gas pipe lines, rigs and platforms.
- spoil grounds.
- level of detail of navigational aids shown on the chart.
- fishing areas and methods used.
- corrections to be applied to satellite derived positions.
- dates of surveys on which the chart is based.

Chart accuracy A chart's accuracy depends on the accuracy of the survey and many Mediterranean charts are based on surveys carried out more than 150 years ago, with more recent local surveys carried out in isolated areas. Some charts show this with a source diagram under the title, especially if it is based on recent surveys, but with most charts it will be coyly but correctly stated in the *Notes* under the title that the chart is based on surveys to the date of the most recent minor survey. Metric charts appear to be up-to-date (heights, depths, contours and depth contours in metres, new chart symbols and abbreviations, new colours and printing techniques etc). Often they are only embellished versions of the old surveys, having retained the original errors in charted positions which may be quite large and important when using accurate navigation systems such as GPS or Loran C.

Chart reference datum The horizontal datum, based on the reference spheroid which gives the best estimate of the shape of the earth in a particular area eg OSGB36 (Ordnance Survey Great Britain, 1936); ED50 (European Datum, 1950); Australian Geodetic Datum, 1966.
  The WGS 84 – World Geodetic System, 1984 – uses the centre of mass of the earth as its datum point and is intended for world-wide use with particular emphasis on GPS.
  When transferring a position from a chart based on one reference datum to a chart based on another do so by the bearing and distance of a terrestrial feature, not by latitude and longitude, otherwise the positions may differ by several hundred metres. When using GPS ensure its positions are based on the same chart reference datum as the chart in use. The reference datum is given under the chart title and with most GPS there is a wide choice of datums available.

Chart corrections are published in a weekly edition of *Notices to Mariners*. Quarterly editions for small boat owners do not cover the Mediterranean. Corrections should be entered on the charts whose number is given in the notice as being affected.

Electronic Charts For information on electronic charts see *9.13 Electronic Chart Plotters*.

Yachtsman's Pilots There is now comprehensive coverage of the Mediterranean in many pilot books and guides in most European languages. They are variable in terms of detail and updates, but most provide more detailed information on harbours and anchorages.

Log book A log book should be kept with details of:
- positions and method of fixing.
- courses, distances and compass errors.

- weather and sea conditions, weather reports and forecasts received.
- events of navigational importance.
- unusual occurrences.

9.3 Course to steer

Set and drift The set and drift is the direction and distance the current has moved a craft from its DR position to its observed position.

Course to counteract current The course can be found by a construction on the chart, but using a calculator is easier, as follows:

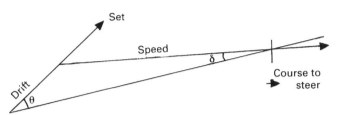

$$\sin \delta = \frac{\text{Drift} \times \sin \theta}{\text{Speed}}$$

$$\text{Speed made good} = \frac{\text{Speed} \times \sin (180° - \theta - \delta)}{\sin \theta}$$

where δ = Course Correction
and θ = Relative Set

Example Find the course to steer to make good 075° when counteracting a current setting 045° at 2 knots. Log speed 6·0 knots.

If the current drift is greater than the speed, the required course cannot be made good.

$$\text{Relative Set} = \theta = 30°$$

$$\sin \text{Course Alteration} = \frac{2 \times \sin 30}{6}$$

$$\therefore \text{Course Alteration} = 9.54°$$

$$\text{Speed Made Good} = \frac{6 \times \sin (180 - 30 - 9.54)}{\sin 30}$$

$$= 7.633 \text{ kts}$$

9.4 Position-fixing

Dead reckoning position (DR) The position is found by laying off from a known position the course steered and the distance by log.

Estimated Position (EP) Found by laying off from a known position the estimated leeway and the distance by log then laying off the estimated current.

To calculate the EP as a bearing and distance from the initial position:

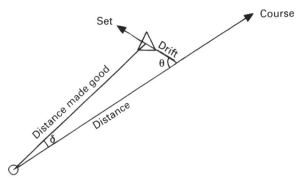

$$\tan \text{Course Made Good} = \frac{(\text{Dist} \times \sin \text{Co}) \pm (\text{Drift} \times \sin \text{Set})}{(\text{Dist} \times \cos \text{Co}) \pm (\text{Drift} \times \cos \text{Set})}$$

$$\text{Distance Made Good} = \frac{\text{Drift} \times \sin \theta}{\sin \delta}$$

where θ = Relative Set
and δ = (CMG ~ Course Steered)
Course and Set are entered using the 360° notation.

Example Course steered 060°, log distance 10 miles, set 305°, drift 2 miles. Calculate the Estimated Position as a bearing and distance from the start point.

$$\tan \text{Course M G} = \frac{(10 \times \sin 60) + (2 \times \sin 305)}{(10 \times \cos 60) + (2 \times \cos 305)}$$

$$= \frac{7.02}{6.15}$$

$$\therefore \text{Course M G} = 48.8°$$

$$(\text{CMG} \sim \text{Course Steered}) = \delta = 11.2°$$

$$\text{Relative Set} = \theta = 65°$$

$$\text{Distance M G} = \frac{2 \times \sin 65}{\sin 11.2}$$

$$= 9.33 \text{ miles}$$

Using a calculator which converts coordinates from polar (course and distance) to rectangular (north/southing and east/westing), the EP is easily calculated. Convert courses and distances to rectangular coordinates, find their sum, and convert this back to polar coordinates. Using the previous example:

$$(10 , 60) \text{ P} \rightarrow \text{R} = (5 , 8.66)$$
$$(2 , 305) \text{ P} \rightarrow \text{R} = (1.15 , -1.64)$$
$$\text{Sum} = (6.15 , 7.02)$$
$$(6.15 , 7.02) \text{ R} \rightarrow \text{P} = (9.33 , 48.8)$$

Both methods can be used to calculate the EP for a passage involving several tracks.

Cross bearings If possible 3 simultaneous bearings should be taken, the third as a check to avoid undetected compass, bearing or laying off errors. Objects should be selected to give a good angle of cut between the bearings.

Cocked Hat When 3 bearings are taken, a 'cocked hat' frequently results. It can be caused by:

- an inaccurate compass.
- bearing errors.
- laying off errors.

- mistaken identification of the object.
- the bearings not being taken simultaneously.
- an inaccurate chart.

It is customary to assume the position to be at the point on the cocked hat nearest to the navigation hazard, but this position must be treated with caution as the true position may be at some distance from the cocked hat.

Running fix The running fix is a method of obtaining a position when only one object is available. Two bearings are taken of the same object with a time interval between. The first P/L is transferred to the end of the run and the position is the point of intersection of the two P/Ls.

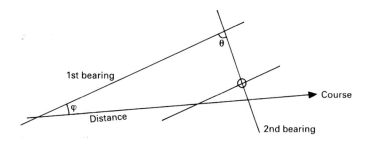

To find the distance off on the 2nd bearing:

$$\text{Distance Off} = \frac{\text{Run} \times \sin \varphi}{\sin \theta}$$

where φ = the 1st bearing (Relative)
and θ = the angle between the bearings

Example When steering 080° a light bears 060°. After a run of 5·5 miles its bearing is 335°. What is the distance off the light on the 2nd bearing?

$$\text{Relative Bearing} = \varphi = 20°$$
$$\text{Angle between Bearings} = \theta = 85°$$
$$\text{Distance Off} = \frac{5.5 \times \sin 20}{\sin 85}$$
$$= 1.88 \text{ miles}$$

Running fix with current The method is the same as for a running fix except that the estimated current is laid off at the end of the run. The 1st P/L is then transferred to the end of the current and the position is at the intersection of the two P/Ls.

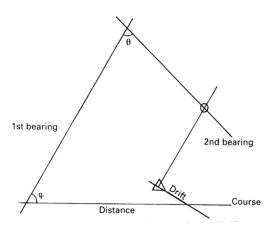

Example A light bore 030°. After sailing 5 miles on a course of 090° it bore 315°, set 300°, drift 1 mile. What is the distance off the light on the 2nd bearing? Solving the two parts separately:

1. Converting from polar to rectangular axes to calculate the EP:

$$(5, 090°) \text{ P} \rightarrow \text{R} = (0, 5)$$
$$(1, 300°) \text{ p} \rightarrow \text{R} = (0.5, -0.866)$$
$$\text{Sum} = (0.5, 4.134)$$
$$(0.5, 4.134) = (4.16, , \angle 83.1)$$
$$\therefore \text{Course Made Good} = 083.1°$$
$$\text{Distance Made Good} = 4.16 \text{miles}$$

2. To calculate the distance off:

$$\text{Relative Bearing, } \varphi = 53.1°$$
$$\text{Angle between bearings, } \theta = 75°$$
$$\text{Distance Off} = \frac{4.16 \times \sin 53.1}{\sin 75}$$
$$= 3.44 \text{ miles}$$

Running fixes are seldom highly accurate because of the difficulty in estimating the current. Currents given in tidal stream data tables are average values and should be treated with caution because no allowance is made for the effect of meteorological conditions.

Doubling the angle on the bow This is a particular form of running fix where the distance run between the 1st and 2nd bearings of an object equals the distance off the object on the 2nd bearing. With the 4 point bearing (4 points = 45°) doubling the angle gives the position when abeam. No allowance is made for set and drift, therefore the accuracy of the position is no higher than for other running fixes.

Horizontal sextant angles The position can be fixed by means of two horizontal sextant angles, using a station pointer or at the intersection of the 2 position circles whose centres can be found by:

$$\text{Radius} = \frac{D}{2 \sin A}$$
where D = Distance between the objects
and A = the horizantal sextant angle

Example Two lighthouses are 2·5 miles apart and the horizontal angle between them is 35°30'. Find the centre of the circle of position.

$$D = 2.5 \text{ miles}$$
$$A = 35°30'$$
$$\text{Radius} = \frac{D}{2 \times \sin 35°30'}$$
$$= 2.15 \text{ miles}$$

With 2·15 miles set on the compasses, draw two arcs with centres the lighthouses. The centre of the circle of position is their point of intersection.

9.5 Waypoints

Way points are positions used in navigation, such as:
- departure positions.
- destination positions.
- positions on route.
- alter course positions.
- tea break positions.

On chart plotters way points can be entered using latitude and longitude, or a bearing and distance of a charted feature. With PCs they can be entered with the mouse.

Waypoints can be obtained from the harbour information section, the latitude and longitude of either the breakwater light or harbour entrance being given for every harbour in the section.

Cautions

1. Charts, even new metric editions and electronic versions, are often based on old surveys (some from the 19th century) and may contain significant errors in latitude and longitude. Check the date of the surveys given under the chart title. Mediterranean charts use different reference data mainly European datum 1950 (ED50); Ordnance Survey of Great Britain 1936 (OSGB36) World Geodetic System 1984 (WGS84). Positions in latitude and longitude will not transfer accurately from one datum to the other.
2. Check the proposed course line on the chart to ensure that it doesn't pass close to or over navigation hazards.
3. If WPs are entered using latitude and longitude, or a bearing and distance, care must be taken to avoid numerical errors. The chart plotter must be set to the same reference datum as the chart from which the positions are obtained.
4. Distance-to-way point alarms where fitted should be used with caution and set for at least 1 mile.

See also *9·12 GPS* and *9·13 Electronic Chart Plotters*

9.6 Speed over measured mile

With the time, in minutes and seconds, taken to complete the measured mile, enter the appropriate minutes column; the speed is read off opposite the seconds.

9.7 Extreme range table

The table gives the dipping distances of lights (geographical range) for heights of eye from 0m to 10m and elevations of objects from 1m to 100m.

By entering the height of object column with the height of eye, the table also gives the distance of the horizon for heights of eye from 1m to 100m. The distance of the horizon is read from the column headed 0m.

The dipping distance of a light can also be found by the formula:

$$\text{Dipping Distance} = 2.0945 \times (\sqrt{h_E} + \sqrt{h_O})$$
where h_E = height of eye in metres
and h_O = height of eye in metres

Example An observer, height of eye 3·2m, raises a light 116m high. What is the range?

$$\text{Raising Range} = 2.0945 \times (\sqrt{3.2} + \sqrt{116})$$
$$= 2.0945 \times (1.79 + 10.77)$$
$$= 26.3 \text{ miles}$$

9.8 Distance off by vertical sextant angle

Using the table, a vertical sextant angle can be used to find the distance of an object, or the sextant angle can be found to ensure a safe distance from a danger. Heights given on the chart are above MHWS so that for all other states of the tide the tabulated distance will be less than the true distance, unless an allowance for the height of the tide is made.

Note The charted height of a lighthouse is measured to the centre of the lantern.

$$\text{Distance} = \frac{\text{Height}}{1852 \times \tan \text{ Sextant Angle}}$$
$$\text{Tan Sextant Angle} = \frac{\text{height}}{1852 \times \text{distance}}$$
where the height is in metres

Example What is the angle to set on a sextant to maintain a distance of 2·5 cables when rounding a 10m high light?

$$\tan \text{ Sextant Angle} = \frac{10}{1852 \times 0.25}$$
$$\text{Sextant Angle} = \tan^{-1}\left(\frac{10}{1852 \times 0.25}\right)$$
$$= 1.237°$$

Note The formula is only correct when the observer's height of eye allows him to see the bottom of the object and when the top of the object is approximately vertically above the bottom.

Speed Over the Measured Mile

Time Secs.	1 kts.	2 kts.	3 kts.	4 kts.	5 kts.	6 kts.	7 kts.	8 kts.	9 kts.	10 kts.	11 kts.	12 kts.	13 kts.	14 kts.	Time Secs.
							Time, Minutes								
0	60.00	30.00	20.00	15.00	12.00	10.00	8.57	7.50	6.67	6.00	5.45	5.00	4.62	4.29	0
1	59.02	29.75	19.89	14.94	11.96	9.97	8.55	7.48	6.65	5.99	5.45	4.99	4.61	4.28	1
2	58.06	29.51	19.78	14.88	11.92	9.94	8.53	7.47	6.64	5.98	5.44	4.99	4.60	4.28	2
3	57.14	29.27	19.67	14.81	11.88	9.92	8.51	7.45	6.63	5.97	5.43	4.98	4.60	4.27	3
4	56.25	29.03	19.57	14.75	11.84	9.89	8.49	7.44	6.62	5.96	5.42	4.97	4.59	4.27	4
5	55.38	28.80	19.46	14.69	11.80	9.86	8.47	7.42	6.61	5.95	5.41	4.97	4.59	4.26	5
6	54.55	28.57	19.35	14.63	11.76	9.84	8.45	7.41	6.59	5.94	5.41	4.96	4.58	4.26	6
7	53.73	28.35	19.25	14.57	11.73	9.81	8.43	7.39	6.58	5.93	5.40	4.95	4.57	4.25	7
8	52.94	28.13	19.15	14.52	11.69	9.78	8.41	7.38	6.57	5.92	5.39	4.95	4.57	4.25	8
9	52.17	27.91	19.05	14.46	11.65	9.76	8.39	7.36	6.56	5.91	5.38	4.94	4.56	4.24	9
10	51.43	27.69	18.95	14.40	11.61	9.73	8.37	7.35	6.55	5.90	5.37	4.93	4.56	4.24	10
11	50.70	27.48	18.85	14.34	11.58	9.70	8.35	7.33	6.53	5.89	5.37	4.92	4.55	4.23	11
12	50.00	27.27	18.75	14.29	11.54	9.68	8.33	7.32	6.52	5.88	5.36	4.92	4.55	4.23	12
13	49.32	27.07	18.65	14.23	11.50	9.65	8.31	7.30	6.51	5.87	5.35	4.91	4.54	4.22	13
14	48.65	26.87	18.56	14.17	11.46	9.63	8.29	7.29	6.50	5.86	5.34	4.90	4.53	4.22	14
15	48.00	26.67	18.46	14.12	11.43	9.60	8.28	7.27	6.49	5.85	5.33	4.90	4.53	4.21	15
16	47.37	26.47	18.37	14.06	11.39	9.57	8.26	7.26	6.47	5.84	5.33	4.89	4.52	4.21	16
17	46.75	26.28	18.27	14.01	11.36	9.55	8.24	7.24	6.46	5.83	5.32	4.88	4.52	4.20	17
18	46.15	26.09	18.18	13.95	11.32	9.52	8.22	7.23	6.45	5.83	5.31	4.88	4.51	4.20	18
19	45.57	25.90	18.09	13.90	11.29	9.50	8.20	7.21	6.44	5.82	5.30	4.87	4.51	4.19	19
20	45.00	25.71	18.00	13.85	11.25	9.47	8.18	7.20	6.43	5.81	5.29	4.86	4.50	4.19	20
21	44.44	25.53	17.91	13.79	11.21	9.45	8.16	7.19	6.42	5.80	5.29	4.86	4.49	4.18	21
22	43.90	25.35	17.82	13.74	11.18	9.42	7.17	7.17	6.41	5.79	5.28	4.85	4.49	4.18	22
23	43.37	25.17	17.73	13.69	11.15	9.40	8.13	7.16	6.39	5.78	5.27	4.85	4.48	4.17	23
24	42.86	25.00	17.65	13.64	11.11	9.38	8.11	7.14	6.38	5.77	5.26	4.84	4.48	4.17	24
25	42.35	24.83	17.56	13.58	11.08	9.35	8.09	7.13	6.37	5.76	5.26	4.83	4.47	4.16	25
26	41.86	24.66	17.48	13.53	11.04	9.33	8.07	7.11	6.36	5.75	5.25	4.83	4.47	4.16	26
27	41.38	24.49	17.39	13.48	11.01	9.30	8.05	7.10	6.35	5.74	5.24	4.82	4.46	4.15	27
28	40.91	24.32	17.31	13.43	10.98	9.28	8.04	7.09	6.34	5.73	5.23	4.81	4.46	4.15	28
29	40.45	24.16	17.22	13.38	10.94	9.25	8.02	7.07	6.33	5.72	5.22	4.81	4.45	4.14	29
30	40.00	24.00	17.14	13.33	10.91	9.23	8.00	7.06	6.32	5.71	5.22	4.80	4.44	4.14	30
31	39.56	23.84	17.06	13.28	10.88	9.21	7.98	7.05	6.30	5.71	5.21	4.79	4.44	4.13	31
32	39.13	23.68	16.98	13.24	10.84	9.18	7.96	7.03	6.29	5.70	5.20	4.79	4.43	4.13	32
33	38.71	23.53	16.90	13.19	10.81	9.16	7.95	7.02	6.28	5.69	5.19	4.78	4.43	4.12	33
34	38.30	23.38	16.82	13.14	10.78	9.14	7.93	7.00	6.27	5.68	5.19	4.77	4.42	4.12	34
35	37.89	23.23	16.74	13.09	10.75	9.11	7.91	6.99	6.26	5.67	5.18	4.77	4.42	4.11	35
36	37.50	23.08	16.67	13.04	10.71	9.09	7.89	6.98	6.25	5.66	5.17	4.76	4.41	4.11	36
37	37.11	22.93	16.59	13.00	10.68	9.07	7.88	6.96	6.24	5.65	5.16	4.76	4.41	4.10	37
38	36.73	22.78	16.51	12.95	10.65	9.05	7.86	6.95	6.23	5.64	5.16	4.75	4.40	4.10	38
39	36.36	22.64	16.44	12.90	10.62	9.02	7.84	6.94	6.22	5.63	5.15	4.74	4.40	4.10	39
40	36.00	22.50	16.36	12.86	10.59	9.00	7.83	6.92	6.21	5.63	5.14	4.74	4.39	4.09	40
41	35.64	22.36	16.29	12.81	10.56	8.98	7.81	6.91	6.20	5.62	5.14	4.73	4.38	4.09	41
42	35.29	22.22	16.22	12.77	10.53	8.96	7.79	6.90	6.19	5.61	5.13	4.72	4.38	4.08	42
43	34.95	22.09	16.14	12.72	10.50	8.93	7.78	6.88	6.17	5.60	5.12	4.72	4.37	4.08	43
44	34.62	21.95	16.07	12.68	10.47	8.91	7.76	6.87	6.16	5.59	5.11	4.71	4.37	4.07	44
45	34.29	21.82	16.00	12.63	10.43	8.89	7.74	6.86	6.15	5.58	5.11	4.71	4.36	4.07	45
46	33.96	21.69	15.93	12.59	10.40	8.87	7.73	6.84	6.14	5.57	5.10	4.70	4.36	4.06	46
47	33.64	21.56	15.86	12.54	10.37	8.85	7.71	6.83	6.13	5.56	5.09	4.69	4.35	4.06	47
48	33.33	21.43	15.79	12.50	10.34	8.82	7.69	6.82	6.12	5.56	5.08	4.69	4.35	4.05	48
49	33.03	21.30	15.72	12.46	10.32	8.80	7.68	6.81	6.11	5.55	5.08	4.68	4.34	4.05	49
50	32.73	21.18	15.65	12.41	10.29	8.78	7.66	6.79	6.10	5.54	5.07	4.68	4.34	4.04	50
51	32.43	21.05	15.58	12.37	10.26	8.76	7.64	6.78	6.09	5.53	5.06	4.67	4.33	4.04	51
52	32.14	20.93	15.52	12.33	10.23	8.74	7.63	6.77	6.08	5.52	5.06	4.66	4.33	4.04	52
53	31.86	20.81	15.45	12.29	10.20	8.72	7.61	6.75	6.07	5.51	5.05	4.66	4.32	4.03	53
54	31.58	20.69	15.38	12.24	10.17	8.70	7.59	6.74	6.06	5.50	5.04	4.65	4.32	4.03	54
55	31.30	20.57	15.32	12.20	10.14	8.67	7.58	6.73	6.05	5.50	5.03	4.65	4.31	4.02	55
56	31.03	20.45	15.25	12.16	10.11	8.65	7.56	6.72	6.04	5.49	5.03	4.64	4.31	4.02	56
57	30.77	20.34	15.19	12.12	10.08	8.63	7.55	6.70	6.03	5.48	5.02	4.63	4.30	4.01	57
58	30.51	20.22	15.13	12.08	10.06	8.61	7.53	6.69	6.02	5.47	5.01	4.63	4.30	4.01	58
59	30.25	20.11	15.06	12.04	10.03	8.59	7.52	6.68	6.01	5.46	5.01	4.62	4.29	4.00	59
60	30.00	20.00	15.00	12.00	10.00	8.57	7.50	6.67	6.00	5.45	5.00	4.62	4.29	4.00	60

Extreme Range Table

Height of Object		Height of Eye														
m		1	2	3	4	5	6	7	8	9	10	12	14	16	18	20
	ft	3	7	10	13	16	20	23	26	30	33	39	46	52	59	66
m	ft	ml	ml	ml	ml	ml	ml	ml	ml	ml	ml	ml	ml	ml	ml	ml
0	0	2.1	3.0	3.6	4.2	4.7	5.1	5.5	5.9	6.3	6.6	7.3	7.8	8.4	8.9	9.4
1	3	4.2	5.1	5.7	6.3	6.8	7.2	7.6	8.0	8.4	8.7	9.4	9.9	10.5	11.0	11.5
2	7	5.1	5.9	6.6	7.2	7.6	8.1	8.5	8.9	9.2	9.6	10.2	10.8	11.3	11.9	12.3
3	10	5.7	6.6	7.3	7.8	8.3	8.8	9.2	9.6	9.9	10.3	10.9	11.5	12.0	12.5	13.0
4	13	6.3	7.2	7.8	8.4	8.9	9.3	9.7	10.1	10.5	10.8	11.4	12.0	12.6	13.1	13.6
5	15	6.5	7.4	8.1	8.6	9.1	9.6	10.0	10.4	10.7	11.1	11.7	12.3	12.8	13.3	13.8
6	20	7.2	8.1	8.8	9.3	9.8	10.3	10.7	11.1	11.4	11.8	12.4	13.0	13.5	14.0	14.5
7	23	7.6	8.5	9.2	9.7	10.2	10.7	11.1	11.5	11.8	12.2	12.8	13.4	13.9	14.4	14.9
8	26	8.0	8.9	9.6	10.1	10.6	11.1	11.5	11.9	12.2	12.6	13.2	13.8	14.3	14.8	15.3
9	30	8.4	9.2	9.9	10.5	11.0	11.4	11.8	12.2	12.6	12.9	13.5	14.1	14.7	15.2	15.7
10	33	8.7	9.6	10.3	10.8	11.3	11.8	12.2	12.6	12.9	13.2	13.9	14.5	15.0	15.5	16.0
12	36	9.4	10.2	10.9	11.4	11.9	12.4	12.8	13.2	13.5	13.9	14.5	15.1	15.6	16.1	16.6
14	39	9.9	10.8	11.5	12.0	12.5	13.0	13.4	13.8	14.1	14.5	15.1	15.7	16.2	16.7	17.2
16	43	10.5	11.3	12.0	12.6	13.1	13.5	13.9	14.3	14.7	15.0	15.6	16.2	16.8	17.3	17.7
18	46	11.0	11.9	12.5	13.1	13.6	14.0	14.4	14.8	15.2	15.5	16.1	16.7	17.3	17.8	18.3
20	49	11.5	12.3	13.0	13.6	14.1	14.5	14.9	15.3	15.7	16.0	16.6	17.2	17.7	18.3	18.7
22	52	11.9	12.8	13.5	14.0	14.5	15.0	15.4	15.8	16.1	16.5	17.1	17.7	18.2	18.7	19.2
24	56	12.4	13.2	13.9	14.5	14.9	15.4	15.8	16.2	16.5	16.9	17.5	18.1	18.6	19.2	19.6
26	59	12.8	13.6	14.3	14.9	15.4	15.8	16.2	16.6	17.0	17.3	17.9	18.5	19.1	19.6	20.1
28	62	13.2	14.0	14.7	15.3	15.8	16.2	16.6	17.0	17.4	17.7	18.3	18.9	19.5	20.0	20.5
30	66	13.6	14.4	15.1	15.7	16.2	16.6	17.0	17.4	17.8	18.1	18.7	19.3	19.9	20.4	20.8
32	72	13.9	14.8	15.5	16.0	16.5	17.0	17.4	17.8	18.1	18.5	19.1	19.7	20.2	20.7	21.2
34	79	14.3	15.2	15.8	16.4	16.9	17.3	17.8´	18.1	18.5	18.8	19.5	20.1	20.6	21.1	21.6
36	85	14.7	15.5	16.2	16.8	17.3	17.7	18.1	18.5	18.9	19.2	19.8	20.4	21.0	21.5	21.9
38	92	15.0	15.9	16.5	17.1	17.6	18.0	18.5	18.8	19.2	19.5	20.2	20.8	21.3	21.8	22.3
40	98	15.3	16.2	16.9	17.4	17.9	18.4	18.8	19.2	19.5	19.9	20.5	21.1	21.6	22.1	22.6
42	105	15.7	16.5	17.2	17.8	18.3	18.7	19.1	19.5	19.9	20.2	20.8	21.4	22.0	22.5	22.9
44	112	16.0	16.9	17.5	18.1	18.6	19.0	19.4	19.8	20.2	20.5	21.2	21.7	22.3	22.8	23.3
46	118	16.3	17.2	17.8	18.4	18.9	19.3	19.8	20.1	20.5	20.8	21.5	22.0	22.6	23.1	23.6
48	125	16.6	17.5	18.1	18.7	19.2	19.6	20.1	20.4	20.8	21.1	21.8	22.4	22.9	23.4	23.9
50	131	16.9	17.8	18.4	19.0	19.5	19.9	20.4	20.7	21.1	21.4	22.1	22.7	23.2	23.7	24.2
55	138	17.6	18.5	19.2	19.7	20.2	20.7	21.1	21.5	21.8	22.2	22.8	23.4	23.9	24.4	24.9
60	144	18.3	19.2	19.9	20.4	20.9	21.4	21.8	22.2	22.5	22.9	23.5	24.1	24.6	25.1	25.6
65	151	19.0	19.9	20.5	21.1	21.6	22.0	22.4	22.8	23.2	23.5	24.1	24.7	25.3	25.8	26.3
70	157	19.6	20.5	21.2	21.7	22.2	22.7	23.1	23.5	23.8	24.2	24.8	25.4	25.9	26.4	26.9
75	164	20.2	21.1	21.8	22.3	22.8	23.3	23.7	24.1	24.4	24.8	25.4	26.0	26.5	27.0	27.5
80	180	20.8	21.7	22.4	22.9	23.4	23.9	24.3	24.7	25.0	25.4	26.0	26.6	27.1	27.6	28.1
85	197	21.4	22.3	22.9	23.5	24.0	24.4	24.9	25.2	25.6	25.9	26.6	27.2	27.7	28.2	28.7
90	213	22.0	22.8	23.5	24.1	24.6	25.0	25.4	25.8	26.2	26.5	27.1	27.7	28.3	28.8	29.2
95	230	22.5	23.4	24.0	24.6	25.1	25.6	26.0	26.3	26.7	27.0	27.7	28.3	28.8	29.3	29.8
100	246	23.0	23.9	24.6	25.1	25.6	26.1	26.5	26.9	27.2	27.6	28.2	28.8	29.3	29.8	30.3
110	262	24.1	24.9	25.6	26.2	26.7	27.1	27.5	27.9	28.3	28.6	29.2	29.8	30.4	30.9	31.3
120	279	25.0	25.9	26.6	27.1	27.6	28.1	28.5	28.9	29.2	29.6	30.2	30.8	31.3	31.8	32.3
130	295	26.0	26.8	27.5	28.1	28.6	29.0	29.4	29.8	30.2	30.5	31.1	31.7	32.3	32.8	33.3
140	312	26.9	27.8	28.4	29.0	29.5	29.9	30.3	30.7	31.1	31.4	32.0	32.6	33.2	33.7	34.2
150	328	27.8	28.6	29.3	29.8	30.3	30.8	31.2	31.6	31.9	32.3	32.9	33.5	34.0	34.5	35.0
160	361	28.6	29.5	30.1	30.7	31.2	31.6	32.0	32.4	32.8	33.1	33.8	34.3	34.9	35.4	35.9
170	394	29.4	30.3	30.9	31.5	32.0	32.4	32.9	33.2	33.6	33.9	34.6	35.2	35.7	36.2	36.7
180	427	30.2	31.1	31.7	32.3	32.8	33.2	33.7	34.0	34.4	34.7	35.4	35.9	36.5	37.0	37.5
190	459	31.0	31.8	32.5	33.1	33.6	34.0	34.4	34.8	35.2	35.5	36.1	36.7	37.3	37.8	38.2
200	492	31.7	32.6	33.3	33.8	34.3	34.8	35.2	35.6	35.9	36.3	36.9	37.5	38.0	38.5	39.0
210	525	32.5	33.3	34.0	34.5	35.0	35.5	35.9	36.3	36.6	37.0	37.6	38.2	38.7	39.2	39.7
220	558	33.2	34.0	34.7	35.3	35.8	36.2	36.6	37.0	37.4	37.7	38.3	38.9	39.5	40.0	40.4
230	591	33.9	34.7	35.4	36.0	36.5	36.9	37.3	37.7	38.1	38.4	39.0	39.6	40.2	40.7	41.1
240	623	34.6	35.4	36.1	36.6	37.1	37.6	38.0	38.4	38.7	39.1	39.7	40.3	40.8	41.3	41.8
250	656	35.2	36.1	36.8	37.3	37.8	38.3	38.7	39.1	39.4	39.7	40.4	41.0	41.5	42.0	42.5
260	689	35.9	36.7	37.4	38.0	38.5	38.9	39.3	39.7	40.1	40.4	41.0	41.6	42.2	42.7	43.1
270	722	36.5	37.4	38.1	38.6	39.1	39.6	40.0	40.3	40.7	41.0	41.7	42.3	42.8	43.3	43.8
280	755	37.2	38.0	38.7	39.2	39.7	40.2	40.6	41.0	41.3	41.7	42.3	42.9	43.4	43.9	44.4
290	787	37.8	38.6	39.3	39.9	40.4	40.8	41.2	41.6	42.0	42.3	42.9	43.5	44.1	44.6	45.0
300	984	38.4	39.2	39.9	40.5	41.0	41.4	41.8	42.2	42.6	42.9	43.5	44.1	44.7	45.2	45.7

Distance Off by Vertical Sextant Angle

Distance Off, Nautical Miles

Height of Object (f)	(m)	0.1	0.2	0.3	0.4	0.5	0.6	0.7	0.8	0.9	1.0	1.1	1.2	1.3	1.4	Height of Object (m)	(f)
16	5	1 33	0 46	0 31	0 23	0 19	0 15	0 13	0 12	0 10						5	16
20	6	1 51	0 56	0 37	0 28	0 22	0 19	0 16	0 14	0 12	0 11	0 10				6	20
23	7	2 10	1 05	0 43	0 32	0 26	0 22	0 19	0 16	0 14	0 13	0 12	0 11	0 10		7	23
26	8	2 28	1 14	0 49	0 37	0 30	0 25	0 21	0 19	0 16	0 15	0 13	0 12	0 11	0 11	8	26
30	9	2 47	1 24	0 56	0 42	0 33	0 28	0 24	0 21	0 19	0 17	0 15	0 14	0 13	0 12	9	30
33	10	3 05	1 33	1 02	0 46	0 37	0 31	0 27	0 23	0 21	0 19	0 17	0 15	0 14	0 13	10	33
36	11	3 24	1 42	1 08	0 51	0 41	0 34	0 29	0 26	0 23	0 20	0 19	0 17	0 16	0 15	11	36
39	12	3 42	1 51	1 14	0 56	0 45	0 37	0 32	0 28	0 25	0 22	0 20	0 19	0 17	0 16	12	39
43	13	4 01	2 01	1 20	1 00	0 48	0 40	0 34	0 30	0 27	0 24	0 22	0 20	0 19	0 17	13	43
46	14	4 19	2 10	1 27	1 05	0 52	0 43	0 37	0 32	0 29	0 26	0 24	0 22	0 20	0 19	14	46
49	15	4 38	2 19	1 33	1 10	0 56	0 46	0 40	0 35	0 31	0 28	0 25	0 23	0 21	0 20	15	49
54	16.5	5 05	2 33	1 42	1 17	1 01	0 51	0 44	0 38	0 34	0 31	0 28	0 26	0 24	0 22	16.5	54
59	18	5 33	2 47	1 51	1 24	1 07	0 56	0 48	0 42	0 37	0 33	0 30	0 28	0 26	0 24	18	59
64	19.5	6 01	3 01	2 01	1 30	1 12	1 00	0 52	0 45	0 40	0 36	0 33	0 30	0 28	0 26	19.5	64
69	21	6 28	3 15	2 10	1 37	1 18	1 05	0 56	0 49	0 43	0 39	0 35	0 32	0 30	0 28	21	69
74	22.5	6 56	3 29	2 19	1 44	1 24	1 10	0 60	0 52	0 46	0 42	0 38	0 35	0 32	0 30	22.5	74
79	24	7 23	3 42	2 28	1 51	1 29	1 14	1 04	0 56	0 49	0 45	0 40	0 37	0 34	0 32	24	79
84	25.5	7 50	3 56	2 38	1 58	1 35	1 19	1 08	0 59	0 53	0 47	0 43	0 39	0 36	0 34	25.5	84
89	27	8 18	4 10	2 47	2 05	1 40	1 24	1 12	1 03	0 56	0 50	0 46	0 42	0 39	0 36	27	89
94	28.5	8 45	4 24	2 56	2 12	1 46	1 28	1 16	1 06	0 59	0 53	0 48	0 44	0 41	0 38	28.5	94
98	30	9 12	4 38	3 05	2 19	1 51	1 33	1 20	1 10	1 02	0 56	0 51	0 46	0 43	0 40	30	98
105	32	9 48	4 56	3 18	2 28	1 59	1 39	1 25	1 14	1 06	0 59	0 54	0 49	0 46	0 42	32	105
112	34	10 24	5 15	3 30	2 38	2 06	1 45	1 30	1 19	1 10	1 03	0 57	0 53	0 49	0 45	34	112
118	36	11 00	5 33	3 42	2 47	2 14	1 51	1 35	1 24	1 14	1 07	1 01	0 56	0 51	0 48	36	118
125	38	11 36	5 51	3 55	2 56	2 21	1 58	1 41	1 28	1 18	1 11	1 04	0 59	0 54	0 50	38	125
131	40	12 11	6 10	4 07	3 05	2 28	2 04	1 46	1 33	1 22	1 14	1 07	1 02	0 57	0 53	40	131
138	42	12 47	6 28	4 19	3 15	2 36	2 10	1 51	1 37	1 27	1 18	1 11	1 05	0 60	0 56	42	138
144	44	13 22	6 46	4 32	3 24	2 43	2 16	1 57	1 42	1 31	1 22	1 14	1 08	1 03	0 58	44	144
151	46	13 57	7 05	4 44	3 33	2 51	2 22	2 02	1 47	1 35	1 25	1 18	1 11	1 06	1 01	46	151
157	48	14 32	7 23	4 56	3 42	2 58	2 28	2 07	1 51	1 39	1 29	1 21	1 14	1 09	1 04	48	157
164	50	15 07	7 41	5 09	3 52	3 05	2 35	2 13	1 56	1 43	1 33	1 24	1 17	1 11	1 06	50	164
171	52	15 41	7 59	5 21	4 01	3 13	2 41	2 18	2 01	1 47	1 36	1 28	1 20	1 14	1 09	52	171
177	54	16 15	8 18	5 33	4 10	3 20	2 47	2 23	2 05	1 51	1 40	1 31	1 24	1 17	1 12	54	177
184	56	16 49	8 36	5 45	4 19	3 28	2 53	2 28	2 10	1 55	1 44	1 34	1 27	1 20	1 14	56	184
190	58	17 23	8 54	5 58	4 29	3 35	2 59	2 34	2 15	1 60	1 48	1 38	1 30	1 23	1 17	58	190
197	60	17 57	9 12	6 10	4 38	3 42	3 05	2 39	2 19	2 04	1 51	1 41	1 33	1 26	1 20	60	197
213	65	19 20	9 57	6 40	5 01	4 01	3 21	2 52	2 31	2 14	2 01	1 50	1 41	1 33	1 26	65	213
230	70	20 42	10 42	7 11	5 24	4 19	3 36	3 05	2 42	2 24	2 10	1 58	1 48	1 40	1 33	70	230
246	75		11 27	7 41	5 47	4 38	3 52	3 19	2 54	2 35	2 19	2 07	1 56	1 47	1 39	75	246
262	80		12 11	8 12	6 10	4 56	4 07	3 32	3 05	2 45	2 28	2 15	2 04	1 54	1 46	80	262
295	90		13 39	9 12	6 56	5 33	4 38	3 58	3 29	3 05	2 47	2 32	2 19	2 08	1 59	90	295
328	100		15 07	10 12	7 41	6 10	5 09	4 25	3 52	3 26	3 05	2 49	2 35	2 23	2 13	100	328
361	110		16 32	11 12	8 27	6 46	5 39	4 51	4 15	3 47	3 24	3 05	2 50	2 37	2 26	110	361
394	120		17 57	12 11	9 12	7 23	6 10	5 17	4 38	4 07	3 42	3 22	3 05	2 51	2 39	120	394
427	130		19 20	13 10	9 57	7 59	6 40	5 44	5 01	4 28	4 01	3 39	3 21	3 05	2 52	130	427
459	140		20 42	14 09	10 42	8 36	7 11	6 10	5 24	4 48	4 19	3 56	3 36	3 20	3 05	140	459
492	150			15 07	11 27	9 12	7 41	6 36	5 47	5 09	4 38	4 13	3 52	3 34	3 19	150	492
525	160			16 04	12 11	9 48	8 12	7 02	6 10	5 29	4 56	4 29	4 07	3 48	3 32	160	525
558	170			17 01	12 55	10 24	8 42	7 28	6 33	5 49	5 15	4 46	4 22	4 02	3 45	170	558
591	180			17 57	13 39	11 00	9 12	7 54	6 56	6 10	5 33	5 03	4 38	4 17	3 58	180	591
656	200			19 48	15 07	12 11	10 12	8 46	7 41	6 51	6 10	5 36	5 09	4 45	4 25	200	656
722	220			21 36	16 32	13 22	11 12	9 38	8 27	7 31	6 46	6 10	5 39	5 13	4 51	220	722
787	240				17 57	14 32	12 11	10 29	9 12	8 12	7 23	6 43	6 10	5 42	5 17	240	787
853	260				19 20	15 41	13 10	11 20	9 57	8 52	7 59	7 16	6 40	6 10	5 44	260	853
919	280					16 49	14 09	12 11	10 42	9 32	8 36	7 50	7 11	6 38	6 10	280	919
984	300					17 57	15 07	13 02	11 27	10 12	9 12	8 23	7 41	7 06	6 36	300	984
1148	350					20 42	17 29	15 07	13 17	11 52	10 42	9 45	8 57	8 16	7 41	350	1148
1312	400						19 48	17 09	15 07	13 30	12 11	11 07	10 12	9 26	8 46	400	1312
1476	450						22 03	19 09	16 54	15 07	13 39	12 27	11 27	10 35	9 51	450	1476
1640	500							21 05	18 39	16 42	15 07	13 47	12 41	11 44	10 55	500	1640

Distance Off by Vertical Sextant Angle

Height of Object f	m	1.5	1.6	1.7	1.8	1.9	2.0	2.1	2.2	2.3	2.4	2.5	2.6	2.7	2.8	m	Height of Object f
		° '	° '	° '	° '	° '	° '	° '	° '	° '	° '	° '	° '	° '	° '		
16	5															5	16
20	6															6	20
23	7															7	23
26	8	0 10														8	26
30	9	0 11	0 10	0 10												9	30
33	10	0 12	0 12	0 11	0 10	0 10										10	33
36	11	0 14	0 13	0 12	0 11	0 11	0 10	0 10								11	36
39	12	0 15	0 14	0 13	0 12	0 12	0 11	0 11	0 10	0 10						12	39
43	13	0 16	0 15	0 14	0 13	0 13	0 12	0 11	0 11	0 10	0 10	0 10				13	43
46	14	0 17	0 16	0 15	0 14	0 14	0 13	0 12	0 12	0 11	0 11	0 10	0 10	0 10		14	46
49	15	0 19	0 17	0 16	0 15	0 15	0 14	0 13	0 13	0 12	0 12	0 11	0 11	0 10	0 10	15	49
54	16.5	0 20	0 19	0 18	0 17	0 16	0 15	0 15	0 14	0 13	0 13	0 12	0 12	0 11	0 11	16.5	54
59	18	0 22	0 21	0 20	0 19	0 18	0 17	0 16	0 15	0 15	0 14	0 13	0 13	0 12	0 12	18	59
64	19.5	0 24	0 23	0 21	0 20	0 19	0 18	0 17	0 16	0 16	0 15	0 14	0 14	0 13	0 13	19.5	64
69	21	0 26	0 24	0 23	0 22	0 21	0 19	0 19	0 18	0 17	0 16	0 16	0 15	0 14	0 14	21	69
74	22.5	0 28	0 26	0 25	0 23	0 22	0 21	0 20	0 19	0 18	0 17	0 17	0 16	0 15	0 15	22.5	74
79	24	0 30	0 28	0 26	0 25	0 23	0 22	0 21	0 20	0 19	0 19	0 18	0 17	0 16	0 16	24	79
84	25.5	0 32	0 30	0 28	0 26	0 25	0 24	0 23	0 22	0 21	0 20	0 19	0 18	0 18	0 17	25.5	84
89	27	0 33	0 31	0 29	0 28	0 26	0 25	0 24	0 23	0 22	0 21	0 20	0 19	0 19	0 18	27	89
94	28.5	0 35	0 33	0 31	0 29	0 28	0 26	0 25	0 24	0 23	0 22	0 21	0 20	0 20	0 19	28.5	94
98	30	0 37	0 35	0 33	0 31	0 29	0 28	0 27	0 25	0 24	0 23	0 22	0 21	0 21	0 20	30	98
105	32	0 40	0 37	0 35	0 33	0 31	0 30	0 28	0 27	0 26	0 25	0 24	0 23	0 22	0 21	32	105
112	34	0 42	0 39	0 37	0 35	0 33	0 32	0 30	0 29	0 27	0 26	0 25	0 24	0 23	0 23	34	112
118	36	0 45	0 42	0 39	0 37	0 35	0 33	0 32	0 30	0 29	0 28	0 27	0 26	0 25	0 24	36	118
125	38	0 47	0 44	0 41	0 39	0 37	0 35	0 34	0 32	0 31	0 29	0 28	0 27	0 26	0 25	38	125
131	40	0 49	0 46	0 44	0 41	0 39	0 37	0 35	0 34	0 32	0 31	0 30	0 29	0 27	0 27	40	131
138	42	0 52	0 49	0 46	0 43	0 41	0 39	0 37	0 35	0 34	0 32	0 31	0 30	0 29	0 28	42	138
144	44	0 54	0 51	0 48	0 45	0 43	0 41	0 39	0 37	0 36	0 34	0 33	0 31	0 30	0 29	44	144
151	46	0 57	0 53	0 50	0 47	0 45	0 43	0 41	0 39	0 37	0 36	0 34	0 33	0 32	0 30	46	151
157	48	0 59	0 56	0 52	0 49	0 47	0 45	0 42	0 40	0 39	0 37	0 36	0 34	0 33	0 32	48	157
164	50	1 02	0 58	0 55	0 52	0 49	0 46	0 44	0 42	0 40	0 39	0 37	0 36	0 34	0 33	50	164
171	52	1 04	1 00	0 57	0 54	0 51	0 48	0 46	0 44	0 42	0 40	0 39	0 37	0 36	0 34	52	171
177	54	1 07	1 03	0 59	0 56	0 53	0 50	0 48	0 46	0 44	0 42	0 40	0 39	0 37	0 36	54	177
184	56	1 09	1 05	1 01	0 58	0 55	0 52	0 49	0 47	0 45	0 43	0 42	0 40	0 38	0 37	56	184
190	58	1 12	1 07	1 03	0 60	0 57	0 54	0 51	0 49	0 47	0 45	0 43	0 41	0 40	0 38	58	190
197	60	1 14	1 10	1 06	1 02	0 59	0 56	0 53	0 51	0 48	0 46	0 45	0 43	0 41	0 40	60	197
213	65	1 20	1 15	1 11	1 07	1 03	1 0	0 57	0 55	0 52	0 50	0 48	0 46	0 45	0 43	65	213
230	70	1 27	1 21	1 16	1 12	1 08	1 5	1 02	0 59	0 56	0 54	0 52	0 50	0 48	0 46	70	230
246	75	1 33	1 27	1 22	1 17	1 13	1 10	1 06	1 03	1 01	0 58	0 56	0 54	0 52	0 50	75	246
262	80	1 39	1 33	1 27	1 22	1 18	1 14	1 11	1 07	1 05	1 02	0 59	0 57	0 55	0 53	80	262
295	90	1 51	1 44	1 38	1 33	1 28	1 24	1 20	1 16	1 13	1 10	1 07	1 04	1 02	0 60	90	295
328	100	2 04	1 56	1 49	1 43	1 38	1 33	1 28	1 24	1 21	1 17	1 14	1 11	1 09	1 06	100	328
361	110	2 16	2 08	2 00	1 53	1 47	1 42	1 37	1 33	1 29	1 25	1 22	1 19	1 16	1 13	110	361
394	120	2 28	2 19	2 11	2 04	1 57	1 51	1 46	1 41	1 37	1 33	1 29	1 26	1 22	1 20	120	394
427	130	2 41	2 31	2 22	2 14	2 07	2 01	1 55	1 50	1 45	1 41	1 36	1 33	1 29	1 26	130	427
459	140	2 53	2 42	2 33	2 24	2 17	2 10	2 04	1 58	1 53	1 48	1 44	1 40	1 36	1 33	140	459
492	150	3 05	2 54	2 44	2 35	2 26	2 19	2 13	2 07	2 01	1 56	1 51	1 47	1 43	1 39	150	492
525	160	3 18	3 05	2 55	2 45	2 36	2 28	2 21	2 15	2 09	2 04	1 59	1 54	1 50	1 46	160	525
558	170	3 30	3 17	3 05	2 55	2 46	2 38	2 30	2 23	2 17	2 11	2 06	2 01	1 57	1 53	170	558
591	180	3 42	3 29	3 16	3 05	2 56	2 47	2 39	2 32	2 25	2 19	2 14	2 08	2 04	1 59	180	591
656	200	4 07	3 52	3 38	3 26	3 15	3 05	2 57	2 49	2 41	2 35	2 28	2 23	2 17	2 13	200	656
722	220	4 32	4 15	3 60	3 47	3 35	3 24	3 14	3 05	2 57	2 50	2 43	2 37	2 31	2 26	220	722
787	240	4 56	4 38	4 22	4 07	3 54	3 42	3 32	3 22	3 13	3 05	2 58	2 51	2 45	2 39	240	787
853	260	5 21	5 01	4 43	4 28	4 14	4 01	3 49	3 39	3 30	3 21	3 13	3 05	2 59	2 52	260	853
919	280	5 45	5 24	5 05	4 48	4 33	4 19	4 07	3 56	3 46	3 36	3 28	3 20	3 12	3 05	280	919
984	300	6 10	5 47	5 27	5 09	4 52	4 38	4 25	4 13	4 02	3 52	3 42	3 34	3 26	3 19	300	984
1148	350	7 11	6 44	6 21	5 60	5 41	5 24	5 09	4 55	4 42	4 30	4 19	4 9	4 0	3 52	350	1148
1312	400	8 12	7 41	7 14	6 51	6 29	6 10	5 52	5 36	5 22	5 09	4 56	4 45	4 34	4 25	400	1312
1476	450	9 12	8 38	8 08	7 41	7 17	6 56	6 36	6 18	6 02	5 47	5 33	5 20	5 9	4 58	450	1476
1640	500	10 12	9 35	9 01	8 32	8 05	7 41	7 20	6 60	6 42	6 25	6 10	5 56	5 43	5 30	500	1640

Distance Off by Vertical Sextant Angle

Distance Off, Nautical Miles

Height of Object f	m	2.9	3.0	3.2	3.4	3.6	3.8	4.0	4.2	4.4	4.6	4.8	5.0	5.2	5.4	m	f
16	5															5	16
20	6															6	20
23	7															7	23
26	8															8	26
30	9															9	30
33	10															10	33
36	11															11	36
39	12															12	39
43	13															13	43
46	14															14	46
49	15	0 10														15	49
54	16.5	0 11	0 10													16.5	54
59	18	0 12	0 11	0 10	0 10											18	59
64	19.5	0 12	0 12	0 11	0 11	0 10	0 10									19.5	64
69	21	0 13	0 13	0 12	0 11	0 11	0 10	0 10								21	69
74	22.5	0 14	0 14	0 13	0 12	0 12	0 11	0 10	0 10							22.5	74
79	24	0 15	0 15	0 14	0 13	0 12	0 12	0 11	0 11							24	79
84	25.5	0 16	0 16	0 15	0 14	0 13	0 12	0 12	0 11	0 10	0 10					25.5	84
89	27	0 17	0 17	0 16	0 15	0 14	0 13	0 13	0 12	0 11	0 11	0 10				27	89
94	28.5	0 18	0 18	0 17	0 16	0 15	0 14	0 13	0 13	0 12	0 12	0 11	0 11	0 10	0 10	28.5	94
98	30	0 19	0 19	0 17	0 16	0 15	0 15	0 14	0 13	0 13	0 12	0 12	0 11	0 11	0 10	30	98
105	32	0 20	0 20	0 19	0 17	0 16	0 16	0 15	0 14	0 13	0 13	0 12	0 12	0 11	0 11	32	105
112	34	0 22	0 21	0 20	0 19	0 18	0 17	0 16	0 15	0 14	0 14	0 13	0 13	0 12	0 12	34	112
118	36	0 23	0 22	0 21	0 20	0 19	0 18	0 17	0 16	0 15	0 15	0 14	0 13	0 13	0 12	36	118
125	38	0 24	0 24	0 22	0 21	0 20	0 19	0 18	0 17	0 16	0 15	0 15	0 14	0 14	0 13	38	125
131	40	0 26	0 25	0 23	0 22	0 21	0 20	0 19	0 18	0 17	0 16	0 15	0 15	0 14	0 14	40	131
138	42	0 27	0 26	0 24	0 23	0 22	0 21	0 19	0 19	0 18	0 17	0 16	0 16	0 15	0 14	42	138
144	44	0 28	0 27	0 26	0 24	0 23	0 21	0 20	0 19	0 19	0 18	0 17	0 16	0 16	0 15	44	144
151	46	0 29	0 28	0 27	0 25	0 24	0 22	0 21	0 20	0 19	0 19	0 18	0 17	0 16	0 16	46	151
157	48	0 31	0 30	0 28	0 26	0 25	0 23	0 22	0 21	0 20	0 19	0 19	0 18	0 17	0 16	48	157
164	50	0 32	0 31	0 29	0 27	0 26	0 24	0 23	0 22	0 21	0 20	0 19	0 19	0 18	0 17	50	164
171	52	0 33	0 32	0 30	0 28	0 27	0 25	0 24	0 23	0 22	0 21	0 20	0 19	0 19	0 18	52	171
177	54	0 35	0 33	0 31	0 29	0 28	0 26	0 25	0 24	0 23	0 22	0 21	0 20	0 19	0 19	54	177
184	56	0 36	0 35	0 32	0 31	0 29	0 27	0 26	0 25	0 24	0 23	0 22	0 21	0 20	0 19	56	184
190	58	0 37	0 36	0 34	0 32	0 30	0 28	0 27	0 26	0 24	0 23	0 22	0 22	0 21	0 20	58	190
197	60	0 38	0 37	0 35	0 33	0 31	0 29	0 28	0 27	0 25	0 24	0 23	0 22	0 21	0 21	60	197
213	65	0 42	0 40	0 38	0 35	0 34	0 32	0 30	0 29	0 27	0 26	0 25	0 24	0 23	0 22	65	213
230	70	0 45	0 43	0 41	0 38	0 36	0 34	0 32	0 31	0 30	0 28	0 27	0 26	0 25	0 24	70	230
246	75	0 48	0 46	0 44	0 41	0 39	0 37	0 35	0 33	0 32	0 30	0 29	0 28	0 27	0 26	75	246
262	80	0 51	0 49	0 46	0 44	0 41	0 39	0 37	0 35	0 34	0 32	0 31	0 30	0 29	0 27	80	262
295	90	0 58	0 56	0 52	0 49	0 46	0 44	0 42	0 40	0 38	0 36	0 35	0 33	0 32	0 31	90	295
328	100	1 04	1 02	0 58	0 55	0 52	0 49	0 46	0 44	0 42	0 40	0 39	0 37	0 36	0 34	100	328
361	110	1 10	1 08	1 04	1 00	0 57	0 54	0 51	0 49	0 46	0 44	0 43	0 41	0 39	0 38	110	361
394	120	1 17	1 14	1 10	1 06	1 02	0 59	0 56	0 53	0 51	0 48	0 46	0 45	0 43	0 41	120	394
427	130	1 23	1 20	1 15	1 11	1 07	1 03	1 00	0 57	0 55	0 52	0 50	0 48	0 46	0 45	130	427
459	140	1 30	1 27	1 21	1 16	1 12	1 08	1 05	1 02	0 59	0 56	0 54	0 52	0 50	0 48	140	459
492	150	1 36	1 33	1 27	1 22	1 17	1 13	1 10	1 06	1 03	1 01	0 58	0 56	0 54	0 52	150	492
525	160	1 42	1 39	1 33	1 27	1 22	1 18	1 14	1 11	1 07	1 05	1 02	0 59	0 57	0 55	160	525
558	170	1 49	1 45	1 39	1 33	1 28	1 23	1 19	1 15	1 12	1 09	1 06	1 03	1 01	0 58	170	558
591	180	1 55	1 51	1 44	1 38	1 33	1 28	1 24	1 20	1 16	1 13	1 10	1 07	1 04	1 02	180	591
656	200	2 08	2 04	1 56	1 49	1 43	1 38	1 33	1 28	1 24	1 21	1 17	1 14	1 11	1 09	200	656
722	220	2 21	2 16	2 08	2 00	1 53	1 47	1 42	1 37	1 33	1 29	1 25	1 22	1 19	1 16	220	722
787	240	2 34	2 28	2 19	2 11	2 04	1 57	1 51	1 46	1 41	1 37	1 33	1 29	1 26	1 22	240	787
853	260	2 46	2 41	2 31	2 22	2 14	2 07	2 01	1 55	1 50	1 45	1 41	1 36	1 33	1 29	260	853
919	280	2 59	2 53	2 42	2 33	2 24	2 17	2 10	2 04	1 58	1 53	1 48	1 44	1 40	1 36	280	919
984	300	3 12	3 05	2 54	2 44	2 35	2 26	2 19	2 13	2 07	2 01	1 56	1 51	1 47	1 43	300	984
1148	350	3 44	3 36	3 23	3 11	3 00	2 51	2 42	2 35	2 28	2 21	2 15	2 10	2 05	2 00	350	1148
1312	400	4 16	4 07	3 52	3 38	3 26	3 15	3 05	2 57	2 49	2 41	2 35	2 28	2 23	2 17	400	1312
1476	450	4 47	4 38	4 21	4 05	3 52	3 40	3 29	3 19	3 10	3 01	2 54	2 47	2 41	2 35	450	1476
1640	500	5 19	5 09	4 49	4 32	4 17	4 04	3 52	3 41	3 31	3 22	3 13	3 05	2 58	2 52	500	1640

Electronic navigation systems

9.9 Hyperbolic position-fixing systems

Theory of hyperbolae

A hyperbola is a line joining all places with the same distance difference. For example the perpendicular bisector of a line is the hyperbola whose distance difference is zero. Every point of the bisector is the same distance from the ends.

With distance from the base line, hyperbola separation increases, resulting in reduced positional accuracy. The effect of hyperbola separation is greatest in the base line extension area, resulting in poor accuracy, accentuated by position line ambiguity.

Errors in hyperbolic systems With all hyperbolic systems, the accuracy depends on knowing the exact velocity of radio signals and the path followed by them.

Fixed errors The lattice drawn on charts is based on the theoretical velocity of radio signals of 299792·5 km/sec, but the velocity of the transmitted signal varies with the conductivity of the ground and sea over which it passes. At any place, the position obtained from the received radio signals will be in error by a constant amount which is determined during the initial commissioning period of the chain.

Variable errors Radio signals arrive at the receiver by two separate paths; the ground wave which follows the curvature of the earth and the sky wave which is reflected by the ionosphere. Simultaneous reception of ground and sky wave signals results in signal fading and variable errors in position. The size of the variable error depends on the time of day, season of the year, the meteorological conditions and position within the chain. For about an hour either side of sunrise/set the large variable errors and fading may make the system unusable.

Transmission synchronisation If a pair of transmitters are not synchronised, errors in position will result. Users are advised of these failures; for Decca by a Decca warning transmitted by coast radio stations; for Loran C by switching on and off the first two pulses of the secondary transmitter.

Chart accuracy See *9.2 Charts and plans.*

Weather effects Anti-cyclonic conditions, thunderstorms and static electricity charges due to rain, snow or hail can affect the accuracy of all radio navigation systems.

9.10 Omega

An ocean navigation aid which gives position lines by phase comparison of very low frequency phase locked transmissions from 8 stations around the world. Expensive equipment together with lattice charts of the area are needed. The accuracy is about ±2 miles by day and ±4 miles at night.

9.11 Loran C

A master and slave pair of transmitters send time locked, pulsed signals on a frequency of 100kHz. The interval between the arrival of the 2 pulsed signals is measured to give a coarse time difference then phase matching of the pulses 100kHz carrier wave gives a fine time difference. These are combined to give the time difference used for position fixing.

The accuracy of Loran C is affected by the terrain over which it passes, poor chain geometry and by the gradual decline in transmitter maintenance in part due to the prevalence of GPS.

9.12 Global Positioning System (GPS)

The first GPS satellites were launched over 25 years ago. Since then GPS has become the cheapest form of position-finding around, with a handheld set now costing less than a decent hand-bearing compass.

There are 24 satellites (21 in use and 3 in reserve) in six orbits, 4 satellites per orbit, at altitudes of 20,000 km. The planes of the orbits are inclined to the equator at 55° with approximately 60° of longitude between each plane. Normally, a minimum of four satellites at suitable elevations are available for position fixing. Transmissions to civilian receivers are on 1575MHz. In the past this contained the coarse and acquisition code (CA) which gives the standard positioning service (SPS).

Until 2000 the signal was degraded by the US military by selective availability (SA) to give an accuracy of around ±100 metres. Selective availability for GPS has been turned off for several years now and a consistent accuracy of ±20 metres is achieved for 95% of the time. This is all dependent on good satellite coverage, an assumption that there are no clock errors for the satellites received and that reception through the ionosphere is within given limits (i.e. the signal is not too degraded by the time it gets to a GPS receiver). In practice errors of up to ±200m still occur.

Modern GPS receivers are all multi-channel and can receive from three to twelve signals at any one time and decode them to determine a position. The speed at which a GPS receiver can do a cold start and produce a position is now around 30 seconds. The ease with which we retrieve data has been simplified by software that enables us to scroll through pages and pick out how we want to view the data. From the stream of position data we get speed over the ground, course heading in true and magnetic, distance off course from a waypoint, and a graphic display of our course.

Positions obtained by GPS are based on the WGS84 Datum and corrections must be applied before plotting on a chart based on a different reference datum (given under the chart title). If the chart's reference datum is selected from those stored in the receiver, the positions displayed will be based on that datum and can be plotted directly on the chart. (See *9.5 Waypoints* for more information on chart reference data).

Dilution of precision (DOP) The numerical indication (on the scale 0 to 10) of the probability of an inaccurate position because of poor satellite geometry

9. NAVIGATION

at that time. 'Satellite geometry' means the altitude of the satellites above the horizon and their positions relative to each other and the receiver. The lower the DOP value, the better the satellite geometry, i.e. the greater the angular separation and altitude. Low altitudes result in unpredictable refraction of the transmitted signal by the earth's atmosphere and a small angular separation gives a small angle of cut between the ranges.

Receivers are programmed to use the satellite group with the smallest DOP value and to warn the user when the DOP value indicates poor geometry. Computing stops if a high DOP value indicates the position would be completely unreliable. Because the satellites are moving rapidly in their orbits, the duration of high DOP value interruptions will only be a few minutes.

Horizontal Dilution of Precision (HDOP), Geometric Dilution of Precision (GDOP), Position Dilution of Precision (PDOP) are similar concepts.

Satellite acquisition Only 3 satellites are needed for position fixing at sea. As the satellites are not stationary the receiver must be able to acquire satellites as they rise above the horizon, discard those which are setting and switch between them to use the group with the lowest DOP value.

Differential GPS A method of improving GPS accuracy which was developed to counter the effects of SA on the accuracy of positions, by the comparison of a shore-side monitoring reference station position with that obtained by a GPS receiver.

The difference can be computed:

i. as a position differential with the corrections fed into a marine GPS receiver which must be using the same satellites as those at the reference position.

ii. as satellite range differentials in the form of range corrections for all the satellites observable at the reference station. The marine station only applies the corrections for the satellites in use.

An additional special receiver is required to receive and decode the DGPS data which will be transmitted in the 285–325kHz marine radio beacon band.

The ranges of the DGPS stations vary between 40 miles and 300 miles depending on transmission power and the range over which the corrections are valid.

Another DGPS system using geo-stationary satellites which transmit range corrections from several reference stations is also available. The range is only limited by the validity of the corrections.

Accuracy close to the monitoring station is now around ±5m, but accuracy decreases with distance from the monitoring station.

SDGPS SDGPS (satellite differential GPS) works by a network of ground reference stations receiving GPS signals and then correcting them for known errors: GPS satellite orbit, clock errors, and transmission errors caused by the atmosphere and ionosphere. A GPS correction signal is then transmitted to geostationary satellites on the same frequency as GPS signals. An accuracy of 2-3 metres is claimed.

In the USA the WAAS (wide area augmentation system) has been approved for some uses. In Europe the EGNOS satellite system will be used in conjunction with ground stations in Europe.

Gallileo The EU alternative to GPS has been approved for start-up costs and operational uses. When the satellites necessary are launched and the system operational (around 2008) it is envisaged users will pay a licensing fee to some authority. Since GPS is free this is hardly likely to catch on too quickly.

GPS Accuracy

You can currently expect an accuracy of around ±20 metres with a standard receiver. Repeated accuracy testing tends to give a figure higher than this though, and in some tests over a 24-hour period errors have been greater than ±200 metres (with SA turned off). SDGPS gives errors of only ±2-3 metres but is presently only available in the US with WAAS equipped receivers. In 2004-2005 SDGPS will use EGNOS satellites in Europe to give a similar accuracy. When Galileo (see above and below) is up and running some time around 2008-2009 it will also give an accuracy of around 5 metres.

For more information on EGNOS and Galileo see the European Space Agency website at www.esa.int

The very accuracy of GPS can be misleading and seeing a position to two or three decimal points can induce a false sense of confidence in the user. The problem is simply that we do not have charts accurate enough to make full use of such precise positions. Read over the caution carefully at the end of this section.

Although satellites are turned off for maintenance every now and again and in places coverage by the satellites is not enough to give an accurate position, in my experience these gaps in coverage have never exceeded an hour. Nonetheless it is worthwhile thinking carefully before linking the GPS to the autopilot so that the autopilot is steering a true course relative to currents, tide, etc., or you may end up like the yacht in the Caribbean which hit a reef because the inattentive owner missed the error warning on his GPS. Without coverage the GPS kept a course using the last data that had arrived from the satellite and without any new data to correct for currents and other errors steered straight towards a reef.

Note Recent research in the US has revealed problems with corruption of GPS signals by some marine television antennas. A small number of marine TV aerials emit spurious radiation which interferes with the Ll GPS frequency at 1575·42MHz. It is only a problem with land-based broadcast TV - satellite TV antennas operate on different frequencies and are not a problem.

9.13 Electronic chart plotters

A number of yachts are fitting dedicated chart plotters which, when interfaced to an electronic position-finding system, show a yacht's position on a chart. Dedicated chart plotters are a useful adjunct to the navigation table or cockpit and I use one on *seven tenths*. Despite the usefulness of a plotter, it does not replace the usefulness of a chart in the cockpit for me. With that old-fashioned paper chart I can put it anywhere, hold it up while looking at a feature or danger to navigation and quickly pan one side of the chart to the other. You can get irritated with the 'please wait, chart loading' message on chart plotters as you either zoom in or out or pan from one part to another. If the chart plotter is located at the chart table then you must constantly run up and down to check the map against the view above and this can make it difficult to mentally fit the 3D real view to the 2D chart view. A chart in the cockpit lets you constantly scan from one to the other and fit the chart to the real world. In addition, the problems outlined below are exacerbated on electronic charts (where an electronically derived 'real' position is displayed on a cartographically inaccurate chart).

Dedicated chart plotters Most have a built-in scaleable world-wide chart which is only intended for use as a background chart or for deep-water navigation. Larger scale charts are available in the form of plug-in cartridges but memory capacity often limits the amount of detail shown when zooming in to a small area. However, both the quality of chart plug-ins and of the displays on modern chart plotters are improving. Some also offer a split screen shared with a radar scanner or depth/log readings, some of which are suitable for mounting in the cockpit.

PC-based chart plotters Many yachts now have laptop computers on board. There are a number of software packages that reproduce charts with detailed route-planning tools, and if GPS, radar and the boat instruments are interfaced this can be a useful navigation tool. Most software now comes on CD-ROM and additional charts or updates can be downloaded from the internet. The latest software also allows weather information (see *10.12 Grib weather files*) to be downloaded and 'layered' over the charts. The following points should be kept in mind when looking at plotting software.

1. Don't go for a chart plotter that has all the bells and whistles. Even a basic plotter has more than enough for practical navigation and the more you squeeze onto a toolbar the more confusing it gets when conditions are a bit bumpy at sea. Even a basic plotter will insert waypoints, construct routes, let you keep an automatic log off the GPS input and an annotated log as well. Just as most of us never use half of the functions on a word processor, so you will never need to use a lot of the functions on some chart plotters.

2. Ease of use and large icons are important when it's blowing half a gale and the boat is bucketing to windward. You don't want to have to work out how to construct a route when the rest of the crew is sick and you are not feeling too bright yourself. And get a mouse for your laptop instead of using the touchpad or that little joystick stuck in the middle of the keys, or every time the boat hits a wave the mouse pointer will shoot across the screen as you twiddle with the touchpad or the miniature joystick.

Electronic Charts You will need to choose between raster and vector charts. Basically, raster charts are scanned originals; vector charts are redrawn digitally from the original. In practice, the best choice is to go for vector charts. They occupy less space on the hard disk, load more quickly and, importantly, can be read when you zoom in or out. Raster charts are scanned at one resolution so when you zoom in or out you lose definition and get a fuzzy pixellated image. That is intensely irritating and the only answer is to buy a large folio of charts, although that means the laptop grinding away to load a chart on a smaller or larger scale. Raster charts also take longer to reload, which is annoying when you are trying to get from one side of the chart to the other on a 15-inch laptop screen.

Both types are based on Hydrographic Department charts, so they have retained errors shown on them which may be large and navigationally important. Information on digitally layered vector charts may also have details omitted in the layering process. Plotted GPS positions may not agree with the position of the land as shown on the chart. You may well appear to be navigating over land.

When planning a passage, and during its execution, it is still necessary to consult an appropriately scaled paper chart. Electronic chart-plotting software carries the disclaimer 'Not to be used for navigation', so if you run aground the manufactures are likely to deny responsibility.

A caution

Most of the charts for the Mediterranean were surveyed in the 19th century using celestial fixes and basic triangulation techniques. Subsequent observations have shown considerable errors, in some cases up to 1 minute of longitude. While you may know your latitude and longitude to within 20 metres, the chart you are plotting it on may contain errors of up to 1 mile, though normally less. The practice of including the datum point for a chart and an offset to be used with electronic position-finding equipment only confuses a very complicated picture because the old charts have varying inaccuracies over the area they cover. For instance, one cape may be in position and another half a mile out of position. For the most part errors have been corrected, but there are still discrepancies and you should not be lulled into a false confidence because everything appears to be turning up in the right place. The next time it may not happen and the situation may be more critical.

The solution to the problem lies in the hands of the relevant hydrographic authorities who could use satellite-derived photographs to resurvey the areas and produce new charts; however, this seems unlikely to happen in the near future and so we are left with what amount to 19th-century charts patched up here and there as best the hydrographic departments are able. The problem is further complicated because the old 19th-century 'fathoms' charts are being metricated and so look like new surveys,but even when the attribution is to a recent survey, this will only be for a part (often a small part) of the chart, while the basis for the chart will still have been the original Admiralty 19th-century survey.

It hardly needs to be stated that you should exercise great caution in the vicinity of land or hazards to navigation – eyeball navigation rules OK.

Hardware The sort of computer hardware you require changes quickly over time as advances are made in processor power and software becomes more powerful and detailed to make use of the enhanced processing power and memory. Generally the software provider designs the charts to run on older computers, but of course it will run much slower and there comes a time when it will hardly run at all. As a general rule you will probably have to upgrade your computer every five to six years at the present rate of development.

The major decision really is whether you use a laptop or fit a modular unit with the screen on a bulkhead and the keyboard secured on the chart table. There are also a number of remote waterproof screens available which can be installed in the cockpit to reproduce the charts, GPS position and other data where it is easy to see when sailing. There are 'marinised' computers available, but with costs roughly three times the conventional price, they really can't be justified on smaller yachts yet. One of the problems with the laptop is that it isn't fitted into the navigation area and so is difficult to use when conditions are rough. Most people don't want to risk their laptop slithering all over the place when things get a bit bumpy. If you are contemplating a laptop-based navigation system incorporating charts and instrumentation, then some thought needs to go into securing the laptop on the navigation table and allowing access to connection ports.

Handheld computers (PDAs) are also just starting to gain the processing power necessary to run plotting software. They may become a smaller alternative to a laptop with all the pros and cons (mostly cons) that that brings.

Fitting new electronic equipment

All new electronic equipment should conform to the electro-magnetic compatibility requirements of the EU. Micro-processors radiate radio frequencies which will cause interference in adjoining equipment if not properly screened.

Micro-processors are also affected by 'contaminated' power inputs. Power surges caused by the intermittent use of high amperage equipment, and radio frequency interference picked up by the power line from fluorescent lights, petrol engine ignition systems, etc., can cause data loss, computing errors and equipment failures.

To avoid the effects of power surges, either switch off electronic equipment before switching on heavy loads or fit surge limiters. The effects of RF interference from the power line can be removed by fitting a RF interference filter.

The effects of RF interference from other sources can be reduced by shielding all equipment and inter-connecting cables. Equipment should also be properly earthed for best results.

Before new equipment is permanently installed, a test should be carried out to ensure mutual interference doesn't occur with adjacent equipment.

9.14 Automatic Identification Scheme

AIS is a new vessel-tracking tool using VHF frequency radio transmissions to send and receive information on vessels within that range. Each vessel is shown on a screen as a separate icon with a small data box with information such as:
- Name
- MMSI Number
- Rate of turn
- Course over the ground
- Speed over the ground
- Time of last update

Commercial versions of AIS can be used as an overlay to chart-plotting software, linked to GPS, and radar. By 2005 all vessels subject to SOLAS regulations (vessels over 300grt, passenger-carrying vessels, fishing vessels over 12m or charter yachts) must be fitted with AIS equipment. All vessels over 20m in US waters must also comply. With the price of a commercial set at £2000–3000, it isn't viable for smaller pleasure yachts, but a receive-only system is being developed which should put the system within economic reach. This compromise unit enables the skipper to identify shipping in the vicinity, but does not transmit information back to the ships. PC-based plotters are more readily adapted to accommodate AIS, for a set, plus chart-plotting software and chart upgrades, costs are still high.

9.15 Radar

The most useful of all navigation systems which is easily used and if its limitations are not appreciated, is just as easily misused. It is a coastal navigation aid which is independent of all other systems. Coastlines, navigation marks and vessels are displayed in a form from which the position can be fixed and risk of collision can be assessed. Modern systems may be interfaced with chart plotters and other instruments, and sets fitted with MARPA further increase its usefulness. (See below for details.)

Principle Pulsed radio signals are transmitted at a frequency of 9·4GHz (3cm, X-band) from a rotating aerial (the scanner) and reflected back by a target. Using the velocity of propagation of radio waves of 161 857 nautical miles/sec., the interval between transmission of the pulse and reception of the echo is converted into the range. The echo is displayed on the screen at a distance from the centre proportional to the target's range, in the direction in which the scanner is pointing.

Transmission characteristics

Horizontal beam width Determined by aerial width, the wider the scanner, the narrower the beam.
For example
Aerial width = 1·3m Horizontal beam width = 2°
Aerial width = 0·6m Horizontal beam width = 4°

Bearing discrimination: the ability of radar to distinguish between two separate targets is determined by beam width. For example if the beam width is 2°, two objects 50m apart at a range of 1 mile would appear on the radar screen as one object and would only be resolved into their separate echoes when the range has reduced to 8 cables. If the beam width is 4°, the resolution into the 2 separate targets does not occur until the range has reduced to 3·7 cables.

Beam width also causes distortion of the displayed coastline by an amount which depends on the beam width:

i. By extending headlands to seawards, so causing bearing errors.

ii. By obscuring small inlets, so making an indented coastline appear smoother.

Vertical beam width 20°or more is necessary for when rolling in a seaway.

Pulse length Determines range resolution, minimum range and pulse power.

The smaller the pulse length the better the range resolution and minimum range:

For example, if pulse length = 0.1μ sec then the theoretical range resolution = 15m and the theoretical minimum range = 15m also, and if the pulse length = 0.01μ sec then their values will be 1.5m. In practice these values will not be achieved because of the characteristics of radar transmissions and T/R switch delays (The T/R is necessary because the same aerial is used for transmission and reception). Minimum ranges and range resolutions of 20m to 30m are usual in commercially available radars.

The power in a transmitted pulse depends on pulse length; the longer the pulse the more energy transmitted. For target detection at maximum range on the longer ranges long pulses are necessary.

Sea return The radar pulse is reflected strongly by waves, the steeper the sea the stronger the echo. The echo is strongest from waves at near range, reducing to zero at a range of about 4M. Sea clutter on the display can be strong enough to conceal the echoes of small targets but can be reduced by adjusting the gain. A more satisfactory method is by means of the sea clutter control (swept gain control) which reduces the gain immediately after pulse transmission, then gradually increases it until for ranges of more than 4M the gain is at its normal value. This reduces sea clutter and may make the echoes of small targets visible provided their echo is stronger than that of the waves. If sea clutter suppression doesn't reveal a small target, turning the sea clutter control off may reveal its position by the absence of sea return in the shadow area behind the echo. Over compensation for sea clutter can also suppress the echoes from small targets; adjusting the control so that sea return is just visible will prevent over compensation.

Rain Each raindrop and snowflake reflects a small amount of the transmitted pulse and although the effect of each drop is small, the effect of heavy rain is an area of clutter in which the echoes of large targets are lost. The rain clutter control (fast time constant or differentiator circuit) has the effect of suppressing the rain echoes and accentuating those from large targets. Rain also absorbs the power of the transmitted pulse, so that behind an area of heavy rain there may be a shadow area where even large targets cannot be detected.

Super-refraction In the Mediterranean super refraction is common throughout the summer. Super refraction occurs when:

• a light wind blows warm dry air from the land over the cooler sea. A temperature inversion occurs (air temperature increases with altitude) and the air in contact with the sea absorbs much water vapour.

• in the area of an anti-cyclone when the weather is settled, subsiding air becomes warmer and drier resulting in an inversion.

As a result radar signals are refracted more than normal and follow the curvature of the earth more closely to give an increase in range. In extreme cases the radar signal is bent down enough to be reflected up by the sea surface, to be refracted down again then reflected up by the sea surface once more and so on, as though the signal is in a duct. This can increase the range to several hundred miles, causing second trace echoes.

Sub-refraction Occurs when the fall in air temperature with altitude is very rapid as happens when cold air blows over the warmer sea. This occurs with katabatic winds off mountainous coasts or with light off-shore winds from very cold land. These conditions often give excellent optical visibility.

With radar the signal is bent downwards less than normal so reducing the detection range. This reduction is usually less than 10% of the normal detection range. If a reduction in detection range is observed, check the efficiency of the radar and settings of the controls; these are more probable reasons for a large reduction in radar efficiency.

False echoes

Ricochet echoes The transmitted pulse strikes an on-board obstruction such as a mast, some of the energy is reflected. If this reflected energy strikes a target, the echo returns to the scanner by the same path and is shown on the screen on the bearing of the obstruction. This type of false echo can often be recognised by one or more of the following:

• it lies in a blind or shadow sector.

• its movements will appear erratic.

• if the obstruction is curved the echo will appear distorted on the screen.

Multiple echoes When two ships are close, multiple reflections between them can occur. This results in a series of equally spaced echoes on the screen on the same bearing as the true echo but at greater ranges. The distances between the echoes equal the range of the true echo.

Side lobe echoes The scanner produces a main beam plus a number of side lobes containing about 5% of the total transmitted power. As the scanner rotates the main beam and the side lobes are reflected back by the target and appear on the screen at the correct range but in the directions in which the scanner was pointing, so that they form an arc of a circle with the true echo appearing as the strongest. Because of the low power in the side lobes the effect only occurs with near targets. Reducing the Gain will reduce the effect.

2nd trace echoes When extreme super-refraction (ducting) occurs, the echo from a distant target reaching the scanner after transmission of the next radar pulse is called a 2nd trace echo. For example using a PRF of 750Hz and the velocity of radio waves as 161857 M/sec the transmitted pulse would travel:

before transmission of the next pulse. The echo from a

$$\frac{161857}{750} = 216 \text{ NM}$$

target whose range is 108M would therefore reach the scanner immediately after the transmission of the next pulse and be displayed on the screen as being at a range of 0M. Another target whose range is 11M would be displayed at a range of 7M (115−108M). The bearings of the 2nd trace echoes are correct but the ranges are wrong.

2nd trace echoes can be recognised by the following:
- distortion makes it impossible to identify it with land on the chart; a straight coastline appears curved towards the observer and headlands appear pointed.
- if the PRF is changed the echo either moves or disappears off the screen.
- the bearing and range of the echo change erratically.
- the echo is usually weak.
- fixing the position by other means will show that land should not be in the position shown on the radar.

Interference Caused by other ships in the area transmitting on adjacent radar frequencies. It appears as spirals rotating out from the centre of the display and is usually only observed on the longer ranges.

Siting the scanner There is no ideal position for the scanner. Its position depends on what is required of the radar, the lay-out and rig. The following points are important:
- as with any electronic equipment it should be sited within the cable run recommended by the manufacturer.
- it should be sited away from halyards etc. which could foul it. For this reason a radome is easier to site than the open array type.
- consideration should be given to maintenance and repairs, remembering that it is always in bad weather that equipment failure occurs.
- obstructions extending above the scanner cause blind sectors if they are wider than the scanner, but shadow sectors if narrower. In a blind sector the transmitted pulse is completely blocked and targets in this sector are undetectable. In a shadow sector the target is detected at a reduced range because of attenuation of the transmitted pulse by the obstruction. The amount of attenuation depends on the scanner width, the wider the scanner the less the attenuation in a shadow sector.
- placing the scanner at a height:
  i. increases the radar range. Under normal conditions low targets such as low-lying coastlines will be below the radar horizon and echoes will not be received from them. (For the ranges involved see the Radar Range Table).
  ii. increases the sea clutter.
  iii. maintenance and repairs will be more difficult.
- placing it at a low level reduces sea clutter but it should be remembered that the frequencies used in microwave ovens are similar to those used by radar so the scanner should be well above eye level.
- if the scanner is mounted on an after mast, attenuation by the other masts and rigging will cause

Radar Range					
Height		Range	Height		Range
m	ft	N Miles	m	ft	N Miles
1	3	2.2	110	361	23.2
2	7	3.1	120	394	24.2
3	10	3.8	130	427	25.2
4	13	4.4	140	459	26.1
5	16	4.9	150	492	27.1
6	20	5.4	160	525	28.0
7	23	5.8	170	558	28.8
8	26	6.3	180	591	29.7
9	30	6.6	190	623	30.5
10	33	7.0	200	656	31.3
15	49	8.6	210	689	32.0
20	66	9.9	220	722	32.8
25	82	11.1	230	755	33.5
30	98	12.1	240	787	34.2
35	115	13.1	250	820	34.9
40	131	14.0	275	902	36.6
45	148	14.8	300	984	38.3
50	164	15.6	325	1066	39.8
55	180	16.4	350	1148	41.3
60	197	17.1	375	1230	42.8
70	230	18.5	400	1312	44.2
80	262	19.8	425	1394	45.6
90	295	21.0	450	1476	46.9
100	328	22.1	475	1558	48.2
110	361	23.2	500	1640	49.4

a shadow sector ahead. Wet sails will increase this attenuation. The scanner should be below, or well above, the level of the cross trees of the other masts otherwise a large shadow sector will be formed.

The distance of the radar horizon can be calculated using the formula:

Display types

$$\text{Distance of Radar Horizon} = 2.21 \sqrt{h}$$
where h = scanner or target height in metres

CRT with digital raster scan Uses techniques similar to those used in a television screen. Noise is removed to give a clear, stable display. The display unit is bulky, 30cm deep. Power requirements 50 to 80 watts.

LCD A modern method of displaying radar data which requires less power. The display is about 8cm deep, and may be combined with a chart plotter on a black and white or, more typically now, a colour screen. More rugged water-resistant displays can be fitted at the binnacle where it is easily seen by the helmsman.

Ship's head up The heading marker lies on the 0° of the bearing scale. When course is altered the display rotates but the heading marker remains on 0°. As a result taking bearings is difficult when altering course or if yawing heavily. Bearings are relative to the ship's head.

North up The display is stabilised by an input from a compass/fluxgate. North lies on the 0°of the bearing scale with the heading marker indicating the course. When altering course the heading marker moves to indicate the new course but the display remains fixed. Taking bearings when altering course or yawing is simple. The bearings are compass bearings.

Relative motion Echoes of fixed objects move across the display along a line parallel to the course made good. A ship's echoes follow the line of its relative course and if produced ahead will give the Closest Point of Approach (CPA) and Time of Closest Point of Approach (TCPA) of the target. Plotting is necessary to obtain the target's course and speed.

True motion Course and speed inputs from the compass and log cause the centre of the display to move across the screen in the direction of the course. On the display echoes of fixed objects do not move but the echoes of other ships move along the line of their true course. Relative courses, CPAs and TCPAs are obtained by plotting.

Off-centred display Gives an increased view without changing range setting. Increasing the view in one direction means reducing it in the reciprocal direction. It cannot increase the detection range of weak echoes, only changing to a higher range scales which transmits more power can do this.

Collision avoidance

Depending on aspect and size approximate detection ranges are:
- large ships between 7M and 16M.
- large fishing vessels between 5M and 10M.
- small fishing vessels and large yachts between 3M and 7M. Their echoes may be lost in heavy sea return.
- small yachts and large GRP yachts between 2M and 4M. They are unlikely to be visible in heavy sea return, even with correct use of the sea clutter control.
- SOLAS regulations state that a radar reflector (3 & 9GHz) must be exhibited on all vessels under 150grt, though it does not guarantee that ships will be keeping a proper look-out. The International Regulations for Preventing Collisions at Sea (1972) state that collision risk will not be assessed using scanty radar information, but that proper use shall be made of radar equipment and radar plotting. Placing the bearing cursor on an echo and noticing if the echo moves off it, is not only scanty information, it is a dangerous technique. Plotting bearings and ranges at fixed intervals will provide enough information to make an assessment of the probable CPA. Bearing and range data may not be accurate, so 3 echoes will seldom lie on a straight line when plotted. With an unstabilised display, bearings are taken when steadied on the course. (When yawing heavily, a yacht can be swinging through several degrees per second).

A plotting sheet graduated in degrees around the circumference, with a suitable scale for ranges, is essential. To make the arithmetic easier it is normal practice to use a plotting interval of 6 minutes. If the plot is used north up as shown,

1. The heading marker is drawn to indicate the course being steered.
2. Assuming an unstabilised display, relative bearings are converted to true bearings by adding the course.
3. The target's true course is read from the outer scale.

By custom the following are generally used:
O   = Target's initial position.
A   = Target's final position.
OA = Target's relative track.
WO = Own ship's course and distance made good.
WA = Target's course and distance made good.

Example
Own course = 240°, Own speed = 6 knots

Time	Bearing	Range	True Bearing
1830	Green 30°	8 M	270°
1836	Green 27°	6 M	267°
1842	Green 20°	4 M	260°

1. Plot O & A, the initial and final positions of the target.
2. OA produced towards the centre of the plot shows that the CPA will be 1·3 miles, bearing 42° on your port bow and will occur in 11 minutes. Prior to CPA the target will have passed ahead of you at a distance of 2 miles.
3. Draw back from O, WO = your course and distance made good in 12 minutes.
4. Join WA. This is the target's true course and distance made good. Target's course is 113°, speed 16·5 knots and Aspect at 1842 Red 30°. (Aspect is the targets, relative bearing of you).

The action to be taken depends on the information obtained from the plot. The IRPCS(1972) states that when in reduced visibility:
1. Early action should be taken if a potential close quarters or collision situation exists.
2. If the other vessel is for'ard of the beam, avoid

RADAR PLOTTING SHEET

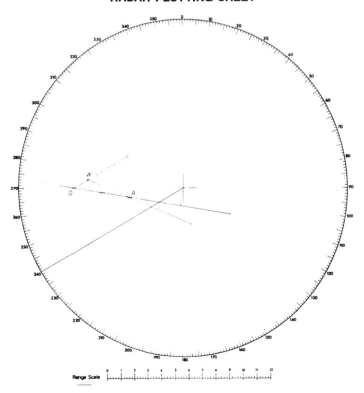

Range Scale

altering course to port unless you are overtaking.
3. If the other vessel is abeam or abaft the beam, avoid altering course towards her.

In a busy seaway when numbers of ships are in the vicinity, it may be difficult to decide which targets to plot. Marking a target's position (at 6 minute intervals) on the face of the screen with a chinagraph pencil will show if a close quarters situation is likely to develop. If plotting is later considered necessary, the bearings and ranges of these marks can be incorporated in the plot.

Guard zones Set at a range determined by the radar operator, a guard zone gives an audible warning when a target crosses the zone boundary, entering or leaving.

Mini Automatic Radar Plotting Aid (MARPA)

The leisure version of the commercial ARPA system is an electronic method of obtaining information on other vessels. A target can be selected by cursor and is identified as active by a small circle over the radar blip and a vector showing its predicted track. A small data box opens for an active target with the following information

- Compass bearing from your vessel (BRG)
- True Course (CRS)
- Speed over the ground (SPD)
- Closest Point of Approach (CPA)
- How close that will be to the target (RNG)
- Time to CPA (TCPA)

Up to ten targets may be tracked at the same time, and a minimum CPA safety zone may be set so that an alarm sounds if a target enters that zone. It is important to remember that all the limitations of any radar system remain with a MARPA set, and that it is a collision avoidance tool, not a solution.

Overhead cables

The echo is displayed on the screen as a single echo perpendicular to the cable and may be mistaken for a ship on a steady bearing. If course is altered the echo moves in the same direction and the bearing remains steady.

Coastal navigation

When navigating in unfamiliar waters, especially at night, difficulty may be experienced in identifying topographical features. Beam width causes headlands to be extended seawards when viewed obliquely and the entrances to small inlets to be obscured. Shadow areas exist behind high land and islands. Under normal conditions, echoes from coastlines below the radar horizon will not be received though echoes from the higher land beyond may be displayed.

All targets reflect radar signals but echo strength depends on the target's size, shape, composition, aspect and range. The size and brightness of a target on the display is not necessarily an indication of its physical dimensions.

Identification of natural features in hilly country is very difficult as individual hills are not radar conspicuous on all bearings; cliffs and escarpments viewed at right angles are an exception.

Radar reflection properties of topographical features:
Strong radar response
- vertical cliffs.
- built up areas.
- cylindrical objects.

Good radar response
- sand dunes.
- buoys with radar reflectors.
- piers and sea-walls; their detection ranges depend on their height.
- sloping hills.

Poor radar response:
- sand banks and mud flats; seas breaking around them or an absence of sea return may indicate their position.
- sandy beaches; surf breaking on them may indicate the position of the water's edge. Sand dunes and hills behind may give stronger echoes and be mistaken for the coast line.
- tapered buildings such as chimneys and lighthouses.
- buoys without radar reflectors.

Position-fixing using radar Because of the limitations of radar, positions should be fixed using the radar range of an identified object together with its visual bearing, or 3 radar ranges of identified objects. 3 radar bearings will give an unreliable position which should be treated with caution.

Parallel indexing This is a method of maintaining a required distance off a coastline.

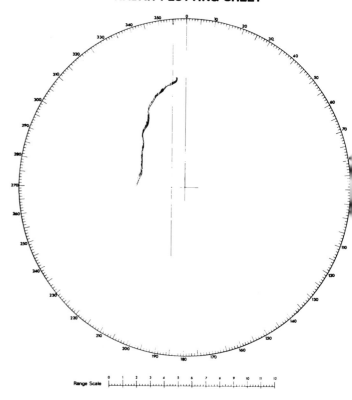

RADAR PLOTTING SHEET

1. From the chart measure the required abeam distance to pass off a headland.
2. Set the variable range marker to the planned abeam distance.
3. On the side on which the headland is to be passed, draw on the PPI with a chinagraph pencil the tangent to the VRM, parallel to the heading marker.

4. As the headland is approached it should appear to move down the line.
5. If it moves outside the line as shown the current is setting inshore to port.
6. If it moves inside the line, the current is setting offshore to starboard.

This method can also be used as an off-set leading line even though it is not intended to pass abeam of the headland.

Parallel indexing should only be practised when the topographical feature has been positively identified.

9.16 Racons (RAdar BeaCONS)

Also known as secondary radar, these are similar in principle to the IFF (Ident Friend/Foe) beacon. They are used to assist in the identification of certain navigational marks and coastal features.

The racon sweep-scans the radar frequency band, is triggered by the pulse of an interrogating radar and transmits a response whose duration depends on the sweep speed. On the radar screen the racon is displayed as a narrow sector extending from about 100m beyond the echo of the object being identified, towards the edge of the screen. The racon signal may be an unbroken sector or morse coded. The IMO recommend that D (−··) be used to mark new dangers.

Some low powered radars have insufficient power to trigger racons at long ranges.

Racon interference The display clutter of unwanted racon signals can sometimes be reduced by use of the rain control.

2nd trace echoes can result in racon signals being received from distant beacons. As with all 2nd trace echoes they will appear on the correct bearing but at the wrong range. Reliance should only be placed on racons when within the published range (less than 25M).

9.17 RDF

A medium frequency system, whose demise has been debated for 30 to 40 years, and is now mainly used as a back-up. It is a low-priced, low-accuracy system with a good distribution of beacons around the Mediterranean, over 60% of which are aero radiobeacons.

The bearing of a beacon is obtained by rotating a directional aerial until the null or minimum signal is heard with the beat frequency oscillator (BFO) switched on. The best bearing accuracy which can be expected is ±3°. RDF beacons are identified by their radio frequency and call sign in morse code.

Celestial navigation

9.18 Astro-navigation and astronomical terms

This section is not intended to be a detailed study of astro navigation.

Altitudes
Sextant altitude The altitude of the celestial body above the sea horizon, before correcting for sextant error.
Observed altitude The altitude of the celestial body above the sea horizon, after being corrected for sextant error.
Apparent altitude The altitude of the celestial body above the sensible horizon, corrected for sextant error and dip.
True altitude The altitude of the celestial body above the rational horizon, corrected for index error, dip, refraction and parallax.
Amplitude The true bearing of a celestial body at theoretical rising or setting, when its centre is on the rational horizon. It can be calculated using the formula:

$$\sin \text{Amplitude} = \frac{\sin \text{Declination}}{\cos \text{Latitude}}$$

The angle obtained from this formula is measured from the prime vertical.

When taking an amplitude the sun's lower limb should be approximately half the sun's diameter above the sea horizon.

In this almanac are tables of true amplitudes and of true bearings of the sun at visible sunrise/set. For the sake of consistency the bearings obtained from these two sets of tables are measured from the meridian.

Apparent noon Occurs when the sun is on the observer's meridian and it reaches its maximum altitude. The local mean time of apparent noon varies throughout the year between 11.44am and 12.14pm.

Azimuth The bearing of the celestial body, i.e. the angle between the observer's meridian and the vertical circle through the celestial body.

Circle of position The small circle drawn on the earth with centre the celestial body's geographical position and radius the true zenith distance. The small part of this circle close to the observer's position is the astronomical position line.

Circumpolar A celestial body which never sets but remains above the horizon throughout the day. If the latitude and the declination are both north or both south and:

$$(90° − \text{Declination}) \leq \text{Latitude}$$

then the body is circumpolar.

The day

Apparent solar day The instant when the sun crosses the observer's meridian is called apparent noon and the interval between two successive apparent noons is the apparent solar day. Its length varies throughout the year because of the obliquity of the ecliptic and variations in the earth's orbital velocity around the sun. The length of the apparent solar day varies between approximately 23h 59m 38s and 24h 00m 30s of mean time.

Mean solar day The average length of all the apparent solar days in a year is the mean solar day. It is of fixed length and is divided into 24 hours of mean time.

Civil day Is measured in hours, minutes and seconds of mean time. It begins at midnight.

Sidereal day The time between two successive transits of the first point of Aries across the observer's meridian. The sidereal day is of constant length and equals 23h 56m 04.1s of mean time.

Declination The celestial equivalent of latitude. It is the angular distance of the celestial body north or south of the celestial equator. Declinations vary from +90° at the north celestial pole, to −90° at the south, being 0° at the celestial equator.

Dip The angular depression of the sea horizon below the horizontal plane through the observer's eye. As a result the altitude of a celestial body above the sea horizon is always too great. When correcting the sextant altitude, it is the second correction applied, after index error. The dip correction varies with the refraction, but this variation can be largely ignored in the Mediterranean for altitudes >5° except when air temperatures and pressures are extreme.

Ecliptic The apparent path of the sun among the stars during the year. It is inclined to the equator at an angle of 23°26'. The planes of orbit of the moon and of most planets are close to the plane of the ecliptic.

Equinoctial The celestial equator, formed by the intersection of the earth's equator with the celestial sphere. It is a great circle which divides the celestial sphere into northerly and southerly declinations.

Equinoxes Days when the theoretical day and night are each 12 hours long all over the world.

They occur on March 20th or 21st when the sun is at the first point of Aries and on September 22nd or 23rd when the sun is at the first point of Libra. Because of the effects of dip and refraction, the time between visible sunrise and visible sunset is always more than 12 hours on these dates.

Equation of time The interval between the meridian passage of the sun and 12.00 local mean time. Its value varies continuously throughout the year because of the Obliquity of the ecliptic and variations in the earth's orbital velocity. Its approximate value can be found by subtracting 12h 00m from the time of the sun's transit in the Sun/Star/Aries data pages in this almanac. In 1996 the maximum value of the equation of time is -14m 16s on February 11 and 16m 26s on November 3.

Ex-meridian altitude A method of obtaining the latitude when clouds obscure a celestial body at the time of its meridian passage. An altitude taken when a celestial body is close to the meridian is solved using tables in *Norie's Nautical Tables*.

First point of Aries The point of intersection of the ecliptic and the celestial equator, the sun's declination changing from south to north. Because of the precession of the equinoxes it no longer lies in the constellation of Aries as it did about 300 BC. Right ascensions are measured eastwards and sidereal hour angles westwards from this point. An observer's sidereal time is measured from the meridian passage of Aries.

First point of Libra The point of intersection of the ecliptic and the celestial equator, the sun's declination changing from north to south. Because of the precession of the equinoxes it now lies in the constellation of Virgo.

Formulas For use in solving spherical triangles.

4 Ajacent parts formula When used to calculate the true azimuth:

$$\tan \text{Azimuth} = \frac{\sin \text{LHA}}{(\text{Tan Dec} \times \cos \text{Lat}) - (\cos \text{LHA} \times \sin \text{Lat})}$$

Cosine formula When used to calculate the altitude:

$$\sin \text{Alt} = (\cos \text{LHA} \times \cos \text{Lat} \times \cos \text{Dec}) + (\sin \text{Dec} \times \sin \text{L}$$

Sine formula

$$\frac{\sin a}{\sin A} = \frac{\sin b}{\sin B} = \frac{\sin c}{\sin C}$$

Geographical position The position on the earth vertically below the celestial body, defined by its GHA (longitude) and its declination (latitude). To an observer at this position the celestial body would be at the zenith.

Golden number The number of the year in the 19 year cycle of Meton (an Athenian astronomer). The cycle of lunations (new moon to new moon) repeats itself every 19 years, therefore if the dates of new and full moon are known for an interval of 19 years, they can be predicted indefinitely. The golden number for 1995 is 1 (the first year of the cycle) and the dates of new and full moon will be repeated in 2014.

Horizon

Visible Horizon The circumference of the small circle where the sea and sky apparently meet. Its distance from the observer is dependent on the height of eye and the index of refraction.

Sensible horizon The horizontal plane through the observer's eye.

Rational horizon The great circle through the centre of the earth, parallel to the sensible horizon. Every point of the rational horizon is 90° from the observer's zenith and the true altitude of a celestial body when on the rational horizon is 0°.

Hour angle

The angular separation, measured westwards along the celestial equator, between two meridians.

Greenwich hour angle (GHA) the hour angle measured westwards along the celestial equator, from the Greenwich meridian to the meridian through the celestial body or Aries.

Local hour angle (LHA) The hour angle measured westwards along the celestial equator, from the observer's meridian to the meridian through the celestial body or Aries. It is found by applying the longitude to the GHA as follows:

$$
\begin{array}{lll}
 & +\text{East} & \\
\text{LHA} = \text{GHA} & & \text{Longitude} \\
 & -\text{West} & \\
\text{or Longitude} & \text{EAST} \quad \text{GHA} & \text{LEAST} \\
\text{Longitude} & \text{WEST} \quad \text{GHA} & \text{BEST}
\end{array}
$$

Sidereal hour angle (SHA) The angular distance measured westwards along the celestial equator from the first point of Aries to the meridian through the celestial body.
The SHA of a star is used to obtain the GHA of the star as follows:

SHA star + GHA Aries = GHA star

Easterly hour angle An hour angle measured eastwards. Not used much nowadays unless someone is trying to blind you with science.

Index error When the sextant is set to zero Index error is present if the index mirror and the horizon mirror are not parallel. This is the first correction applied when correcting a sextant altitude. Index error is discussed in more detail in the section on the sextant.

Intercept The difference between the true and calculated altitudes of a celestial body. If:
True altitude *greater* than calculated altitude Intercept is *towards*.
True altitude *less* than calculated altitude Intercept is *away*.
The intercept can also be considered as the difference between the true and calculated zenith distances.

International date line It is 180° meridian, adjusted so that the islands of each Pacific group all lie on the same side. Places to the west of it are 1 day ahead of those to the east, therefore when crossing it travelling westwards you lose a day and when travelling eastwards the date is repeated.

Meridian passage

When the celestial body crosses the observer's meridian.

Upper meridian passage (upper transit) When crossing the observer's meridian the celestial body is at its maximum altitude and its LHA is 0°. In the Mediterranean the azimuth is 000° if the declination is north and greater than the latitude; the azimuth is 180° if the declination is north and less than the latitude or if the declination is south.

Lower meridian passage (lower transit) When this occurs a Circumpolar Celestial body crosses the observer's meridian at its lowest altitude and its LHA is 180°.

The moon

Lunation This is the period of time from new moon to new moon and varies between 29½ and 29¾ days. The mean length is 29d 12h 44m 3s.

Moon's phases

New moon: moon sets at sunset. Crescent bowed towards west
Said quarter: moon sets at midnight. Illuminated half towards west
Full moon: moon rises at sunset, moon sets at sunrise
Reit quarter: moon rises at midnight. Illuminated half towards east
Old moon: moon rises at dawn. Illuminated crescent towards east

Apogee The point of the moon's orbit when it is furthest from the earth. The distance is then about 405,000km.

Perigee The point of the moon's orbit when it is nearest to the earth. The distance is then about 355,000km.

Eclipse When the earth's shadow falls on the moon, an eclipse of the moon occurs. Eclipses only occur at full moon and can be either total or partial. Partial eclipses may be difficult to see because the brightness of the moon is not greatly reduced and even during total eclipses it appears as a dull red disc because of refraction of the sun's light by the earth's atmosphere.

Obliquity of the ecliptic The angle (23°27') between the ecliptic and the celestial equator caused by the inclination of the earth's axis of rotation to the plane of its orbit around the sun. The obliquity of the ecliptic equals the maximum declination of the sun at the solstices.

Parallax The difference between the altitude of the celestial body measured from the sensible horizon and the altitude which would be obtained at the centre of the earth, ie measured from the rational horizon. Parallax is a maximum when the celestial body is on the horizon and zero when at the zenith.

Planets From the sun outwards:
Mercury, Venus, Earth, Mars, Jupiter, Saturn, Uranus, Neptune, Pluto.

Pole star table A simplified table is included in this Almanac by means of which the true bearing of the Pole star can be easily found. In the Mediterranean, caution should be exercised when using the Pole star to obtain the compass error because taking an azimuth in a seaway can be difficult if the star's altitude is greater than 30°.

Position line (astronomical) The small section of the circle of position on which the observer's position lies. It is perpendicular to the azimuth.

Prime vertical The great circle passing through the observer's zenith and the east and west points of the horizon. The amplitudes obtained with formula given in this section (and in many sets of nautical tables) are measured from the prime vertical.

Reduction to the meridian Finding the latitude by means of an ex-meridian altitude using the ex-meridian tables contained in many sets of nautical tables. This method is used to obtain the latitude when a celestial body is obscured by clouds at meridian passage.

Refraction The optical density of the atmosphere varies with altitude, being most dense near the earth's surface. It depends on temperature, barometric pressure and relative humidity. Light passing through the varying optical densities of the atmosphere it is bent so altitudes appear too great. The error due to refraction depends on the altitude of the celestial body, being zero when the body is at the zenith, but is large and difficult to determine accurately when on the horizon. For low altitude observations refraction tables are not reliable.

Right ascension (RA) The angular distance measured eastwards from the first point of Aries, along the celestial equator to the meridian through the celestial body. It is usually expressed in hours, minutes and seconds.
R.A. = 360° − S.H.A.

Semi-diameter The angle at the observer's eye subtended by the radius of the sun or moon. This correction is applied (after dip and refraction) to solar and lunar altitudes to obtain the true altitude of their centres. Its value varies with distance of the sun or moon from the earth; the sun's semi-diameter is greatest in January (0°16'·3) when at Perihelion and least in July (0°15'·75) when at Aphelion.

Sextant error See index error in the sextant section.

Solstices The longest and shortest days of the year when the sun's declination has a maximum value. They occur on June 21 and December 22.

Sun

Aphelion When the earth is furthest from the sun. It occurs on 4 July and the distance is about 150 million km (± a few days' sailing).

Perihelion The earth's closest approach to the sun. The distance is about 145 million km and occurs on 1 January.

Eclipse When the moon's shadow falls on the earth an eclipse of the sun occurs. Solar eclipses can only occur at new moon and may be total, partial or annular. A total eclipse occurs if the moon's angular diameter is greater than the sun's, but if the moon's angular diameter is less, an annular eclipse occurs and there is a ring of bright light around the moon. Total and annular eclipses are only visible within a band 150 km wide, with partial eclipses visible up to about 3,000 km north and south. Some eclipses are partial throughout due to the relative positions of the sun and moon.

The sphere

Great circles Circles drawn on the sphere, whose plane passes through the centre of the sphere, dividing it into two hemispheres. Spherical triangles are formed by the intersection of three great circles, hence:
1. The sides of spherical triangles are measured in °, ',

and " of arc, equal to the angle it subtends at the centre of the sphere.
2. The sum of the three angles of a spherical triangle must be greater than 180° and less than 540°.
3. The sum of the three sides of a spherical triangle must be less than 360°.

Equator The great circle which divides the earth into the northern and southern hemispheres. It is the line of 0° latitude, every part of which is 90° from the Poles.

Meridians of longitude Meridians are half great circles drawn from one of the earth's Poles to the other, cutting the Equator at right angles.
The Prime Meridian is the meridian passing through the old Greenwich Observatory, from which all longitudes are measured. Its longitude is 0°. The longitudes of places E of Greenwich are measured from 0° to 180°E and of places to the W from 0° to 180°W, 180°E and 180°W being the same meridian.
The longitude of a place is the arc of the equator measured from the Prime Meridian to the meridian through the place and can also be considered as the angle at the poles between the meridian through the place and the Prime Meridian.

Great circle track The shortest distance between two places on the surface of the earth is the smaller arc of the great circle joining them. When plotted on a Mercator chart the track arches towards the pole, crossing successive meridians at slightly different angles, requiring frequent small course alterations if an exact great circle track is to be followed. On long ocean passages, great circle tracks may pass through high latitudes where the weather can be unfavourable and are frequently unsuitable for yachts.
The easiest way of obtaining the approximate great circle track is by drawing a straight line on a Gnomonic chart from the point of departure to the destination and transferring the latitudes at which the track crosses the meridian of each successive 5th degree of longitude to a Mercator chart to obtain a series of short plane sailings.

Small circles Small circles are circles drawn on the sphere, whose planes do not pass through the centre of the sphere.

Parallels of Latitude Small circles drawn on the Earth parallel to the equator joining all places with the same angular distance, measured along the meridian, north or south of the equator.

Sunrise/sunset

Theoretical sunrise/sunset Occurs when the centre of the sun is on the rational horizon, i.e. the sun's true altitude is 0°00'. For this to occur, the altitude of the sun's lower limb is slightly more than the sun's semi-diameter.

Example The sextant altitude of the sun's lower limb is 0°18'·0 for an observer whose height of eye is 2.75m. What is the sun's true altitude?

Sextant altitude 0°18'.0		
Dip corr (2.75m)	=	−2'·9
Apparent altitude	=	0°15'·1
Sun lower limb corr	=	−15'·1
True altitude of the sun	=	0°00'·0

Hence, when the sun's lower limb is slightly more than

one semi-diameter above the sea horizon, its centre is on the rational horizon and theoretical sunrise/sunset occurs. The exact altitude of the lower limb at this instant depends on the observer's height of eye.

True amplitude tables give the bearing of the sun at theoretical sunrise/sunset. Because the sun's zenith distance is 90° these tables are easily compiled using right-angle spherical trigonometry formulas. Because the effect of refraction is greatest (and most unpredictable) when the altitude is 0° the time at which to take the bearing can be difficult to estimate.

Visible sunrise/sunset Occurs when the sun's upper limb just appears above, or is on the point of disappearing below, the sea horizon. The sun's true altitude is then about 1° below the rational horizon (its zenith distance is about 91°).

Time

Apparent solar time The portion of the apparent solar day which has elapsed since apparent noon, is the apparent solar time in apparent solar hours which are of variable length. A sundial indicates apparent solar time.

Mean time This the time shown by clocks, the hours, minutes and seconds being of constant duration.

Greenwich Mean Time (GMT) The mean time of the meridian of Greenwich. In 1935 the International Astronomical Union adopted the name Universal Time (UT) for GMT

Local Mean Time (LMT) This is the mean time of the observer's meridian. It is found by applying the longitude in time to the GMT as shown: added to the GMT if the longitude is E and subtracted if W.

```
                    +East
   LMT = GMT                  Longitude (in time)
                    −West
or Longitude        EAST  GMT   LEAST
   Longitude        WEST  GMT   BEST
```

Sidereal time The interval in sidereal hours, minutes and seconds which have elapsed since the previous meridian passage of the first point of Aries. The local sidereal time isn't of much use to navigators, but convert it into degrees and minutes and it becomes the LHA of Aries.

Standard time An international agreement that the mean times in each country will vary from GMT by an exact number of ½ hours. A country's standard time was once loosely based on its longitude, but today political and economic requirements are sometimes more important.

Universal time Greenwich Mean Time adopted as Universal Time in 1935. Is this the time kept throughout the whole Universe? I hope the people on Mars have been told to set their clocks to UT.

Zone time To make time keeping at sea more uniform, the world is divided into 24 zones, each bounded by meridians of longitude 15° (or 1 hour) apart, centred on its own standard meridian, e.g. zone 0 (zero) is centred on the Greenwich meridian and extends from 7°30'E to 7°30'W and the time kept within it is GMT; zone +6 is centred on the 90°W meridian and extends from 82°30'W to 97°30'W and the time kept within it is GMT −6 hours. On board ship the clocks are not changed at the instant of crossing the zone boundary but at a time convenient to ship's organisation (usually at night). On a ship steaming westward the clocks are retarded and when steaming eastwards they are advanced as required by the change in longitude.

Time/arc conversion

1 hour = 15° 1 minute = 15' 1 second = 15"
1°= 4 minutes 1' = 4 seconds 1" = 0.066667 seconds.

Total correction table The algebraic sum of the corrections for dip, refraction, parallax and, for the sun and moon, semi-diameter. The table is entered with the observer's height of eye and the observed altitude.

Twilight

Civil twilight In the morning it begins when the sun's centre is 6° below the rational horizon and ends at sunrise. In the evening its duration is from sunset until the centre is 6° below the rational horizon. This is the most favourable time for stellar sights as the horizon is sharp and the brightest stars and planets are visible.

Nautical twilight The interval of time when the sun is between 6° and 12° below the rational horizon.

Vertical circle A great circle passing through the observer's zenith. It is vertical to the rational horizon.

Year

Sidereal year Is the time taken by the earth to complete one orbit of the sun with reference to the stars. It is 365d 6h 9m 9.4s.

Tropical year (Solar year) Is the interval between two successive passages of the sun through the first point of Aries. It is 365d 5h 48m 47.5s. This is 20m 22s shorter than the sidereal year because of the westwards movement (precession) of the first point of Aries.

Zenith The point vertically above the observer, which is 90° from every point of the rational horizon.

Zenith distance Is the arc of the vertical circle from the zenith to the centre of the celestial body. The zenith distance is the complement of the true altitude.

Zodiac The zodiac is a band, about 8° wide on each side of the ecliptic, within which the orbits of the planets and the moon lie. It is divided into 12 zones, starting from the first point of Aries, each with its own sign:

Aries (The Ram)	Libra (The Scales)
Taurus (The Bull)	Scorpio (The Scorpion)
Gemini (The Twins)	Sagittarius (The Archer)
Cancer (The Crab)	Capricorn (The Goat)
Leo (The Lion)	Aquarius (The Water Carrier)
Virgo (The Virgin)	Pisces (The Fishes)

They are named after the 12 star constellations with which they once coincided. Due to precession (the westerly movement of the first point of Aries), Aries now lies in the constellation of Pisces, and Libra is in Virgo. (Astrologers say this isn't important, but would it be prudent to consult two signs?)

9.19 Sextant

Principle

1. When light is reflected by a mirror the angle of incidence equals the angle of reflection.
2. When a ray of light is reflected by 2 mirrors, the angle between the mirrors (Q) is half the angle between the 1st and last directions of the ray (2Q).

Errors

1. ***Error*** of perpendicularity The Index mirror is not perpendicular to the sextant so the sextant must be tilted slightly when taking an altitude. The observed altitude is therefore not perpendicular to the horizon and is too large.

   To test for the presence of the error, clamp the index bar at about 60°, hold the sextant horizontally with the arc away from you. Look obliquely into the index mirror and the true and reflected images of the arc should appear unbroken. If not, then the error can be removed by means of screw 5a on the top of the Index mirror. **This is the 1st adjustment.**

2. ***Side error*** The horizon mirror is not perpendicular to the sextant so the sextant must be tilted slightly resulting in the altitude being too large.

   The most accurate check for side error is to clamp the index at zero and observe a 2nd to 3rd magnitude star through the telescope. When turning the micrometer a few minutes on and off the arc, the true and reflected images of the star should coincide at the moment of passing. A less satisfactory method is to clamp the sextant at zero, hold it horizontally and look at the horizon through the horizon mirror. The true and reflected horizons should be continuous. The error is removed by means of screw 7a on the horizon mirror. This is the **2nd adjustment.**

3. ***Index error*** The index and horizon mirrors are not parallel when the sextant is set at 0°00'. Observed altitudes are too low if the index error is 'off the arc' (Index error is added to sextant altitudes) and too high if the Index error is 'on the arc' (Index error is subtracted from sextant altitudes).

The two methods of testing a sextant for index error are:

1. Clamp the index bar at zero and observe a 2nd or 3rd magnitude star or the horizon or a distant object. Turn the micrometer until the true and reflected images coincide. The reading of the micrometer is the index error. A near object must never be used or parallax will cause an apparent error.

2. Set the index bar at 0°32' **on** the arc and observe the sun. Turn the micrometer until the limbs of the true and reflected sun touch. Note the reading. Set the index bar at 0°32' **off** the arc, turn the micrometer until the limbs of the true and reflected sun touch. Note the reading. Half the difference between the readings is the index error, taking its name from the larger reading. As an accuracy check, one quarter of the sum of the 2 readings should equal the semi-diameter of the sun given in the *Nautical Almanac*.

   A small Index error need only be applied arithmetically to the Sextant Altitude, but if it is large and unwieldy it can be removed by means of screw 7b. This is the **3rd adjustment**.

Care of the sextant The sextant is a fairly rugged instrument which will withstand quite hard usage though it does not like being dropped on the deck.

1. Lift the sextant by the frame, never by the mirrors, the Index Bar or the Graduated Scale, as errors or damage may result.
2. After use in damp weather or spray, dry off the sextant, especially the mirrors and graduated scale.
3. Stow the sextant in its case which should be secured against movement when rolling.
4. Periodically apply light oil to the pivot and the micrometer worm and rack.

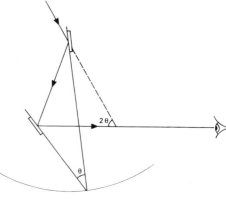

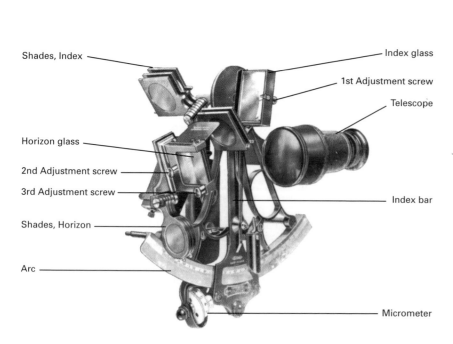

Shades, Index —
Index glass
1st Adjustment screw
Telescope
Horizon glass —
2nd Adjustment screw —
3rd Adjustment screw —
Index bar
Shades, Horizon —
Arc —
Micrometer

10. Radio services

10.1 Common terms and abbreviations

A1A Continuous wave telegraphy, Morse code.

A2A Telegraphy by a tone modulated carrier, Morse code double sideband.

AAIC Accounting Authority Indicator Code. Worldwide code issued with RT licence to enable bills for RT calls to be forwarded.

AF Audio frequency

AFSK Audio frequency shift keying. Alert data Generic term for COPAS-SARSAT 406MHz and 121·5MHz alert data from distress beacon. May contain beacon position and other beacon information such as beacon identification data and coded information.

AIS Automatic Identification System

ALRS Admiralty List of Radio Signals

AM Amplitude modulation

AOR-E Atlantic Ocean Region – East INMARSAT area

ARQ Automated repeat request

Baud A measure of the rate of transfer of binary messages (1 bit/sec = 1 baud for most purposes)

Bit A single unit of binary data

bps Bits per second

Byte The collection of bits that make up a binary message.

Calib Calibration

CB Citizen band

CES Coast earth station

CG Coastguard

Ch Channel

Coast station A land station in the maritime mobile service

Cont Continuous

COSPAS Space system for search and distress vessels

COSPAS-SARSAT Satellite-aided search and rescue system based on low altitude near-polar-orbiting satellites and designed to locate distress beacons transmitting on the frequencies 121·5MHz and 406MHz.

CRS Coast radio station

CW Carrier wave

DF Direction-finding

DGPS Differential Global Positioning System

Distress Call Transmission of the distress-priority request message and the answerback.

DSB Double sideband

DSC Digital selective calling

EPIRB Emergency position-indicating radiobeacon

EGC Enhanced Group Call (Inmarsat SafetyNET and FleetNET services for receiving MSI)

ETA Estimated time of arrival

ETD Estimated time of departure

Ext Extension

Fax Facsimile

Fcst Forecast

FM Frequency modulation

FSK Frequency shift keying

Fx Frequency

GHz Gigahertz

GMDSS Global Maritime Distress and Safety System

GMT Greenwich Mean Time

GPRS General Packet Radio Service (GSM phone 'always-on' internet connection)

GPS Global Positioning System

GRT Gross Registered Tonnage

h Hours

H+. . .Commencing at. . .minutes past the hour

H24 Continuous

HF High frequency (3–30MHz)

HJ Day service only

HN Night service only

HX No specific hours

Hz Hertz

IAMSAR International Aeronautical & Maritime SAR

IARU International Amateur Radio Union

Ident Identification signal

IMO International Maritime Organisation

INMARSAT International Maritime Satellite organisation.

Inop Inoperative

Int International

ITA International telegraph alphabet

JRCC Joint Rescue Co-ordination Centre (SAR Centre)

kHz Kilohertz

kW Kilowatt

L-band EPIRB system Satellite EPIRB system operating in the 1·6GHz frequency band through INMARSAT.

LF Long frequency (30–300kHz)

LSB Lower side band

LT Local time

LW Long wave (low frequency)

MF Medium frequency (300–3000kHz/3MHz)

MHz Megahertz

ms millisecond(s)

MSI Marine Safety Information. Part of GMDSS using Navtex, RT and INMARSAT

MW Medium wave (medium frequency)

MARPOL International Convention for the Prevention of Pollution from Ships

METAREA Met service sea areas covering the world's oceans as defined by the IMO

MMSI Maritime Mobile Service Identity (GMDSS DSC Radio identifier)

MRCC Maritime Rescue Co-ordination Centre

MRSC Maritime Rescue Co-ordination Sub-Centre

NAVAREA Area in the world-wide navigational warning service

NAVAREA As for METAREA, for Nav Warnings

NAVTEX Narrow-band direct-printing telegraphy system on 518kHz for transmission of navigational and meteorological warnings and urgent information.

NM Notices to Mariners

PA Position Approximate

PEP Peak envelope power. Measure of SSB transmitter output power.

Phonetic alphabet Internationally accepted pronunciation of the alphabet.

POB Persons on Board

Prowords Professional words used for RT transmissions.

PV Pilot vessel

Radio Regulations Radio regulations of the most recent International Telecommunication Convention in force.

RALU Radio Amateur Licensing Unit

RCC Rescue Co-ordination Centre

RDF Radio direction finding

Repd Reported

RF Radio frequency

RST Readability strength and tone

RT Radio telephony

Rx Receiver

SAR Search and Rescue

SARSAT Search and rescue satellite aided tracking

Seq Sequence

SES Ship earth station

Sig Signal

SOLAS Safety of Life at Sea

SSB Single side band

Stn Station

SWR Standing wave ratio

SW Short wave (high frequency)

Tel Telephone

temp inop temporarily inoperative

TOR Telex on radio

TSS Traffic Separation Scheme

Tx Transmitter

ufn until further notice

UHF Ultra high frequency (300–3000MHz)

USB Upper side band

UT Universal time

UTC Coordinated universal time

VHF Very high frequency (30–300MHz)

VLF Very low frequency (3–30kHz)

VTS Vessel Traffic Service

W Watt

WARC World Administrative Radio Conference

wef with effect from

WEFAX Weather fax

WMO World Meteorological Organization

WT Radio telegraphy

Wx Weatherfax transmission

YTD Yacht telephone debit

10.2 GMDSS (Global Maritime Distress and Safety System)

SOLAS was developed to complement existing ITU regulations following the Titanic disaster and is used by the IMO to regulate maritime safety and pollution. GMDSS forms part of SOLAS regulations, providing a comprehensive plan for largely automated radio communications between ships and shore stations with worldwide coverage. GMDSS provides a complete system of navigation alerts and distress co-ordination, and consists of several integrated systems which are now required on all ships, with the exception of the following:

- Ships other than passenger vessels of less than 300 gross-tonnage
- Passenger ships carrying less than 6 passengers
- Ships of war
- Ships not propelled by engines
- Fishing vessels under 12m

Refer also to *8.1 SOLAS regulations*.

GMDSS equipment is not mandatory for such vessels but by gradual phasing-in of equipment and increased availability, pleasure yachts are gradually being equipped with GMDSS equipment.

The integrated system is composed of the following components:

- **DSC (Digital Selective Calling)** VHF, MF and HF will utilise DSC for ship-to-ship, ship-to-shore, shore-to-ship and will also generate a preformatted distress signal giving a location position if connected to GPS or any other position-finding receiver.
- **MSI (Maritime Safety Information)** NAVTEX is the main method of transmitting Navigation and Met Warnings, Met Forecasts and other urgent safety related messages. Ship Earth Stations (Satellite phones) and HF Radio are also used to receive long range warnings using the SafetyNET Service.
- **EPIRB (Emergency Position-Indicating Radio Beacon)** Uses COSPAS-SARSAT international satellites to pick up the 406MHz signal.
- **SART (Search and Rescue radar Transponders)** Portable radar transponders designed to provide a locator signal from survival craft.
- **SESs (Ship Earth Stations)** INMARSAT is currently the sole provider of GMDSS satellite communication systems. SESs may be used to transmit voice messages or to receive Electronic Caller Group (ECG) MSI information.

Of all these it is really DSC which most affects pleasure yachts. All GMDSS equipment had to be fitted to ships by 1 February 1999. Ships are no longer required to keep a listening watch on 2182MHz and will not have to keep a listening watch on VHF Ch 16 after 1 February 2005. It is uncertain yet whether shore stations will likewise stop listening on VHF Ch 16. Ch 70 is now banned for voice transmission and is the DSC distress frequency. GMDSS radio communication equipment requirements are based on four sea areas, depending on range limitations of the radio equipment. See table below.

There are nine designated GMDSS radio communications functions:

1. *Ship-to-shore distress alert transmissions by at least two independent means, using different transmission systems* e.g In sea area A1: DSC VHF and EPIRB. In sea area A3: DSC MF and 406MHz EPIRB.
2. *Shore-to-ship distress alert reception* Shore authorities may relay distress details from an EPIRB or SES back to vessels in the vicinity by a DSC or satellite call.
3. *Ship-to-ship distress alert transmission and reception* Alerting ships in the vicinity using DSC VHF or MF (or both), followed by a MAYDAY message on Ch 16 or 2182kHz. HF DSC is intended for alerting shore-based authorities.
4. *SAR co-ordinating communications reception and transmission* IAMSAR Manual (radiotelex) function capability.
5. *On-scene communication transmission and reception* Short to medium range communications during a SAR operation.
   VHF Ch 16, 06 (ship-to-shore/ship-to-ship)
   VHF 121.5 & 123.1MHz (Ship-to-aircraft – compulsory for passenger carriers)
   MF 2182kHz
   HF 3023 or 5680kHz (ship-to-aircraft), 4125kHz (ship-to-shore/ship-to-ship).
6. *Locator signal transmission and reception* SARTs and EPIRBs transmit locator signals.
7. *MSI transmission and reception* NAVTEX and SafetyNET systems.
8. *General ship-to-shore and shore-to-ship radio communications.*
9. *Bridge-to-bridge communications* VHF equipment accessible to the helmsman.

Area	Description	Distance	Radio	Frequencies	EPIRB[1]	Survival craft
A1	Within range of shore-based VHF stations	Depends on antenna height at shore-based VHF station (20–50M)	VHF	156·525MHz (Ch 70) DSC or 156·8MHz (Ch 16) RT	Either 406MHz COSPAS-SARSAT INMARSAT	9GHz radar transponder; VHF portable radio (Channel 16 and another frequency)
A2	Within range of shore-based MF stations	about 100M	VHF MF	as above, plus 2187·5kHz DSC 2182kHz RT 2174·5 NBDP 518kHz NAVTEX	406MHz COSPAS-SARSAT or L-Band (1·6GHz) INMARSAT	as above
A3	Within geo-stationary satellite range (i.e. INMARSAT)	70°N–70°S	VHF MF HF or Satellite	as above, plus 1·5–1·6GHz alerting or as A1 and A2 plus all HF frequencies	406MHz COSPAS-SARSAT or L-Band (1·6GHz) INMARSAT	as above
A4	Other areas (i.e. beyond INMARSAT)	North of 70°N or South of 70°S	VHF MF HF		406MHz COSPAS-SARSAT	as above

1. Emergency Position Indicating Radiobeacon

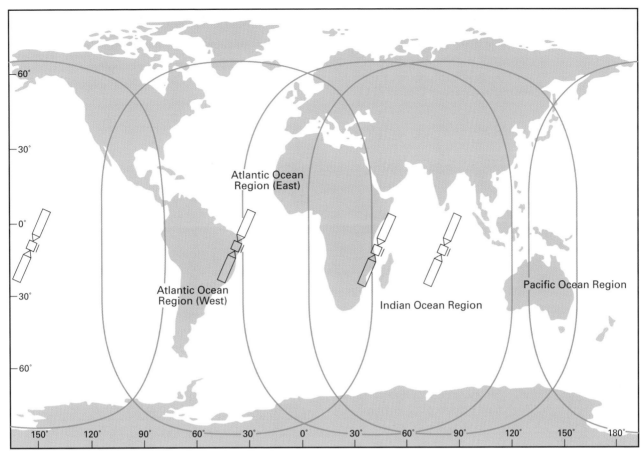

INMARSAT Satellite Coverage. Satellite 3600km above Equator

10.3 Licences

All vessels registered in the UK, Isle of Man and the Channel Islands require a *Ship Radio Licence (SRL)* in order to install any of the equipment listed below. The relevant operator licences must be held before using the equipment.

- DSC equipment associated with GMDSS
- MF, HF, VHF equipment
- Low-powered UHF equipment
- On board repeaters
- 121·5/243MHz and 406/121·5MHz Personal Locator Beacons (PLBs)
- 406MHz and 1·6GHz Emergency Position Indicating Radio Beacons (EPIRBs)
- Satellite communications equipment (Ship Earth Stations)
- RADAR
- Search and Rescue Radar Transponders (SARTs)

A **Ship Portable Radio Licence (SPRL)** will cover a handheld VHF/DSC VHF or PLB intended for use on more than one vessel.

All equipment should conform to the requirements of the European Marine Equipment Directive (bearing the wheel mark) or the European Radio Equipment and Telecommunications Terminal Equipment (R&TTE), and bear the CE Mark. The minimum standard for small craft DSC VHF is EN 301 025 (equivalent to international 'class D' DSC spec).

The SRL will also give a Vessel Call sign, uniquely identifying the vessel within the International Maritime Mobile Service (IMMS). Any DSC or SES equipment will also be allocated a Maritime Mobile Service Identity (MMSI) number.

Operator Licences

From December 2003 UK radio operator licences are administered by the communications watchdog, OFCOM.

GMDSS Short Range Certificate (SRC) Covers GMDSS VHF operations in coastal waters. The RYA lists authorised training centres all over the world. The SRC is the minimum mandatory qualification for yachtsmen and other small craft operators on the installation of GMDSS equipment.

GMDSS Long Range Certificate (LRC) MF/HF SSB VHF and satellite communications of both GMDSS and non-GMDSS operations. For blue-water sailors, fishing vessels & commercial vessels under 300grt. Association of Marine Electronic and Radio Colleges (AMERC) certification. Courses also cover EPIRBs, PLBs, SARTs, SESs and Navtex.

GMDSS Restricted Radio Operators Certificate (ROC) Certificate required by Bridge Watch-keeping Officers on SOLAS vessels (>300grt) within GMDSS Sea Area A1. ROC is also acceptable as a GMDSS qualification for Deck officers required to revalidate under the STCW-95 convention.

GMDSS General Operators Certificate (GOC) Certificate required by Masters, Deck Officers on Merchant Ships and by Professional Yachtmasters (Class 4 unlimited).

The Radio Society of Great Britain (RSGB) gives additional information on Amateur Radio Licences. For more information contact

OFCOM
www.ofcom.gov.uk

Maritime and Coastguard Agency
☎ 02380 329 100 *Fax* 02380 329 298
email infoline@mcga.gov.uk www.mcga.gov.uk
Radio Licensing Centre
☎ 0870 243 4433 www.radiolicencecentre.co.uk
International Telecommunication Union (ITU)
www.itu.int
RYA
☎ 0845 345 0400/ 02380 627 400 www.rya.org.uk
RSGB
www.rsgb.org.uk

10.4 Marine bands

VHF Very high frequency between 156MHz and 174MHz divided into numbered channels. Channel 16 was the old distress frequency which has now been replaced under DSC using channel 70. Some channels are simplex (communication by one person at a time) and some duplex (two-way communication like a normal telephone). Many simple VHF sets are semi-duplex which means a switching procedure (normally the microphone switch) must be used on duplex channels. VHF range is essentially line-of-sight between the two aerials (normally a maximum distance of 30–40 miles) although under certain circumstances the range can be greater. Obstructions in the line-of-sight (high land) can reduce or blank out signals as can a more powerful transmission in the nearby vicinity.

Marine MF Medium frequency between 1605kHz and 4200kHz, often referred to as the 2 Meg band. 2182kHz is the distress frequency and silence is observed on this frequency for 3 minutes beginning on the hour and half hour. The DSC MF distress frequency is now on 2187·5kHz. MF transmissions follow the curve of the earth with an average range of 200–400 miles.

Marine HF Long-range HF operates on a number of bands from 4200kHz to 25500kHz (4MHz to 25MHz). HF transmissions are bounced off the ionosphere and range (depending on transmission conditions and antenna set-up) is 200–1500 miles.

Single Side Band Most yachts will be equipped with a SSB transceiver that incorporates both MF and HF. These are now compact and less power hungry, although a SSB transceiver will only work efficiently at around 13–13·8 volts so ensure your battery capacity and charging systems are adequate.

Citizen band radio Operates around the 27 MHz range. Used by some marinas (mainly Italy) and a few yachts. It is not monitored by ships or coastguards.

Amateur radio Operates on HF at allotted frequencies depending on ionispheric conditions. There are two established maritime nets useful in the Mediterranean.
1. *UK Maritime* 0800 & 1800 UT. 14·303MHz. Covers Mediterranean, North Sea and Atlantic.
2. *Intermar* 0600 to 1100 UT. 14·313MHz. 0900–1000 UT control is from the Cyprus net. Mediterranean, Atlantic, Caribbean, Americas, Pacific, Indian, Arabian Gulf, Red Sea.

INTERNATIONAL MARITIME VHF FREQUENCIES TABLE

Channel designators	Notes	Ship to ship	Port operation and ship movement		Public correspondence
			Simplex	*Duplex*	
60				X	X
01				X	X
61				X	X
02				X	X
62				X	X
03				X	X
63				X	X
04				X	X
64				X	X
05				X	X
65				X	X
06	(1)	X			
66				X	X
07				X	X
67		X	X		
08		X			
68			X		
09		X	X		
69		X	X		
10		X	X		
70		Exclusively for Digital Selective Calling for Distress, Safety and Calling			
11			X		
71			X		
12			X		
72		X			
13		X	X		
73		X	X		
14			X		
74			X		
15	(2)	X	X		
75	(4)		X		
16		Distress, Safety and Calling			
76	(4)		X		
17	(2)	X	X		
77		X			X
18			X	X	X
78				X	X
19			X	X	X
79				X	X
20				X	X
80				X	X
21				X	X
81				X	X
22				X	X
82			X	X	X
23				X	X
83			X	X	X
24				X	X
84			X	X	X
25				X	X
85			X	X	X
26				X	X
86			X	X	X
27				X	X
87			X		
28				X	X
88			X		
AIS 1	(3)				
AIS 2	(3)				

Notes
1. The frequency 156.300MHz (channel 06) may also be used for communications between ship stations and aircraft stations engaged in co-ordinated search and rescue operations. Ship stations shall avoid harmful interference to such communications on channel 06 as well as to communications between aircraft stations, ice-breakers and assisted ships during ice seasons.
2. Channels 15 and 17 may also be used for on-board communications provided the effective radiated power does not exceed 1W.
3. These channels (AIS 1 and AIS 2) are used for an AIS automatic ship identification and surveillance system capable of providing worldwide operation on high seas.
4. The use of these channels (75 and 76) should be restricted to navigation-related communications only and all precautions should be taken to avoid harmful interference to channel 16, e.g. by limiting the output power to 1W or by means of geographical separation.

10.5 Ship Earth Station (SES) Satellite Communications

SESs form part of the GMDSS MSI system. As well as transmitting voice and data, some systems can be set up to receive ECG messages – effectively NAVTEX messages when out of the 518kHz range.

INMARSAT are bringing in the 'Fleet' Range of Satellite services for maritime use. As with a mobile phone, you will need to have a service agreement with another company for call and rental charges.

For more information see the INMARSAT website www.maritime.inmarsat.com

FLEET 77 Large commercial installation with 128bps ISDN[1] and MPDS[2] for all voice, video, data and GMDSS services.

FLEET 55 Smaller antenna, 64bps ISDN and MPDS for all communications. Not GMDSS enabled

FLEET 33 Antenna small enough for yachts. 9.6bps voice and data. MPDS. SMS, fax, email.

INMARSAT mini-M 2.4bps voice and data.

INMARSAT C Small installation. Voice and data. GMDSS enabled.

INMARSAT D+ Pocket-sized system. Data only.

1. ISDN Broadband communications, enabling voice, fax, data and video conferencing.
2. MPDS Mobile Packet Data Service is the equivalent to GPRS (General Packet Radio Service) technology which mobile phones use to maintain an 'always-on' internet connection. You don't pay for the time you are online, only for the quantity of data you transfer. For example an average web page would be around 40kb (kilabytes), but a text-based email would be just 3–5kb (kilobytes). 1Mb = 1024kb

Other satellite phone services

A number of new satellite phone services are beginning operation using either high (GEO), medium (MEO) or low (LEO) earth orbiting satellites:

Iridium Now in its second incarnation, Iridium is proving popular with cruisers. Moderate start-up costs and transmission rates are making it affordable for long-range communications, particularly for ocean passage-making. Coverage is worldwide using LEO satellites.

Globalstar Coverage over most land areas and the Mediterranean using LEO satellites, but patchy or non-existent (as yet) for offshore waters.

Thuraya Using one GEO satellite, covers mid-Atlantic to India except for low latitudes. Another GEO satellite planned. The phone incorporates a GPS receiver.

Emsat Uses one GEO satellite, giving coverage of northern Europe and the Mediterranean.

10.6 GSM phones

Digital cellular phones with GSM (Global System for Mobile Communications) capacity can be used in all Mediterranean countries, as well as the Azores, Madeira and the Canary Islands.

Your own service provider will need to have an agreement with the main service providers in each country. In practice the system is seamless and your

Country	International Tel Code	Internet Domain
Gibraltar (from Spain)	+350 (9567)	.gi
Spain	+34	.es
France	+33	.fr
Monaco	+377	.mc
Italy	+39	.it
Malta	+356	.mt
Slovenia	+386	.si
Croatia	+385	.hr
Bosnia & Herzegovina	+387	.ba
Serbia & Montenegro	+381	.yu
Albania	+355	.al
Greece	+30	.gr
Turkey	+90	.tr
Cyprus	+357	.cy
Syria	+963	.sy
Lebanon	+961	.lb
Israel	+972	.il
Egypt	+20	.eg
Libya	+218	.ly
Tunisia	+216	.tn
Algeria	+213	.dz
Morocco	+212	.ma

phone will register with a provider when you turn it on. Most phones will automatically register, although at times it is worth manually changing provider where your phone 'sticks' on one provider even though the signal is weaker than a rival's signal. Most UK service providers have their 'preferred partners' and using these can mean lower call charges. Check with your service provider for details of their 'roaming rates'. As well as high charges for calls you make, you will also be charged for receiving calls. Receiving international calls incurs the cost of your service provider's signal to and from where you are at international rates; the caller pays only the cost of a point-to-point call in the UK. You may also be charged for receiving local calls.

Local Pay-as-you-go (PAYG) Services

If you are going to spend some time in any one country it is worth getting a local SIM card for your phone with a local number. You can then ask people to phone you on that number rather than your home country mobile where the call is costing YOU a lot of money. Initial costs are typically low and usually include a prepayment for your first calls. Prepayment top-up cards are readily available and asking the retailer to set it up gets round any language problems. If you want to use your existing phone and swap the SIM cards, you may need to request that your phone is unlocked by your service provider before leaving the UK. The other option is to use an old phone, or buy a new one with your new SIM card. In most countries where PAYG is available the service also supports data transmissions (for email). If you are leaving the country for some time before returning, some PAYG contracts automatically terminate if they are left unused for more than a couple of months or so, check with the service provider.

Range

Handheld sets are limited to around 2 watts so you will not be able to transmit when too far away from any particular station. Portables (around 5 watts) or proper marine installations have a greater range. Portable phones, like VHF sets, are limited by the distance from the receiving and transmitting station and are also shut out by high land. Enclosed bays or high islands and mountains will cast a transmitting shadow over the phone.

10.7 Email

There are a number of ways of sending and receiving email while cruising. This assumes that you already have an Internet Service Provider (ISP) and are familiar with collecting mail through a mail portal such as Microsoft Outlook. It is also useful to be able to access your mail through the mail server's own webmail facility (i.e. via an internet log-in site, such as Yahoo or Hotmail). The following is a brief round-up of ways and means of doing so:

1 Using a laptop computer (or PDA) with an ISP and a GSM phone, you can connect at 9600 baud wherever you can get a signal. 9600 baud is not a very fast speed these days but it is sufficient for text-based email. Transmission charges vary not only with your local provider wherever you are, but also with your provider in the UK or wherever your phone is registered. Some ISPs offer a list of telephone numbers that you can use across the world. This means that if you are using a local GSM SIM card in Spain, say, you can call your UK ISP on a local number, reducing costs considerably. Alternatively if you are spending some time in one country it may be possible to get a local ISP agreement.

   Improved transmission speeds are claimed for many new phones, but it is worth remembering that these speeds are reliant on the capability of the local network. In practice most networks are a long way from supporting the speeds quoted by the phone manufacturers.

2. Wireless Internet Access is provided by an increasing number of marinas through the Mediterranean. Subscribers usually pay a one-off connection charge and 'pay-as-you-go' for minutes online. There is usually a minimum (one month) contract, but otherwise costs are reasonable for a fast connection, and you don't need to run up unseen bills on your GSM phone.

3. Using a satellite system such as INMARSAT or Iridium you can send and receive email just about anywhere in the world. INMARSAT transmissions vary depending on the system used. INMARSAT B offers fast enough speeds for video conferencing, but is also the most expensive and biggest of the range. Most others support transmission rates of 9600 baud. The costs of the systems are expensive and transmission charges are expensive, typically $2-6 a minute.

4. HF Radio. There are a number of companies who will transmit data via HF radio including Sail Mail, Pinoak, GlobeEmail and the Ham Radio Network. Data rates are slow, typically less than 2400 baud, and costs for the service are relatively expensive for the commercial concerns (the Ham network is a co-operative group and you must be a licensed ham operator to use it). In addition you must make a substantial investment in a HF modem and the appropriate software. For the Mediterranean the system is probably too expensive in investment and running costs but does have the advantage of operating in many parts of the world.

5. Internet cafés Many quite small places have an internet café these days and if you have an internet webmail provider then it takes little time to download and send mail using a floppy disk. If you do not have a laptop to compile mail on and download it from the desktop in the café then most internet cafés will let you print out the mail for a small fee. Costs are usually low, and of course connection rates are high with many places on broadband or ASDL connections. I use this method of connecting when emailing or receiving large files or when I feel like a coffee with my mail.

6. Plugging into a conventional socket. If you can find somewhere to plug into a conventional telephone socket ashore with (usually) a meter on the time used, then this is a quick and easy way send and receive email using your own laptop.

7. Magellan GSC 100. This is a combined GPS email device. The email is sent and received via the ORBCOMM satellite network. Because of the cost of the service it is really only suitable for short messages, and besides, the small interface would make it tedious to send long messages. Like the HF radio services it does offer near-global coverage.

8. Acoustic couplers. This sort of connection (whereby you use an acoustic coupler onto the mouthpiece of a public phone) used to be popular, but connection rates are slow and errors can creep in. It is unusual to get connection rates much over 2400 baud.

10.8 Navtex

A dedicated service on 518kHz giving information on navigation and weather reports, Navtex forms part of the GMDSS Maritime Safety Information (MSI) service. Data is received on a dedicated receiver on screen with storage or by a print-out. The system is in operation in the Mediterranean with information in English and (in some cases) the language of the country of origin. There are a number of message categories as follows:

A	Navigational warnings
B	Gale warnings
C	Ice reports
D	Distress information
E	Weather forecasts
F	Pilot Service messages
G	Decca messages
H	Loran-C messages
I	Omega messages
J	Satnav messages
L	Oil and gas rig information
Z	No messages on hand at present time

See Imray *Mediterranean Almanac* for Navtex coverage.

10.9 SafetyNET

SafetyNET is the SES-based MSI service for GMDSS. A receiver can be fitted to an INMARAST SES in order to facilitate reception of satellite-transmitted Enhanced Group Calls (EGC) MSI broadcasts. The Mediterranean comes under the Area of Responsibility NAV/METAREA III which is covered by the Atlantic Ocean Region – East Satellite footprint. All messages are issued from the LES Thermopylae, Greece.

Transmission schedule
Nav Info   1200, 2400 & on receipt (AOR-E)
Met Info   1000, 2200

10.10 Weatherfax

Weatherfax services are usually accessed using a HF receiver and appropriate computer and software or a dedicated weatherfax receiver. The quality of the charts obtained will depend on the strength of the radio signal, and on the quality of the printer (if used). Some Mediterranean weatherfax stations have been shut down and it is likely that more will go as the information is increasingly sourced from the internet.

For weatherfax station frequencies, transmission times and data please consult:
Imray *Mediterranean Almanac*
Admiralty *ALRS Small Craft NP289*
or the following websites:
HF-Fax. Listing of stations, frequencies and data
www.hffax.de
Frank Singleton. Links and explanations
www.franksingleton.clara.net
NOAA. World-wide stations. PDF download.
www.nws.noaa.gov/om/marine/radiofax.htm

10.11 Weather on the internet

There are a number of services on the Internet which provide up-to-date surface forecasts, text forecasts and satellite pictures. The options for connecting to the internet are the same as for email (see *10.7 Email*), only transmission rates really need to be at least 14400 baud. The cost of using a mobile phone and laptop are prohibitive unless transmission rates improve.

1. Laptop and GSM phone using GPRS (where network support exists). Speeds around 115bps. Cost based on amount downloaded, not time online.
2. Wireless Internet Access (Wi-Fi). One-off connection charge and 'pay-as-you-go' for minutes online. Costs are reasonable for a fast connection.
3. Using a satellite system such as IMMARSAT. At present only the very top-range systems have the capacity to access the internet.
4. Cyber-Cafés. If you know the sites you are looking for then half an hour will be more than sufficient to get weather data. Most cyber-cafés will let you print out surface charts for a small fee
5. Plugging into a conventional socket. This is a quick and easy way to access the internet using your own lap-top and a modem, preferably a PC card modem.

10.12 Grib weather files

Grib files are highly compressed weather files which cut download speeds compared to earlier compression formats. They can contain all sorts of data though commonly they have information on wind speed and pressure. The files can be downloaded off the internet or received by email and their small size makes them particularly suitable for receiving using slow modems such as SSB or GSM phone. You will need a Grib viewer and for some forecasts you will have to pay a subscription fee to the provider.
The first thing you will need is a Grib viewer.

- A number of software plotting systems have a Grib viewer including later versions of Raytech Navigator (this is the software I use), Max-Sea, and Nobeltec. In the future other software plotting systems are likely to include a Grib viewer.
- There are a number of free Grib viewers available including Airmail's Weather Fax Companion at www.siriuscyber.net/wxfax/ and I'm sure there are others out there.

Weather on the internet

Internet sites

Nemoc (Naval European Meteorology and Oceanography Center)
www.nemoc.navy.mil/ Click on 'weather charts'
This is the US navy site based in Rota which has good unclassified forecasts and maps for the Mediterranean. Many other private sites use the forecasts and maps from NEMOC (often without a source signature) so this is a good place to go first. Here you can get excellent text forecasts, surface analysis maps showing lows, highs and wind strength for next 36 hours, surface maps showing wave height and surface currents for next 36 hours, Meteosat photos updated hourly, satellite loop mpegs, wind and sea warnings, and much more. Excellent site which is quick to load.

Met Office site
www.meto.govt.uk/weather/charts/animation.html
Provides a B&W surface analysis map for pressure, highs and lows from Bracknell. Satellite photos of Europe. Updated daily. Difficult site to navigate because of all the pay features included. Basically you pre-pay for units to navigate some pages for data.

Frank Singleton's Weather Site
www.franksingleton.clara.net
An excellent overview of weather for sailors, with comprehensive links to weather sources.

Weather Online
www.weatheronline
Gives surface wind direction and strength up to a week ahead. Also synoptic charts. Good site.

Spain (Spanish Met Office)
www.inm.es/web/infmet/predi/metmar/indpuer1.html

France (Meteo France)
www.meteo.fr/meteonet/

Italy (Eurometeo)
www.eurometeo.com/english/meteomar

Greece (Poseidon)
www.poseidon.ncmr.gr/weather.html

Turkey (Turkish Met. Service)
www.meteor.gov.tr

Grib files are generated by various agencies, including NOAA, which many of the other sources rely on for their raw data. You can download free Grib files from various sources, but typically you will have to pay for some email services and for longer range data. Raytech, for example, allow free internet downloads (usually 3- day forecasts), but you must subscribe to the email service (up to 7-day forecasts). Have a look at the list below for sourcing Grib data.

- It is important to know that Grib files are entirely computer generated and have no human at the helm interpretting the data.
- Grib files are compressed in different ways and you may need some software to decompress the files depending on the viewer you are using. Compression can be .zip (use Winzip), .grb, or .bz2 and there may be others. Shareware or relatively cheap software can be downloaded to decompress the file formats.
- These weather files are all fairly broad stroke and do not provide the sort of detailed information found in more dedicated websites for a country or sea area. They provide an overall picture for a large sea area rather than detailed data for planning your sailing within a country.

For more information and Grib data sources look at
Airmail www.siriuscyber.net/wxfax/
Meteo-France www.meteofrance.com
Unzipping software
EF Commander www.bhs.com or WinRar 3.0 www.rarlab.com
Raytech Navigator (all-in-one Grib viewer and receiver) www.raymarine.com
Xaxero (I use their weatherfax software, the Grib viewer is a later addition) www.xaxero.com/gribplot
Maxsea (via Setsail which has a good site for the basics) www.setsail.com/maxsea
Sailmail www.sailmail.com
Marinenet www.marinenet.net
Navcenter www.navcenter.com

10.13 Coast radio

All Mediterranean countries operate coast radio stations which monitor the distress frequencies and the working frequencies used for services (port authorities, pilots, tugs, medical help, weather, navigation warnings, telephony services). Some work for limited hours and some are 24 hours. Some stations operate automatic direct dialling from ship to shore to national and international telephone networks. Schedules, frequencies, and services are listed in the *Imray Mediterranean Almanac*.

10.14 Radiotelephony rules

General rules governing radiotelephony:
1. Follow the correct voice procedures using prowords. Do not use CB terms.
2. Do not obstruct distress signals.
3. Do not use Ch 16 or 2182 when another working channel or frequency is available.
4. Identify the yacht by name and call sign when transmitting.
5. Do not transmit over another station already transmitting.
6. All transmissions are confidential and not for re-transmission.

7. Do not use bad language or obscenities.
8. In most harbours RT transmission is prohibited. In some countries there are heavy penalties for doing so.

In many of the Mediterranean countries correct procedures are not used by local craft but this does not excuse a visiting yacht from observing proper radio procedures.

10.15 Normal radiotelephony procedure

1. Select the required channel. Use a listed working channel in preference to Channel 16 or 2182.
2. Call the station as follows: (Call sign for station, e.g. *Hellas Radio*) this is (Name of vessel and call sign e.g. yacht *Fiddlers Green*) over.
3. If you get no reply after several attempts try: Do you read me? Another station may be able to relay your message or a reply if either is not being received.
4. When contact is made give your message spelling out any difficult words (if asked to) using the phonetic alphabet.
5. Confirmation of the message received will be: Received.
6. Finish your message with: Vessel name and call sign (e.g. yacht *Fiddlers Green*) out.

10.16 GMDSS Distress procedure

There are two categories:
MAYDAY Priority distress call at any time of serious and imminent danger when there is the possibility of loss of life.
PAN-PAN Urgent emergency where medical or other aid is required but loss of life is not likely.
1. DSC Distress and Urgency signals are automatically transmitted on Ch 70 or MF 2187.5 kHz when the DSC signal is sent.
2. Non-DSC Distress or Urgency RT calls are as for step 5.

For a DSC *MAYDAY* distress alert
1. Press DSC distress button   Procedure varies on
2. Select DISTRESS category   different sets
3. Press DSC distress button for 5 seconds
4. Wait 15 seconds, or after DSC acknowledgement if sooner
5. Transmit Distress call on VHF Ch 16 or MF 2182MHz:
MAYDAY MAYDAY MAYDAY
This is (yacht name or call sign 3 times e.g. . . . FIDDLERS GREEN . . . FIDDLERS GREEN . . . FIDDLERS GREEN).
MAYDAY (yacht name or call sign, and MMSI number) in position (give latitude and longitude/bearing and distance from a fixed point/close to. . . / distance off a major port).
I am (give brief description of problem e.g. I am sinking) OVER.
Listen for a reply and follow coastguard/ rescue authorities instructions.

For a DSC *PAN-PAN* call:
1. Press DSC distress button   Procedure varies on
2. Select URGENCY category   different sets
3. Press DSC distress button for 5 seconds
4. Wait 15 seconds, or after DSC acknowledgement if sooner
5. Transmit Pan-Pan call on VHF Ch 16 or MF 2182MHz:
PAN-PAN, PAN-PAN, PAN-PAN
ALL STATIONS, ALL STATIONS, ALL STATIONS,
This is (yacht name or call sign and MMSI)
Position
Nature of urgency (medical, tow needed, etc) and request assistance OVER
Listen for a reply and follow coastguard/rescue authorities instructions.

For a DSC Safety Message:

1. Press DSC distress button   Procedure varies on
2. Select SAFETY category   different sets
3. Press DSC distress button for 5 seconds
4. Wait 15 seconds, or after DSC acknowledgement if sooner
5. Transmit Securité call on VHF Ch 16 or MF 2182MHz:

SECURITÉ, SECURITÉ, SECURITÉ,
ALL STATIONS, ALL STATIONS, ALL STATIONS,
This is (yacht name or call sign and MMSI)
Position
Safety Message (restricted ability to manoeuvre)
Request (vessels to keep clear) OUT
Listen for a reply and follow coastguard/rescue authorities instructions.

For known MMSI routine or group call:
1. Enter MMSI number of the other vessel or group
2. Indicate ship-to-ship channel to be used for RT
3. Send message
4. Called vessel should initiate the RT on the requested channel

If the MMSI is not known:
1. Call on Ch 16
2. If there is no response try Ch 13
(GMDSS allocated bridge-to-bridge communications)

10.17 Ship-to-shore telephone calls

1. Have all information to hand including your AAIC (Accounting Authority Indicator Code).
2. Call a coast station which can make link calls to the telephone network. For many Mediterranean coast stations you will be allocated a channel or frequency for the call.
3. When answered give the vessels' name, call sign, and AAIC.
4. The operator will indicate if you have to wait or can proceed.
5. You may be allocated a duration time if there are a lot of calls queued up.

10.18 Prowords (procedure words)

All after	Used after the proword SAY AGAIN to request a repetition of a portion of a message
All before	Used after the proword SAY AGAIN to request a repetition of a portion of a message
Correct	Reply to a repetition of a message that has been preceded by the prowords READ BACK FOR CHECK when it has been correctly repeated
Correction	Spoken during transmission of a message means an error has been made in this transmission. Cancel the last word of group and substitute . . . .
In figures	See standard phonetic numerals.
In letters	The following numeral or group of numerals are to be written in letters, as spoken
I read back	If the receiving station is doubtful about the accuracy of the whole or any part of the message it may repeat it back to the sending station, preceding the repetition with the prowords I READ BACK
I say again	I am repeating a transmission or portion, as indicated
I spell	I SHALL SPELL OUT the next word or group of letters phonetically
Out	This is the end of working to you. The end of work between two stations is indicated by each station adding the word OUT to the end of its reply.
Over	The invitation to reply
Radio check	Please tell me the strength and clarity of my transmission
Received	Used to acknowledge receipt of a message, e.g. YOUR NUMBER. . .RECEIVED. In the case of language difficulties the word ROMEO is used
Say again	Repeat your message or portion referred to, e.g. SAY AGAIN ALL AFTER . . . OR SAY AGAIN ADDRESS, etc.
Station calling	Used when a station receives a call which is intended for it but is uncertain of the identification of the calling station
This is	This transmission is from the station whose call sign immediately follows. In the case of language difficulties the abbreviation DE spoken as DELTA ECHO is used
Wait	If a call station is unable to accept traffic immediately it will reply to you with the words WAIT . . . MINUTES. If the probable duration of the time exceeds 10 minutes the reason for the delay should be given
Word after or *word before*	Used after the prowords SAY AGAIN to request a repeat of a portion of a radio telegram or message
Wrong	Reply to a radio telegram that has been preceded by the words I READ BACK when it has been incorrectly repeated

10.19 The standard phonetic alphabet

Letter		Pronunciation			
A	alfa	ALfah	N	november	noVEMber
B	bravo	BRAHvoh	O	oscar	OSScar
C	charlie	CHARlee	P	papa	pahPAH
D	delta	DELLtah	Q	quebec	keyBECK
E	echo	ECKoh	R	romeo	ROWmeoh
F	foxtrot	FOKStrot	S	sierra	seeAIRrah
G	golf	golf	T	tango	TANgo
H	hotel	hohTELL	U	uniform	YOUneeform
I	india	INdeeah	V	victor	VIKtah
J	juliett	JEWleeETT	W	whisky	WISSkey
K	kilo	KEYloh	X	x-ray	ECKSRAY
L	lima	LEEmah	Y	yankee	YANGkey
M	mike	mike	Z	zulu	ZOOloo

STANDARD PHONETIC NUMERALS

Figure	Pronunciation
1	Wun
2	too
3	tree
4	FOW-er
5	fife
6	six
7	SEV-en
8	ait
9	NIN-er
0	zero

10.20 Morse Code

A	·—	N	—·	1	·————
B	—···	O	———	2	··———
C	—·—·	P	·——·	3	···——
D	—··	Q	——·—	4	····—
E	·	R	·—·	5	·····
F	··—·	S	···	6	—····
G	——·	T	—	7	——···
H	····	U	··—	8	———··
I	··	V	···—	9	————·
J	·———	W	·——	0	—————
K	—·—	X	—··—		
L	·—··	Y	—·——		
M	——	Z	——··		

Period (full stop) ·—·—·—
Comma   —·—·——
Colon   ———···
Interrogation (Also used for 'please repeat after...' when interrupting long messages) (IMI)   ··——··
Apostrophe ·————·

11. Weather

11.1 About weather data

Weather data in the Mediterranean is complicated by a number of factors.

1. The Mediterranean is subject to rapid changes in the weather generally not experienced elsewhere in Europe. Strong mountain gap winds like the *mistral* or coastal slope winds like the *bora* can appear out of nowhere from a clear sky and go from a flat calm to Force 8 in an hour.
2. There are big local variations in the weather which means that while you have a good Force 6 in one

area, in another there may be a gentle Force 3. Many of the recording stations are situated in atypical places for the generalised wind strengths and directions and so give a false picture of the overall weather pattern for the section of coast they represent. For example Sète in the Golfe du Lion sits in a pocket of comparative tranquillity compared to the coast on either side which is exposed to the full violence of the *tramontane* and *mistral*. Often a *tramontane* and *mistral* can blow at Force 6–7 at 50 miles either side of Sète whereas at Sète itself there is only a Force 3–4.

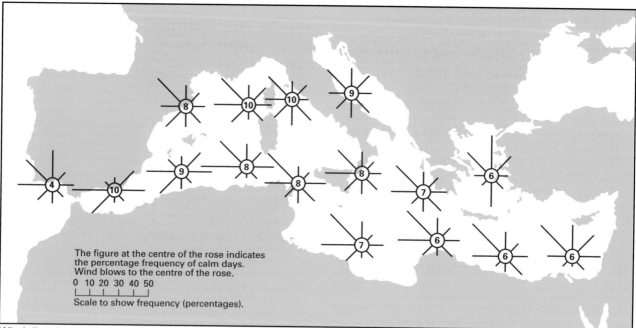

The figure at the centre of the rose indicates the percentage frequency of calm days.
Wind blows to the centre of the rose.
0 10 20 30 40 50
Scale to show frequency (percentages).

Wind direction and frequencies. April

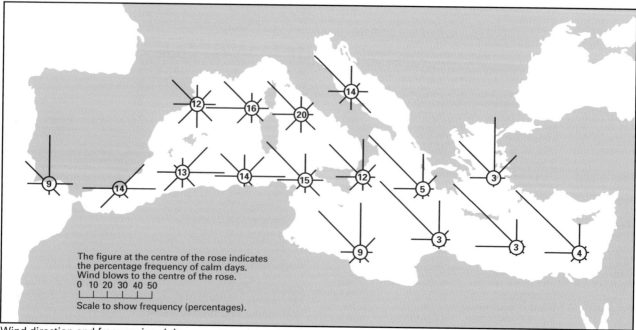

The figure at the centre of the rose indicates the percentage frequency of calm days.
Wind blows to the centre of the rose.
0 10 20 30 40 50
Scale to show frequency (percentages).

Wind direction and frequencies. July

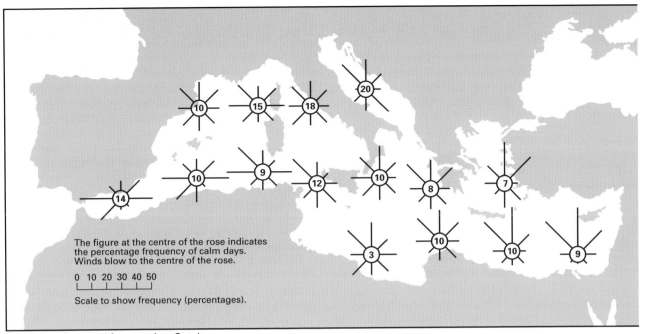

Wind directions and frequencies. October

The figure at the centre of the rose indicates the percentage frequency of calm days.
Winds blow to the centre of the rose.

0 10 20 30 40 50
Scale to show frequency (percentages).

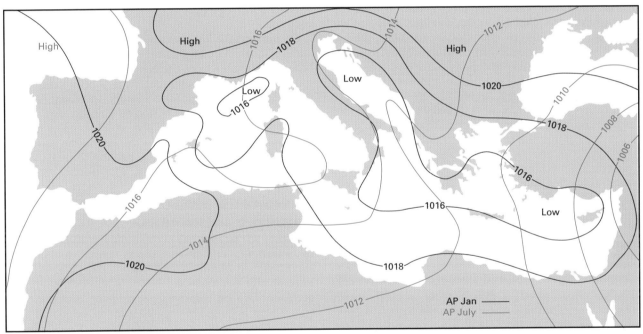

Air Pressure. January & July

AP Jan ———
AP July ———

3. In common with other weather recording stations elsewhere, many in the Mediterranean are often situated some distance inland, often at airports, and so give a false idea of wind strength and direction over the sea. In general wind strengths recorded 5 or more miles inland can be nearly doubled over the open sea assuming there are no funnelling or channelling effects at the recording station.

4. The effect of comparatively high land around much of the northern Mediterranean significantly alters wind directions and strengths. See *11.4 Coastal effects* for why wind strength seems greater around high coasts than the recorded figures might otherwise indicate.

11.2 Global Warming

Global warming refers to an increase in the overall average temperature of the world that is at least partly the result of human activity. The big culprit in all this is carbon dioxide emissions which have increased significantly since the industrial revolution began in the middle of the 19th century. Carbon dioxide stays in the upper atmosphere and while it lets light through, it does not let very much heat out. This is the greenhouse effect. It is just one factor in climate change which can be affected by all sorts of things, but it is an important issue because of the catastrophic influence global warming could have on the world's weather in the next century and indeed may be having on weather patterns today. Global warming and cooling has always been around, but what is significant here is the scale of the change over a comparatively short period of time and how that will affect the weather that we as yachtsmen take to be the norm.

Without going into all the ramifications of the debate it is possible to say that most climatologists believe that global warming is occurring and that some general conclusions can be drawn from the data that is available.

Is it really happening?

The Intergovernmental Panel on Climate Change (IPCC) set up in 1988 by the UN and the World Meteorological Organisation concluded in 1997 that: 'The balance of evidence suggests a discernible human influence on global climate'. Studies of *El Niño* off the South American coast point to the longest warming of waters from 1990-1995 in 130 years of records, an event expected to occur only once every 2000 years given normal conditions. In the last century the average global temperature rose by 0·5°C. A conservative estimate of the rise in global warming by 2100 is for temperatures to be 2°C higher than 1990 and for sea levels to be 50cm higher than present levels. This might not seem much but small changes in temperature over a relatively short period of time can lead to dramatic changes in the weather. Some of the counter arguments to the global warming models which point to climatic temperature changes in the past are talking about time periods for these changes measured in thousands of years, not in decades.

For those yachtsmen, especially in the northern hemisphere, who imagine that global warming will lead to a pleasant Mediterranean climate along the south coast of England, the bad news is that it does not work this way. The effects of global warming for northern waters is that weather patterns become more disturbed with big fluctuations between hot and cold temperatures. Rain becomes less evenly distributed and there is a high likelihood of heavy downpours followed by long periods of drought. And the weather in terms of depressions and storms becomes less clearly defined between the seasons.

Tropical storms and mid-latitude hurricanes

The simplistic model is that because tropical storms arise in waters with temperatures in the region of 26°C and above, then an increase in sea temperature could mean that tropical storms will increase in number and affect areas not normally within tropical storm zones. This scenario is not completely ruled out but the models need to take into account a lot of other variables like wind flows and different wind speeds in the atmosphere (vertical wind shear). For the records, the number of hurricanes in the Atlantic has gone down (despite the bad years of 1994–1995) but the number of typhoons in the Pacific has gone up. The few models which have been run are unsatisfactory and in world terms there seems to be no overall increase in tropical storms predicted although some areas may have an increase in numbers and others a decrease. There also appears to be no corresponding increase in intensity although the variation in hurricane tracks appears to be more erratic.

Hurricanes and typhoons grab the headlines, but mid-latitude hurricanes or extratropical storms which originate outside normal hurricane breeding grounds are of more concern to the yachtsman as they affect seas and coasts not normally in hurricane areas. Coasts and yacht harbours can be devastated by the effects of a hurricane as happened with the October hurricane that hit Britain in 1987. While the models point to fewer hurricanes they also predict these will be of increased intensity in areas like the North Atlantic. Studies of the hard data point to an increase in storm intensity and a trend to increasing winds and wave heights in the North Atlantic since the 1980s.

Depressions

One of the consequences of global warming is likely to be less settled weather in the summer season. Are the seasons becoming less settled or is the weather pretty much as it always was?

Backed by some 20 years of observation in the Mediterranean, I and others believe that weather patterns are shifting. The number of depressions passing through the eastern Mediterranean in the late spring and early summer also seems to be on the increase. The Azores high seems to take a longer time period to stabilise the weather patterns so that the seasons seem to occur about a month later than they used to.

Of importance to yachtsmen in the Aegean is the *meltemi*, the prevailing summer wind which normally blows predictably from the NE through N to NW from mid-June to early September. It is a boisterous wind that often blows up to 30–35 knots. In recent years it seems to have moved its period to late July through to October and it now often blows at 40 knots or dies to a paltry 10 knots. Likewise in the spring the unsettled weather caused by depressions passing through seems to go on longer than it used to. The trouble with this type of observation is that it is short term and statistically means little over the longer period.

Waterspouts and tornadoes

Evidence for an increase in the numbers and intensities of waterspouts and tornadoes which hit coastal locations is difficult to find statistically. Waterspouts have always been around but it is difficult to gather accurate data on numbers because the duration of a waterspout is normally only 20 minutes or so and they are localised phenomenon. Windspeeds are calculated to be in the 50-100 knot band. However a new breed of waterspout, the 'water' tornado or double funnel spout is more like a land tornado over the water with possible wind speeds up to 400 mph. A number of these have been recorded and studied, notably on the east coast of the USA, with one figuring in the news in 1997 at Miami. These water tornadoes are significantly bigger and more violent than waterspouts and do not appear to break up when moving from the land to the sea or vice versa.

Whether they are connected to global warming is difficult to know, but theoretically it would seem likely that localised patches of hot and cold air resulting from global warming could produce bigger and more violent waterspouts.

The *meltemi* in the eastern Mediterranean is a special case and in the summer months it can get quite boisterous at times

Rainfall

One thing the models for global warming can predict with some accuracy is a disruption to normal rainfall patterns. Rainfall already appears to be conforming to predictions with heavy precipitation over short periods becoming common and a shift in regional precipitation patterns occurring. Global warming will cause more rain overall but it will fall in different regions and in heavy downpours.

Flooding of river estuaries will become more common and flash floods can cause a lot of damage to craft moored in an estuary and to marinas within rivers and estuaries. After a period of dry weather large amounts of rain inland can back up until a flood wave sweeps down the river carrying trees and other debris with it to an estuary where yachts may be moored.

For yachtsmen cruising to lower latitudes water shortages are likely to become a real problem. While global warming brings more rain, it will mostly be distributed in high northerly latitudes. Water shortages in the Mediterranean are a likely scenario, indeed are already a reality in some areas of the Mediterranean, and it will be more and more difficult to find good potable water.

For users of inland waterways short periods of heavy rain can close sections of a waterway where it is close to a river or where there is heavy run-off, and periods of prolonged drought mean that at other times waterways may be closed because there is insufficient water. This already occurs in the Canal du Midi which has been closed at certain times of the year because of lack of water. Ironically warmer temperatures mean that the Alpine snows melt more quickly producing strong currents in rivers like the Rhone.

Destruction of natural habitats

For most people, going sailing is as much about arriving at a quiet beautiful place as putting up sails and pulling on ropes. Increased sea levels affect natural habitats like estuarine wetlands and it is likely that many of these will disappear along with the bird and marine life associated with them. In tropical waters coral reefs will likely be effected by global warming as slightly warmer tropical water may kill the algae which reef animals feed on. In the Mediterranean there has been some discussion over whether weed growth has occurred in the comparatively shallow water where yachts anchor.

Weather conditions can change quickly in the Mediterranean and you need to take care that what was a peaceful berth when you arrived does not turn into a dangerous situation when you go shopping in town

11.3 Prevailing summer winds

Sea breezes In the Mediterranean most of the prevailing winds in the summer are sea breezes. There are a number of special cases and a few interruptions from depressions passing over Europe or unseasonally through the Mediterranean, but for most observations the sea breeze prevails and can be relied upon for over 50% of the time in most places and for up to 75% of the time in a few places during the summer months.

The sea breeze blows because of the pressure difference set up by the variable effect of the sun on the land and sea. By day the land heats up more quickly than the sea and causes air to flow in over the hotter land from the cooler sea. By night a gentle land breeze may blow when the land cools mor quickly than the sea and so air flows from the cooler land to the warmer sea. The following should be noted in relation to the sea breeze:

1. The relatively high temperatures of the Mediterranean mean that sea breezes are not the gentle zephyrs of northern Europe. In many places the temperature differences generate winds up to Force 5–6 and can reach up to 50 miles off the coast.
2. There is a fairly accurate wind clock for the sea breeze. As the land warms up in the morning the sea breeze will begin to blow at 1100–1200 local time at around Force 2–3. Usually within an hour the wind will get up to Force 4–6 and will blow through the afternoon until early evening. The wind will die off fairly quickly around 1900–2000 local time. The abruptness of the change is linked to the air temperatures and geography of a region. In general the higher the temperature the more abrupt the transition between morning calm and the onset of the full force of the sea breeze. The terrain affects the sea breeze according to altitude. Low-lying plains or gentle S-facing slopes will heat up more quickly than mountain ranges with valleys in shadow for much of the day, and so generate greater pressure differences and stronger winds.
3. Where there are other winds or light winds generated by other pressure effects, the sea breeze will often reverse the light winds or will introduce a diurnal thermal effect on special case winds.
4. At night a light land breeze may blow off the land but it rarely exceeds 10 knots except where there is a katabatic effect.
5. The Coriolis effect. The earth spinning on its axis deflects objects from a straight line. In the northern hemisphere this deflection is to the right and introduces a slight westerly component into the wind equation. Thus a sea breeze which might blow from the SW onto a coast will be deflected so it blows from the WSW at a slight angle to the land.

The *meltemi* is a special case in that it is the prevailing wind over the Aegean caused by pressure differences at a macro level. It blows throughout most of the summer, starting gently in June and ending around the end of September. It can blow at Force 6–7 and although there may be a slight thermal component lessening its strength in the late evening, it usually blows night and day for up to two weeks before there is a brief respite for a few days. It is caused by a pressure gradient between the Azores high and the monsoon low over Pakistan. Only in the Aegean is the pressure gradient pronounced enough to produce these constant summer winds. From the Dardanelles it blows from the NE curving down through the Aegean to blow from the N and NW before curving to blow from the W around Rhodes.

11.4 Coastal effects

The steep-to indented coast and offshore islands produce pronounced effects on winds near it. Moving air takes the path of least resistance so any land in its way can alter the strength and/or direction of the wind. The following is a very general round-up of coastal effects on wind blowing out to sea with a comparatively constant direction and strength.

1. *Lifting effects* Where a light wind blowing off the sea hits the land it tends to lift, leaving a calm area close to the coast. Not until the wind gets up to Force 3–4 will the calm patch be filled in. Where a sea breeze meets an opposing wind there will also be a calm patch or variable light winds until the sea breeze overcomes the opposing wind.
2. *Straight coast* Wind blowing onto the coast at an oblique angle will often be deflected along it if high land prevents it blowing over the land. Until the wind gets up to sufficient strength to blow over any obstacles it can often be deflected by up to 90° along the coast.
3. *Headlands* Wind blowing onto a headland will be deflected around it until it gets to sufficient strength to blow over it. The wind tends to flow around a headland until it meets the main air-flow again. It will also increase in strength as it is compressed onto the headland and around it. When the wind gets up to a sufficient strength it will lift over the headland and fall off the lee side in strong gusts. These can be severe in places.
4. *Funnelling* When wind lifts over land it will often be funnelled down a valley or other path of least resistance on the lee side, often resulting in severe gusts. In general the lee sides of islands and peninsulas will have more wind gusting off them than the wind out to sea on the windward side.
5. *Channelling* Where wind is forced into a channel by high land on either side it will increase in strength and will often come from variable directions, frequently squalls off the high coast on either side. The Strait of Messina is a classic example of channelling.
6. *Katabatic winds* A katabatic wind occurs at night when the land breeze on high cold slopes flows down to the sea. As it cools further with dropping night temperatures and cool land it acquires mass and accelerates down valleys. At sea level it can blow at Force 6–7, usually for 2–4 hours. It occurs most frequently in the spring and autumn when there are comparatively large differences between day and night temperatures.
7. *Anabatic winds* Normally the sea breeze blowing up a coastal slope which tends to reduce its strength.

Cloud Types

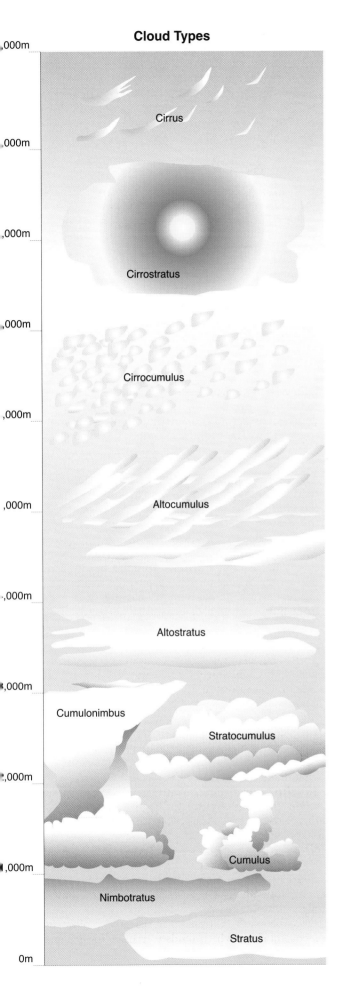

,000m

,000m

,000m

,000m

,000m

,000m

-,000m

,000m

,000m

,000m

0m

Cirrus

Cirrostratus

Cirrocumulus

Altocumulus

Altostratus

Cumulonimbus

Stratocumulus

Cumulus

Nimbotratus

Stratus

Coastal effects

Wind is compressed by high coast and increases in strength

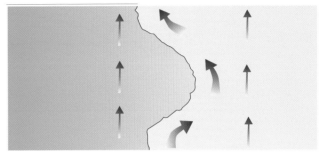

Wind is compressed near high coast and follows contours of the land

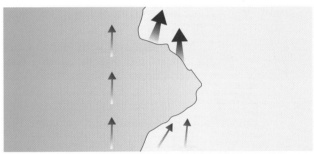

Wind gusts off lee side of high headland

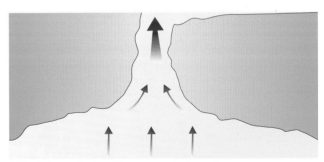

Wind channelled and increases in strength

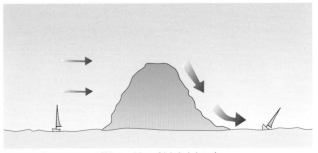

Wind often gusts off lee side of high islands

11. WEATHER

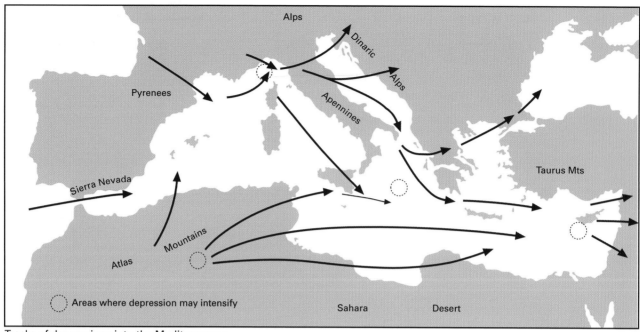

Tracks of depressions into the Mediterranean

11.5 Gales

Between summer and winter there is a marked difference in weather patterns. In the summer pressure gradients are relatively stable and there are few cyclonic changes. In the winter nearly all weather is from disturbed cyclonic patterns, with depressions entering the Mediterranean and directly causing bad weather or passing over Europe or North Africa and indirectly causing bad weather. The following points are general observations on gales in the Mediterranean.

1. Depressions from the Atlantic tend to enter the Mediterranean directly through the Strait of Gibraltar, drop down from Europe into the Golfe du Lion or Gulf of Genoa, or swing up from North Africa across the east coast of Tunisia. Because depressions passing through the Mediterranean follow an erratic path at an erratic speed compared to the fairly predictable tracks and plodding speed of depressions across the Atlantic, they are difficult to track and weather forecasts cannot be relied upon to give accurate predictions of the speed and direction of a depression.

2. There are a number of places where depressions tend to linger and deepen. The most well known are the Gulf of Genoa, around the Atlas Mountains, in the Ionian, and to a lesser extent in the SE Mediterranean off Cyprus.

3. The map of gale force winds in the Mediterranean shows the likely percentage of gales in any area in the winter. Many of these gale force winds are the indirect result of depressions passing over Europe from mountain gap or coastal slope winds and are

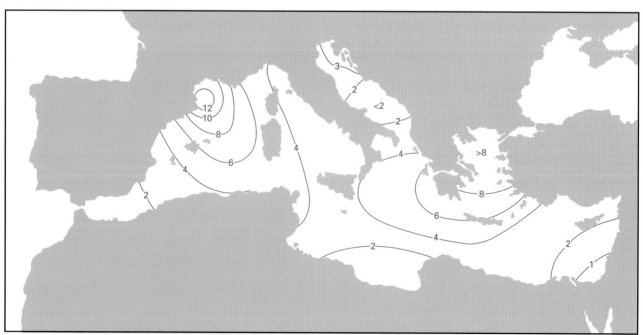

Percentage frequency of gales in the winter

not from actual depressions in the Mediterranean itself.

4. *Mountain gap winds* These winds result when cold air from a depression passing across Europe is bottled up behind mountains until it finds a gap to escape through. The classic examples are the *mistral* and *tramontane*. These result from a depression passing across central France and cold air finding an escape route down the Rhône valley between the Massif Central and the Alps (producing the *mistral*) and/or through the Toulouse Gap between the Massif Central and the Pyrenees (producing the *tramontane*). In the winter these two winds are much to be feared, blowing out of a clear sky with little warning and often reaching gale force and sometimes Force 10–11. The *levanter* blowing in the Strait of Gibraltar is another example of a mountain gap wind.

5. *Coastal slope winds* These winds result when cold air from an unstable airstream falls off plateaux and coastal slopes onto a warm sea. The classic example is the *bora* in the Adriatic which can blow at gale force and up to Force 10–11 out of a clear sky with little warning. The *vardaarac* blowing out of the Gulf of Thessaloniki is another example.

6. *Desert winds* Blow off the hot desert when a depression passes through the Mediterranean. The classic example is the *sirocco* which off the North African coast is dry and dusty but is more often sultry and humid by the time it passes over the sea and reaches Europe. It will often blow at gale force though rarely more.

7. *Thunderstorms* May be associated with a cold front or in the summer result from thermal instability ('heat thunderstorms').

11.6 Named Mediterranean winds

Named winds do not indicate frequency nor force, although they do often reflect strong winds from a specific direction. For more details on locally named winds see *14 The Mediterranean Countries*. Winds are listed in alphabetical order.

Arifi Strong *sirocco* in Morocco.
Bise Cold dry NE blowing into the Golfe du Lion.
Bora Coastal slope N–NE wind blowing into the Adriatic off the Dinaric Alps.
Borasco General term for gales in Italy although often applied to W–SW gales.
Borino Small *bora* in the Adriatic.
Chergui Warm dry *sirocco* in Morocco.
Chili Hot dry *sirocco* in Algeria and Tunisia.
Chom Hot dry southerly in Algeria.
Dzhani Generally a warm dry southerly in Algeria.
Etesians Ancient name for the *meltemi* from the Greek *etos* (annual).
Gharbi Strong moist SW wind in Morocco. Known as the *gharbis* in Italy and Greece where it brings the 'red rain' containing Saharan dust.
Ghibli Strong *sirocco* in Tunisia.
Gregale Strong NE wind blowing over the Ionian as far as Malta. From *grecale*, the 'Greek wind'.
Imbat Sea breeze in North Africa. Local name for the *meltemi* around Izmir.
Khamsin Hot dry *sirocco* in Egypt.
Levante Strong E–NE winds in Spain.
Levanter Strong E mountain gap wind blowing in the Strait of Gibraltar.
Leveche Hot, dry dusty SE wind in Spain.
Llevantades NE gale in Spain.
Libeccio Moderate to strong W–SW winds in the Tyrrhenian and Corsica.
Maestral General term for northerlies in France.
Maestrale Cold dry wind in the Gulf of Genoa.
Maistro (Maestro) N–NW sea breeze in the southern Adriatic and Greek Ionian.

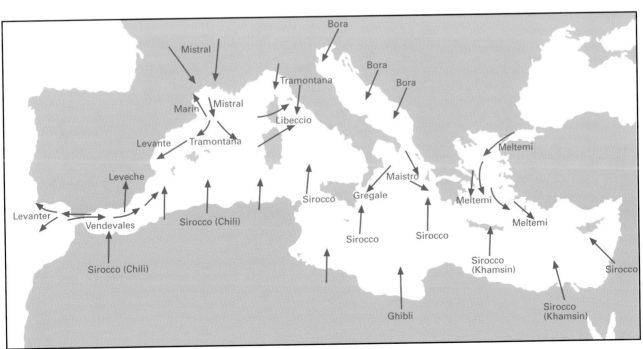

Local Winds

Marin S–SE sea breeze in France.

Meltemi The prevailing summer northerlies in the Aegean.

Mestral General term for northerlies in Spain (see *maestral*).

Mistral Strong N mountain gap wind blowing down the Rhône Valley.

Ponente Westerlies in Italy and Greece.

Sharav Hot dry *sirocco* in Israel.

Simoon Hot dry S winds usually associated with dust storms. Literally means 'the poisoner'.

Sirocco General term for the S desert wind blowing off North Africa.

Tramontane A N mountain gap wind blowing into the Golfe du Lion and along the Spanish coast. Also *tramontana*.

Vardaarac N Coastal slope wind blowing out of the Gulf of Thessaloniki.

Vendeval W winds in the Strait of Gibraltar. Also *vendevales*.

11.7 The Beaufort Scale

BEAUFORT SCALE OF WIND STRENGTH

Sea State	Beaufort No.	Description	Velocity in knots	Velocity in km/h	Term	Code	Wave height in metres
Like a mirror	0	Calm, glassy	<1	<1	Calm	0	0
Ripples	1	Light airs Rippled	1–3	1–5	Calm	1	0–0.1
Small wavelets	2	Light breeze Wavelets	4–6	6–11	Smooth	2	0.1–0.5
Large wavelets	3	Gentle breeze	7–10	12–19	Slight	3	0.5–1.25
Small waves, breaking	4	Moderate breeze	11–16	20–28	Moderate	4	1.25–2.5
Moderate waves, foam	5	Fresh breeze	17–21	29–38	Rough	5	2.5–4
Large waves, foam and spray	6	Strong breeze	22–27	39–49			
Sea heads up, foam in streaks	7	Near gale	28–33	50–61	Very rough	6	4–6
Higher long waves, foam in streaks	8	Gale	34–40	62–74			
High waves, dense foam, spray impairs visibility	9	Strong gale	41–47	75–88	High	7	6–9
Very high tumbling waves, surface white with foam, visibility affected	10	Storm	48–55	89–102	Very high	8	9–14
Exceptionally high waves, sea covered in foam, visibility affected	11	Violent storm	56–62	103–117	Phenomenal	9	Over 14
Air filled with spray and foam, visibility severely impaired	12	Hurricane	>63	>118			

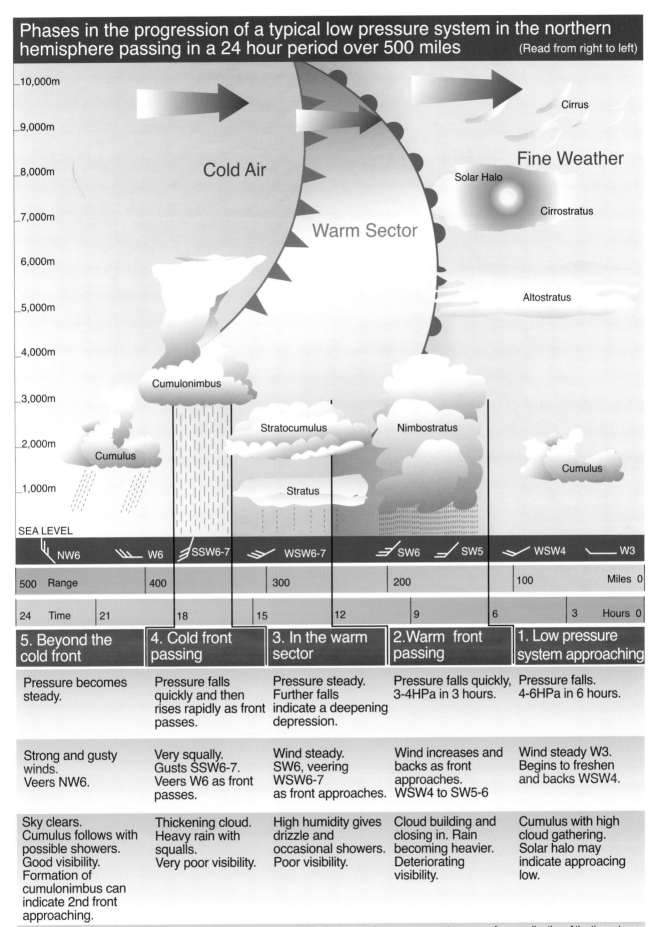

Phases in the progression of a typical low pressure system in the northern hemisphere passing in a 24 hour period over 500 miles

(Read from right to left)

Cold Air

Warm Sector

Fine Weather

Cirrus

Solar Halo

Cirrostratus

Altostratus

Cumulonimbus

Stratocumulus

Nimbostratus

Cumulus

Cumulus

Stratus

SEA LEVEL

NW6	W6	SSW6-7	WSW6-7	SW6	SW5	WSW4	W3

500	Range	400		300		200		100		Miles 0

24	Time	21		18		15		12		9		6		3	Hours 0

5. Beyond the cold front	4. Cold front passing	3. In the warm sector	2. Warm front passing	1. Low pressure system approaching
Pressure becomes steady.	Pressure falls quickly and then rises rapidly as front passes.	Pressure steady. Further falls indicate a deepening depression.	Pressure falls quickly, 3-4HPa in 3 hours.	Pressure falls. 4-6HPa in 6 hours.
Strong and gusty winds. Veers NW6.	Very squally. Gusts SSW6-7. Veers W6 as front passes.	Wind steady. SW6, veering WSW6-7 as front approaches.	Wind increases and backs as front approaches. WSW4 to SW5-6	Wind steady W3. Begins to freshen and backs WSW4.
Sky clears. Cumulus follows with possible showers. Good visibility. Formation of cumulonimbus can indicate 2nd front approaching.	Thickening cloud. Heavy rain with squalls. Very poor visibility.	High humidity gives drizzle and occasional showers. Poor visibility.	Cloud building and closing in. Rain becoming heavier. Deteriorating visibility.	Cumulus with high cloud gathering. Solar halo may indicate approacing low.

Note. Weather systems vary enormously in their size and speed. Mediterranean low pressure systems are often smaller than Atlantic systems.

11. WEATHER

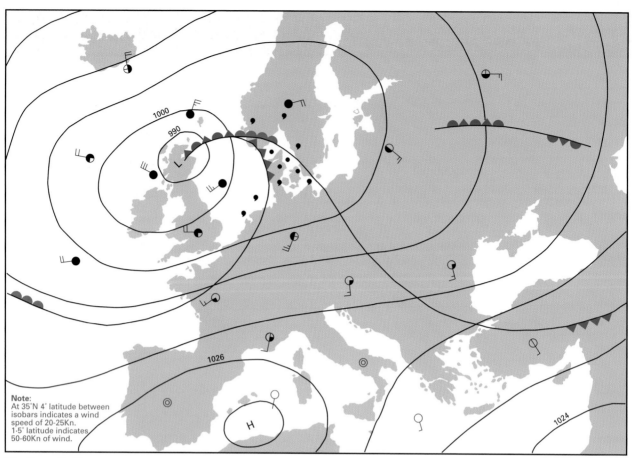

Note:
At 35°N 4° latitude between
isobars indicates a wind
speed of 20-25Kn.
1·5° latitude indicates
50-60Kn of wind.

The Synoptic Chart

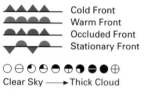

▲▲▲▲	Cold Front	●	Rain
●●●●	Warm Front	✳	Snow
▲●▲●	Occluded Front	◗	Drizzle
▼▼▼	Stationary Front	◖	Hurricane
		≡	Fog

Clear Sky ──► Thick Cloud

◎   ◯⌐ ◯⌐ ◯⌐ ◯⌐ ◯⌐ ◯◥
Calm 5Kn 10Kn 15Kn 20Kn 25Kn 50Kn from NE

| ⊺ | Thunderstorm |
| ↳ | Squall |

12. Routes to the Mediterranean

12.1 Northern Europe

There are three main routes to the Mediterranean from Northern Europe.

The outer sea passage

The outer sea passage across Biscay and down the coast of Spain and Portugal to the Strait of Gibraltar is the quickest route. It is used by delivery skippers, those who do not want to bother with the inland waterways routes, or those whose draught, breadth or air height bars them from the inland waterways.

For those who like port-hopping it is possible to cruise around the coast with few long passages between harbours or anchorages. The Atlantic coasts of France, Spain and Portugal provide a wonderful cruising area and a significant number of foreign boats are permanently based on the Iberian peninsula to take advantage of the cruising to be had there.

For those not port-hopping the intermediate route is normally to La Coruña on the NW corner of Spain and then in shorter stages to Bayona (Spain), Leixões, Lisbon, Vilamoura (all in Portugal), Puerto Sherry, Algeciras (in Spain) and into the Mediterranean through the Strait of Gibraltar.

For the outer passage the following should be noted.

Weather For the most part passages across the Bay of Biscay are trouble-free in the summer but there is still the risk of a gale and Biscay gales can be fearsome. The incidence of gales in Biscay increases dramatically either side of the equinox and if at all possible passage should be made in the settled summer months. The incidence of gale force winds decreases dramatically in the summer with about a 3% chance of gale force winds in July and August compared to 20% in May and October.

Fog The Spanish and Portuguese coasts, especially from La Coruña to Lisbon, are prone to coastal fog. Fog is most common in July and August when there can be a 10–12% chance of fog along the coast.

Shipping From the English Channel to Gibraltar there is a constant risk of encountering shipping. In the English Channel separation zones operate and a yacht is required to cross the shipping lanes as near to a right angle as possible. A traffic separation scheme bends SW at Ouessant and there will be numerous ships heading into or out of the channel. Across Biscay no traffic separation scheme operates and shipping may be encountered heading in either direction. Off Cabo de Roca, Lisbon, Cabo de São Vicente and in the approaches to the Strait of Gibraltar separation schemes operate. There is substantial traffic along the Spanish and Portuguese coasts but it is not until the Strait of Gibraltar that things get crowded. There is always a lot of traffic in the Strait of Gibraltar and care must be taken of rogue ships outside the proper lane.

Fishing boats There are usually concentrations of fishing boats S of Ouessant and off the Spanish and Portuguese coasts from La Coruña to Cádiz. The danger from fishing boats is from their often erratic handling which can be frightening when a large trawler emerges at speed from fog, and from the variety of lights shown at night which do not always conform to international regulations or to any regulations at all.

Offshore hazards Apart from the jagged rocks and reefs fringing Ouessant (not to mention the strong tidal streams) there are few hazards if 10M off the Spanish and Portuguese coasts.

Strait of Gibraltar As you approach the Strait of Gibraltar care must be taken of the large amount of shipping entering or leaving the Mediterranean, the tidal streams in the strait, and worst of all a *levanter* blowing out of the strait.

Pilots

Bay of Biscay (NP22) (Admiralty)
West Coast of Spain and Portugal (NP66) (Admiralty)
Ocean Passages and Landfalls Rod Heikell and Andy O'Grady (Imray)
The Cruising Almanac (Cruising Association/Imray)
North Brittany K. Adlard Coles/John Lawson (RCC Pilotage Foundation/Imray)
North Biscay Mike and Gill Barron (RCC Pilotage Foundation/Imray)
South Biscay John Lawson (RCC Pilotage Foundation/Imray)
Atlantic Spain and Portugal Anne Hammick (RCC Pilotage Foundation/Imray)

French Inland Waterways

There are two main arterial routes, with variations along the way.

1. The main route is from Le Havre or Calais to Paris, the central canals along one of three routes (the most direct being the Yonne and Canal de Bourgogne), and the rivers Saône and Rhône.

2. The 50–50 route from the Bay of Biscay and then the Canal Latéral à la Garonne and Canal du Midi from Bordeaux to Sète.

When planning to traverse the waterways passage time is largely dictated by the number of locks. There is a speed limit in most of the older canals of 8km/hr for craft under 20 tons and 6km/h for craft over 20 tons although it is not always closely observed. In the commercial waterways on canalised rivers like the Seine and Rhône, speed limits are higher, at around 8 knots up to 20 tons and 13 knots over 20 tons.

Waterways dimensions are as follows:

Length Effectively the length of the locks determines the maximum LOA for the inland waterways. In most of the locks the maximum length that will fit is 30m (98·4ft) or more. In the European Class IV Waterways (the Seine, Oise, lower Saône, Rhône and part of the Gironde) locks are 144m (472·43ft) long. In the Brittany canals the maximum length that will fit is 25m (82ft). Unless you own a *péniche* designed for the French waterways it is likely that breadth, draught, and air height are the limiting factors.

See
*Inland Waterways
of France*
for dimensions
and routes

IRELAND

ENGLAND

*North
Sea*

London

Lek

Waal

Maas

Calais • Dunkerque

St Valéry • *Nord*

English Channel

Le • Rouen
Havre

Somme

Meuse

Moselle

Rhine

• Regensburg

Paris •

Seine

Oise

Marne

Nancy •

*Marne au
Rhin*

Ouessant •

St Malo •

Rance

Vitry-
Le-F •

Toul •

Danube

Brest •

Brittany

Vilaine

Montereau •

Loing

*C de
l'Est*

• Donaueschingen

*Lat à la
Loire*

*Marne à
Saône*

Saône

• Basle

St Nazaire •

Nantes à Brest

Nantes •

*Rhône au
Rhin*

La Rochelle •

Decize •

• Châlon

*Atlantic
Ocean*

Bourgogne

Gironde

Royan •

Bordeaux •

FRANCE

Centre

Lyon •

Rhône

ITALY

*Bay of
Biscay*

*C. lat à la
Garonne*

Avignon • Nice •

• La Coruna

Toulouse •

Arles •

C. Finisterre

• Bayona

Sète •

P. St Louis

Marseille

Corsica

SPAIN

*Islas
Baleares*

Sardinia

• Lisbon

PORTUGAL

*Mediterranean
Sea*

From
the Azores

• Vilamoura

Gibraltar

0   100   200

Strait of Gibraltar

NORTH AFRICA

Kilometres

NOTHERN EUROPEAN ROUTES

Breadth The width of the locks (and some bridges) determines the maximum breadth for the inland waterways. The maximum breadth for most of the locks (without fenders) is 5m (16·4ft). European Class IV waterways are 12m (39·4ft) wide. In the Brittany canals the maximum breadth for the locks is 4·50m (14·75ft).

Draught and air height

The maximum dimensions for draught and air height vary as follows:

St Malo to St Nazaire 1·30m (4·26ft) max. draught and 2·40m (7·87ft) air height.

Le Havre to Paris 2·50m (8·2ft) max. draught and 5·97m (19·6ft) air height.

St Valéry to Paris 1·80m (5·9ft) max. draught and 3·40m (11·15ft) air height.

Calais to Paris 2·18m (7·15ft) max. draught and 3·68m (12·07ft) air height.

Paris to the Saône (Yonne and Canal de Bourgogne) 1·80m (5·9ft) max. draught and 3·40m (11·15ft) air height.

Paris to the Saône (Canal du Loing, Canal Latéral à la Loire, and Canal du Centre) 1·80m (5·9ft) max. draught and 3·48m (11·41ft) air height.

Paris to the Saône (Marne, Canal Latéral à la Marne and Canal de la Marne a la Saône) 1·80m (5·9ft) and 3·50m (11·48ft) air height.

Rivers Saône and Rhône 3·0m (9·8ft) max. draught and 7·0m (23·0ft) air height (using the Macon bypass, otherwise max. air height on the Saône is 3·70m (12·1ft) under the Pont Saint-Laurent).

Bordeaux to Sète (Canal Latéral à la Garonne and Canal du Midi) 1·60m (5·25ft) max. draught and 3·25m (10·66ft) air height 3·0m (9·8ft) at the sides). In 1990/91 the section of the Canal du Midi between Toulouse and Trèbes was closed because of a prolonged drought. In 1992 a depth of only 1·40m (4·6ft) was guaranteed. In 1994 the water supply was back to normal and 1·60m (5·25ft) was again the norm.

Note Depths in the canals can be reduced by silting although with sufficient power a yacht can usually push through. The debris on the bottom is usually dead leaves from the autumn forming a sludge that you can carve a channel through with a yacht keel. Water shortages may also effect the available depths so if you are on the margin try to go through in the spring when feeder reservoirs and rivers will have been topped up from melting winter snow and spring rainfall. There may also be other waterways debris such as old bicycles, water–logged logs, park benches, etc.

Effectively this means that for the two main routes the limiting dimensions are as follows:

1. Le Havre to the Mediterranean via the Seine, Paris, central canals, Saône and Rhône. Max LOA 30m (98·4ft). Max breadth 5m (16·4ft). Max draught 1·80m (5·9ft). Max. air height 3·40 to 3·50m (11·15 to 11·48ft).
2. Bordeaux to the Mediterranean via the Canal Latéral à la Garonne and Canal du Midi to Sète. Max. LOA 30m (98·4ft). Max. breadth 5m (16·4ft). Max. draught 1·60m (5·25ft). Max air height 3·25m (10·66ft).

Hours of navigation Effectively daylight hours determine lock operation. In the summer locks are open 0630–1930. On canals where there is no commercial traffic the locks are not manned in the winter and navigation stops. From around November to March you will have to make special arrangements, normally this means contacting the first lock-keeper who will telephone the others although there can be hiccups if a lock-keeper has decided to go to see his mother or do some shopping.

Chômages Periodically the canals will be drained or closed for maintenance, usually in the winter or late autumn/early spring. In most cases only a section of the canal is drained. Work usually takes around 6–8 weeks for a drained section.

Waterways charges Charges are levied on a Day Rate, Holiday Rate (16 days inclusive with specified dates), Leisure Rate (30 days which need not be consecutive), or an Annual Rate. Charges are based on boat length x breadth (m²) and may be paid by post to any VNF regional or head office, or directly at any of nearly forty offices along the waterways. Payment may be made by cheque (in Euros), or by Visa, Mastercard or Eurocard.

Note There is no charge for craft under 5 metres and powered by an engine of 9.9 HP or less.

Offices have been set up in the major ports to administer the paperwork and collect the fees.

Note A CEVNI certificate is mandatory for travelling on European waterways. Details of the Certificate may be obtained from the RYA.

For information on all French canals, *chômages* and up-to-date charges, the VNF website (with English text version) is excellent at www.vnf.fr or at the VNF head office. Voies Navigables de France (VNF), 175 rue Ludovic Boutleux BP 820, 62400 Bethune Cedex ☎ 03 21 63 24 54 *Fax* 03 21 63 24 42.

Harbours Secure places to berth for the night vary from waterway to waterway. Some of the waterways have numerous harbours or village quays suitable for the night whereas on others it is necessary to plan where to stop for the night. For the two main routes there are few difficulties in the canals where there are

Lock and sluice on the Canal du Midi

INTERNATIONAL WATERWAY SIGNS

LOCK SIGNALS

 No entry

 Opening soon

 Enter now

 Lock not in operation

SOUNDS

—	Attention
•	I am turning to starboard
••	I am turning to port
•••	I am going astern
••••	I am incapable of manoeuvring
•••••	Danger of collision
— — —	(repeated) Distress signal
— •	I am turning round to starboard
— ••	I am turning round to port

WARNING SIGNS (RED)

 or red lights — No entry

 No overtaking

 No passing

 No long-term mooring

 No anchoring

 No mooring

 No turning

 Making waves forbidden

 Pleasure craft forbidden

 Rowing boats forbidden — Motor boats forbidden

 Mandatory direction sign

 Stop

 Speed limit (km/h)

 Sound horn

 Danger

 Major waterway ahead

 Height (m)

 Depth (m)

 Width (m)

 Keep away from bank (m)

 Keep out of port and tributary

 Must contact waterways staff by radio (VHF 11)

 Channel is 40m from the right bank

 Cross to left-hand side

 Cross to right-hand side

 Keep on right-hand side

 Keep on left-hand side

 Head for left-hand side

 Head for right-hand side

Do not cause wash or

Keep within limits (red)

OTHER SIGNS

 or green lights — Entry allowed

 Electricity cable

 Weir

 Ferry

 Side turning

 Turning place

 Anchoring place

 Mooring place (long term)

 Advisory direction sign

 End of prohibited area

 Mooring against bank permitted

   Junctions or crossings of secondary waterways

     Priority waterway ahead (junction or crossing)

 Keep within limits (green)

 Recommended channel (in both directions)

 Passage only in direction indicated (other direction prohibited)

---

numerous places to stop for the night, but on the Seine, Saône and Rhône there are fewer places to stop. For the latter the following may be useful.

Le Havre to Paris on the Seine

Seine Estuary Le Havre Marina or Honfleur (8 km from start of km marks at km348).

km 245·5 Rouen. Bassin Saint-Gervais. Pontoon.

km 241·7 Pré au Loup yacht basin.

km 175·7 Val St-Martin yacht harbour.

km 173·6 Les Andelys yacht harbour.

Paris Bras de la Monnaie

km 3·4 Touring Club de France. Quay.

km 168·2 Paris. Port de Plaisance de Paris-Arsenal. Marina basin. All facilities.

km 81·5 Junction with Canal du Loing

km 67·7 Junction with the Yonne.

Chalon-sur-Saône to Lyon on the Saône

km 223·4 Chalon-sur-Saône. Harbour in the Genise arm. All facilities.

km 282·1 Macon. Yacht club

km 322 Fareins. Boat harbour. Facilities.

km 342·5 St-Germain-au-Mont d'Or. Yacht club.

km 365·4 Junction with the Rhône.

Lyon to Port-St-Louis-du-Rhône on the Rhône

km 2·6 Port de Lyon-Edouard Herriot. Commercial basins.

km 39·7 Les Roches-de-Condrieu. Boat harbour. All facilities.

km 54·8 Quay near Serrières.

km 70 Hire boat base.

km 106·7 Valence. Quay.

km 109 Valence. L'Epervière Marina. All facilities.

km 196·8 St-Etienne-des-Sorts. Mooring.

km 269·2 Arles. Pontoon. Facilities.

km 310 Port-St-Louis-du-Rhône. Shallow patches alongside quay before lock. Marina in basin. All facilities.

Useful books

Les Cartes Guide Vagnon de Navigation Fluviale (Vagnon. Les Editions du Plaisancier). Strip maps for the different canals and navigable rivers.

Les Cartes Guides de la Navigation Fluviale (Editions Grafocarte). Strip maps for the different canals and navigable rivers.

Inland Waterways of France David Edwards-May (Imray)

Tablet commemorating the Emperor Trajan in the Gorge of Kazan on the Danube

Fishing on the Danube delta

Through the French Canals Phillip Bristow (Adlard Coles Nautical)

Cruising French Waterways Hugh McKnight (Adlard Coles Nautical)

Through France to the Med Mike Harper (Gentry)

River Seine Cruising Guide Derek Bowskill (Imray)

12.2 The Danube

It is possible to take a boat clear across Europe from the North Sea to the Black Sea via the waterways system based on the Rhine, Main and Danube rivers. Much of these three rivers has already been canalised to Waterway Category IV standards (craft up to 185m long and 11·4m breadth) and the rest to Category III. The Main and the Danube are now connected by the Rhine-Main-Danube Canal (to Category IV). Effectively craft with a breadth of 10m and a draught of 2–2·5m (varies with the time of year in the upper Danube) can transit from the North Sea to the Black Sea. For most LOA will be immaterial.

The Danube is now a little-frequented route but with some revival in pleasure traffic following the end of the fighting in the former Yugoslavian Republics.

Rhine The Rhine has long been canalised and pleasure craft regularly use it. There are numerous club-marinas and town quays along it. The Rhine runs at 6 knots in places so you will need a powerful engine or assistance from a barge to get up parts of it.

Main The Main is canalised for 297km from Aschaffenburg to Bamberg. There are 27 locks. The current is negligible. Club-marinas and town quays.

Main-Danube Canal The new 171km canal, partly purpose cut and partly a canalisation of the River Altmühl. There are 20 locks. The current is negligible. Two marinas (at Berching and Beilngries) and town quays.

Danube Partly canalised with varying depths and current depending on the section. The upper Danube from Kelheim to Passau is the critical section with depths of around 2–2·5m although there have been reports of depths as little as 1·5m in parts during a dry summer. Depths vary according to the time of year with low water on the upper Danube in January and February and high water in July and August; on the lower Danube low water is September and October and high water in April and May. Despite canalisation there are considerable currents, up to 7–8 knots in places. The river is well buoyed from Germany to Austria, reasonably so from Austria to Croatia, less well so from Croatia to Romania. Club-marinas in Germany and Austria, club-marinas and town quays from the Czech Republic to Croatia, town quays and anchorages from Croatia to Romania.

Useful books

Inland Waterways of Germany Barry Sheffield (Imray)

Main and Main-Donau Kanal Karin Brundlers/Gerd Fleischauer (Verlag Rheinschiffahrt). In German

The Danube – A River guide Rod Heikell (Imray). Strip maps for the Danube from Kelheim to the Black Sea

Slow Boat through Germany Hugh McKnight (Adlard Coles Nautical)

Black Sea Cruising Guide Rick and Sheila Nelson (Imray). Pilotage for all of the Black Sea.

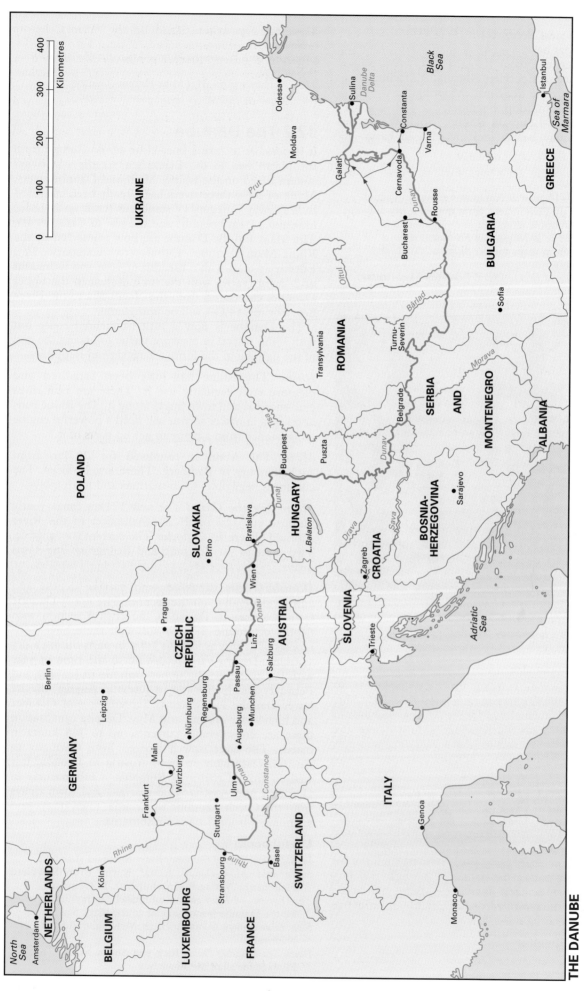

North Sea

NETHERLANDS
Amsterdam
Köln
BELGIUM
LUXEMBOURG
FRANCE
Strasbourg
Rhine
SWITZERLAND
Basel
GERMANY
Berlin
Leipzig
Frankfurt
Würzburg
Main
Nürnburg
Regensburg
Ulm
Stuttgart
Donau
L.Constance
Passau
Augsburg
München
Salzburg
Linz
Donau
Wien
AUSTRIA
SLOVENIA
Trieste
ITALY
Genoa
Monaco
Adriatic Sea
CZECH REPUBLIC
Prague
POLAND
SLOVAKIA
Brno
Bratislava
Dunaj
HUNGARY
L.Balaton
Puszta
Budapest
Tisa
Drava
Sava
CROATIA
Zagreb
BOSNIA-HERZEGOVINA
Sarajevo
SERBIA
AND
MONTENEGRO
Belgrade
Dunav
Morava
ALBANIA
Turnu-Severin
ROMANIA
Transylvania
Oltul
Bârlad
Dunav
Cernavoda
Rousse
Bucharest
BULGARIA
Sofia
Varna
Constanta
Black Sea
Sulina
Danube Delta
Galati
Moldava
Prut
UKRAINE
Odessa
GREECE
Istanbul
Sea of Marmara

0 100 200 300 400
Kilometres

12.3 From across the Atlantic

For those heading eastwards from the USA and the Caribbean there is a fairly standard route to the Azores with a few variations along the way. Crossing the Atlantic from west to east is certainly not as enjoyable as the east–west trade wind passage with less favourable winds and current and a greater possibility of gale force winds. For the west to east passage, the following should be kept in mind:

Seasons From the USA and the Caribbean yachts normally head for Bermuda in April-May in order to leave for the Azores sometime in May-June. The hurricane season runs from June to November although August and September are the worst months. Hurricanes can affect Bermuda and early hurricanes seem to track closer to Bermuda than those later in the season. In May and June winds are predominantly SW or N–NE which combined with the Gulf Stream running NE means that boats leaving from the USA should aim to leave from somewhere like Norfolk in Virginia rather than more northerly destinations like Newport, Rhode Island.

USA/Virgin Islands to Bermuda

From the USA to Bermuda is around 650–700M and from the Virgin Islands to Bermuda is around 850M. Most yachts head for St Georges. Normally a route is plotted to cross the Gulf Stream as near to right angles as possible to avoid the unpleasant lumpy seas it generates. A northerly gale blowing against the NE–going Gulf Stream produces potentially dangerous seas.

Bermuda to the Azores

Bermuda to the Azores is around 1820 to 1850M depending on how high you go looking for westerlies. The normal advice on leaving Bermuda is to head NE to around 38°N to 40°N before turning E to the Azores. This should ensure a favourable W–WNW–going current and a fair proportion of SW–W winds. Most yachts will head for Horta. Often a belt of calms surrounds the Azores and most yachts have to motor the last 50–100M.

Caribbean to the Azores

Traditionally yachts crossing from the Caribbean to Europe leave the Caribbean in late April or early May for Bermuda and then head for the Azores sometime in May to early June. Many yachts now leave the Caribbean and sail direct for the Azores. Traditionally this route has less wind and you will have to be more patient than on the Bermuda-Azores route. Many yachts take on additional fuel although yachts which sail well in light conditions can make good passage times.

From St Maarten or Antigua to Horta is around 2100 miles and yachts normally take around 21 days for the passage. You can either head north for a bit before curving east to the Azores or sail a rhumb line. There seems to be little practical evidence that more calms will be encountered on the rhumb line route as opposed to heading north first.

Azores to Gibraltar

Most yachts go to Ponta Delgada on São Miguel, the most easterly major island of the Azores, before heading off eastwards. Yachts normally head for somewhere on the Iberian peninsula like Lisbon or Puerto Sherry or make the voyage direct to Gibraltar. A few drop down to Madeira and then proceed on to Gibraltar. From Ponta Delgada to Lisbon is around 790M and to Gibraltar around 980M. From Ponta Delgada to Funchal on Madeira is around 560M and from Funchal to Gibraltar around 590M. For the most part the voyage from the Azores to Iberia or Gibraltar will be made with favourable S–going currents and northerly winds. From Madeira to Gibraltar there is an unfavourable S–SSW–setting current and the prevailing winds are N–NNE making the passage largely a windward one.

Pilots

The Atlantic Crossing Guide revised by John Lawson and Gavin McLaren (RCC Pilotage Foundation/Adlard Coles Nautical)

Street's Transatlantic Crossing Guide Don Street (W W Norton)

Atlantic Islands Anne Hammick (RCC Pilotage Foundation/Imray). Covers the Azores, Madeira, Canaries and Cape Verde Islands.

The Yachtsman's Guide to the Bermuda Islands Michael Voegli. PO Box 1699, Hamilton 5, Bermuda.

Yachting Guide to Bermuda J & E Harris (Bermuda Maritime)

World Cruising Routes Jimmy Cornell (Adlard Coles Nautical)

Ocean Passages and Landfalls Rod Heikell and Andrew O'Grady (Imray).

Horta on Faial in the Azores

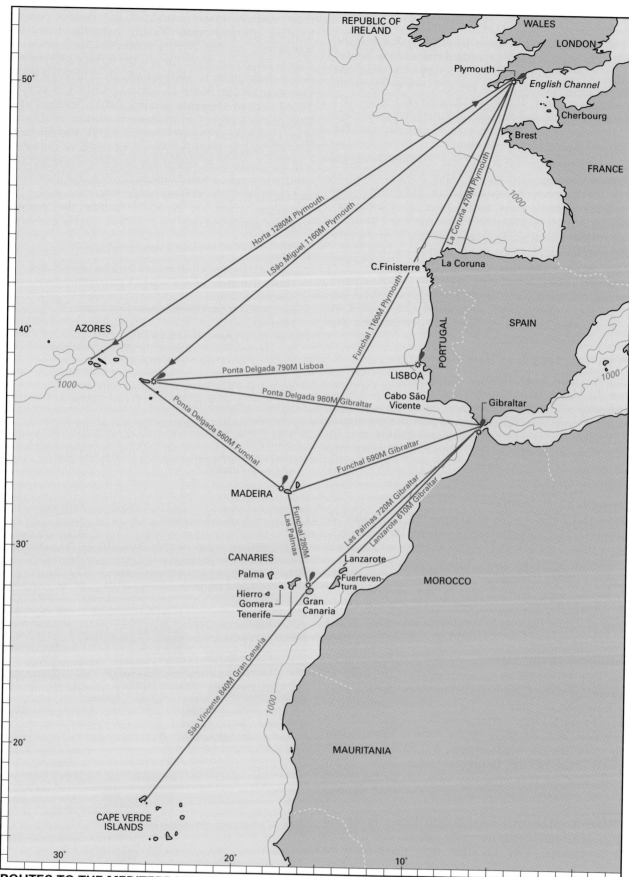

REPUBLIC OF
IRELAND

WALES

LONDON

Plymouth

English Channel

Cherbourg

Brest

FRANCE

Horta 1280M Plymouth

I.São Miguel 1160M Plymouth

La Coruña 470M Plymouth

C.Finisterre

La Coruna

Funchal 1160M Plymouth

AZORES

SPAIN

PORTUGAL

Ponta Delgada 790M Lisboa

LISBOA

Ponta Delgada 980M Gibraltar

Cabo São
Vicente

Gibraltar

Ponta Delgada 560M Funchal

Funchal 590M Gibraltar

MADEIRA

Las Palmas 720M Gibraltar

Lanzarote 610M Gibraltar

Funchal 280M
Las Palmas

CANARIES

Lanzarote

Palma

Fuerteven-
tura

MOROCCO

Hierro
Gomera
Tenerife

Gran
Canaria

São Vincente 840M Gran Canaria

MAURITANIA

CAPE VERDE
ISLANDS

ROUTES TO THE MEDITERRANEAN

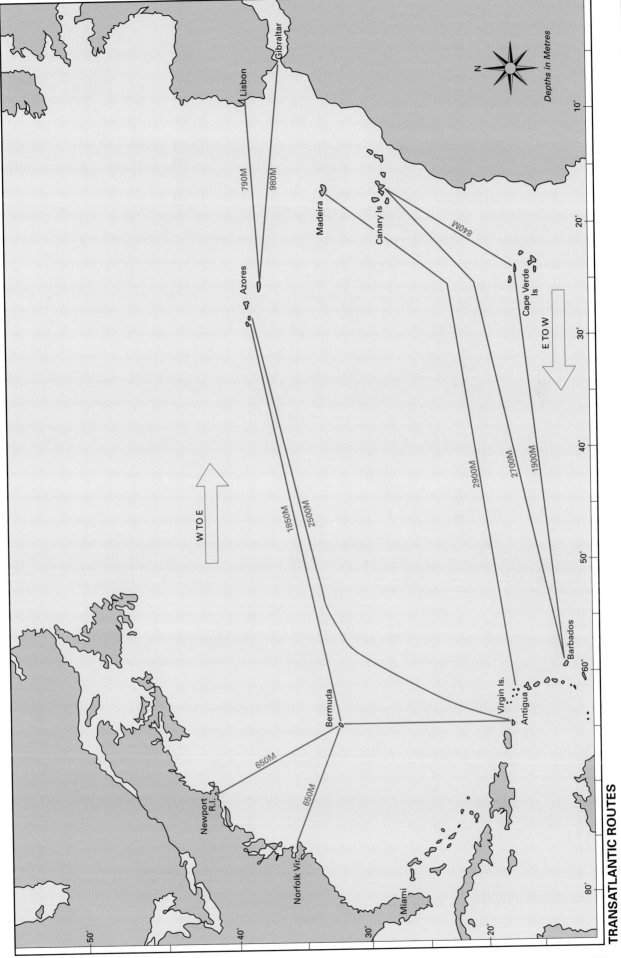

Lisbon

Gibraltar

790M

980M

Madeira

Canary Is

840M

Cape Verde
Is

E TO W

Azores

1900M

2700M

2900M

1850M

2500M

W TO E

Barbados

Virgin Is.

Antigua

Bermuda

650M

650M

Newport
R.I.

Norfolk Vir.

Miami

N

Depths in Metres

TRANSATLANTIC ROUTES

137

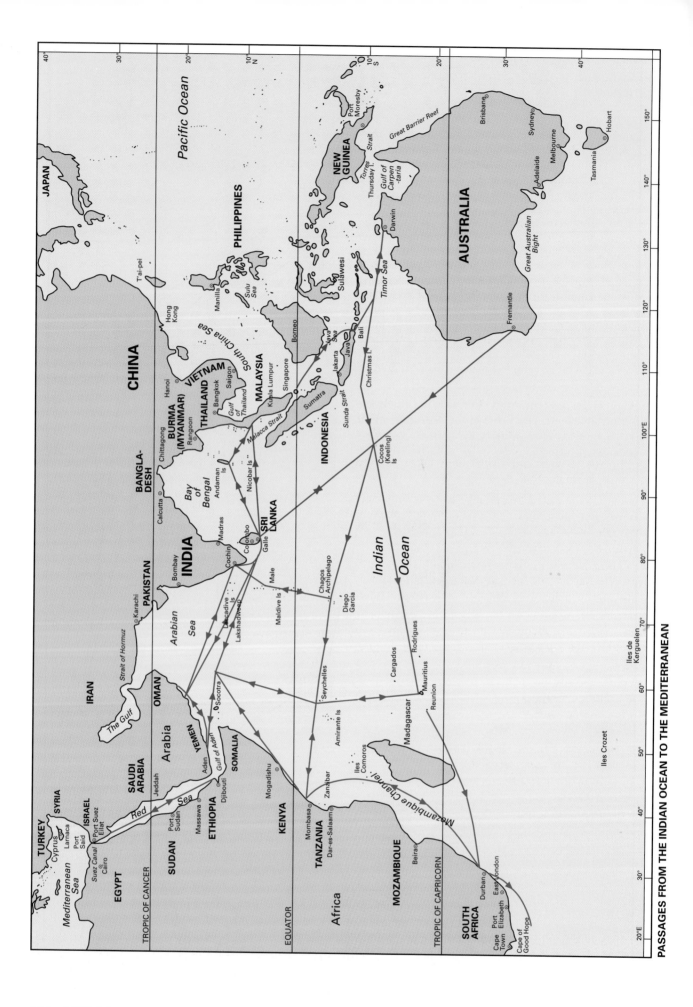

PASSAGES FROM THE INDIAN OCEAN TO THE MEDITERRANEAN

12.4 From the Red Sea

Most yachts that started a circumnavigation across the Atlantic finish it via the Red Sea and the Suez Canal and so into the Mediterranean. Many yachts based in the Pacific and particularly Australasian yachts are in the first half of a circumnavigation by the time they come up through the Red Sea and through Suez into the Mediterranean. Routes in the Red Sea are straightforward although there appears to be a fairly extreme difference of opinion over cruising in the area. Some consider it an unpleasant option that must be overcome between the Indian Ocean and the Mediterranean, while others consider the Red Sea one of the best cruising areas in the world.

At the moment some care is needed over the political situation in Somalia and Sudan. Most yachts heading up here exchange information on a regular basis and many head up the Red Sea in company. Like many places the political turmoil emanating from the capital of a country or civil strife inland may not necessarily rule out putting in at harbours and anchorages along its coast. For the Red Sea the following should be noted:

Winds From April to December northerlies are the prevailing winds throughout the Red Sea. Normally the winds blow at around Force 4–6 at the northern end of the Red Sea, less at the southern end. From December to April northerlies blow down to around the Sudan/Eritrea border and from there there will be southerlies, normally SSE–SE.

Haze Much of the Red Sea is hazy and visibility over the mostly low-lying coast can make fixing a position (from geographical features or a sextant) difficult. GPS has much to recommend it in the Red Sea.

Suez Canal Nearly all yachts now employ an agent to process the paperwork for transiting the Suez Canal. The transit normally takes two days with an overnight stop at Ismalia.

From Suez Most yachts will head for Cyprus from Port Said. Some head for Israel and a few for Greece or Turkey.

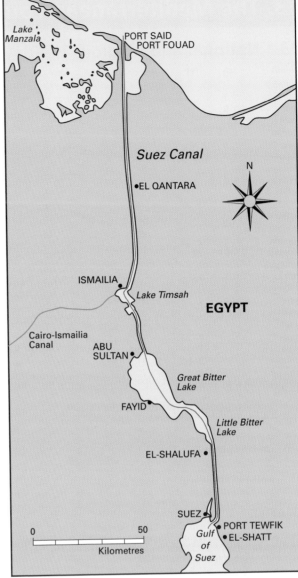

THE SUEZ CANAL

Pilots

Red Sea and Gulf of Aden Pilot (NP64) (Admiralty)
Red Sea Pilot Elaine Morgan and Stephen Davies (Imray). Detailed pilotage for the Red Sea
Indian Ocean Cruising Guide Rod Heikell. Cruise planning and pilotage for the Indian Ocean (Imray).

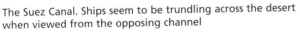

The Suez Canal. Ships seem to be trundling across the desert when viewed from the opposing channel

13.1 National and religious holidays

Month / Country	Jan	Feb	Mar	Apr	May	Jun	Jul	Aug	Sep	Oct	Nov	Dec
Gibraltar	1	8		2	1, 3	21		30	10			25, 26
Spain	1, 6			2	1			15		12	1	6, 8, 25
France	1			2	1, 8³		14	15			1, 11	25
Monaco	1, 27			2	1³	3		15¹			1, 19	8, 25
Italy	1, 6			25, 2	1	2		15			1	8, 25, 26
Malta	1	10	19, 31¹	2	1	7, 29		15	8, 21			8, 13, 25
Slovenia	1, 2	8		27, 2	1,2	25		15		31	1	25, 26
Croatia	1, 6			2	1	10, 22, 25		5,15		8	1	25
Bosnia & Herzegovina	1	2¹,22¹	1		1, 2¹, 9			15	8		1, 8, 14¹, 25	25
Serbia & Montenegro	1, 7¹,14¹			27, 2	1, 9					29		
Albania	1, 2	2¹, 22¹			1, 2¹						14¹, 28, 29	25
Greece	1, 6	23	25	2	1, ³31			15		28		25, 26
Turkey	1	2¹	21⁴	23	19			30		29	14¹, 15	
Cyprus	1, 6	23	25	2,4	1,³31		20	15		1,28		25
N. Cyprus	1	2¹		23	1			1, 30		29	14¹	
Syria ᴬ	1	2¹, 22¹	8, 21⁴	17,2	1, 2¹, 6		17			6	14¹	25
Lebanon ᴮ	1, 6⁴, 7	2¹, 9, 22¹	2⁴	2	1, 2¹, 6			15			1, 14¹, 22	25, 31
Israel ᶜ			7¹	6¹,12¹,27	26¹		27¹	16¹, 17¹, 25¹, 30¹	1¹, 7¹			
Egypt ᶜ	7⁴	2¹, 22¹		12^{1,2,4},25	1, 9	18	23	15	11^{1, 4}	6,24	14¹	23
Libya ᴬ		2¹, 22¹	2⁴, 3, 28		2¹	11, 13			1	7	14¹	
Tunisia	1	2¹, 22¹	20, 21	19	1, 2¹		25,13				7, 14¹	
Algeria ᴰ	1	22¹	8		1, 2¹	19	5				1, 14¹	
Morocco	1, 5¹, 11	2¹, 22¹			1, 2¹		30	14, 20, 21			6, 14¹, 18	

1   Islamic holidays base year 2004. See note below.
2   Easter: Maundy Thursday (Spain only), Good Friday (not France, Monaco, Italy, Slovenia), Easter Monday (not Malta).
3   Ascension Day (40 days after Easter) & Whit Monday (7weeks after Easter Monday). Corpus Christi (Monaco only).
4   May only apply to certain communities.
A   Weekend: Friday.
B   Weekend: Sat pm-Sun. (Thur-Fri in some areas).
C   Weekend: Fri-Sat.
D   Weekend: Thur-Fri (banks closed Fri-Sat).
When a Spanish National holiday falls on a Sunday, the autonomous regions have the choice of either celebrating the holiday the following Monday, or using it to celebrate a regional festival.

Islamic holidays
The Islamic calendar is lunar based, the year consisting of 12 months, each month beginning when the new moon is first sighted in Mecca. The months are 29 or 30 days long. The year has either 354 or 355 days, hence the Islamic year is 10, 11 or 12 days shorter than the Gregorian year. The dates of Islamic festivals are fixed in the Islamic months, but by the Gregorian calendar they occur approximately 11 days earlier each year. www.national-holidays.com has detailed data by country.

13.2 GIBRALTAR   TIME ZONE UT+1   ☎ IDD +350 (9567 FROM SPAIN)

Area 2·25M² (6·5km²)
Frontiers 1·2km with Spain
Coastline 6·5M (12km)
Maritime claims 3M. Exclusive fishing zone 3M
Population 29,500. Growth rate 0·1%
Government Dependent colony of the United Kingdom. Gibraltar Council and Cabinet
Disputes Occasional friction over land border with Spain
Capital Gibraltar
Time zone UT+1 DST Apr–Sep.
Language English and Spanish primary languages. Also Italian and Portuguese. English used for official purposes.
Ethnic groups Italian, English, Maltese, Portuguese and Spanish descent.
Religion 75% Roman Catholic, 8% Church of England.
Public holidays
  Jan 1 New Year's Day

  Last weekend in May: Spring holiday
  Last weekend in August: Summer holiday
  Dec 25, 26 Christmas
Moveable
  Good Friday
  Easter Monday
  Commonwealth Day
  Queen's Birthday
Economy Depends heavily on the United Kingdom. Tourism. Shipping services. Banking and finance.
  Exports commodities (mostly re-exports of oil, beverages, tobacco, and manufactured goods).
  Imports Nearly everything.
Environment and pollution Affected by industrial pollution in Spain. Local hydrocarbon pollution.
Internal travel Bus and taxi.
International travel Flights to the United Kingdom. Flights and ferries to Morocco. The land border with Spain is open.
Mail Reliable. Preferably sent to one of the marinas

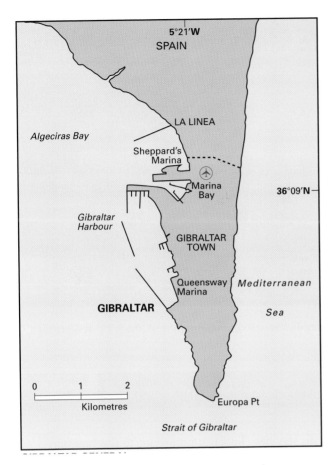

or a private address. Poste restante service.

Telecommunications Automatic dialling. Country code +350, (9567 from Spain). Adequate system. GSM PAYG mobile phones. Internet cafés.

Currency Gibraltar pound (£) or UK sterling which is legal tender.

Banks Open 0900–1530 Mon–Thur and 0900–1530/1630–1800 Fri. All major cheque cards, credit cards, charge cards and travellers cheques accepted. ATM which work with major credit cards.

Medical Good treatment. UK nationals are treated free of charge within 30 days of leaving UK. Reciprocal agreements with most EU countries.

Temperature and precipitation

	Av max °C	Av min °C	Record	Rel. humidity	Days 1mm rain	Sea temp °C
Jan	16	10	37	70%	10	14
Feb	17	11	24	67%	7	14
Mar	18	12	27	66%	10	15
Apr	20	13	28	64%	6	16
May	23	15	31	62%	4	17
Jun	25	18	33	62%	1	18
Jul	28	20	38	60%	0	20
Aug	29	21	37	60%	1	21
Sep	26	19	33	65%	2	20
Oct	23	17	33	69%	5	18
Nov	19	14	29	72%	7	17
Dec	17	11	24	70%	10	15

Electricity 240V 50Hz AC.

Geography

A conspicuous mountainous promontory surrounded by a narrow coastal strip on the north side of the Strait of Gibraltar.

Seismic activity Seismic activity is evident although there has been no great loss of life or damage to buildings. In 1755 the great Lisbon earthquake (which levelled the city) was felt in Gibraltar. Recently on February 28 1969 an earthquake of considerable magnitude in the Strait of Gibraltar caused damage in Portugal, Spain and Morocco with the death of 13 people.

Weather Midway between a Mediterranean and continental Atlantic climate. Summers are warm and mild. Winters temperate.

Winds About 80% of the winds in the Strait of Gibraltar are funnelled into an ENE or W direction.
Levanter The predominant easterly wind. It is stronger in the narrow part of the Strait compared to either side. It is usually caused by an approaching Atlantic depression and is most frequent in spring and late summer and autumn. Can blow at gale force for several days or more.
Poniente The W wind. Usually less strong than the *Levanter* Can last for 5 days or a week.

Tides and currents

Tides in the Strait of Gibraltar are significant enough to be taken into account by most craft. In the Strait of Gibraltar there is a permanent E–going current which is modified by the tidal stream. See *Straits Sailing Handbook* for the best information on transiting the Straits.

Harbours

There are three marinas in Gibraltar: Sheppard's Marina, Marina Bay and Queensway Quay Marina, with another, Ocean Village, under development.

Facilities

Everyday

Water In all marinas.
Fuel Near Waterport and to be installed at Queensway.
Electricity At all marinas.
Gas Camping Gaz available. Gas containers can be refilled in Spain.
Paraffin Available.

Boat repairs

Engines Most spares for the major makes of marine engines available or can be obtained. Competent workshops.
Electrics and electronics Spares and repair facilities available.
Engineering Steel and stainless steel fabrication possible.
Wood and GRP Most wood repairs and fabrication possible. GRP repairs including osmosis treatment possible.
Paints and antifouling All paints and antifouling available.
Hauling 44-ton travel-hoist. Dry dock for 45m LOA at

ex-Naval yard. Hard standing.

Gardiennage Several companies can arrange gardiennage and general yacht care.

Provisioning

All provisions can be found although fresh fruit and vegetables are not always the best. Shopping hours 0900–1300 and 1500–1900 Mon–Fri and 0930–1300 Sat. Some shops remain open outside these hours.

Charts and pilots

Mediterranean Pilot Vol 1 (NP45) (Admiralty).

Straits Sailing Handbook Colin Thomas. Annual publication, published locally in Gib.

Atlantic Spain and Portugal Anne Hammick (RCC Pilotage Foundation/Imray).

Costas del Sol and Blanca Robin Brandon. Revised by John Marchment (RCC Pilotage Foundation/ Imray).

Charts Admiralty charts and publications and Imray charts and publications available from chandlers and bookshops locally.

Leaving the unforgettable outline of 'the Rock' at Gibraltar

13.3 SPAIN

TIME ZONE UT+1 ☎ IDD+34

Area 194,329M² (504,750km²) includes Balearic Islands, Canary Islands, Ceuta, and Melilla

Frontiers 1903·2km total. Andorra 65km, France 623km, Gibraltar 1·2km, Portugal 1214km.

Coastline 2680M (4964km)

Maritime claims 12M

Inland waterways 649M. (1045km)

Population 42.7m. Growth rate 0·3%

Government Parliamentary monarchy.

Disputes Gibraltar question. Controls two *presidos*, Ceuta and Melilla, on the N coast of Morocco

Capital Madrid

Time zone UT+1. DST Apr–Sep.

Language Castillian Spanish. Others include 17% Catalan, 7% Galician, some English and French

Ethnic groups Composite Mediterranean. Catalan in the E around Barcelona.

Religion 99% Roman Catholic.

Public holidays

Fixed

Jan 1 New Year's Day
Jan 6 Epiphany
Mar 19 St Joseph's Day
May 1 Labour Day
Jul 18 National Day
Jul 25 St James Day
Aug 15 Festival of the Assumption
Oct 12 Columbus' Day
Nov 1 All Saints Day
Dec 8 Festival of the Immaculate Conception
Dec 24, 25 Christmas

Moveable

Maundy Thursday
Good Friday

Economy Joined EU in 1986. Work force is 16% in agriculture, 24% in industry and commerce, 52%

in services. Tourism important to the economy with approximately 50 million visitors annually.

Exports Fruit and farm produce, iron and steel products, vehicles, footwear, textiles, wood, chemicals, refined petroleum.

Imports Petroleum, machinery, cotton, chemicals, grain, coffee, tobacco, iron and steel, timber, cellulose, vehicles.

Crops Cereals, grapes, citrus, olives, vegetables.

Environment and pollution Mediterranean polluted with heavy metals. Fishing techniques affect dolphins and sea turtles. Bottom trawling destroying sea grasses. Much sewage pumped raw into the sea. Nine nuclear power stations. Heavy use of pesticides and fertilisers which reach the sea via the rivers. Six marine reserves including Isla Cabrera.

Internal travel Internal flights to all major cities including Islas Baleares. Extensive train network with efficient service. Local bus and taxi services are good. Hire cars and motorbikes in the main coastal resorts.

International travel Madrid is the centre for international flights to most major airports in the world. Also European flights, including low-cost airlines, to Malaga, Almeria, Murcia, Alicante, Barcelona and Palma de Mallorca. Ferries to Islas Baleares and Morocco.

Mail Reliable. Best sent to a marina or private address. Poste restante (*lista de correos*) service.

Telecommunications Automatic dialling. Code +34. Good telephone system throughout Spain. GSM PAYG mobile phones. Internet cafés.

Currency Euro.

Banks Open 0900–1400 Mon–Fri 0900–1300 Saturday. Exchange offices and travel offices

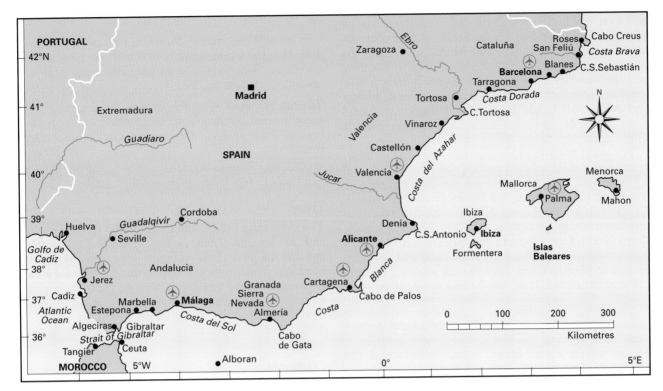

operate outside these hours. All major credit cards, charge cards, Traveller's cheques accepted. ATM in larger towns and resorts which work with most major credit cards.

Medical Good medical care system. Reciprocal medical care for EU nationals with Form *E111* although you will have to pay for a part of any treatment costs.

Electricity 220/125V 50Hz AC.

Geography

The Mediterranean Spanish coast stretches from Gibraltar to the border with France in the Golfe du Lion. The country is basically a high plateau surrounded by high mountains with the Pyrenees on the Spanish–French border reaching 3404m (11,172ft) (Aneto). Along the Mediterranean coast the terrain varies from low and marshy to mountainous. A group of islands (the Balearics/ Islas Baleares) lie approximately 50M off the coast. The mainland coast has traditionally been divided into five *costas* which conveniently slice up the coast: Costa del Sol, Costa Blanca, Costa del Azahar, Costa Dorada, and Costa Brava.

Costa del Sol The sunny coast. Mostly flat near the coast although high mountains follow the coast a short distance inland.

Costa Blanca The white coast. The coast is bordered by white cliffs for part of its length from which it takes its name.

Costa del Azahar Mostly low-lying with several major river deltas.

Costa Dorada The golden coast. It takes its name from the numerous fine golden beaches along its length.

Costa Brava A more mountainous coastline.

Islas Baleares The group of four major islands and several smaller groups lying off the Mediterranean coast. Ibiza, Formentera, Mallorca and Menorca are the four major islands. Cabrera is now a marine reserve and tourism (including yachting) is strictly controlled.

Weather Of the typical Mediterranean type with hot dry summers and mild wet winters. The Costa del Sol has exceptionally mild winters. In general summer temperatures are in the range 25°–35° and winter temperatures 5°–20°. The relative humidity is moderate at 60–90%. Most of the rainfall occurs in the autumn and winter.

Prevailing winds The prevailing wind, the *brisa de mar*, is a sea breeze blowing onto the coast. It typically begins around midday, blows strongest by mid-afternoon, and dies in the evening. This wind may increase or diminish the effects of other winds depending on their direction. Because of the effects of other winds or local topography it will often blow at a slant to the coast or even along it. Typically it blows from the NE through E to SE along the mainland coast

Temperature and precipitation (at Palma)

	Av max °C	Av min °C	Record	Rel. humidity	Days 1mm rain	Sea temp °C
Jan	13	6	23	61%	5	12
Feb	14	7	21	58%	5	12
Mar	16	9	24	60%	8	13
Apr	19	10	26	66%	6	13
May	22	13	31	67%	5	14
Jun	26	17	37	65%	3	17
Jul	29	20	39	65%	1	21
Aug	29	20	37	65%	3	24
Sep	27	18	35	69%	5	23
Oct	23	14	31	71%	9	22
Nov	18	10	26	47%	8	19
Dec	13	8	21	62%	6	15

and from the E–SE around the Balearics. As the coast of Spain reaches down to the Strait of Gibraltar the land on either side (Spain and Morocco) funnels the wind into pretty much a westerly or easterly direction and the wind strength increases. Consequently a NW wind in the Atlantic will be a west wind after Gibraltar and NE or SE winds around the Balearics will tend more towards the east as you progress towards Gibraltar.

The wind most feared is the *tramontana* or *mestrale*. It is generated when a depression passes across central France and the wind drops down through the Toulouse Gap between the Pyrenees and the Massif Centrale. It blows from the NW into the Golfe du Lion and fans out to blow from the NW–N–NE over the Costa Brava, Costa Dorada and Balearics. It can reach gale force in a short time from a flat calm and has been known to blow at Force 10–11 in the winter.

Other strong winds are the *levante* and *poniente*.

Locally-named winds

Tramontana, mestrale Strong NW–N–NE wind. Arrives with little warning and can quickly reach gale force. Mostly affects Costa Brava, Costa Dorada and the Balearics. The warning signs are a clear, glaring visibility and a dry almost electric atmosphere with a steady or slightly rising barometer. Rarely preceded by a swell. Usually lasts 2–7 days.

Levante, llevantade, levanter Strong E–NE wind. Can blow strongly in the Strait of Gibraltar. Blows strongly in the sea area around Valencia where there are on average eight or nine gales a year from this direction. It is caused by a depression passing along the North African coast. The warning signs are a heavy swell, a cold damp atmosphere and low cloud and poor visibility. Usually lasts 1–3 days.

Vendevales, poniente Strong W–SW wind. Blows strongly in the Strait of Gibraltar, Costa del Sol and Costa Blanca. Most frequent in spring and autumn. Caused when a depression crossing over Spain causes W winds to funnel into the Strait of Gibraltar. Usually lasts 1–2 days.

Sirocco The hot humid S wind blowing off the Sahara. Most common in the Balearics and Costa Blanca. It is accompanied by bad visibility and low cloud. If it rains there will often be 'red rain' containing dust particles from the Sahara. May blow up to gale force. Usually lasts 1–3 days.

Garbi A warm humid wind from the SW–W. Mostly affects the Balearics and *Costa Brava*. Often blows in the spring up to Force 5–6. In the winter it will often blow at Force 6–8. Usually lasts 1–3 days.

Brisa de mar The normal sea breeze. May blow up to Force 5.

Terral The offshore land breeze that may blow at night. Light wind Force 1–3, seldom more.

Gales

The *tramontana* is the most feared source of gale force winds, being relatively common and strong. The effects of the *tramontana* die off towards the S coast although a heavy swell may be felt. The *levante* mostly effects the Costa del Sol and Strait of Gibraltar where it is funnelled and increases in force. Yachts attempting to enter the Mediterranean from the Atlantic should wait for the *levante* to die before entering the Strait of Gibraltar.

In general the annual percentage frequency of gales dies off in the winter from N to S with 10–12% around the Costa Brava, 6–8% in the Balearics, and 2% around the Costa del Sol.

Thunderstorms Most frequent in the autumn. Often accompanied by strong winds of short duration (1–3 hours). Rain or hail often accompany the associated squall.

Waterspouts Have been recorded along the Spanish coast and in the Strait of Gibraltar.

Tides

The tidal range at Gibraltar at springs is 0·9m (2·9ft) and at Málaga 0·5m (1·7ft). This is considerable enough to take into account when anchoring or berthing. This range can be modified by strong winds blowing from one direction over a period of days which increase or decrease the range depending on the wind direction. The tidal range drops to 0·15m (0·5ft) at Alicante and can for all practical purposes be ignored on the east coast.

Currents

The Atlantic inflow into the Mediterranean causes an E–going current of 1–2 knots along the S coast of Spain. On the east coast there is a SSW–going counter-current of 1–1½ knots caused by the main E–going current around the S side of the Balearics. There is an E–NE–going current of 1–1½ knots on the S and E sides of the Balearics and a WSW current of 1–1½ knots on the N side.

Around some of the harbours, especially the *calas*, a freak seiche called the *resaca*, similar to the *marrobio* in Sicily, occurs from time to time. Under certain meteorological conditions the water level will abruptly rise and fall as much as 1·5m (5ft) every few minutes. The *resaca* has been known to occur when two major wave trains meet and the resonance set up causes a rapid 'tidal wave'. Most *resacas* are minor affairs and occur infrequently but in 1984 a *resaca* at Ciudadela in Menorca was estimated to have a tidal wave of 3m and caused around three million dollars worth of damage. 35 boats were sunk, 4 were missing, and another 42 craft sustained major damage. Perhaps unrelated but just as devastating was the earthquake that struck in Algeria in May 2003. It sent a tsunami across the Mediterranean that caused substantial damage to yachts in Mahon. Surges of 2-3m every ten minutes over a period of four hours trapped yachts under jetties and sunk many others.

Harbours and anchorages

Along the mainland coast and around the Balearics there are numerous marinas with more planned or being built. These marinas vary from huge conglomerations with an associated apartment complex to smaller more humdrum harbours. Many of the commercial or fishing harbours have a part of the harbour allocated to a yacht club which will often organise berths for visiting yachts. These yacht clubs are usually run as a business and aim to provide facilities similar to private marinas at similar prices. There are still a number of commercial and fishing harbours where yacht facilities are not developed. There are a number of anchorages, many offering good shelter and others useable depending on the wind and sea. The Balearics afford a large number of useful anchorages.

With few exceptions most marinas have visitors berths. Some marinas have visitors berths numbered in three figures while others have just a few visitors berths. There has been some ire expressed over the fact that yachts arriving in the high season cannot find a berth at a chosen marina and there has been some muttering about whether these berths exist at all. It is important to remember that visitor's berths apply equally to local boats in transit as well as to boats from outside the country. I may be stating the obvious, but a visitor's berth is for any boat not permanently berthed at the marina in question.

In my experience all marina managers will try to squash you into a berth whenever it is possible in the high season. Many of them go out of their way to find visiting yachts a berth. If at all possible try to arrange a berth in known crowded marinas in advance. If you intend to base yourself for a week or more in a marina in the high season then book ahead. Alternatively try to avoid popular parts of the coast in the high season from mid-June to mid-September.

Facilities

Everyday
Water Readily available in all marinas and most commercial and fishing ports. Is potable from taps unless marked otherwise.
Fuel Fuel quays in nearly all marinas, the larger yacht clubs and some commercial and fishing ports. Duty free fuel available to fishermen is not available to yachts.
Electricity 220V at all marinas, yacht clubs and some commercial and fishing harbours. 380V available at some marinas and yacht clubs, usually for berths 15m and above.
Gas Camping Gaz widely available. Spanish gas bottles can be refilled at most places and other gas bottles in the larger towns.
Paraffin Not widely available and difficult to find in some places. Sold in general stores, usually in the poorer quarter of town. Methylated spirits also sold in general stores.

Boat repairs
Engines Most spares for the major makes of marine engine are available or can be obtained at the larger marina yards. Smaller yards may take longer to obtain spares. Competent workshops in many of the marina yards.
Electrics and electronics Spares and repair facilities available in the larger marina yards. Some items may take a little while to obtain and if you can locate it elsewhere and get it to Spain quickly this may be worth doing.
Engineering Steel and stainless steel fabrication in some yards and larger towns.
Wood and GRP Good wood repairs and fabrication to yacht standards in many yards. GRP repairs and osmosis treatment in some of the larger marina yards.
Paints and antifouling Locally manufactured paints and antifouling of good quality widely available. Imported paints and antifouling also widely available.
Hauling A large number of yacht yards with travel-hoists and slipways. Most have a large area for hardstanding and good security.
Gardiennage Most of the larger marinas and yacht clubs can arrange gardiennage and general yacht care. Ask around for recommendations.

Provisioning
Generally there are few problems in even quite small places. Some of the marinas built away from a village or town do not have good shopping within the marina and you really need a car to get to a nearby town to stock up. Good fruit and vegetables and other produce will be found in the markets. Shopping hours vary but generally are 0800/0900–1200 and 1400–1800/2000 Mon–Sat.

Charts and pilots
Mediterranean Pilot Vol 1 (NP45) (Admiralty). Covers the south and east of Spain and Islas Baleares.
Costa del Sol and Blanca, Costa del Azahar, Dorada and Brava. Islas Baleares Robin Brandon, revised by John Marchment. (RCC Pilotage Foundation/Imray). Detailed pilotage information for the Spanish Mediterranean coast and offshore islands.
The Yachtsman's Directory (The Coast of Spain and the Algarve) editor Richard Ashton (PubliNautic). In English and Spanish covering marinas and ports around the Mediterranean coast.
Charts Admiralty charts provide adequate coverage. Spanish charts provide better coverage. They are available from some chandlers authorised as agents for the Spanish hydrographic service or from the Commandancia Militar de Marina at major ports. Imray publish five small-scale charts for Spanish Mediterranean waters.

Almerimar on the Costa del Sol is a popular place for cruisers to overwinter

Area 209,836M² (545,630km²)

Frontiers 2,892 miles total. Andorra 60km, Spain 623km, Monaco 4·4km, Italy 488km.

Coastline 918M (1700km) (includes Corsica)

Maritime claims 12M.

Inland waterways 14,932km. Larger waterways much used for transportation of cargo, mostly oil, gravel, sand and cereals. Lesser waterways used mostly for tourism.

Population 60.1m. Growth rate 0·4%

Government Democratic republic. 22 regions. 96 *départements*.

Disputes None in Mediterranean.

Capital Paris

Time zone UT+1; +1 DST Apr–Sep

Language French. Declining regional languages, Catalan in the SW, Basque and Corsican.

Ethnic groups Mediterranean and northern. Minorities of North Africans (3 million), Indochinese and Basque.

Religion Roman Catholic (90%), Protestant (2%), Jewish (1%), Muslim (3–5%).

Public holidays

Jan 1 New Year's Day
May 1 Labour Day
Jul 14 Bastille Day
Aug 15 Festival of the Assumption
Nov 1 All Saints Day
Nov 11 Armistice Day
Dec 25, 26 Christmas
Moveable
Good Friday
Easter Monday
Ascension Day
Whit Monday
In addition there are numerous regional holidays.

Economy Highly developed economy. Net exporter of agricultural products. Net exporter of electricity from nuclear power stations. Modern industrial sector including vehicle production (Renault, Peugeot, Citroën), electrical and electronic goods, aircraft production (Airbus in Toulouse). Finance services. Tourism. France has the largest yacht manufacturing company (Bénéteau) in the world. Work force is 9% in agriculture, 45% in industry and commerce, 46% in services.

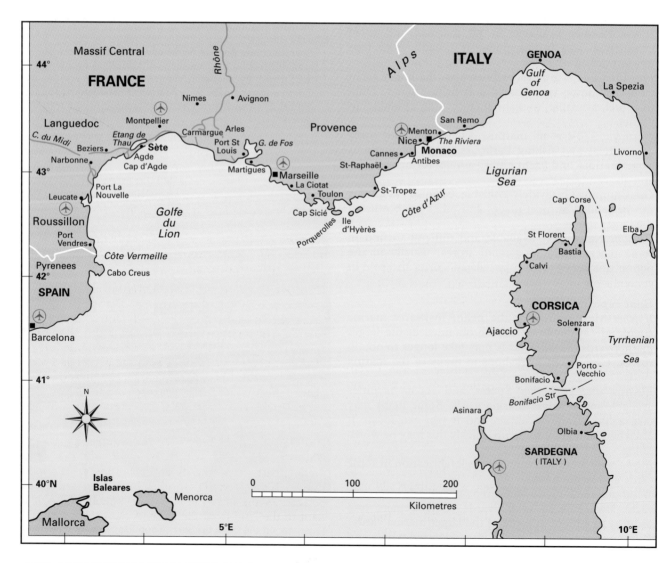

Exports Farm produce especially dairy, wine, machinery, chemicals, vehicles, textiles, clothing and related products.

Imports Oil, chemicals, machinery, minerals, agricultural products, and vehicles.

Minerals Oil, coal, iron, bauxite.

Crops Cereals, rice, fruit, sugar beet, grapes.

Environment and pollution Heavy metal pollution of the Rhône and hence into the Golfe du Lion. Pesticides and fertilisers heavily used. Nuclear power stations provide over 80% of electricity. Few controls on car emissions. Sewage is rarely treated before being discharged into the sea. Laws exist governing the environment and pollution but enforcement is rare. Several maritime reserves, most notably around Corsica where collaboration between fishermen and environment bodies has been successful.

Internal travel Internal flights to most major cities including Perpignan, Toulouse, Montpellier, Marignane (Marseille), Hyères and Nice. Train and bus travel is reliable, comfortable and efficient. Taxis can be found everywhere. Hire cars in the major towns and resorts. Ferries to Ajaccio and Bastia on Corsica and flights to Ajaccio.

International travel Paris is the hub for international flights but some European flights, including low-cost airlines, go to Perpignan, Toulouse, Marignane, Ajaccio (Corsica) and Nice. Ferries to Algeria and Tunisia. Rail system connects other European destinations.

Mail Reliable efficient system, if a little slow at times. Use a marina address or Poste restante.

Telecommunications Automatic dialling. Country code +33. Good public telephone (phone cards) and fax (*télécopier*) service widely available. GSM PAYG mobile phones. Limited internet cafés.

Currency Euro.

Banks Open 0830–1200 and 1400–1700 Mon–Fri although hours may vary. Exchange offices and travel offices operate outside these hours. Post offices will change Traveller's cheques and cash. All major credit cards, charge cards, Eurocheques and Traveller's cheques accepted. ATMs common and work with most credit cards.

Medical Good medical care system. Reciprocal medical care for EU nationals with form *E111* although you will have to pay a part of any treatment costs. Medical costs high.

Electricity 220V 50Hz AC.

Geography

The coast from the Spanish border to the Italian border is composed of a long flat sandy shore around the Golfe du Lion, limestone *calanques* from Golfe de Fos to Hyères, and a rocky and often cliffy coast from Hyères to Menton and the Italian border. The latter part of the coast to the Italian border is steep-to with the foothills of the Alps-Maritime rising sharply from the coast. The island of Corsica has been described as a mountain surrounded by sea, a description difficult to better.

The coastline can be divided up as follows: Languedoc-Roussillon, Provence, Côte d'Azur and

Temperature and precipitation (at Marseille)

	Av max °C	Av min °C	Record	Rel. humidity	Days 1mm rain	Sea temp °C
Jan	10	2	18	68%	8	11
Feb	12	2	22	60%	6	11
Mar	15	5	24	57%	7	12
Apr	18	8	29	54%	7	12
May	22	11	31	54%	8	13
Jun	26	15	37	50%	4	17
Jul	29	17	39	45%	2	20
Aug	28	17	37	49%	5	22
Sep	25	15	34	54%	6	22
Oct	20	10	29	61%	8	20
Nov	15	6	23	66%	9	17
Dec	11	3	20	66%	10	15

Riviera.

Languedoc-Roussillon From the Spanish border to the Rhône delta. Except for the southernmost part where the foothills of the Pyrenees come down to the sea (the *Côte Vermeille*), the coast is a long flat sandy coast with salt lakes (*étangs*) behind the coastal dunes. The French government began a development programme in the 1960s to build large marina-apartment complexes which now ring the Golfe du Lion.

Provence The area from the Rhône delta to La Ciotat. Marseille-Fos is a large commercial and oil port (second only to Amsterdam). Numerous marinas and some anchorages in the *calanques* between Marseille and Cassis.

Côte d'Azur From Toulon to St Laurent du Var. There are many old established resorts and numerous marinas, either purpose built or part of older commercial and fishing ports.

The Riviera The short stretch of coast extending from Nice to Menton and the Italian Riviera. Numerous old established marinas. The principality of Monaco is on this coast.

Corsica The large island lying approximately 100M off the NE coast. Some marinas and numerous picturesque anchorages.

Weather Of the typical Mediterranean type with hot dry summers and mild wet winters. The winter climate along the Riviera is exceptionally mild. In general summer temperatures are in the range 25°–35°C and winter temperatures 2°–20°C. The relative humidity is moderate at around 75% (80% in the winter and 53% in the summer). These figures are increased by onshore winds and reduced by offshore winds. Mean sea temperatures vary from 12°C in February to 23°C in August.

Prevailing winds The prevailing winds are from the NW or SE. NW winds blowing off the land predominate from the Spanish border to Toulon. Further E the prevailing wind is the *vent du midi*, a sea breeze blowing onto the land. It generally blows at a slant to the land from the SE and can even be turned E by the local topography along the coast. This sea

Fréjus Marina on the Côte d'Azur

breeze is also common around the Golfe du Lion when a NW breeze is not blowing.

Around the Golfe du Lion and as far as Toulon the NW winds (*tramontane* from the Spanish border to Sète, *mistral* from Sète to Toulon) can blow up to Force 10 and more and are much to be feared, especially in the winter and spring.

The *mistral* blows down the Rhône Valley from the N and fans out over the Rhône delta to blow from the NE around Cap Bear near the Spanish border and from the NW around Toulon. It can reach as far as the Balearics and Corsica. In the Golfe du Lion it blows at Force 8 or more for over 10% of observations. A *mistral* is caused by a depression passing over central France when cold air finds an outlet down the Rhône Valley and is funnelled down to the Mediterranean. It arrives with little warning and can quickly rise to gale force from a flat calm.

The *tramontane* is first cousin to the mistral and blows out over the Golfe du Lion between the Pyrenees and Sète. Like the *mistral* it is caused by a depression passing over central France and cold air escaping between the Massif central and the Pyrenees through the Toulouse Gap.

In the summer there is often a mild *tramontane* or *mistral* with a diurnal component so that it lessens by day with the sea breeze.

Locally-named winds

Mistral The strong (often gale force) N wind blowing down the Rhône and fanning out to blow as far as Corsica and Sardinia in the E and the Balearics in the W. By the time it has reached Corsica it is blowing from the W and in the Balearics it blows from the NE–E. Arrives with little warning and can quickly reach gale force. Mostly affects the area around the mouth of the Rhône as far as Toulon. The warning signs are a very dry almost electric atmosphere, a clear sky and very clear visibility. Caused by a depression passing over central France and the barometer may rise slightly. Raises a heavy sea. Usually lasts 3 days to a week.

Tramontane The NW wind blowing out over the Golfe du Lion between the Pyrenees and Sète. It fans out to blow as far as the Balearics. Arrives with little warning and can quickly reach gale force. Warning signs are much the same as the *mistral*. Raises a heavy sea. Usually lasts 2–4 days.

Levante A strong E wind accompanied by wet weather. Caused by a depression passing along the North African coast. Preceded by a swell, low cloud forming over the hills and poor visibility. Usually lasts 1–3 days.

Ceruse A strong SE wind similar to the *levante*.

Marin A strong southerly (SW–S–SE) wind bringing a warm humidity with it.

Vent du Midi, vent du solaire The normal day breeze blowing onto the land.

Gales The *mistral* and the *tramontane* are the most feared source of gale force winds because they arrive with little warning, can blow up to gale Force 8 and more, and raise bad seas. For all observations there is a 12% frequency of gales in the winter in the Golfe du Lion, the highest in the Mediterranean. Most of these are from the N–NW. Gales from the S also occur and these raise a heavy sea along the coast making entry to some harbours difficult or dangerous. Again this is especially so in the Golfe du Lion where the water shallows at the entrance to some of the harbours and there are breaking waves at the entrance with S gales.

Thunderstorms Most frequent in the autumn although they do occur in the summer. Often accompanied by strong winds of short duration (1–3 hours). Rain or hail often accompany the associated squall.

Tides

Tides are on average around 0·15m (0·5ft) at springs and for all practical purposes can be ignored. The sea level is raised by onshore winds (up to 1 metre in exceptionally strong and prolonged winds) and is decreased by offshore winds.

Currents

Along the Riviera the current follows the coast in a westerly direction. In the Golfe du Lion the current flows out of the gulf in a SW direction with a lesser easterly counter-current close to the coast.

Harbours and anchorages

Much of the French Mediterranean coast is built up with resorts strung out along the whole coast. Around the Golfe du Lion are numerous large marina and apartment complexes developed with government assistance. Around the Côte d'Azur and Riviera there are numerous old established resorts from the 19th century. There are probably more marinas per mile of coast than anywhere else in the Mediterranean, or the world for that matter. Corsica by comparison, is little developed, with just 14 marinas around a coastline comparable in length with the French Mediterranean coast.

With few exceptions most marinas have visitors berths. Some marinas have visitors berths numbered in three figures while others have just a few visitors berths. There has been some ire expressed over the fact that yachts arriving in the high season cannot find a berth at a chosen marina and there has been some muttering about whether these berths exist at all. It is important to remember that visitor's berths apply equally to local boats in transit as well as to boats from outside the country. I may be stating the obvious, but a visitor's berth is for any boat not permanently berthed at the marina in question.

In my experience all marina managers will try to squash you into a berth whenever it is possible in the high season. Many of them go out of their way to find visiting yachts a berth. If at all possible try to arrange a berth in known crowded marinas in advance. If you intend to base yourself for a week or more in a marina in the high season then book ahead. Alternatively try to avoid popular parts of the coast in the high season from mid-June to mid-September.

Nice on the French Riviera

Facilities

Everyday

Water Readily available in all marinas and most commercial and fishing ports. Is potable from taps unless marked otherwise.
Fuel Fuel quays in nearly all marinas.
Electricity 220V at all marinas. 380V available in some marinas, usually for berths 15m and above.
Gas Camping Gaz widely available. French gas bottles widely available. Other gas bottles difficult to refill.
Paraffin Difficult to obtain. Ask for *petrole kerdane*. Wood alcohol, methylated spirits without the blue dye, can be purchased in supermarkets and grocery shops - ask for *alcool à brûler*.

Boat repairs

Engines Most spares for the major makes of marine engine are available or can be obtained at the larger marina yards. Smaller yards may take longer to obtain spares. Competent workshops in many of the marina yards.
Electrics and electronics Spares and repair facilities available in the larger marina yards. Most items can be obtained quickly although some British and American spares take a while.
Engineering Steel and stainless steel fabrication in some yards and larger towns.
Wood and GRP Good wood repairs and fabrication to yacht standards in many yards. GRP repairs and osmosis treatment in some of the larger marina yards.
Paints and antifouling Locally manufactured paints and antifouling of good quality widely available. Imported paints and antifouling also widely available.
Hauling A large number of yacht yards with travel-hoists and slipways. Most have a large area for hardstanding and good security.
Gardiennage Most of the marinas can arrange gardiennage and general yacht care. Ask around for recommendations.

Provisioning

Most provisions can be found in even very small places in the summer. In the cities and larger towns there are excellent supermarkets (Géant Casino, Continent, Carrefour, Auchan) where all prices are clearly marked and everything you need can be bought. Some of the marinas built away from a village or town do not have good shopping within the marina and you will need a car to get to a nearby town to stock up. In the winter many of the shops, restaurants and cafés close down completely in some of the large purpose-built marina and apartment complexes and the places are effectively ghost towns. This is especially true of the developments around the coast in Languedoc-Roussillon. Good fresh fruit and vegetables, fish and shellfish, and farm produce will be found in the markets. Shopping hours vary but generally are 0830–1200 and 1400–1800 Mon–Sat. Some shops will close on Mon. afternoon. In the summer some shops remain open for longer hours. Many towns have a Sunday morning market.

Charts and pilots

Mediterranean Pilot Vol II (NP47) (Admiralty). Covers the French Mediterranean coast and Corsica.

Mediterranean France and Corsica Pilot Rod Heikell (Imray). Detailed pilotage of the southern French waterways, Mediterranean coast and Corsica.

Corsica and North Sardinia John Marchment (RCC Pilotage Foundation/Imray)

Votre Livre du Bord – Méditerranée (Bloc Marine Interval Editions). Annual almanac for France. Gives price lists for French marinas. Available locally.

Bateaux Skipper (Bateaux). Annual almanac for France. Available locally.

Charts Admiralty charts provide just adequate coverage. French charts provide better coverage. French charts (SHOM) do not have compass roses on them and so require the use of a Portland Plotter, Douglas Protractor or similar. French charts are widely available from chandlers and maritime bookshops in the larger ports. *Cartes-Guide* charts (published by Editions Grafocarte), which fold up, are widely available from chandlers and bookshops. Admiralty charts and Imray publications are available from Riviera Charts, Galerie du Port, 26-30 Rue Lacan, 06600 Antibes
☎ (04) 93 34 45 66
Fax (04) 93 34 43 36
www.riviera-charts.com

13.5 MONACO ☎ IDD +377

Area 0·75M² (2km²)
Frontiers France
Coastline 6M
Population 32,000
Government Constitutional monarchy
Capital Monaco-Ville
Time zone UT+1 DST Apr-Sep
Language French, Italian, English
Economy Tax haven for the extremely wealthy.
Telecommunications Code +377. GSM capability.
Currency Euro

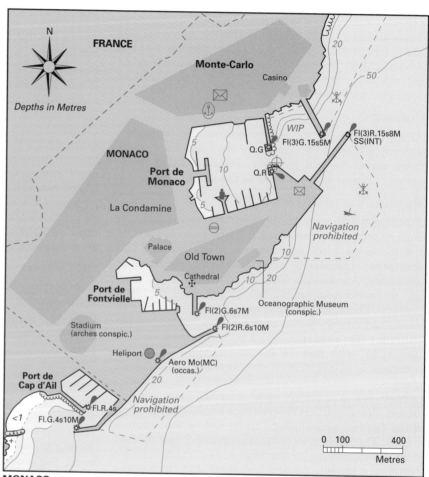

MONACO

Area 115,973M² (301,230km²)
Frontiers 1902km total. Austria 430km, France 488km, Switzerland 740km, Slovenia 202km, San Marino 39km, Vatican City 3·2km

Coastline 2698M (4996km)
Maritime claims 12M
Inland waterways 2400km. Limited commercial traffic.

Population 57·4M. Growth rate 0·2%

Government Democratic republic; 20 *regioni*

Disputes South Tyrol question with Austria. Friction with N African states over illegal immigration to the Italian islands of Lampedusa and Pantellaria

Capital Rome

Time zone UT+1 DST Apr–Sep

Language Italian. Some French spoken on the Riviera. Some English and German spoken

Ethnic groups Primarily Italian with clusters of German, French and Slovenes in the north and Albanians in the south

Religion Almost 100% nominally Roman Catholic

Public holidays
Jan 1 New Year's Day
Apr 25 Liberation Day
May 1 Labour Day
Aug 15 Festival of the Assumption
Nov 1 All Saints Day
Dec 8 Festival of the Immaculate Conception
Dec 25, 26 Christmas
Moveable
Easter Monday

Economy Highly developed industrial economy in the north and poorer agricultural economy in the south. There is some friction between the affluent north who feel they should not have to subsidise the poorer south. Work force is 5% in agriculture, 32% in industry and commerce, 58% in government and services. Most raw materials and 75% of energy requirements must be imported. Tourism is important.

Exports Machinery and transport equipment, chemicals, textiles, metals, food products, vehicles (Fiat).

Imports Ore, oil, machinery, chemicals, food.

Crops Grapes, olives, citrus, vegetables, wheat, rice.

Environment and pollution Heavy metals and toxic waste dumped into rivers and washed down to the sea. Heavy use of pesticides and fertilisers. The nitrate rich waters of the Po emptying into the N Adriatic have produced severe algal blooms in recent years. Italian waters are over-fished and Italian fishermen regularly poach in other areas. Drift nets cause many dolphin and turtle deaths annually. Several marine reserves although these are not very well policed. 'Pelican' boats to scoop up surface rubbish exist in many harbours but are not always effective.

Internal travel Internal flights link major cities. Extensive rail network with an efficient train service. Regular bus services to most destinations. Hire cars in the major towns and tourist resorts. Regular ferries to Sardinia and Sicily.

International travel Rome and Milan are the principal airports for international flights. Some European flights, including low-cost airlines, to Genoa, Pisa, Pescara, Brindisi, Bari, Olbia (Sardinia), Naples, Catania (Sicily), and Venice. Ferries from Ancona, Bari and Brindisi to Greece. Ferries from Venice to Greece and Turkey. Ferries from Reggio di Calabria and Siracusa (Sicily) to Malta. Ferries from Trapani (Sicily) to Tunisia. Ferries to Corsica.

Mail Not always reliable. Best sent to a marina or private address. Poste restante service.

Telecommunications Automatic dialling. Code +39. Adequate service. Public telephones can be used with phonecards. GSM PAYG mobile phones. Internet cafés.

Currency Euro.

Banks Open 0830–1330 Mon–Fri. Exchange offices and travel offices operate outside these hours. Major credit cards and charge cards can be used in most places. Traveller's cheques accepted. ATM's common and work with major credit cards.

Medical Generally good. Reciprocal care for EU nationals with Form *E111* although you will have to pay a part of the costs. Medical costs high.

Electricity 220V 50Hz AC.

Geography

Italy is a long peninsula jutting SE into the Mediterranean for some 500M from the Alps. On the W side are the Ligurian and Tyrrhenian seas, at the S end the Ionian sea, and on the E side the Adriatic. On the western side the Republic of Italy encompasses Sicily and Sardinia, two of the largest islands in the Mediterranean. The backbone of the Italian peninsula is the Apennine range of mountains which terminates in the Calabrian massif and the mountains of Sicily. The coast varies dramatically from place to place, but in general the W coast is mountainous with high land close to the coast and the E coast is largely low-lying with a shallow shelf extending seawards.

The coast and islands can be divided up as follows: the Ligurian coast, Tuscan Islands and adjacent coast, Tyrrhenian Sea, Sardinia, Sicily, Ionian Sea, and the Adriatic coast.

Ligurian Coast From the French border to the Magra River just before Carrara. The Italian Riviera runs around to Genoa and is backed by the foothills of the Alps rising steeply from the sea. From Genoa down to the Magra River the land also rises steeply from the coast. Numerous old established marinas. Genoa is Italy's largest commercial port.

Tuscan Islands and adjacent coast Capraia, Elba, Pianosa, Giglio and Montecristo are the principal islands. Much of the adjacent coast is comparatively low-lying. Some marinas, commercial and fishing harbours and some anchorages.

Tyrrhenian Sea The coast from Civitavecchia to Reggio di Calabria in the Strait of Messina. Numerous off-lying islands including Ponza, Ventotene, Ischia, Procida, and Capri. Rome and Naples lie on this coast. A mix of marinas, commercial and fishing harbours and a few anchorages.

Sardinia The large offshore island (second largest in the Mediterranean) at $9303M^2$ ($24,100km^2$) lying immediately S of Corsica. Marinas on the NE coast but otherwise there is a mix of marinas, commercial and fishing harbours and numerous anchorages.

Sicily The largest island in the Mediterranean, $9920M^2$ ($25,700km^2$), lying a short hop across the Strait of Messina from the toe of Italy. A few marinas, commercial and fishing harbours, and a few anchorages.

Ionian Sea A few commercial, fishing harbours and marinas scattered sparsely along the coast.

Adriatic coast The long and fairly straight coast from Capo Santa Maria di Leuca to the border with Slovenia. Much of it is comparatively low-lying with shoal water extending some distance off the coast, especially around the lagoons of Venice. Marinas and commercial harbours with few anchorages.

Seismic activity The W coast stretching from Naples down to Sicily lies along a major fault line where the North African plate rubs up against the Italo-Yugoslav plate. There have been regular and severe earthquakes in the region, notably the disastrous 1908 earthquake at Messina and recently, on 23rd November 1980, the Calabria quake which killed 5000 and left nearly half a million homeless.

Volcanic activity Around Naples and extending down to Sicily there are a number of active volcanoes, most notably Vesuvius in the Bay of Naples, Stromboli, Vulcano, and Etna near Catania on Sicily. Etna is the most active of these, but all of them regularly release gas and cinders.

Weather Summers are of the Mediterranean type but winters vary from continental to the more normal Mediterranean mild winter. The head of the Adriatic around Venice and Trieste can be very wet and cold in the winter. The Italian Riviera from the French border to past Genoa has its own mild winter micro-climate. In the south in Calabria and Sicily the winter climate is particularly mild. In Sicily the January average temperature is 13°C and the August average 29°C.

Prevailing winds In the summer winds are predominantly from the NW–W–SW. On the W coast of Italy this is a sea breeze getting up around midday and dying at night. It can be much altered by the local topography so that in some places it blows from the N or S. It is typically Force 3–5. On the E coast the wind is more variable but is usually N–NW in the S of the Adriatic and SE in the N of the Adriatic. In the Ionian the wind direction is variable throughout although NW–W winds predominate.

Locally-named winds

Maestrale The predominant NW wind. It gets its name from the gales that blow from the NW but has now been generalised to any wind from this direction.

Libeccio The SW–W wind that blows over Corsica and in the Ligurian and N half of the Tyrrhenian seas. It frequently blows at Force 5–8. Accompanied by cloud and often rain in the autumn and winter. Usually lasts 1–4 days.

Tramontana A N–NE wind which mostly blows in the autumn and winter along the W coast of Italy. It can blow at gale force and there can be severe gusts off high land. Often associated with a depression in the Adriatic. Usually lasts 1–2 days.

Gregale Strong NE wind. Blows principally down the Adriatic and across to Malta. The warning signs are a heavy swell and low cloud with rain. Often blows at gale force. Usually lasts for 2–5 days.

Sirocco The hot humid S wind blowing off the Sahara. Most common in southern Italy. It is accompanied by

Temperature and precipitation (at Naples)

	Av max °C	Av min °C	Record	Rel. humidity	Days 1mm rain	Sea temp °C
Jan	12	4	20	68%	11	12
Feb	13	5	20	67%	10	12
Mar	15	6	25	62%	9	13
Apr	18	9	27	61%	8	13
May	22	12	32	63%	7	15
Jun	26	16	35	58%	4	17
Jul	29	18	36	53%	2	22
Aug	29	18	37	53%	3	24
Sep	26	16	34	59%	5	23
Oct	22	12	29	63%	9	22
Nov	17	9	26	68%	11	19
Dec	14	6	20	70%	12	15

bad visibility and low cloud. If it rains there will often be 'red rain' containing dust particles from the Sahara. May blow up to gale force. Usually lasts 1–3 days.

Bora A strong N wind similar to the *mistral*. Mainly affects the N Adriatic. Most frequent in winter although it can blow at other times of the year. Often blows at gale force. Can last from 2–12 days. See *13.8 Croatia* for more information.

Gales Depressions entering the Mediterranean follow several different tracks over Italy. Frequently a depression will enter Golfo di Genoa and deepen, spawning the notorious Genoa lee cyclone. This depression will then move off, typically across the N Adriatic. It brings gale force winds and heavy rain. It can raise a vicious sea in the Ligurian. Other depressions will come directly across the Mediterranean and usually slide off around the bottom of Italy and across the Ionian to Greece. These can bring gale force winds to the Tyrrhenian (particularly in the Aeolian triangle around the Aeolian Islands) and the Ionian, usually from the SW–W–NW. In the Adriatic the *bora* is the wind most feared and frequently blows at gale force. In Trieste hurricane force gusts (Force 11) have been recorded.

Thunderstorms Most frequent in the summer and autumn and may be associated with a cold front or result from an unstable thermal air mass (heat thunderstorm). Heat thunderstorms can occur on successive evenings in some areas. They are more common close to land than out to sea. Often accompanied by strong winds of short duration (1–3 hours). Rain or hail may accompany the associated squall.

Waterspouts These have been recorded around the Italian coast along the Italian Riviera, the Bay of Naples, Aeolian Islands, Strait of Messina, and Golfo di Cagliari. There are few accounts of yachts being struck by a waterspout and in the few recorded instances damage has been limited to damage to rig and sails and other items on deck. However in larger waterspouts the wind speeds must be great enough to cause severe damage.

The miniature harbour at Ventotene, carved out of rock in Roman times

Tides

Tidal differences around the coast vary considerably. On the W coast down to the Strait of Messina the tidal difference is on average around 0·3m (1·0ft) at springs though mostly less. For all practical purposes this can be ignored except in the Strait of Messina and the Northern Adriatic.

In the Strait of Messina the tidal difference causes strong tidal streams at springs. The most appreciable rate, up to 4 knots at springs, is in the narrow section between Punta Pezzo and Capo Peloro. To the N and S of this narrow section the stream diminishes appreciably although a lessened stream (around ½–1 knot) may be encountered as far away as Capo dell'Armi and Taormina. Under normal conditions the N–going stream begins at 1 hour 45 minutes before high water Gibraltar. The S–going stream starts at 4 hours 30 minutes after high water Gibraltar. Strong winds from N or S can increase or diminish the stream. At each turn of the tide there is a brief stand followed by one or more bores or *tagli* caused by the particular submarine nature of the strait. In the narrow part of the strait the *tagli* is accompanied by eddies and whirlpools which can bother small craft. Of general interest is the fact that the tide tables published by official bodies (and reproduced in this almanac) do not seem to tally with local tables (at Reggio di Calabria) nor with locally derived times for the tidal streams.

In the S Adriatic tidal differences can again be ignored for all practical purposes. In the N Adriatic tidal differences at springs are more significant at 0·2–1·3m (0·66–4·26ft) at springs. At Venice the tidal range is 1·0m (3·3ft). This tidal range is much augmented or decreased by strong winds. At Venice a strong SE wind can raise the sea level by as much as 1·8m (5·9ft) and a strong N wind can decrease it by 0·8m (2·62ft). The *bora* causes the sea level to rise along the E coast of Italy.

Currents

Currents are complex around the long peninsula of Italy with added complications from the offshore islands.

In general there is a weak N–NNW–going current, usually around ½–1 knot, flowing up the W coast. In the Ligurian the current is turned E and then flows SE down the W side of Corsica. Off the coast in the Tyrrenhian there is a counter-current flowing back down to the SE along the coast of Sardinia. This splits at Sicily to flow east-about along the N and S coasts of Sicily.

In the Ionian there is a SW current flowing down the coast which can reach 1–2 knots in places such as around Capo Santa Maria di Leuca.

In the Adriatic there is, roughly, a circular anticlockwise current flowing N–NW up the coast of Albania and Croatia before turning to flow roughly SE down the mainland coast of Italy. The currents are much modified by the coast and wind. In the upper N of the Adriatic there are variable circular currents easily modified by strong winds from any direction.

Around the S of Sicily a form of seiche known as the

Scario on the west coast of Italy

berths. Some marinas have visitors berths numbered in three figures while others have just a few visitors berths. There has been some ire expressed over the fact that yachts arriving in the high season cannot find a berth at a chosen marina and there has been some muttering about whether these berths exist at all. It is important to remember that visitor's berths apply equally to local boats in transit as well as to boats from outside the country. I may be stating the obvious, but a visitor's berth is for any boat not permanently berthed at the marina in question.

In my experience all marina managers will try to squash you into a berth whenever it is possible in the high season. Many of them go out of their way to find visiting yachts a berth. If at all possible try to arrange a berth in known crowded marinas in advance. If you intend to base yourself for a week or more in a marina in the high season then book ahead. Alternatively try to avoid popular parts of the coast in the high season from mid-June to mid-September.

Facilities

Everyday

Water Readily available in all marinas and many commercial and fishing harbours, although in the latter the water point may be some distance away. Some marinas have dual water points with potable water on one and non-potable water suitable for washing down boats on the other. In some of the off-lying islands there are shortages in the summer and you should not rely on obtaining supplies. In some areas, especially around Naples and in Calabria, water is also in short supply and may be of suspect quality (Naples especially).

Fuel Fuel quays in nearly all marinas. Fuel can be delivered to some of the commercial and fishing harbours although in the S of Italy and parts of Sardinia and Sicily you may have difficulties finding a supply in places.

Electricity 220V at all marinas. 380V available in some marinas, usually for berths 20m and above. Some of the yacht clubs in commercial or fishing harbours can arrange for electricity.

Gas Camping Gaz widely available in the N and at larger towns and resorts in the S. Italian gas bottles widely available. Other gas bottles can be filled in a few places.

Paraffin Not readily available. Try in the larger towns or some of the fishing harbours where the fishermen use it for their lamps. Ask for *petrolio* or *paraffina*. Methylated spirits available in general grocery and hardware shops.

Boat repairs

Engines Most spares for the major makes of marine engine are available or can be obtained in the larger marina yards in the N. In the S it is more difficult to obtain spares. As a general rule the main distributor for Italy will be in the N (often in Milan) and most distribution outlets are concentrated in the N. Most of the major Italian manufacturers of marine engines and associated equipment are also in the N. Competent workshops in many of the marina yards in the N. Good workshops willing to tackle engine problems without necessarily having all the requisite equipment will be

marrobio can occur. It is a form of tidal wave which quickly raises the level of the water and then recedes again. The cycle may be repeated at intervals of a few minutes. It can raise the water level as much as 1m (3·3ft). It is probably caused by two wave trains meeting and the resonance set up causes a rapid 'tidal wave'. H M Denham reported it can be associated with humid conditions, a falling barometer and the onset of southerlies. Since southerlies are often preceded by a swell it could be that this S–going wave train meeting a N or W–going wave train sets up the resonance to cause a *marrobio*.

Harbours and anchorages

Harbours in Italy vary dramatically from N to S. As a general rule the numbers of marinas decrease the further S you go. In the N there are numerous purpose built marinas or commercial and fishing harbours converted in part or whole to a marina. There are also numerous fishing harbours and some anchorages. This pattern holds true for the northern Adriatic where there are large numbers of marinas clustered around Venice. S of Naples there are fewer yacht marinas and fishing harbours and commercial harbours with a few yacht club berths become the norm.

In Sardinia there is a cluster of yacht marinas on the N and E coast but for the rest of the coast fishing and commercial harbours become the norm. Around the Sicilian coast there are yacht marinas on the N coast but for the rest there are mostly fishing and commercial harbours. Along the boot of Italy there are fishing and commercial harbours with few anchorages.

With few exceptions most marinas have visitors

Tropea in Calabria on the western coast of Italy. The coast from Tropea right up to Amalfi is comparatively little cruised by yachts.   Lu Michell

found in the S.

Electrics and electronics Spares and repair facilities available in the larger marina yards in the N. Fewer repair facilities in the S. Some British and American spares may take a while to arrive if ordered from source.

Engineering Steel and stainless steel fabrication in many yards in the N. Steel fabrication in the S.

Wood and GRP Excellent wood repairs and fabrication to yacht standards, possibly to the highest standards in the Mediterranean. Yards noted for their work exist at San Stefano, Rome and around Venice. GRP repairs and osmosis treatment in some of the larger yards in the N and S.

Paints and antifouling Locally manufactured paints and antifouling of good quality widely available. Imported paints and antifouling also widely available.

Hauling A large number of yacht yards with travel-hoists and slipways in the N. Fewer yacht yards with travel-hoists in the S although some fishing boat yards will haul yachts either by travel-hoist or on a slipway.

Gardiennage Many of the marinas in the N can arrange gardiennage and general yacht care. In the S it is more difficult to obtain gardiennage although reliable guardians exist. Ask around for recommendations. In the S Salerno and Sibari Marina have been recommended.

Provisioning

Most provisions can be found except in some of the out-of-the-way places in Calabria, Sardinia and Sicily. In the cities and larger towns there are excellent supermarkets (Standa, Upim) where all prices are clearly marked and you can obtain everything you need. Some of the marinas built away from a village or town do not have good shopping facilities and you will need a car to get to the shops. In the S there is not the range of goods to be found in the N. Good fresh fruit and vegetables, fish and shellfish, will be found in the markets. Shopping hours are generally 0900–1230 and 1500–1930 Mon–Sat. Shops often close on Monday mornings and/or Wednesday afternoons.

Charts and pilots

Mediterranean Pilot Vol I (*NP45*) (Admiralty). Covers Sicily and Calabria.

Mediterranean Pilot Vol II (*NP46*) (Admiralty). Covers the W coast of Italy and Sardinia.

Mediterranean Pilot Vol III (*NP47*) (Admiralty). Covers the E coast of Italy.

Italian Waters Pilot Rod Heikell (Imray). Detailed pilotage of the W and S coasts of Italy including Sardinia and Sicily (and Malta).

Adriatic Pilot T & D Thompson (Imray). Detailed pilotage of the E coast of Italy.

The Tyrrhenian Sea H M Denham (John Murray). Covers the area bordered by the Tyrrhenian Sea. OP.

Porticcioli d'Italia Bruno Ziravello. In Italian.

Navigare Lungocosta Mauro Mancini. Five volumes covering the Italian coast with pen and ink sketches. In Italian.

Pagine Azzure Il Portolano dei Mari d'Italia. Covers all Italian harbours. Published annually. In Italian.

Charts Admiralty charts provide adequate coverage. Istituto Idrografico Della Marina (Italian Hydrographic Department) charts provide better coverage and are beautifully produced, though at a price. Italian charts are available from chandlers in the larger ports. Nauticard produce a number of charts of smaller size for Italy and are widely available in chandlers.

Area 123M² (320km²)
Coastline 75·6M (140km)
Maritime claims 24M. 25M exclusive fishing zone
Population 400,000. Growth rate 0·9%
Government Parliamentary democracy. EU member since May 2004
Capital Valletta
Time zone UT+1 DST Apr–Sep
Language Maltese and English (official). Some Italian spoken
Ethnic groups Mixture of Arab, Sicilian, Italian, Norman, Spanish, and English
Religion 98% Roman Catholic
Public holidays
Jan 1 New Year's Day
Mar 31 National Day
May 1 May Day
Aug 15 Festival of the Assumption
Dec 13 Republic Day
Dec 25 Christmas
Moveable
Good Friday
Economy Largely dependent on tourism. A large shipyard and minor light industry. Most agricultural goods must be imported. 35% in industry and commerce, 30% in services, 22% in government, 4·5% in agriculture and fisheries.
Exports Ships, textiles, yarns.
Imports Nearly everything.
Minerals Limestone, salt.
Crops Some fruit and vegetables.
Environment and pollution Fertilisers and pesticides are beginning to be used. Raw sewage is dumped untreated into the sea. Minor dumping of toxic waste from industry. Fishermen catch sea turtles and coral is taken for tourist trinkets. Dolphins are caught in drift nets.
Internal travel Buses are cheap and run everywhere. Hire cars. Taxis. Ferry to Gozo.
International travel Some international flights and connections to Rome and London where all international flights can be found. Ferries to Siracusa (Sicily) and Reggio di Calabria.
Mail Reliable. Mail can be sent to Msida Creek Marina, Manoel Island Marina, Manoel Island Yacht Yard, or Poste restante.
Telecommunications Automatic dialling. Code +356. Telephone and fax services available at the marinas and Manoel Island Yacht Yard.
Currency Maltese pound (£M) = 100 cents. Euro.
Banks Open 0800–1200 Mon–Sat. All major credit cards, charge cards, and traveller's cheques accepted. ATMs common and work with most credit or debit cards.
Medical Reciprocal agreement with United Kingdom. Good treatment. Fees are moderate.
Electricity 240V.

Geography

Malta consists of two major islands, Malta and Gozo, and two smaller islands, Comino and Filfla. They lie

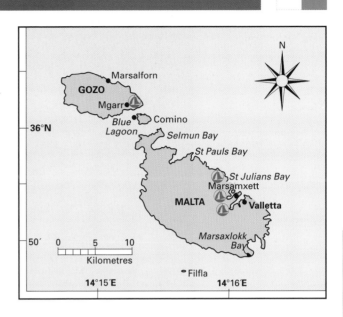

approximately 60M S of Sicily and 220M N of Libya. The strategic position of the islands between the W and E Mediterranean basins and between Africa and Europe has made them militarily important over the centuries. Malta is not so much a cruising area as a base for yachts with cruising grounds in Italy and Greece nearby.

Weather Typically Mediterranean with hot dry summers and wet mild winters. In July and August temperatures can be very high, often reaching 40°.

Prevailing winds Winds from the NW prevail in the summer although winds from the N and NE also blow. The prevailing wind is modified by the local topography so that in places it gusts over the land from the N–W–SSW. Normally it gets up around midday, blows Force 4–5 through the afternoon, and dies at night.

Locally-named winds
Majjistral The prevailing NW wind. It is commonly believed to be the same wind as the *mistral* although this is not the case. It is in fact a sea breeze set up by the pressure difference between Sicily and Tunisia.
Rih fuq N winds.
Rih isfel S winds.
Xlokk The *sirocco*.
Gregale The NE wind often blowing at gale force.

Gales In the winter the NE *gregale* is the wind most feared as Marsamxett is open to this direction (as is Grand Harbour) and a considerable surge is set up. The *gregale* regularly blows up to gale force and can reach Force 9–10 on occasion. It can blow from 2–5 days. The *sirocco* (*xlokk*) also blows in winter and summer bringing an enervating humidity in the summer. It can blow at gale force and raises a considerable sea.

Thunderstorms Most frequent in the autumn and winter. Frequently associated with a cold front. Often accompanied by strong winds of short duration (1–3

Mgarr on the smaller
Maltese island of Gozo
Lu Michell

hours). Rain or hail may accompany the associated squall.

Waterspouts Have been recorded in the Sicilian and Malta Channels.

Tides

Tidal difference at Valletta is 0·4m (1·3ft) at springs which for all practical purposes can be ignored. The sea level is only slightly affected by onshore and offshore winds.

Currents

The predominant set through the Sicilian Channel is to the SE at ½–1 knot although strong W–NW winds can push the current up to as much as 2 knots. A S–SE–going current flows down the E side of Sicily to join the main current passing along the North African coast and through the Sicilian channel. Because the sea bottom is comparatively shallow and irregular over the sill in the Sicilian channel there can often be lumpy seas and a disproportionate swell.

Facilities

Everyday

Water Available at all marinas. It is often in short supply in the summer and can be brackish.

Fuel Can be delivered by mini-tanker as required. There is also a fuel barge in Marsamxett.

Electricity 220V at yacht berths.

Gas Camping Gaz available. Most gas bottles can be refilled in 2–3 days.

Paraffin Easily available from mini-tankers which do the rounds of Gzira and Valletta. Methylated spirits also available from the same vendors.

Boat repairs

Engines Most spares for the major makes of marine engine are available or can be ordered. It may pay to check on the origin of the spares and the estimated time for them to arrive in Malta if ordered from overseas. Competent workshops and contractors.

Electrics and electronics Spares and repair facilities. Many items are held in stock but if not check to see how long it will take for items to arrive.

Engineering Steel and stainless steel fabrication but check around as standards vary.

Wood and GRP Adequate wood repairs and fabrication. Check on the credentials of the contractor. GRP repairs and osmosis treatment to adequate standards.

Paints and antifouling Locally manufactured paints and antifouling (Hempels manufactured under licence) of adequate quality. Imported paints and antifouling also widely available.

Hauling Manoel Island Yacht Yard has a 25-ton travel-hoist and slipways up to 500 tons. Hard standing ashore. Also private yards.

Gardiennage Several agencies can arrange gardiennage (essential if a yacht is left afloat in Manoel Island Yacht Marina where damage can occur to an unattended yacht when the *gregale* blows) and general yacht care. Ask around for recommendations.

Provisioning

Good shopping in Msida, Gzira and Sliema. Fruit and vegetables can be of poor quality depending on supply.

Charts and pilots

Mediterranean Pilot Vol I (*NP45*) (Admiralty). Covers Malta.

Italian Waters Pilot Rod Heikell (Imray). Detailed pilotage for harbours and anchorages around Malta.

North Africa Compiled by Hans van Rijn, revised by Graham Hutt (RCC Pilotage Foundation/Imray). Information on Malta.

Charts Admiralty charts cover the islands well.

13.8 Slovenia

Area: 7836sM² (20,296km²)

Frontiers: Total 998km. Austria 262km, Croatia 455km, Italy 199km, Hungary 83km

Coastline: 16M (32km)

Maritime claims 12M

Population 2M. Growth rate 0·26%

Government Parliamentary democracy. EU member since May 2004

Disputes Dispute with Croatia over fishing rights in the Adriatic

Capital Ljubljana

Time zone UT+1. DST Apr–Sep

Language 91% Slovene. Serbo-Croat. Italian widely spoken

Ethnic groups 91% Slovene. 3% Croat. 2% Serb. 1% Muslim

Religion 94% Roman Catholic. 2% Orthodox Catholic. 1% Muslim

Economy Most prosperous of the old Yugoslav republics. Joined the EU in May 2004. Output has declined 10% plus since the split from ex-Yugoslavia. Work force is 46% in manufacturing and mining, 2% in agriculture.

Environment and pollution Sava River polluted by raw sewage and industrial waste products. Heavy metal and toxic chemical pollution along the coast. Fertiliser and pesticides run off into the sea. Air pollution from industry.

Internal travel Good bus and train services.

International travel Ljubljana Airport has flights from British and other international destinations. Bus connections to nearby countries. Trieste airport can also be used for easy connections to the coast.

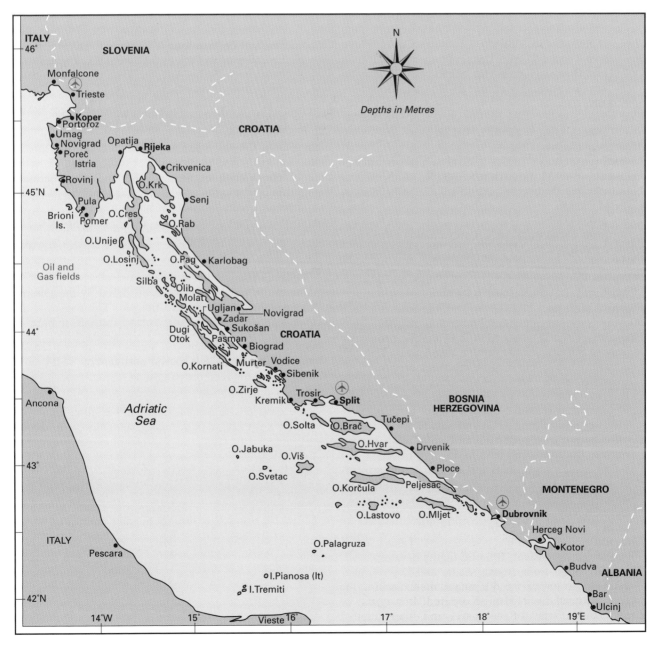

Mail Reasonable. Best sent to a marina.

Telecommunications International and national connections possible. Code +386. GSM capability.

Currency Slovene Tolar. Euro.

Banks Traveller's cheques and credit cards can be used in most places. It is advisable to carry cash (Euros) for most transactions. Most marinas charge in Euros.

Medical Adequate facilities. No data on costs or reciprocal agreements.

Electricity 220V.

Geography

Low rolling hills. Coast fringed by rocks and shoal water.

Weather Mediterranean climate in the summer along the coast. Continental type winters. See *13.9 Croatia*.

Tides and currents

See *13.9 Croatia*.

Facilities

Good facilities for yacht care and repair available. Italy is nearby if services and spares are not available.

Charts and pilots

Mediterranean Pilot Vol III (NP47) (Admiralty). Covers Slovenia.

Adriatic Pilot T & D Thompson (Imray). Detailed pilotage for Slovenia.

Kustenhandbuch Jugoslawien (DK Edition Maritim). Covers Slovenia. In German.

Charts Admiralty charts provide adequate coverage at a reasonable scale. Italian and ex-Yugoslav charts provide more detail.

13.9 CROATIA

TIME ZONE UT+1 ☎ IDD +385

Area 21,829M² (56,538km²)

Frontiers Total 1843km. Bosnia Herzogovina E 751km. Bosnia Herzegovina SE 91km. Hungary 292km. Serbia and Montenegro 254km. Slovenia 455km

Coastline Total 3127M (5790km). Mainland 960M (1778km). Islands 2166M (4012km).

Maritime claims 12M

Inland waterways 785km. Of varying importance

Population 4·4M. Growth rate 0·05%

Government Democratic republic

Capital Zagreb

Time zone UT+1

Language Croat 96%. Italian spoken along the coast

Ethnic groups Croat 78%, Serb 12%, Muslim 1%. Also Hungarian and Slovenian

Religion Roman Catholic 76·5%, Orthodox 11%, Muslim 1·2%, Protestant 1·4%

Public holidays
30 May National Statehood Day

Economy Croatia was second in economic prosperity only to Slovenia in the former Yugoslavia. The economy has stablised although there are still question marks over some areas. Tourism along the coast that once contributed significantly to the economy has returned in parts. Work force is industry and mining 37%, agriculture 4%.

Environment and pollution Industrial waste is run off into the rivers and the sea. Hydrocarbon pollution at oil terminals and from passing tankers cleaning out their tanks. Air pollution around industrial sites. Unknown environmental damage both directly and to the infrastructure from the armed conflict with Serbia.

Internal travel Good bus connections. Taxis (although expensive). Internal flights between Zagreb, Split, Pula, Rijeka, Zadar and Dubrovnik. Hire cars at airports and large towns. Coastal ferries Rijeka, Split, Hvar, Korcula, Dubrovnik.

International travel British and some other continental connections to Zagreb. Charter flights in the summer to Pula and Dubrovnik. Ferries Split-Ancona, Zadar Ancona, Dubrovnik-Greece.

Telecommunications Generally good. Code +385. Card phones are being introduced. Phonecards can be bought from post offices and bars. GSM PAYG. Internet cafés.

Currency Croation Kuna. 1 kuna = 100 lipa. Euro.

Banks Banks and marina offices will change traveller's cheques, $US, £GBP or Euros to kuna. Some credit cards and charge cards accepted along the coast although not yet widespread.

Medical Variable. No data available on costs and reciprocal agreements.

Electricity 220V.

Geography

Most of the Croatian coast is bordered by the Dinaric Alps which drop sheer into the sea. The coast for the most part is steep-to and rocky and often bare of

Temperature and precipitation (at Dubrovnik)

	Av max °C	Av min °C	Record	Rel. humidity	Days 1mm rain	Sea temp °C
Jan	12	6	19	59%	13	12
Feb	13	6	21	63%	13	12
Mar	14	8	23	63%	11	13
Apr	17	11	26	66%	10	14
May	21	14	29	69%	10	18
Jun	25	18	34	66%	6	21
Jul	29	21	37	61%	4	23
Aug	28	21	37	61%	3	25
Sep	25	18	34	63%	7	25
Oct	21	14	28	63%	11	23
Nov	17	10	24	65%	16	21
Dec	14	8	19	65%	15	15

Zadar in Croatia

Peter Kleinoth

vegetation. In a few places there are coastal flats where a river meets the sea but on the whole there are few coastal plains. Lying in serried ranks off the coast are numerous islands increasing the coastline by some 3 times. Both the coast and islands are much indented providing numerous sheltered bays and natural harbours.

Seismic activity The European plate butts up against the Italo-Yugoslav plate running down the Adriatic coast of Croatia and Montenegro into Albania. The area is prone to earthquakes of significant magnitude which have caused widespread damage in the past. The last significant earthquake was in 1979 which caused damage to harbours and changed the coastline and submarine features S of latitude 42°30'.

Weather The summer climate is of the Mediterranean type with settled weather and temperatures in the region of 28° to 35° C. The winter climate is continental with low temperatures, snow over the high land and often violent winds. The winter climate becomes more mild to the S. Average air temperatures on the coast in August are 23°C in the N, 28°C in the S. Average air temperatures on the coast in February are 7°C in the N, 10°C in the S. Average annual rainfall is 150cm (59") in the N, 50cm (20") in the S.

Prevailing winds The prevailing wind in the summer is the *maestral*, a sea breeze blowing onto the islands and coast. It is much modified by the local topography so that it can blow from NW–W–SW. Like all sea breezes it starts in the late morning or midday, blows strongest in the afternoon at around Force 3–5, although it can be channelled to Force 6 between the islands, and dies off in the evening. A light land breeze may blow in the early morning, but it is usually less than Force 2–3.

The wind most feared in the Adriatic is the *bora*. It occurs when a depression passes N over continental Europe and cold air escapes between the Italian Alps and the Dinaric Alps into the Adriatic. It typically blows from the N–NE and there is a cascade effect as cold air tumbles down the steep-to land to the sea. It frequently blows at gale force and can reach hurricane force in squalls along the coast. Fortunately it is rare in the summer (normally lasting a day or less) and is typically a winter wind.

The *yugo* is the Serbo-Croat term for the *sirocco* which often blows in the spring and autumn. (Perhaps it will now be called the 'croat'). It normally occurs when a high pressure sits over the Balkans and draws air up the Adriatic. It normally blows from the S–SE, can blow at gale force, occasionally more, and brings with it a heavy swell which can be dangerous in some harbours. Because the wind has travelled some distance over the sea it normally brings a sultry humidity.

Locally-named winds

Maestral, maestrale, maestro, mestral NW–W–SW sea breeze blowing onto the coast.
Smorac Alternative name for the *maestral*.
Bora, bura The violent N–NE wind blowing down the Adriatic. Typically blows from the NE along the Croatian coastline, often at gale force, and has been recorded at hurricane force at Trieste. It blows throughout the Adriatic although it is strongest around Trieste and in the Velebitski Kanal. It is most frequent in the winter although it also blows in the summer, though at less strength and shorter duration. Caused by a depression passing to the N of the Adriatic when cold air trapped behind the mountains escapes through the gap between the Italian Alps and Dinaric Alps and

161

lesser mountain valleys. Arrives with little warning and quickly gets up to gale force from a flat calm. Care is needed after a *bora* dies down in case a secondary cold front comes along when the *bora* can suddenly start blowing again. A low-lying cloud cap over the high mountain tops along the coast usually means a *bora* is imminent. Blows for up to 2 weeks in the winter but usually only 1–2 days in the summer.

Burano The name given to a little *bora* in the summer. Usually blows at less than gale force.

Jugo, yugo Name for the *sirocco* in Croatia. Blows from the S–SE. Often blows at gale force. Most common in the spring and autumn. Raises a heavy sea along the coast.

Libeccio As for the *libeccio* in Italy.

Tramontana Squally N wind.

Levanat E wind that normally blows in the northern Adriatic. Associated with a depression passing over the Adriatic. Usually accompanied by rain and cloud.

Gales The *bora* and *jugo* are the two most feared gale force winds, the *bora* in particular. In the summer gales are rare but in winter they occur for 5–10% of observations. Northerly gales (*bora*) are most frequent in the N while southerly gales (*jugo*) are most common in the S. In the centre gales are around 50–50 from the N or S. Depressions intensify in the Gulf of Genoa and northern Italy and in the Ionian. The direction and speed of depressions is erratic giving rise to great difficulty for weather forecasters.

Thunderstorms Occur frequently throughout the area. In the centre and N the highest reported frequency is in July and August suggesting these are 'heat' thunderstorms. Also occur frequently in June and September. Often accompanied by strong winds of short duration (1–3 hours). Rain or hail often accompany the associated squall.

Waterspouts Have been reported in the region.

Tides

Tides are on average around 0·3m (1ft) at springs. Tidal differences are greatest at the NW end and least along the SE coast. At Trieste tides are around 0·8m (2·4ft) at springs. The sea level can be significantly altered by barometric pressure and constant winds from one direction. With prolonged SE winds the sea level may rise 0·3–0·6m (1–2ft) above normal levels at the northern end of the Adriatic. At Venice the sea level can rise by 1m (3·3ft) with prolonged S–SE winds.

Currents

There is much variability in the current flow in the Adriatic and also a difference between summer and winter patterns. Basically there is a counter-clockwise flow with an area of great variability, depending on the prevailing winds, in the northern Adriatic. Currents around the islands are much complicated by particular submarine features and again by the prevailing wind. In the summer there will usually be a SE–going current down the outside of the islands in the northern Adriatic and a weak N–NW–going current in southern Croatia. In the winter the counter-clockwise current is more pronounced.

Harbours and anchorages

The area is well developed with the provision of numerous marinas along the coast and islands and generally good yacht facilities. It provides a useful 'break' for non-EU yachts from the EU VAT restrictions.

European yachts have now returned to the Croatian coast and marinas are operating at full capacity. There are 50 marinas operating in Croatia with an average capacity of 400 berths.

Facilities

Everyday

Water Available at all marinas and ashore at most harbours or anchorages. Care needed in some areas where war damage may have made supplies suspect.

Fuel Fuel quays in most marinas and larger harbours.

Electricity 220V at marinas.

Gas Gas bottles can be refilled at major ports.

Paraffin Available at hardware shops.

Boat Repairs

Engines Few spares available. Competent repair yards in the larger towns.

Engineering Good steel fabrication.

Wood and GRP repairs Range from adequate to poor. Most wood repairs are not up to yacht standard.

Paints and antifouling Locally manufactured paints and antifouling available.

Hauling Good facilities with travel-hoists in many of the marinas.

Gardiennage Can be arranged in some marinas. Ask around for recommendations.

Note Italy is close by for spares.

Provisioning

Good shopping for all basics in the larger towns and resorts. Fresh fruit and vegetables adequate.

Charts and pilots

Mediterranean Pilot Vol III (*NP47*) (Admiralty). Covers Croatia.

Adriatic Pilot T & D Thompson (Imray). Detailed pilotage for Croatia.

Navigational guide to the Adriatic – Croatian coast Miroslav Krleža Lexicographical Inst. Distributed by Imray

Charts Admiralty charts provide adequate coverage at a reasonable scale. Italian and Croat charts provide more detail.

The Croatian Hydrographic Office publishes charts for the Adriatic including two folios of Male Karte (little charts) at 1:100,000 scale. Folio 1 of 12 charts covers Monfalcone to Zadar. Folio 2 of 17 charts covers Zadar to Ulcinj. They are sold in a plastic envelope and are reasonably priced. Available at chandlers or from: Naval Adria, Budicinova 7, 51000 Rijeka, Croatia. ☎/*Fax* (51) 267 635. Available from Imray.

13.10 BOSNIA-HERZEGOVINA
TIME ZONE UT+1 ☎ IDD +387

12 km coastline on the Adriatic. Few facilities for yachts.

13.11 MONTENEGRO
TIME ZONE UT+1 ☎ IDD+381

Area 5381M^2 (13,938km^2)

Frontiers Total 599km. Albania 173km, Bosnia-Herzegovina 215km, internal boundary with Serbia 211km

Coastline 107M (199km)

Maritime claims 12M

Population 10·5M

Government The two Republics of Serbia and Montenegro exist with a single State Union president. Montenegro is a parliamentary democracy with its own president and prime minister. A referendum is planned for 2006 in which the future of the Union will be questioned. With the coastal tourism to boost the economy, the more developed Montenegro may wish for devolution from the Union with Serbia

Disputes The border disputes with Croatia and Bosnia-Herzogovina are calm at the time of writing, but it cannot be assumed there will be no further conflict given the problems of resettling refugees. Dubrovnik has been shelled on numerous occasions. Border tensions with Albania

Capital Belgrade. The capital of Montenegro is Podgorica

Time zone UT+1

Environment and pollution Raw sewage runs untreated into the sea (Gulf of Kotor particularly effected). Unknown war damage to the environment and infrastructure

Currency Yugoslav New Dinar (YD). 1 Dinar = 100 paras. The Euro is commonly used in Montenegro

Electricity 220V 50Hz AC

Geography

Mountainous steep-to coastline. No significant off-lying islands.

Seismic activity Area prone to earthquakes.

Weather See *13.9 Croatia*.

Tides and currents

See *13.9 Croatia*.

Facilities

Formerly good facilities for yacht care and repair were available.

Charts and pilots

Mediterranean Pilot Vol III (NP47) (Admiralty). Covers Montenegro.

Adriatic Pilot T & D Thompson (Imray). Detailed pilotage for Montenegro.

Charts Admiralty charts provide adequate coverage at a reasonable scale. Italian and ex-Yugoslav charts provide more detail.

13.12 ALBANIA
TIME ZONE UT+1 ☎ IDD+355

Note The faltering steps of this post-communist republic make its future hard to determine, but finally some stability seems to be establishing itself. Even so, there are still border disputes with Montenegro and Kosovo, and these areas should be avoided. Consult the UK Foreign and Commonwealth Office for the latest travel advice before visiting, on www.fco.gov.uk A yacht should not be left unattended while in Albanian waters. The following information is subject to change and should be interpreted with care and attention to the latest information on the ground.

Area 11,100M^2 (8,750km^2)

Frontiers Total 720km. Macedonia 151km, Serbia and Montenegro 287km, Greece 282km

Coastline 195M (362km)

Maritime claims 12M. Note: According to the Admiralty and to Albanian sources, the minefields noted on some charts have been cleared. In fact it now seems doubtful that many of them existed in the first place

Inland waterways 43km plus sections of Lake Scutari, Lake Ohrid, Lake Prespa
Population 3·2M. Growth rate 1·9%
Government Parliamentary democracy.
Disputes Border tensions with Montenegro. Kosovo question with Serbia and Montenegro. Northern Epirus question with Greece. Dispute with Greece over the Greek population in Albania
Capital Tirane
Time zone UT+1
Language Albanian (official dialect is *Tosk*). Greek along the border with Greece. Some Italian in coastal areas
Ethnic groups Albanian 90%, Greek 8%
Religion All mosques and churches were closed in 1967. In 1990 religious observance was again allowed. Estimates are Muslim 70%, Greek Orthodox 20%, Roman Catholic 10%
Public holidays
  Nov 29 Liberation Day
Economy Provided the poorest standard of living in Europe under the communists. After the elections in 1991 the economy constricted even further. Largely dependent on foreign aid at the present. At the time of publication there had been some foreign investment, principally Italian and German, but the economy remains sluggish and bogged down by the confused politics of the country.
Environment and pollution Little reliable data available. Rivers and coast are believed to suffer from industrial and domestic waste pollution. Air pollution around industrial sites. Kune wetlands and the coastal lagoon at Divjaka are nature reserves.
Internal travel Buses are infrequent and hopelessly crowded. Taxis.
International travel Some European flights to Tirana. Ferries from Italy and Greece.
Mail No data.
Telecommunications Rudimentary. Code +355.
Currency Lek (L) = 100 qintars
Banks Cash (in $US, or Euros) should be carried.
Medical Poor. Few Western drugs available.
Electricity 220V 50Hz AC.

Geography

Most of the coast is flat marshy land (usually part of a river delta) except for higher land near the Greek border. Much of the coast is bordered by shallows.

Seismic activity The coastal area is prone to earthquakes and, it is reported, to *tsunami*.

Climate and weather

See *13.9 Croatia*.

Tides and currents

See *13.9 Croatia*.

Charts and pilots

Mediterranean Pilot Vol III (*NP47*) (Admiralty). Covers Albania.
Adriatic Pilot T & D Thompson (Imray). Brief coverage of Albania.
Charts Admiralty charts provide adequate coverage at a reasonable scale. Italian charts provide more detail.

13.13 GREECE

TIME ZONE UT+2   ☎ IDD +30

Area 50,796M² (131,940km²)
Frontiers 1228km total. Albania 82km, ex-Yugoslavia 246km, Bulgaria 94km, Turkey 206km
Coastline 7385M (13,676km) (includes some 7000km islands)
Maritime claims 6M. A 12M claim is under review.
Inland waterways 80km system of three coastal canals and three unconnected rivers. Little used
Population 11M. Growth rate 0·2%
Government Parliamentary democracy. 51 *nomoi* (departments)
Disputes Complex maritime and air disputes with Turkey in the Aegean. Cyprus question. Stand-off over the question of the islet between Kalimnos and the Bodrum peninsula. Northern Epirus question with Albania. Dispute with Albania over the Greek population in Albania. Some trouble with people-smuggling across the extensive sea borders.
Capital Athens
Time zone UT+2 DST Apr–Sep
Language Demotic Greek. English and German also spoken
Ethnic groups Greek, Albanian
Religion 98% Greek Orthodox
Public holidays
  Jan 1 New Year's Day
  Jan 6 Epiphany
  Mar 25 Independence Day
  May 1 Labour Day
  Aug 15 Assumption Day
  Oct 26 St Dimitrius Day
  Oct 28 *Ochi* Day
  Dec 25, 26 Christmas
Moveable
  1st day of Lent
  Good Friday
  Easter Monday
  Ascension
Economy Mixed economy with some agriculture, industry, and shipping (Greece has one of the largest merchant fleets in the world). Tourism is a vital part of the economy (over 20% of GDP). As one of the poorest members of the pre-2004 EU large amounts of EU funds went into developing the infrastructure of the country. Work force is 28% in agriculture, 29% in industry, 42% in services (the government is the largest employer).
Exports Manufactured goods, fruit and vegetables, tobacco, refined petroleum products.

Imports Oil, machinery, vehicles, chemicals, food products, consumer goods.

Minerals Bauxite, iron, oil, lignite, manganese.

Crops Cereals, rice, cotton, tobacco, olives, fruit.

Environment and pollution Heavy use of fertilisers and pesticides pollutes the sea, particularly around Thessaloniki and in the Ionian. Fertiliser factories, olive oil processing plants and tanneries dump waste products untreated into the sea. Some sewage is untreated and runs off into the sea. Air pollution is a major problem in Athens. Oil pollution from tankers passing through Greek waters is an ever present problem. Fishing stocks are depleted from illegal fishing methods (fine mesh nets and dynamite). There are a few Mediterranean monk seal maritime reserves in Zakinthos and around the Northern Sporades some wetlands have a protected status.

Internal travel Internal flights to most of the major towns and islands from Athens. An extensive ferry network connects most of the islands with mainland ports. There is a limited rail network but the service is irregular and slow. Coach travel is widespread and cheap. Taxis everywhere. Hire cars and motorbikes in most tourist resorts.

International travel Athens is the principal airport with flights to most international destinations. European flights in the summer to Corfu, Preveza, Zakinthos, Thessaloniki, Thira, Mikonos, Rhodes, and Iraklion. Ferries to Italy, Turkey and Cyprus.

Mail Mostly reliable if a little slow at times. Use a marina or private address if possible. Poste restante service.

Telecommunications Automatic dialling. Country code +30. Adequate public telephone service with phonecards. Telephone and fax services from travel agents or other private agencies. GSM PAYG mobile phones. Internet cafés in most towns, even some in remote villages.

Currency Euro.

Banks Open 0800–1300 Mon–Fri. Exchange offices and travel agents operate outside these hours. Post offices will change Traveller's cheques and cash. All major credit cards, charge cards, and Traveller's cheques accepted. ATM's can be found in the larger towns and resorts and work with most credit cards.

Medical Ranges from poor to good in the cities. Reciprocal medical care for EU nationals with Form *E111*. Medical costs moderate.

Electricity 220V 50Hz AC.

Geography

Most of Greece is mountainous with steep land close to the coast. Often mountains drop precipitously into the sea. These chains of mountains extend into the sea where the peaks form a huge archipelago of islands in the Aegean and to a lesser extent in the Ionian. There are three major seas: the Ionian on the W, the Cretan Sea in the S, and the Aegean. Estimates of the number of islands in Greek waters vary from around seventy to hundreds; it depends how small you want to go when counting islands.

The coast and islands can be divided up as follows:

Northern Ionian The Ionian Islands from Corfu down to Zakinthos and the adjacent coast.

Southern Ionian The W and S Peloponnese from Katakolon to Cape Malea and off-lying islands.

Gulf of Patras and Gulf of Corinth The two gulfs separating the Peloponnese from mainland Greece.

Saronic and eastern Peloponnese The Attic coast from the Corinth Canal through Athens to Cape Sounion, the enclosed islands from Aigina to Spetsai, and the adjacent coast of the eastern Peloponnese.

Cyclades Split into Northern Cyclades (Kea to Mikonos), Middle Cyclades (Serifos to Amorgos), and Southern Cyclades (Milos to Anafi).

Evia and the Northern Sporades Evia and the adjacent mainland coast from Cape Sounion to Volos and the Northern Sporades.

Northern Greece Thessalonikos Kolpos to Alexandroupolis near the Greek–Turkish border and off-lying islands.

Eastern Sporades Limnos to Samos.

Dodecanese Patmos to Rhodes and Astipalaia.

Crete N and S coasts.

Seismic activity There are three major fault lines in Greece along either side of the roughly triangular Greek plate. One side runs down the Ionian from Corfu to the E end of Crete. Another runs from Levkas in the Ionian across northern Greece to the Dardanelles. The last side runs from the E end of Crete up into Asia Minor through Kos. In effect all of Greece is subject to earthquakes and has the highest number in the Mediterranean, although many of these are minor. Some can be severe. In the Ionian a severe earthquake in 1954 flattened most of the towns in Levkas, Cephalonia and Zakinthos with great loss of life. In 2003 another smaller earthquake hit Levkas, causing damage through the town and marina, but with no loss of life: a testament to anti-earthquake building regulations. In 1956 an earthquake with its epicentre near Amorgos caused a tsunami that deposited flotsam

Temperature and precipitation (at Athens)

	Av max °C	Av min °C	Record	Rel. humidity	Days 1mm rain	Sea temp °C
Jan	13	6	21	62%	16	13
Feb	14	7	23	57%	11	12
Mar	16	8	28	54%	11	13
Apr	20	11	32	48%	9	14
May	25	16	36	47%	8	15
Jun	30	20	42	39%	4	18
Jul	33	23	42	34%	2	22
Aug	33	23	43	34%	3	24
Sep	29	19	38	42%	4	24
Oct	24	15	37	52%	8	23
Nov	19	12	28	56%	12	20
Dec	15	8	22	63%	15	16

17m above sea level on Amorgos and caused damage with a 3 metre tsunami in Crete. On February 20 1968 a severe earthquake rocked the islands of Ayios Evstratios and Limnos killing 19 and causing widespread damage. In 1989 an earthquake near Kalamata caused significant damage to buildings.

Volcanic activity There are no large active volcanoes in Greece as there are in Italy, but there are numerous dormant volcanoes and plenty of evidence of volcanic activity where hot springs bubble to the surface. Thira (Santorini) is the largest known caldera in the Mediterranean. Kammeni, the plug in the middle of Thira, appeared in 236BC and in 1711–1712 Nea Kammeni appeared. In 1866 a violent eruption lasted two years. In 1925–26 an eruption joined Kammeni to Nea Kammeni. Other areas of recorded volcanic activity are in Amvrakikos Kolpos (19th century), on the Methana peninsula (Kaimeni in the 1st century BC), Milos which is also an old caldera, and Niseros (last eruption 1888).

Weather Summers are of the Mediterranean type, hot and dry, and winters mild with most of the rainfall occurring during the winter months. Northern Greece can be very cold in the winter and snow regularly falls on the mountains. Crete and Rhodes have the mildest winters. In the summer air temperatures regularly reach 35–40°C and sea temperatures 23–24°C.

Prevailing winds Winds in the summer are from the NE–N–NW–W throughout most of Greece with only a few minor exceptions. The summer wind pattern is exceptionally stable and can be counted on for around 70% of the time from June through to the end of September. In the Ionian a sea breeze sets in from the NW–W from Corfu down to Cape Malea. In the Aegean the *meltemi* (*etesians*) is the prevailing wind. It blows from the N–NE in the northern Aegean describing an arc down through the Cyclades to Rhodes and the Turkish coast where it blows from the NW–W. It can reach as far across as Aigina and Poros and down to Cape Malea.

The *meltemi* is a consequence of a pressure gradient between the monsoon low over Pakistan which extends

Fiskardho in the Ionian

Maistro The prevailing NW–W wind blowing down through the Ionian in the summer.
Sirocco The hot humid S wind blowing off the Sahara. Occasionally blows up to gale force.
Greek names for the winds are as follows:
North winds *vorias, boreas, tramontana.*
Northeast winds *vorias anatolikos, gregorio, gregoa.*
East winds *anatolikos, levante, ageliotes.*
Southeast winds *notios anatolikos, sirocco, euros.*
South winds *notios, ostra.*
Southwest winds *notios ditikos, garbis.*
West winds *ponente, ditikos, zephyros.*
Northwest winds *vorias ditikos, maistro, schiron.*

Gales There are few gales in the summer although the *meltemi* can produce gale force gusts in the Aegean. Gales in the winter result from depressions moving in an easterly direction either SE towards Cyprus or NE towards the Black Sea. Many of these depressions are small by Atlantic standards but nevertheless can give rise to violent winds. The depressions can intensify, rapidly move off and then stop again, making tracking them a difficult task. Depressions often linger in the Ionian and the southern Aegean. Southerly gales will often turn around and blow with renewed force from the N.

Thunderstorms These occur most often in the spring and autumn. The distribution of thunderstorms is reported to vary over the mainland and islands: thunderstorms are more frequent over the mainland in spring and autumn and over the islands in the winter. The thunderstorms are often accompanied by strong winds of short duration (1–3 hours). Rain and hail often accompany the associated squall.

Waterspouts These have been recorded in parts of Greece, especially at Corfu, the entrance to the Gulf of Patras, the Gulf of Corinth, the Evia Channel, and the S coast of Crete.

Tides

The tidal differences around the coast vary considerably. For the most part the tidal difference at springs is around 0·2m (0·6ft). However in Pagasitikos Kolpos (Gulf of Volos) and Evvoikos Kolpos (Gulf of Evia), there is a tidal difference at springs of 0·8m (2·5ft). This gives rise to the only significant tidal stream at Khalkis where rates can reach 6–7 knots at springs in the narrow gap between the N and S Evia channels. Even at slack water there may be a stream of 1–3 knots running. It should be remembered that strong offshore or onshore winds can decrease or increase sea levels significantly (as much as 1 metre in parts of northern Greece).

Currents

In general there is an anticlockwise current turning around the Aegean but the myriad islands and headlands jutting out into the sea complicate the overall picture. From the Ionian the E–going current follows the North African coast except for a branch which turns to become a N–NW–going current up the eastern Peloponnese and through the Ionian Islands. Across the S coast of Crete there is a W–SW–going counter-current and S of Rhodes an E–NE–going

its influence over the eastern Mediterranean and the stable summer high pressure over the Azores which effects the western Mediterranean. The pressure gradient between these two stable air masses produces the constant N–NW winds in the Aegean.

In the winter the pressure gradients over the eastern Mediterranean are not pronounced and winds are not from any constant direction. You can expect almost equal proportions of northerlies and southerlies.

Where the *meltemi* is not found or when it is not blowing a sea breeze predominates, though the direction is much affected by the local topography. For the most part the sea breeze is from the SW–S–SE.

Locally-named winds

Meltemi The NE–N–NW–W wind that blows over the Aegean in the summer. It can blow at Force 4–7 but gusts off the lee side of an island can be stronger. It is caused by a pressure gradient between the monsoon low over Pakistan and the Azores high. Typically it begins in June, blows strongest in the latter half of July, August, and the first half of September, and dies off at the end of September. A long cigar-shaped cloud over an island heralds a strong *meltemi*.
Etesians The older Greek name for the *meltemi* (Turkish in origin) from the Greek *etos* (annual).

The picture postcard port of Simi in the Dodecanese

Harbours and anchorages

For the most part there are few marinas in Greece. There are numerous commercial and fishing harbours and a large number of safe anchorages everywhere. There are more anchorages around the islands and mainland of Greece than anywhere else in the Mediterranean.

Facilities

Everyday

Water In all the marinas. In most harbours there will be a water tap on the quay, but it may be some distance away and unless you have a very long hose you will have to carry it in jerry-cans. In many places water is in short supply in the summer and its distribution is regulated. Often there is a 'water-man' who makes a few drachma supplying water. He will usually have a long hose that can reach most boats. In some places a fairly hefty charge is made for supplying yachts with water. In places where water is in short supply it should not be abused even if you are paying for it. In most places water is potable although it can be brackish or heavily chlorinated in a few places.

Fuel A few places have a fuel quay but mostly fuel is delivered by mini-tanker. In some of the more out-of-the-way places it can be difficult to obtain large quantities. In some places there is a significant amount of water in the diesel and bacterial contamination ('diesel bug') is an increasing problem.

Electricity Apart from the marinas, few of the harbours have electricity points and for the most part you will have to rely on generating it yourself.

Gas Camping Gaz is fairly widely available in the main towns and resorts. The supply is sometimes uncertain at peak periods. Greek gas is widely available. Gas bottles can be refilled at Preveza, Kalamata, Piraeus, Thessaloniki, Kavala, Kalimnos and Iraklion.

Paraffin Can be found in some villages and in bulk in the cities and larger towns. Ask for *petroleon katharon*. Methylated spirit is widely available in grocery shops.

Boat repairs

Engines Most spares for the major makes of marine engine are available or can be obtained. The main distributors are mostly in Athens or Piraeus so parts normally come from there. For the lesser well known makes spares will have to be imported and this can take a while. Competent workshops but also not-so-competent ones around. Ask for recommendations. Even quite small workshops can generally accomplish make-do minor repairs.

Electrics and electronics Some spares available, mostly from Athens or Piraeus. Few good electronic repair workshops so be prepared to send items back to the manufacturer.

Engineering Steel fabrication in many towns. Stainless steel fabrication to yacht standards in a few places.

Wood and GRP Some wood repairs and fabrication to yacht standards in a few places. Some GRP repairs and osmosis treatment carried out at the old Olympic Yard near Lavrion.

Paints and antifouling Locally manufactured paints and antifouling of adequate quality depending on the brand. Imported paints and antifouling widely available.

current. In the Aegean Sea the current roughly follows the coast of Asia Minor with a N–NNW going current until encountering the inflow from the Dardanelles which turns the current W–SW–going down through the islands to flow out through the gap between Cape Malea and the W end of Crete. For the most part these currents can be ignored as they are variable in strength, easily turned by surface drift currents set up by winds blowing for several days from a constant direction, and almost impossible to determine with any accuracy. There are a few exceptions. At Preveza where Amvrakikos Kolpos empties into the Ionian there is always an outgoing current of ½–2 knots. Around Cape Malea the W–SW–going current can raise confused heavy seas with wind against current. Through the Doro Channel between Evia and Andros there is usually a SW–going current of 1–4 knots and with wind against current heavy seas are raised. Around Limnos and Lesvos there is often a strong W–SW set from the current out of the Dardanelles. In the Samos Channel there can be overfalls when the prevailing N–NW wind is blowing against the E–NE current setting through the channel.

Kasos is a little gem of a place in the wind-tossed southern Dodecanese

Provisioning

Most provisions can be found except in some of the out of the way places. Fruit and vegetables are seasonal but now Greece is part of the EU more imported fruit and vegetables are to be found. Shopping hours vary but generally are 0800–1300 and 1630–2000 Mon–Sat. Some shops close on Mon mornings and Wednesdays.

Charts and pilots

Mediterranean Pilot Vol III (NP47) (Admiralty). Covers the Ionian Sea.

Mediterranean Pilot Vol IV (NP48) (Admiralty). Covers the Aegean Sea.

Greek Waters Pilot Rod Heikell (Imray). Detailed pilotage for all Greek waters from the Ionian to the Aegean.

Ionian Rod Heikell (Imray). Detailed pilotage and other information for the Ionian from Corfu to Methoni and the adjacent coast.

West Aegean Rod Heikell (Imray). Detailed pilotage and other information for the Saronic, eastern Peloponnese from the Corinth Canal to Cape Sounion, off-lying islands from Aigina to Spetsai and western Cyclades.

The Ionian to the Anatolian Coast H M Denham (John Murray). Covers the Ionian and Crete. OP.

The Aegean H M Denham (John Murray). OP.

Charts Admiralty charts provide adequate coverage, better in some areas than others. Admiralty charts available in Piraeus. Waterproof Imray-Tetra charts cover the area on a scale practical for yachtsmen when used in conjunction with Imray yachtsman's pilots. Imray-Tetra charts are available in Corfu, Levkas, Piraeus, Athens and Rhodes.

Hauling There are travel-hoists in marinas and independent yards in Greece. More are planned for the future and a few yards use hydraulic trailers to lift boats. In other yards boats are hauled in the traditional way on a sledge and greased runners and while it looks primitive, it is perfectly safe and there are few accidents.

Gardiennage There are many places offering gardiennage services of one sort or another, but few reliable places where proper care and attention is paid. Ask around for recommendations.

Area 300,088M²(779,450km²)

Frontiers Total 2715km. Bulgaria 240km, Greece 206km, Georgia and Armenia 617km, Iran 499km, Iraq 331km, Syria 822km

Coastline Total 3888M (7200km) Mediterranean coast 2808M (5200km), Black Sea coast 1080M (2000km)

Maritime claims 6M. 12M in eastern Mediterranean and Black Sea

Inland waterways About 1200km. Not well documented and little used

Population 71·3M. Growth rate 2·2%

Government Republican parliamentary democracy. 67 *iller* (provinces)

Disputes Complex maritime and air (but not territorial) disputes with Greece in the Aegean. Northern Cyprus question (Turkey is the only country to recognise Northern Cyprus). Downstream riparian disputes with Syria and Iraq over the Euphrates and Tigris rivers. Kurdish question in the east

Capital Ankara

Time zone UT+2 DST Apr–Sep

Language Turkish (using Roman alphabet since 1928). Kurdish and Arabic. English, German and some French spoken in the western coastal strip.

Ethnic groups 85% Turkish, 12% Kurd

Religion Nominally 98% Muslim (mostly Sunni), 2% other (mostly Christian and Jewish)

Public holidays
Jan 1 New Year's Day
Apr 23 Childrens Day
May 1 May Day
May 19 Youth Day
May 27 Freedom and Constitution Day
Aug 30 Victory Day
Oct 29,30 Republic Days

Moveable
Seker bayrami (sugar holy days)
Kurban bayrami (holy days of sacrifice)

Economy Fast growing mixed economy which in 1993 had one of the highest percentage increases for economic growth in the world. Aiming for EU membership, but is unlikely to join before 2012.

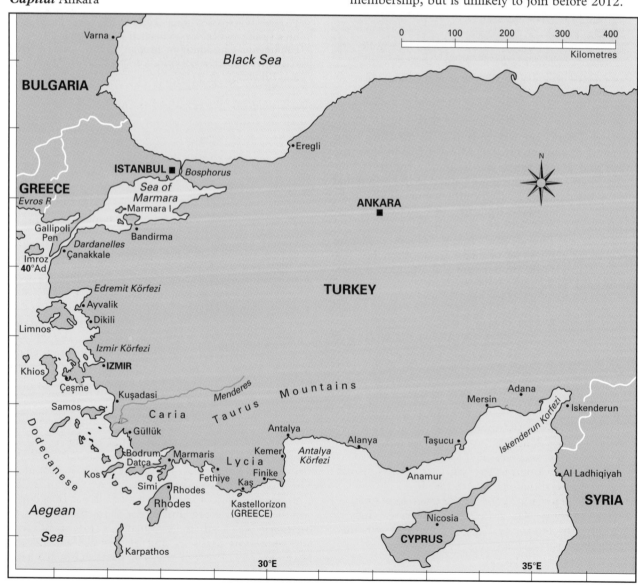

Agriculture is important and Turkey exports fruit and vegetables, cereals and cotton products. Fast growing industrial sector. Tourism is important. Work force is 56% in agriculture and fisheries, 14% in industry, 12% in services.

Exports Cotton, tobacco, fruit and vegetables, nuts (largest exporter of hazel nuts in the world), livestock, minerals, textiles, glass, cement.

Imports Machinery, oil, iron and steel, medicines, chemicals, fertilisers, consumer goods.

Minerals Coal, oil, phosphates, iron ore, copper, boron.

Crops Cotton, cereals, sugar beet, olives, citrus, tea, hazel nuts.

Environment and pollution Industrial effluent is dumped into the sea around the Sea of Marmara, Izmir, and Iskenderun. Fertiliser and pesticide use is increasing. Oil pollution in the Bosphorus, Sea of Marmara, around Izmir, and the Gulf of Iskenderun. Low grade coal is used for power stations and causes heavy environmental damage. Monk seals and loggerhead turtles are threatened by tourist development along the coast. Several coastal reserves though these are not well policed.

Internal travel Internal flights to some of the major cities, mostly from Istanbul, Izmir and Ankara. Limited rail network and slow unreliable service. Most internal travel is by coach or minibus (*dolmuş*) and you can get everywhere by public transport on the roads. Taxis in the towns and tourist resorts. Hire cars and motorbikes in the larger resorts.

International travel Istanbul and Ankara are the main airports with international flights to many destinations. European flights in the summer to Bodrum, Izmir, Dalaman, Antalya and Ankara. Train network connects through Bulgaria with the European network. Ferries to Greece and northern Cyprus.

Mail Generally reliable but slow. Packages are opened by customs and take some time to arrive. Have mail sent to a marina or private address. Poste restante service.

Telecommunications Automatic dialling to most areas. Country code +90. An improving and adequate system. Public telephone system with phonecards. Telephone and fax service from marinas and travel agents. GSM PAYG mobile phones. Internet cafés in most towns.

Currency Yeni Turkish lira (YTl). Revaluation in January 2005 reduced the face value of notes by a factor of one million lira i.e. 1000,000TL (2004) = 1YTL (2005). Marinas usually charge in Euros.

Banks Open 0830–1200 and 1330–1700 Mon–Fri. Exchange offices and travel agents operate outside these hours. All major credit cards, charge cards, Eurocheques, and Traveller's cheques accepted. ATM can be found in the larger towns and resorts and work with major credit cards.

Medical Ranges from good in the cities to poor in out-of-the-way places. Fees are moderate. Many drugs restricted in the EU can be bought over the counter in pharmacies.

Electricity 220V 50Hz AC.

Kizakalesi on the Turkish Pamphilian Coast

Geography

Two mountain chains traverse the N and S sides of Turkey hemming in the central Anatolian plateau. Most of the coast is bordered by high mountainous terrain except where river deltas form low coastal plains. Much of the steep-to coast drops off sheer into the sea. There are a few off-lying islands and for the most part cruising is around the much indented coast.

Turkey has four seas bordering its coasts:

The Black Sea Coast Mostly a straight coast with few natural indentations. The coast is mostly steep-to, spectacularly so in places, except for a few coastal plains around river mouths. There are numerous artificial fishing harbours or commercial ports along its length such that day-hopping is feasible for most of the coast. Little cruised by yachts.

Marmara Sea The sea locked in by the narrow Bosphorus in the NE and by the Dardanelles in the SW. The coast varies with mostly low rolling hills on the N side and higher land on the S side. Istanbul sits astride the Bosphorus straddling Europe and Asia Minor. A yacht must contend with the current in the Dardanelles (up to 4 knots) and again in the Bosphorus (up to 4 knots) when proceeding from the Aegean to the Black Sea. There are two marinas close to Istanbul and numerous harbours and anchorages around the Marmara Sea. Parts of the sea, particularly the area

171

around the Marmara Islands, offer a superb cruising ground little visited by yachts.

Aegean Sea This coast stretches from the Evros River that forms the frontier between Greece and Turkey to Marmaris where the coast angles south and east along the southern Mediterranean. There are numerous large gulfs cutting into the coast which provide a wealth of natural anchorages. The area south of Kuşadasi is the most popular with the deep gulfs of Güllük Körfezi, Gokova Körfezi and Hisarönu Körfezi providing superb cruising grounds. The land is mostly steep-to and much of it is covered in pine. There are six marinas and numerous municipal harbours with good facilities.

The Mediterranean Coast Less indented than the Aegean coast with the exception of Fethiye Körfezi and Kekova Adasi. There are five marinas and numerous municipal harbours.

Along both the Aegean and Mediterranean coasts there are numerous interesting sites from the Graeco-Roman periods.

The coast can be divided up as follows:
Dardanelles to Istanbul (Marmara Sea)
The Dardanelles to Çeşme (Northern Aegean)
Çeşme to Güllük Körfezi (Middle Aegean)
Güllük Körfezi to Marmaris (Southern Aegean)
Marmaris to Antalya (Northern SE Mediterranean)
Antalya to the Syrian border (Southern SE Mediterranean).

Seismic activity There are three major fault lines in Turkey along either side of the roughly triangular Asian plate. One side runs from the coast around Güllük Körfezi (Bodrum) up to a point on the Sea of Marmara around Gemlik Körfezi. Another is an extension of the northern side of the Greek plate through the Dardanelles along the S shore of the Sea of Marmara and across N Turkey inland of the Black Sea. The last side runs from Bodrum and curves around E to run through a point above Anamur Burnu following the coast inland in a NE direction to join up with the N side of the plate near Iran.

Many areas of Turkey are subject to earthquakes but the most severe are along the N side of the plate especially in the E. In recent times there have been numerous severe earthquakes in eastern Turkey: in August 1966 a violent earthquake in eastern Turkey levelled 139 villages and killed 2400 people; in July 1967 earthquakes killed hundreds in NW Anatolia; in March 1970 shocks registering over 7 on the Richter scale killed over a 1000 in Kutahya province in Anatolia; in September a shock registering 6·8 on the Richter scale killed 2300 around Lice in eastern Turkey; and in 1991 a severe earthquake around Ezerum caused severe damage and killed over a 1000 people. In 1999 two further 'quakes, one in Izmit on the Marmara Sea coast, again claimed 17,000 lives.

Volcanic activity There are no active volcanoes along the Turkish coast but there is plenty of evidence of low level activity under the surface where hot springs bubble to the surface.

Weather The climate varies considerably from N to S. In the N summers are mild and mostly dry except along the Black Sea coast where there can be

Temperature and precipitation (at Izmir)

	Av max °C	Av min °C	Record	Rel. humidity	Days 1mm rain	Sea temp °C
Jan	13	4	23	62%	10	13
Feb	14	4	23	51%	8	12
Mar	17	6	29	52%	7	13
Apr	21	9	33	48%	5	14
May	26	13	41	45%	4	15
Jun	31	17	41	40%	2	18
Jul	33	21	42	31%	0	22
Aug	33	21	42	37%	1	25
Sep	29	17	39	42%	1	24
Oct	24	13	37	49%	4	23
Nov	19	9	32	58%	6	20
Dec	14	6	26	64%	10	16

considerable rainfall at times. In the S Aegean and along the Mediterranean coast it is normally very hot in the summer with temperatures around 35–40°C. Winters on the E coast of Turkey around Iskenderun are very mild in the winter. For all of the region most of the rain falls in the winter months.

Prevailing winds Winds in the summer are predominantly from the NE–N–NW–W from Istanbul to Kaş. This is the same *meltemi* which blows over the Greek islands in the Aegean. As in Greece the wind pattern is exceptionally stable and can be counted on for the majority of observations from June to September. It blows from the NE in the Sea of Marmara and the Dardanelles before curving to blow from the N–NW down the Aegean coast before turning to blow from the NW–W around Bodrum and along to Kaş. The direction of the wind is much determined by the local topography and tends to blow into gulfs and large bays. From Kaş to the E the prevailing winds are land and sea breezes which are well developed in the summer. The onshore sea breeze gets up about midday and blows at Force 3–5 from the SE–S–SW before dying at night. The offshore land breeze begins to blow in the early morning at around Force 3–4, occasionally more, and may blow until midday.

Locally-named winds

Meltemi (meltem) The NE–N–NW–W wind that blows from Istanbul to Kaş. It can blow at Force 4–7 but gusts off high land can be stronger. It is caused by a pressure gradient between the monsoon low over Pakistan and the Azores high. Typically it begins in June, blows strongest in the latter half of July, August and the first half of September, and dies off at the end of September except in the Sea of Marmara when it can blow strongly through September to early October. *Imbat* Local name for the *meltemi* when it blows into Izmir Körfezi.

Turkish names for the winds (from the points of the compass) are as follows:
North winds *yildiz* (the pole star)
Northeast winds *poyraz*
East winds *Gündoğusu*

Date Duration	Name	Dir	Type	
27 Sept	El Saleeb	W	Cross	3 days
21 Oct	El Saleebish	W	Crusade	3 days
26 Nov[1]	El Micness	W	Broom	3 days
6 Dec[1]	Kaāsim	SW	Gale	7 days
20 Dec	El Fadrel Saggra	SW	Small gale	
11 Jan[1]	El Fadrel Saggra	S	Strong gale	3 days
		S	Strong gale	3 days
19 Jan	El Fedra El Kibirain	W	Feeder	5 days
27 Jan	El Fedra El Kibirain	W	Feeder	2 days
18 Feb[1]	El Shams El Saggira	NW	Feeder	5 days
10 Mar	El Hossom	SW	Brings the Equinox	8 days
20 Mar[1]	El Shams El Kabira	E	Big Sun gale	2 days
25 Mar	Hawa	E	A wind	
29 April	Khaseen	E	Sand wind	2 days
16 July	El Nogia	E	Black wind	2 days

Notes
1. Indicates a severe gale.
2. Local directions of winds vary from the general direction given with a greater proportion of S in the wind than appears in the table.
3. Strictly the calendar applies to the Levant further S and deviation from the dates is usually around 24–48 hours later. It can be applied as is to Syria, Lebanon, Israel, and Egypt.
4. For the full table incorporating Turkish and Coptic sources, see *Turkish Waters & Cyprus Pilot.*

Southeast winds *keşişleme*
South winds *Kible* (towards Mecca)
Southwest winds *lodos*
West winds *bati, günbatisi*
Northwest winds *karayel*

Gales There are few gales in the summer although the *meltemi* can produce gale force gusts off high land. Gales in the winter result from depressions passing across the Sea of Marmara or under Crete and along the Turkish coast towards Syria. For much of the Aegean and Mediterranean coast, gale force winds are from the S and can send heavy seas onto parts of the coast. In the Sea of Marmara and northern Aegean there are more gale force winds from the N. A calendar of gale force winds for the winter has been assembled over time and commonly the Coptic Calendar for gales is used. A concise version is reproduced opposite.

Thunderstorms These occur most often in the spring and autumn. The thunderstorms are often accompanied by strong winds of short duration (1–3 hours). Rain and hail often accompany the associated squalls.

Waterspouts These have been recorded in parts of Turkey, especially along the coast from Antalya to Marmaris. Most close to the land have been of small dimensions. In 1992 a small waterspout at Marmaris caused superficial damage to yachts. Further out to sea waterspouts of larger dimensions have been recorded.

Tides

The tidal range at springs does not exceed 0·5m (1·64ft) and is mostly less than 0·3m (1·0ft). For all practical purposes tides can be ignored.

Currents

A strong current flows down through the Bosphorus and along the N side of the Sea of Marmara and out through the Dardanelles into the northern Aegean. In the Bosphorus and the Dardanelles this SW–S–going current can reach 3–4 knots and in exceptional circumstances has been recorded at 7 knots. At the entrance of the Dardanelles there is usually a SW–W going current. A S–SSW–going current of ½–1½ knots runs down the coast past Bozcaada to Lesvos. For the rest of the Mediterranean and Aegean coast the current follows the anticlockwise flow in the eastern

Kizil Kuyruk in Skopea Limani on the Turkish Lycian coast

Turkish carpets

wind against the SW–W–NW–going current there can be confused seas. In the channel between Samos and the Turkish coast there can be overfalls when the prevailing N–NW wind is blowing against the E–NE–going current.

Harbours and anchorages

There are 20+ marinas around the Turkish coast with more planned. However many of the municipal harbours provide some of the facilities of a marina and make a charge to visiting yachts. There are numerous commercial and fishing harbours and a large number of anchorages along the much indented coast.

Facilities

Everyday

Water In all marinas and many of the municipal harbours. Supply is not always guaranteed in the summer when considerable demands are made on water supplies. In other places there may be a tap nearby where you can obtain water, although a long hose may be needed. Some restaurants supply water if you eat there. Water is normally potable, but on occasion there has been contamination (Marmaris and Bodrum have had problems) and at the height of summer care is needed.

Fuel Most of the marinas and a few municipal harbours have a fuel quay. In some of the other harbours fuel can be delivered by mini-tanker. In some out of the way places it can be difficult to obtain fuel.

Electricity All the marinas and some of the municipal harbours have electricity points. Elsewhere you will have to rely on generating it yourself.

Gas Camping Gaz is available in some resorts. In most places your bottles can be sent away to be refilled. Turkish gas is widely available.

Mediterranean basin. This current is variable in direction and rate. In a few places the rate is noticeable.

Along the coast between Antalya and Fethiye, the flow can be ½–2 knots and with the prevailing NW–W

Ayvalik on the Aeolian coast of Turkey

Paraffin Widely available in the larger towns, usually from a pump at one of the petrol stations. Methylated spirit is available from hardware and grocery shops.

Boat repairs

Engines Spares can be ordered for most major makes of marine engine. The main distributors are usually in Istanbul or Izmir. If spares have to be ordered from outside Turkey they can take a while to arrive so it is best to plan in advance before undertaking major work. Some competent workshops and some not-so-competent ones around. Even quite small workshops can accomplish make-do repairs and the mechanics are adept at adapting or even fabricating bits to make repairs.

Electrics and electronics Few spares available. Few good electronic workshops so be prepared to send items back to the manufacturer.

Engineering Steel fabrication in many towns. Stainless steel work to an acceptable standard can be carried out in a few places.

Wood and GRP Some wood repairs and fabrication to yacht standards in a few places. Some GRP repairs possible.

Paints and antifouling Locally manufactured paints and antifouling of adequate quality depending on the brand. Imported paints and antifouling can be obtained.

Hauling There are travel-hoists in most Turkish marinas, including: Ataköy (Istanbul), Kuşadasi, Yalikavak, Turgutreis, Bodrum, Keçi Bükü, Marmaris (2), Kemer, and Setur Antalya Marina. More are planned for the future. For the rest boats are hauled in the traditional way on a sledge and runners or by crane with slings.

Gardiennage There are a number of places offering gardiennage services of one sort or another, but not all provide proper care and attention. Ask around for recommendations.

Provisioning

Most provisions can be found except in some out-of-the-way places. Local produce, especially fruit and vegetables, is excellent. Imported goods can be found in the larger towns and resorts. In the larger villages and towns there is a market day once a week (usually Friday) where fruit and vegetables, dried fruit and nuts, local cheeses, herbs and spices, and local handicrafts are brought in from the surrounding countryside for sale. The quality is generally excellent. Shopping hours vary but are usually 0830–1530 and 1600–1930 Mon–Sat. Some shops remain open outside these hours and on Sundays.

Charts and pilots

Mediterranean Pilot Vol IV (*NP48*) (Admiralty). Covers the Aegean.

Mediterranean Pilot Vol V (*NP49*) (Admiralty). Covers the Mediterranean coast of Turkey.

Black Sea Pilot (*NP24*) (Admiralty). Covers the Dardanelles to Istanbul.

Turkish Waters and Cyprus Pilot Rod Heikell (Imray). Detailed pilotage for all Turkish waters from Istanbul to the Syrian border and the Turkish Black Sea coast. With colour aerial photographs.

The Ionian Islands to the Anatolian Coast H M Denham (John Murray). OP.

The Aegean H M Denham (John Murray). OP.

Black Sea Cruising Guide Rick and Sheila Nelson (Imray).

Charts Admiralty charts provide adequate coverage, better in some areas than others. Difficult to obtain in Turkey. Turkish Hydrographic charts are mostly metricated larger scale versions of Admiralty charts. They provide good coverage and are available in the larger towns and at marinas. Waterproof Imray-Tetra charts cover the popular areas on a scale practical for yachtsmen when used in conjunction with Imray yachtsman's pilots. Imray-Tetra charts are available in Istanbul and Bodrum.

13.15 Cyprus

TIME ZONE UT+2 ☎ IDD (N) +90 ☎ IDD (S) +357

In 1974 Cyprus was partitioned into northern Cyprus (Turkish) and southern Cyprus (Greek) after the Turkish army invaded the island. Northern Cyprus is recognised only by Turkey. The dividing line between the north and south is policed by the UN. Only the southern part of Cyprus joined the EU in May 2004. Some progress towards reconcilliation has been made, and there is now access between the two halves of the country by land at least. The current regulations regarding yachts have been retained here.

The following should be noted:

The government in southern (Greek) Cyprus considers any visit by a yacht to northern (Turkish) Cyprus to be illegal. It should be pointed out that under UN Resolution 34/30 (1979) and 37/253 (1983) the UN views the Government of Cyprus (i.e. presently southern Cyprus) as the legal government of all Cyprus. If a yacht does visit northern Cyprus and then goes to southern Cyprus it can incur heavy penalties. Under the laws of the Republic of Cyprus a fine of up to C£10,000 and/or 6 months imprisonment can be imposed. It is legal to proceed from mainland Turkey directly to southern (Greek) Cyprus.

Area 3561M² (9250km²)

Frontiers None, but divided into Northern (Turkish) Cyprus and Southern (Greek) Cyprus since 1974

Coastline 432M (800km)

Maritime claims 12M

Population 802,000 (population of Northern Cyprus difficult to assess because of an influx of Turkish settlers). Growth rate 1%

Government Parliamentary democracy in Southern (Greek) Cyprus. Parliamentary democracy in Northern (Turkish) Cyprus (recognised only by Turkey)

Disputes The 1974 invasion by Turkey effectively

divided the island into two *de facto* autonomous areas: the Greek south (60% of the island) and the Turkish north (35% of the island) are divided by a narrow UN buffer zone. Negotiations to reunite the island are currently deadlocked despite indications from the UN that they will reduce the number of UN troops there. Two UK sovereign bases (at Akrotiri and Dhekelia, about 5% of the island) over which some hostility has been expressed

Capital Nicosia (Lefkosia, Lefkosa)

Time zone UT+2

Language Southern Cyprus: Greek but English commonly spoken. Northern Cyprus: Turkish

Ethnic groups 78% Greek, 18% Turkish, 4% other

Religion 78% Greek Orthodox, 18% Muslim, 4% other

Economy Southern Cyprus: Mixed economy with tourism playing an important role. Work force is 35% in industry, 19% in services, 18% in commerce, 21% in agriculture.
Exports Southern Cyprus: Clothing, machinery.
Imports Southern Cyprus: Manufactured goods, machinery, vehicles, oil, food products.
Minerals Copper, asbestos, gypsum, salt.
Crops Cereals, citrus, fruit, olives, grapes.

Environment and pollution Increasing use of fertilisers and pesticides. Tourism threatens beaches where loggerhead turtles nest although the government has promised to protect Akamas Beach. Raw sewage runs off into the sea although some treatment stations are being built. Two coastal wetland reserves.

Internal travel Buses and taxis in the N and S. Hire cars and motorbikes in the S.

International travel Flights from many European destinations to Southern Cyprus. Ferries to Greece, Egypt and Israel from Limassol. Flights to Northern Cyprus from Turkey. Ferries from Tasuçu and Mersin to Kyrenia (Girne).

Mail Reliable in Southern Cyprus. Send mail to Limassol Sheraton Marina or Larnaca Marina. Poste restante service. For Northern Cyprus mail must be addressed to Mersin 10, Turkey and not to Northern Cyprus.

Telecommunications Automatic dialling to Southern Cyprus. Country code +357. Calls to Northern Cyprus are routed through Turkey. GSM PAYG mobile phones. Internet cafés in most towns.

Currency Southern Cyprus: Cypriot pound (C£). Euro. Northern Cyprus: Turkish lira or Cypriot pound.

Banks Southern Cyprus: Open 0800–1300 Mon–Fri. Branches of Barclays, Co-op, Grindleys, and Lombard. All major credit cards, charge cards, Eurocheques and Traveller's cheques accepted. ATM.

Medical Adequate to good service in Southern Cyprus. Poor in Northern Cyprus.

Electricity 220V 50Hz AC.

Geography

Cyprus is the third largest island in the Mediterranean. Despite its size it has few indentations and no natural harbours affording good shelter. Cyprus is not so much a cruising area as a base for yachts with good access to Greece, Turkey and Israel.

Weather Typically Mediterranean with hot dry summers and mild winters. In July and August temperatures can be very high, often reaching 40°.

Prevailing winds The prevailing summer wind is a sea breeze that normally blows in from the W. It gets up about midday, blows between Force 3–6 and dies down at night. Away from the coast the wind tends to be SW but closer in it follows the contours of the coast so that at Larnaca it blows from SSW–S.

Gales Gales can blow from all directions, but most frequently blow from the S or E. See the Coptic Calendar in the section on Turkey.

Sea fog In the summer there is frequently a sea fog in the early morning which can reduce visibility to less than a mile. It has usually dispersed by midday.

Thunderstorms Most frequent in the autumn and winter. Frequently associated with a cold front. Often

Temperature and precipitation (at Kyrenia)

	Av max °C	Av min °C	Record	Rel. humidity	Days 1mm rain	Sea temp °C
Jan	16	9	24	70%	13	15
Feb	17	9	31	67%	10	16
Mar	19	10	27	67%	7	16
Apr	22	12	31	68%	4	17
May	26	16	36	68%	2	19
Jun	30	20	41	65%	0	21
Jul	33	22	41	62%	0	25
Aug	33	23	42	60%	0	27
Sep	31	21	39	60%	1	26
Oct	27	17	36	62%	3	24
Nov	23	14	32	66%	7	22
Dec	18	11	24	69%	11	19

accompanied by strong winds of short duration (1–3 hours). Rain or hail may accompany the associated squall.

Waterspouts Have been recorded in the sea area between Cyprus and Turkey.

Tides

The tidal difference at Limassol is around 0·3m (1ft) at springs which for all practical purposes can be ignored as atmospheric pressure or constant winds from one direction can cancel the range or increase it.

Currents

The anticlockwise current in the Mediterranean turns N up the coast of Lebanon and Syria and then abruptly W–going between Cyprus and the Turkish coast to flow towards Rhodes. The anticlockwise current is also turned to a N–NW–going current around the W end of Cyprus. Currents off the coast are variable and rarely exceed 1 knot. They are easily reversed or augmented by surface drift currents.

Facilities (Southern Cyprus)

Everyday

Water At Limassol and Larnaca. In the summer water may be rationed.
Fuel At Limassol and Larnaca.
Electricity 220V at Limassol and Larnaca.
Gas Camping Gaz available. Most gas bottles can be refilled.
Paraffin Can be found. Enquire at Larnaca.

Boat repairs

Engines Most spares for the major makes of marine engine are available or can be ordered. If they have to be ordered from Greece or further afield it may pay to check what the estimated time of arrival is likely to be. Competent workshops and contractors.
Electrics and electronics Limited spares and repair facilities available.
Engineering Steel and stainless steel fabrication to adequate standards.
Wood and GRP Basic wood repairs. GRP boats are built in Limassol.
Paints and antifouling Locally manufactured paints and antifouling. Imported paints and antifouling available.
Hauling A 40-ton travel-hoist and hardstanding at Larnaca.
Gardiennage Several agencies can arrange gardiennage. Ask around for recommendations.

Provisioning

Good shopping in Limassol (town) and Larnaca. The British bases mean that all sorts of British foodstuffs are available.

Charts and pilots

Mediterranean Pilot Vol V (NP49) (Admiralty). Covers Cyprus.
Turkish Waters and Cyprus Pilot Rod Heikell (Imray). Detailed pilotage for harbours and anchorages around Cyprus.
The Ionian Islands to the Anatolian Coast H M Denham (John Murray). OP
Charts Admiralty charts provide adequate coverage of Cyprus.

Area 71,294M^2 (185,180km^2)
Frontiers Total 2253km. Iraq 605km, Turkey 822km, Jordan 375km, Israel 76km, Lebanon 375km.
Coastline 108M (200km)
Maritime claims 35M
Population 17·8M. Growth rate 4%
Government Effectively single party where the President is also head of the ruling Ba'ath Party. Other parties may stand for election
Disputes Separated from Israel by the 1949 Armistice Line. Golan Heights is occupied by Israel. Hatay question with Turkey. Dispute over riparian rights for Euphrates and Tigris rivers with Turkey and Iraq. Kurdish question with Turkey and Iraq. Real threat of terrorism in parts of the country. Latest travel advice may be obtained on the FCO website www.fco.gov.uk

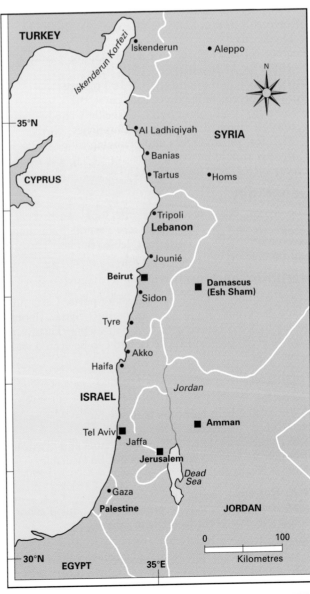

Capital Damascus

Time zone UT+2

Language Arabic. Also Kurdish, Armenian, Aramaic. Some French spoken

Ethnic groups 90% Arab. Others include Kurds and Armenians

Religion 74% Muslim (Sunni), 10% Christian (various), 16% Alawite, Druze and other Muslim sects

Economy Largely oil based. Also agriculture and some industry. Work force is 32% in agriculture, forestry and fishing, 29% in industry, 39% in services.

   Exports Oil (50%), textiles, tobacco, fruit and vegetables, cotton.

   Imports Food products, minerals, machinery, chemicals, fertilisers.

   Minerals Oil, natural gas, chrome, manganese, iron, phosphates.

   Crops Cotton, cereals, olives, fruit and vegetables.

Environment and pollution Oil refineries cause significant pollution in the sea. Fertiliser and pesticide use is increasing and much of it runs off into the sea via rivers.

Internal travel Some internal flights. Most public transport is by bus.

International travel Some international flights to Damascus.

Telecommunications Automatic dialling. Code +963. GSM capability.

Currency Syrian pound (S£) = 100 piastres

Banks There is only one official bank, the Commercial Bank of Syria. Traveller's cheques can only be changed in designated branches. Carry $US for SHIPCO fees and changing money. Black market should be avoided.

Electricity 220/110V 50Hz AC.

Geography

The Syrian coast is virtually one long sandy beach except for the N end. There are several man-made harbours, notably at Lattaquie, Jeble, Banias, Tartous and the fishing harbour at Rouad.

Harbours and anchorages

There are only commercial or fishing ports. Lattaquie is the best port for a first entry into Syria. Banias fishing harbour can be used by small yachts. Tartous is a commercial port and Ile de Rouad can be visited with permission.

Facilities

Everyday

Water Available in harbours and potable.

Fuel Can be arranged.

Gas Bottles can be filled at Lattaquie and Tartous although the correct fittings may not be available.

Paraffin Available.

Boat Repairs

In an emergency it may be possible to be hauled ashore by a crane. No yacht facilities or spares.

Provisioning

Excellent markets for fresh produce, fish and meat. Soft cheeses, yoghurt, humus and tahini readily available. Staples readily available. Few canned foods. No toilet paper.

General note

Few yachts visit Syrian waters but those that have report no problems as long as proper formalities are observed.

Charts and pilots

Mediterranean Pilot Vol V (NP49) (Admiralty). Covers Syria.

Mediterranean Almanac (Imray).

The Eastern Mediterranean H M Denham (John Murray). OP.

Charts Admiralty charts are adequate but SHOM charts have a larger scale and better detail.

13.17 LEBANON
TIME ZONE UT+2 ☎ IDD +961

Note The peace accord with Israel had brought comparative peace to the region until the recent retaliatory attacks by Israel on hard-line Palestinian groups on Lebanese soil. At the time of publication it appeared safe to go to Lebanon. No yacht coming from Israel can enter a Lebanese port.

Area 4004M² (10,400km²)

Frontiers 454km total. Syria 375km, Israel 79km.

Coastline 121M. 225km

Maritime claims 12M

Population 3·6M. Growth rate 1·3%

Government Democratic republic. The National Assembly has seats reserved for both Christians and Muslims

Disputes Separated from Israel by the 1949 Armistice Line. Israeli troops in Southern Lebanon since 1982. Syrian troops in Northern Lebanon since 1976. From 1975 Lebanon was torn by Civil War between its Christians and Muslims and between factions of these two groups amongst one another. In recent years there has been some terrorism threat in certain areas, and there is still conflict between the Palestinians in the south and Jewish settlers on disputed land. Latest travel advice is available on the FCO website www.fco.gov.uk

Capital Beirut

Time zone UT+2

Language Arabic and French. Some English spoken.

Ethnic groups 82% Arabs, 5% Armenian, 10% Palestinian

Religion 57% Muslim (1 million Shi'ite, ½ million Sunni, 200,000 Druze). 42% Christian (Maronite, Roman Catholic, Syrian Catholic, Armenian Catholic, Greek Catholic, Caldean, Protestant, Armenian Orthodox, Greek Orthodox, Nestorian, Syriac Orthodox)

Economy The economy is recovering gradually, with both business and tourism providing growth, although there is a long way to go before Beirut may become the 'Paris of the East' again.

Environment and pollution Toxic waste from an unknown source (but suspected to be one of the large EU countries) has been dumped on the Lebanese coast and this is a serious environmental threat to the sea. Increasing use of fertilisers and pesticides.

Internal travel Taxi.

International travel Limited flights to Beirut Airport.

Telecommunications Automatic dialling. Code +961. GSM capability.

Currency Lebanese pound (L£) = 100 piastres

Electricity 220 and 110V AC.

Geography

Like Syria, the coastline is mostly straight with few indentations. There are several man-made harbours, notably at Tripoli, Jounie Yacht Marina, and Beirut.

Harbours and anchorages

New marinas are being developed, particularly around Beirut, where a super-yacht marina is near completion.

Facilities

Yacht facilities in the marinas are generally excellent.

Charts and books

Mediterranean Pilot Vol V (NP49) (Admiralty). Covers Lebanon.

Mediterranean Almanac (Imray).

The Eastern Mediterranean H. M. Denham (John Murray). OP.

Charts Admiralty charts provide adequate coverage of Lebanon.

13.18 ISRAEL
TIME ZONE UT+2 ☎ IDD +972

Area 7996M² (20,770km²) (Does not include occupied Arab territories)

Frontiers Total 1,006km. Syria 76km, Jordan 238km, Lebanon 79km, West Bank 307km, Gaza Strip 51km.

Coastline 147M (273km)

Maritime claims 6M

Population 6·4M (est). Palestine 3·5M (est). Growth rate 1·5%

Government Parliamentary democracy.

Disputes Separated from Lebanon, Syria and the West Bank by the 1949 Armistice Line. West Bank, Gaza Strip, and the Golan Heights occupied by Israel. Israeli troops in southern Lebanon since 1982. Riparian dispute with Jordan. Ongoing threats of Palestinian suicide bombing and Israeli retribution. Latest travel advice is available on the FCO website www.fco.gov.uk

Capital Israel proclaimed Jerusalem its capital in 1950 but most political business is carried out in Tel Aviv. Most embassies are located in Tel Aviv.

Time zone UT+2

Language Hebrew is the official language. Arabic. English commonly spoken

Ethnic groups 80% Jewish. 17% Arab. Christians and Druze

Religion 80% Judaism. 17% Muslim (mostly Sunni). Christians. Druze

Public holidays

The Jewish calendar is lunar rather than the Julian calendar used in Europe

Independence Day 14 May 1948 (falls in April or May)

The Jewish Sabbath is on Saturday

Economy Mixed economy with a developed industrial and agricultural base. Tourism of some importance. Work force is 25% in industry, 6% in agriculture, 12% in commerce, 16% in financial services, 28% in government.

Exports Polished gems, military equipment, electronics, fruit and vegetables, textiles, fertilisers and chemicals.

Imports Rough gems, oil, chemicals, iron and steel, cereals, vehicles, machinery, ships, military equipment.

Minerals Copper, phosphates, potash.

Crops Citrus and other fruit, vegetables.

Environment and pollution Heavy use of fertilisers and pesticides which run off into the sea. Most of the population live along the coast which is much built up. Israel has not signed the Nuclear Non-proliferation Treaty and is thought to possess nuclear weapons. Seven protected coastal and river reserves.

Internal travel Internal flights connect the major towns. Buses to most destinations. Hire cars in the cities and resorts.

International travel Flights to some international (mostly European) destinations from Tel Aviv. Ferries to Cyprus and Piraeus.

Mail Reliable. Send it to a marina if possible. Poste restante service.

Telecommunications Automatic dialling. Code +972. Good public telephone service. Fax machines at most of the marinas or at travel agents or other agencies. GSM capability.

Currency New Israeli Shekel = 100 new agorot.

Banks Open 0830–1230 Sun to Fri. Also 1600–1800 Sun, Tues. All major credit cards, charge cards and traveller's cheques accepted. ATM in the cities and larger towns which work with major credit cards.

Medical Very good. Fees are expensive and private insurance is essential.

Electricity 220V AC.

Geography

The coastline is a long straight strip of low-lying sand and shingle with no indentations forming natural harbours. There are six marinas or harbours with yacht facilities either built or under construction along the Mediterranean coast and a marina at Eilat in the Red Sea. Most yachts visit one or perhaps two places in Israel, staying in one harbour and taking trips inland to sites in the Holy Land. However the local yacht clubs and cruising community have an active club and racing programme for those who want to get involved.

Temperature and precipitation (at Haifa)

	Av max °C	Av min °C	Record	Rel. humidity	Days 1mm rain	Sea temp °C
Jan	18	9	26	56%	13	18
Feb	19	10	31	56%	11	17
Mar	22	12	40	56%	7	18
Apr	25	14	43	57%	4	19
May	28	18	44	59%	1	20
Jun	29	22	43	66%	0	22
Jul	31	24	36	68%	0	26
Aug	32	24	37	69%	0	28
Sep	31	23	42	66%	0·2	27
Oct	29	20	41	66%	2	26
Nov	26	16	36	56%	7	23
Dec	20	12	29	56%	11	20

Weather Summers are hot and sometimes humid. The winters are warm although temperatures can plummet at night.

Prevailing winds The predominant wind is a sea breeze getting up about midday and dying at night. Normally it blows at Force 3–5 from a westerly direction, mostly W–NW. At night the land breeze is usually from the SE and in fact the morning breeze will frequently be SW turning to W–NW later in the day as the sea breeze effect sets in. The wind blowing onshore raises a difficult sea close to the coast. In the winter there can be periods of E winds which are reported to bring low temperatures to the region.

Gales Strong winds are predominantly from the NW or E. Gales are rare in the summer and for all observations infrequent in the winter. Occasionally a depression passing across Cyprus will deepen and move off over Israel. Also see the Coptic calendar in the section on Turkey.

Tides

The tidal range is on average 0·3m (1ft) for the area but is easily modified by atmospheric pressure or constant winds from one direction. For all intents and purposes tides can be ignored.

Currents

Currents are weak and variable in this area. There are no observations of more than 1 knot and surface drift currents predominate.

Harbours and anchorages

There are marinas at Akko (Acre), Haifa, Herzlia, Tel Aviv, Jaffa, Ashdod, Ashkelon and Eilat in the Red Sea. There are plans to enlarge Akko and expand facilities elsewhere.

Facilities

Everyday

Water Available in marinas and at yacht clubs. Potable unless marked otherwise.
Fuel Can be supplied at yacht marinas and yacht clubs.
Electricity 220V at the marinas and yacht clubs.
Gas Camping Gaz and other bottles can be refilled.

Paraffin Can be obtained.

Boat repairs

Engines Spares for marine engines are limited to the basics. Spares can be imported but may take some time to arrive. Competent workshops available which will carry out make-do repairs if necessary.
Electrics and electronics Spares common to electrics and electronics generally are easily found, but specific items will have to be imported. Competent repair facilities.
Engineering Steel and stainless steel fabrication.
Wood and GRP Wood and GRP repairs. Materials are expensive and good wood hard to find.
Paints and antifouling Locally manufactured paints. Some imported paints and antifouling available.
Gardiennage Can be arranged at the marinas or yacht clubs. Generally conscientious.

Provisioning

Supermarkets in Haifa and Tel Aviv. In general it is better to go beyond the shops near the waterfront to the more modestly priced shops further into the city. Carmel Market in Tel Aviv has good fruit and vegetables.

General note

In the past Israel has had raging inflation, up to 1000% at one time, but now inflation is under 20%. Prices on the whole are relatively high compared to its neighbours and Israeli yachts go to Cyprus, Greece or Turkey to buy equipment.

Charts and pilots

Mediterranean Pilot Vol V (NP49) (Admiralty). Covers Israel.
Imray Mediterranean Almanac Edited by Rod Heikell (Imray).
Red Sea Pilot Elaine Morgan and Stephen Davies (Imray).
Southern Turkey, the Levant and Cyprus H M Denham (John Murray). OP.
Charts Admiralty charts cover the coast adequately.

Area 385,558M² (1,001,450km²)

Frontiers Total 2689km. Gaza Strip 11km, Israel 255km, Libya 1150km, Sudan 1273km

Coastline 1323M (2450km)

Maritime claims 12M

Inland waterways 3500km of varying importance. Suez Canal is 193·5km and can take vessels up to 16m draught. The Nile (including the Nubaraya Canal) from the coast to Cairo is of importance for shallow draught cargo vessels. Tourist boats of varying size ply the Nile. The Nubaraya Canal has 1·65m depth

Population 71·9M. Growth rate 2·5%

Government Democratic republic. The president is head of state and appoints a Council of elected Ministers

Disputes Boundary dispute with Sudan. International terrorism from fundamentalist Muslim groups. The latest travel advice is available on the FCO website www.fco.gov.uk

Capital Cairo

Time zone UT+2

Language Arabic. English and French spoken in tourist resorts and by educated classes

Ethnic groups 90% Eastern Hamitic. 10% Greek, Italian, Syrian, Lebanese, Bedouin

Religion 94% Muslim (mostly Sunni). 6% Coptic Christian and other

Public holidays
Jan 1 New Year's Day
Feb 22 Unity Day
Mar 8 Revolution Day
May 1 Labour Day
Jun 18 Republic Day
Jul 23 Revolution Day
Sept 1 September Revolution Day
Oct 6 Armed Forces Day
Oct 24 Suez Day
Dec 23 Victory Day
Moveable
First Monday after Coptic Easter
Sham-en-Nessim (National spring festival)

Economy Oil is important. Large agricultural sector. Much of the heavy industry is under government control. Suez Canal important. Tourism important although currently declining because of attacks by fundamentalist Muslim groups. Work force is 44% in agriculture, 22% in services, 14% in industry.

Exports Oil (65%), cotton, citrus, rice, cement, textiles.

Imports Food products, machinery, vehicles, fertiliser, wood.

Minerals Oil, phosphates, gypsum, limestone, iron, manganese.

Crops Cotton, cereals, rice, beans, citrus, other fruit and vegetables.

Environment and pollution Oil pollution along the coast is a persistent problem from refineries, loading platforms and tanker traffic. Heavy use of fertilisers and pesticides which run off into the sea, chiefly down the Nile which is intensively farmed around the delta and along the banks. Toxic waste (principal contaminants chlorine, cadmium, mercury and oil) is emptied into the sea. Most sewage is untreated and empties directly into the sea or rivers. Sardine catches around the Nile delta have plummeted dramatically with the completion of the Aswan Dam which means the delta no longer floods and distributes nutrients out to sea. Four marine and coastal reserves.

Internal travel Internal flights to some destinations. The rail network serves important cities and towns, but is very crowded. Buses serve all destinations, but are invariably overcrowded. Taxis in the larger towns and resorts.

International travel Flights to many international destinations from Cairo. Ferries from Port Said and Alexandria to Cyprus.

Mail Not always reliable. Have mail sent to Alexandria Yacht Club or Port Fouad Yacht Centre.

Telecommunications Automatic dialling. Country code +20. Telephone services at travel agents or other agencies. GSM capability.

Currency Egyptian pound (E£) = 100 piastres

Banks Open 0900–1230 Mon–Thur and Sat. 1000–1200 Sun. Major credit cards and charge cards can be used in some places. Traveller's

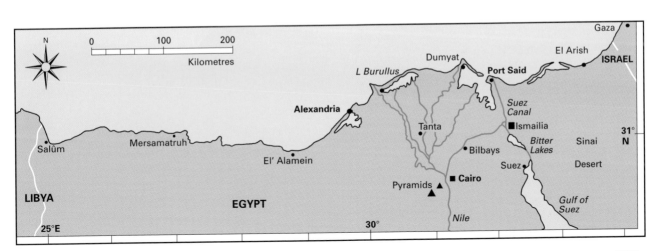

cheques widely accepted. Some ATMs.

Medical Adequate in Cairo and Alexandria, poor in the country. Medical fees are expensive so private insurance is essential.

Electricity 220/110V 50Hz AC.

Geography

The coastline is mostly straight with a bulge where the Nile delta has pushed out into the Mediterranean. Most of the coast is a low-lying sandy shore or low limestone cliffs with few natural indentations affording shelter. Most yachts will be heading either for Port Said to transit the Suez Canal or for Alexandria. It is possible for suitable yachts to voyage up the Nile although not without difficulty. To voyage up the Nile a yacht must draw 1·5m or less (you will still run aground on shifting sandbanks), must have an air height of less than 3m to pass under the low bridges, and will need a powerful engine to push against the current (3–4 knots in places).

Weather The climate is of the North African type with very hot dry summers and warm dry winters. Summers can be oppressive with high humidity near the coast and temperatures often reach 40°C. Rainfall in the winter can be variable.

Prevailing winds The prevailing wind over the long fairly straight coast is a sea breeze blowing from the NW–N with some NE along the Gaza Strip. The wind gets up around midday, blows around Force 3–4, with a fair percentage of calm days. The land breeze is of little consequence.

Locally-named winds

Khamsin Simoon The sirocco blowing off the desert.

Temperature and precipitation (at Alexandria)

	Av max °C	Av min °C	Record	Rel. humidity	Days 1mm rain	Sea temp °C
Jan	18	11	28	61%	7	17
Feb	19	11	33	59%	5	15
Mar	21	13	40	57%	3	16
Apr	23	15	42	60%	1	19
May	26	18	44	64%	0·5	20
Jun	28	21	44	68%	0	21
Jul	29	23	40	70%	0	26
Aug	31	23	41	68%	0	27
Sep	30	23	41	63%	0·1	27
Oct	28	20	40	61%	1	25
Nov	25	17	35	60%	4	22
Dec	21	13	31	60%	7	19

Normally associated with a depression. Most common in the spring and often blows at gale force.

Simoon The sirocco when associated with a dust storm off the desert. Often occurs under a clear sky and brings hot, dusty conditions. Normally lasts 1–4 days.

Gales Rare in the summer and usually occur in the winter and spring. Normally come from the NW or SW. Also see the Coptic Calendar in the section on Turkey.

Red Sea sunset in Egypt

Charts and pilots

Mediterranean Pilot Vol V (NP49) (Admiralty). Covers Egypt.

Red Sea Pilot (NP64) (Admiralty). Covers the Suez Canal and the Red Sea.

Red Sea Pilot Elaine Morgan and Stephen Davies (Imray). Detailed pilotage for Egypt in the Red Sea and transitting the Suez Canal.

Indian Ocean Cruising Guide Rod Heikell (Imray).

Imray Mediterranean Almanac Edited by Rod Heikell (Imray)

Egypt for Yachtsmen A booklet issued by the Egyptian Tourist Office. Yachtsmen using the booklet report that the information in it should be treated with caution.

Charts Admiralty charts cover the coast adequately. There are large scale plans of the Suez Canal and approaches.

13.20 LIBYA
TIME ZONE UT+1 ☎ IDD +218

General note A yacht should not attempt to visit Libya without prior permission from Tripoli and a valid visa. There have been reports that it is now easier to get a visa for Libya and that yachts can now visit without too many hassles. However, check with the Foreign Office before heading for Libya. Keep well outside the territorial waters when on passage.

Area 677,423M² (1,759,540km²)

Frontiers Total 4383km. Egypt 1150km, Sudan 383km, Niger 354km, Chad 1055km, Algeria 982km, Tunisia 459km

Coastline 956M (1770km)

Maritime claims 12M. Gulf of Sidra closing line 32°30'N

Population 5·5M. Growth rate 3·1%

Government Jamahiriya (literally 'state of the masses'). Only one permitted political party, the Arab Socialist Union Organisation whose head, Col. Muammar Abu Minyar al Gadafy, is head of the state and of the army

Disputes Claims and occupies a portion of the Aozou Strip in northern Chad. Maritime boundary dispute with Tunisia. Claims a large part of northern Niger and SE Algeria. Gadafy was perpetually at odds with the western world, principally the USA, but is recently building bridges with the EU. The latest travel advice is available on the FCO website www.fco.gov.uk

Capital Tripoli

Time zone UT+2

Language Arabic. Italian and English widely understood in the major cities.

Ethnic groups 97% Arab and Berber

Religion 97% Muslim (Sunni)

Public holidays
Sept 1 (1969) Revolution Day

Economy Largely oil based. Petrochemical industry. Heavy industry (iron, steel and aluminium). Agriculture against the odds. Work force is 18% in agriculture, 30% in industry, 27% in services, 24% in government.

Yemeni fishermen in the Red Sea. They look piratical but most are just curious and want simple items like tea and sugar

Tides

The tidal range is around 0·3m (1ft). The range is easily altered by atmospheric pressure or winds from a constant direction. For most purposes the tidal range can be ignored.

Currents

Generally there is a weak ENE current across the top of the Nile delta which is easily altered by surface drift currents.

Harbours and anchorages

Yachts will usually head for the Port Fouad Yacht Centre or Alexandria Yacht Club. There are a number of small fishing harbours and oil terminal harbours, but little information is available on them.

Facilities

Yacht facilities are virtually non-existent. Basic engine repairs. Some wood repairs at Port Said and Alexandria.

Provisioning

Stores can be obtained at Port Said/Fouad. Good shopping in Alexandria.

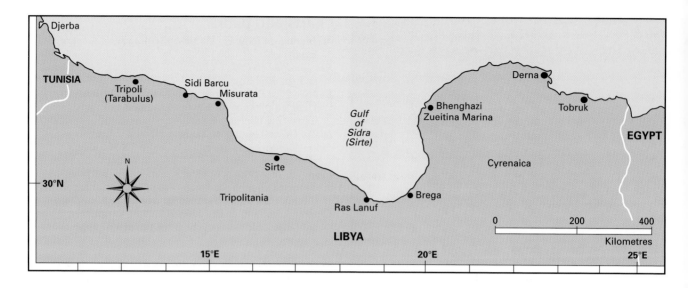

Exports Oil (1 million barrels a year).
Imports Food products, machinery, vehicles, manufactured goods.
Minerals Oil, natural gas, gypsum.
Crops Cereals, dates, olives, citrus, peanuts.
Environment and pollution Severe oil pollution along the coast. Saline spoilage of the land where subterranean aquifers have been over-exploited for agriculture. The Great Manmade River Project, the largest water development scheme in the world, is under construction to bring water from large aquifers under the Sahara.
Internal travel Buses connect most destinations.
International travel There are currently sanctions against international flights to Libya.
Telecommunications Automatic dialling. Country code +218.
Currency dinar (D) = 1000 dirhams
Medical Generally good. Private insurance is essential.
Electricity 220/125V 50Hz AC.

Geography

The long coastline is mostly low-lying with few indentations affording good shelter. The large Gulf of Sirte (Sidre) is considered to be Libyan territorial waters outside the 12M zone to 32°30'N. There are manmade ports and oil terminals at Port Bardia, Marsa El Hariga, Tobruch, Dernah, Benghasi, Ez Zueitina, Marsa El Brega, Ras Lanuf, Es Sider Misurata, Tripoli, Zawia, Zuara, and Abu Kammash Sidi Said.

Weather The climate is of the North African type with very hot dry summers and warm dry winters. Summers can be oppressive with temperatures often around 40°C. Rainfall in the winter can be variable.

Harbours and anchorages

Many of the oil terminals are unsuitable for yachts with no small craft basin. Tripoli is really the only viable port. At one time there were plans to build a string of marinas along the coast, not for tourists, but to keep the idle young occupied. With declining oil revenues it is unlikely the marinas will be built.

Facilities

Yacht facilities are non-existent. Basic engine repairs.

Provisioning

Most stores can be obtained. Some items are in short supply.

Charts and pilots

Mediterranean Pilot Vol V (NP49) (Admiralty). Covers Libya.

Area 62,990M² (163,610km²)

Frontiers Total 1424km. Libya 459km, Algeria 965km.

Coastline 620M (1148km)

Maritime claims 12M

Population 9·8M. Growth rate 2·2%

Government Democratic republic. Elected president is head of state. 23 *wilayat* (governorates)

Disputes Maritime boundary dispute with Libya

Capital Tunis

Time zone UT+1

Language Arabic (official). French commonly spoken

Ethnic groups 98% Arab, 1% European

Religion 98% Muslim, 1% Christian, less than 1% Jewish

Public holidays
Jan 1 & 18
Mar 20 National Day
Apr 9
May 1 Labour Day
Jun 1
Jul 25
Aug 3 & 13
Sept 3
Oct 15

Moveable
Festival of the sheep
Ramadan
Prophet's Birthday
Moslem New Year

Economy Partly oil based, with phosphates and tourism also important. Agriculture employs a large number of people, but droughts make systematic yields difficult. Work force is 35% in agriculture and fisheries, 22% in industry, 11% in trade and finance.

Exports Oil, phosphates, textiles, fruit, olive oil.

Imports Machinery, vehicles, metals, fertiliser, chemicals, textiles, food products.

Minerals Oil, phosphates, iron, lead, zinc.

Crops Cereals, fruit and vegetables, olives, dates.

Environment and pollution
Increasing use of fertilisers and pesticides which run off into the sea from the cultivated coastal strip. Industrial waste (mostly oil and phosphate residues) in Gulf of Gabes and around Tunis. Air pollution bad in Tunis. Most sewage is now treated. Three coastal reserves, although tourist development

impinges on these.

Internal travel Some internal flights. Limited rail network. Buses run everywhere but are often overcrowded. *Louages* are shared taxis (six people normally) covering a more or less fixed route. Hire cars in a few resorts.

International travel Tunis is the centre for international flights. In the summer there are some European flights to Monastir and Djerba. Ferries run to Marseille, Genoa, Naples, and Palermo. Hydrofoil service in the summer from Kelebia via Pantelleria to Trapani.

Mail Generally reliable. Have mail sent to a marina address if possible. Poste restante letters are returned after 2 weeks.

Telecommunications Automatic dialling. Country code +216. Telephone and fax services in the marinas and at some travel agents. GSM capability.

Currency Tunisian Dinar (D) = 1000 millimes

Banks Open 0800–1100 Mon–Fri in the summer. Open 0800–1100 and 1400–1615 Mon–Thur, 0800–1100 and 1330–1515 Fri in the winter. Exchange offices outside these hours. Major credit cards, charge cards and Traveller's cheques

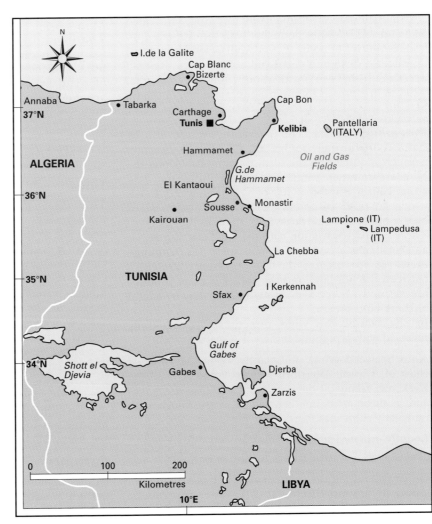

accepted in the cities and major resorts.

Medical Adequate in the cities and poor in the country. Medical fees are cheap to moderate. Private insurance essential.

Electricity 220V 50Hz AC.

Geography

The coast of Tunisia juts out to form the S side of the waist between the western and eastern Mediterranean. It has numerous natural indentations and a number of off-lying islands. The N coast between Tabarka and Cap Bon is flanked by mountains although there are extensive coastal flats and some shallows extending seaward. This area is more fertile than the eastern seaboard, with extensive cultivation along the coast including market gardens and citrus orchards. The eastern seaboard becomes progressively more low-lying with the Sahara meeting the sea between Chebba and the Libyan border. Shallows extend seaward for some considerable distance along this coast.

The coast is simply divided into two: the north coast from Tabarka to Cap Bon and the east coast from Keliba to the Libyan border.

Weather The climate is of the North African type with hot dry summers and mild winters. Summer temperatures often reach 40°C. Most of the rainfall occurs in the winter and there can be violent downpours. Between Sept 28 and Oct 8 1969 there were 10 days of torrential rain after 5 years of drought. Nearly 500 were killed and half a million homes destroyed. Again on Dec 4 1969 torrential rain killed 542 and left 300,000 homeless with an estimated 40 million dollars of damage. On April 7 1972 torrential rain left 86 dead and destroyed 6000 homes. Rainfall decreases from N to S with about 750mm in Tabarka, 420mm in Tunis, 325mm in Sousse and less in the far S.

Prevailing winds The prevailing winds in the summer are the daily sea breeze, although its direction is much modified by the local topography. Along the N coast summer winds are mainly from the NW around Bizerte and the Gulf of Tunis. However E–NE winds are also common. Along the E coast a sea breeze blows onto the coast from the E in the summer. There is a daily variation with the wind starting at NE and swinging around to E and then SE. Although these are sea breezes the high pressure differences between the hot land and the cooler sea can produce breezes up to Force 5–6. At night there may be a light offshore land breeze.

In the winter the wind directions are generally reversed with a preponderance of W winds.

Note Seaweed grows abundantly along the entire E coast of Tunisia. South of Monastir and around the Kerkenah Islands it has a calming effect on the waves and in these areas one can sail in strong winds with unusually calm seas.

Locally-named winds

Chihli/ghibli Tunisian names for the *sirocco*.

Gales Are rare in the summer although not unknown, especially around Bizerte. In the winter depressions

Temperature and precipitation (at Tunis)

	Av max °C	Av min °C	Record	Rel. humidity	Days 1mm rain	Sea temp °C
Jan	14	4	25	52%	3	15
Feb	17	4	32	42%	3	14
Mar	21	7	35	42%	3	14
Apr	25	11	37	41%	3	15
May	29	15	43	36%	3	18
Jun	34	19	49	33%	1	20
Jul	38	21	53	30%	1	23
Aug	38	21	48	31%	1	25
Sep	33	18	45	40%	3	25
Oct	27	14	39	45%	3	23
Nov	21	9	33	46%	3	20
Dec	15	4	29	55%	3	17

passing between Sicily and Tunisia can give rise to violent winds, especially over the N coast, although the severity along the Tunisian coast varies with location. Depressions do pass over Tunisia itself and can linger in the Gulf of Gabes giving rise to strong winds.

Gales passing westwards through the Sicilian Channel can generate heavy seas which pile up over the comparatively shallow water to produce high and confused waves. A wave height of 12m has been recorded in the Sicilian Channel, the highest recorded in the Mediterranean.

Thunderstorms Occur in the summer but are most frequent in the autumn. Summer thunderstorms are usually of the thermal instability (heat thunderstorm) type and are less violent than the autumn variety which are normally associated with a cold front. The thunderstorms are often accompanied by strong winds of short duration (1–3 hours).

Waterspouts Have been recorded in Tunisian waters and in the Sicilian Channel.

Tides

The tidal differences around the coast vary considerably. Along the N coast the tidal range is negligible at springs with a difference of around 0·25m (0·8ft) at Bizerte. South of La Chebba in the Gulf of Gabes the range starts to become appreciable and in Gabes the spring range can be 1·8m (6·0ft). In the shallow waters around the Kerkenah Islands the spring range can be 1 metre (3·3ft). The comparatively shallow water off the coast and around the islands means that care must be taken over depths when anchoring or when navigating in approach channels. This is especially so when channel buoys or markers may be missing or difficult to make out. The tidal range along the E coast gives rise to tidal currents of a mostly variable nature and care is needed when on passage not to be set off course. For tidal range data see *Imray Mediterranean Almanac*.

Currents

In the Sicilian Channel there is a constant SE–going current of around 1 knot. Currents off the Tunisian coast are weaker and of unpredictable direction. Along the E coast currents are mostly generated by the tidal range, but are also much affected by strong winds which set up appreciable surface drift currents in the shallow water.

Under certain conditions there may be a form of seiche similar to the *marrobbio* in southern Sicily. It normally occurs when two opposing wave trains meet in the Sicilian Channel. It has been reported as occurring every 10 and 26 minutes with a range of 0·6 to 0·9m (to 2·95ft).

Harbours and anchorages

Tunisia is a popular destination, and provides a useful break for non-EU boats from EU VAT restrictions.

Four marinas have been developed in Tunisia at Sidi Bou Said, Hammamet, El Kantaoui, and Monastir. There are a number of fishing harbours where facilities have been developed for yachts and numerous commercial and fishing harbours which a yacht can use. There are also a useful number of safe anchorages.

Facilities

Everyday

Water Readily available in the marinas and yacht clubs. Water points at most fishing harbours although they may be some distance from a berth. In most places the water is potable unless marked otherwise.

Fuel Generally available in the marinas and a number of fishing ports. In other places a mini-tanker can deliver and jerry cans can be delivered back full. It is reported that Tunisian diesel has a high sulphur content and is often contaminated by water.

Electricity Apart from the marinas, yacht clubs and a few fishing harbours, you will have to rely on generating it yourself.

Gas Gas bottles can be filled at Bizerte and Gabes, but sometimes foreign bottles, including Camping Gaz, will be refused. It is reported that staff will decant local bottles into foreign bottles at El Kantaoui and Monastir.

Paraffin Widely available from petrol stations. Ask for *petrole bleu*.

Boat repairs

Engines Few spares for marine engines are available. It can take some time to get spares into Tunisia and some yachts find it worthwhile going to Malta or Italy to have major work done. A few competent workshops, but most mechanics are not familiar with marine engines. Make-do repairs can be carried out in most places.

Electrics and electronics Spares virtually non-existent. Most yachts go to Malta to have work done.

Engineering Basic steel fabrication and galvanising.

Wood and GRP Some wood repairs though usually not to yacht standards. Hardwoods are hard to find. Basic GRP repairs.

Paints and antifouling Locally manufactured paints and antifouling available. Trans-Ocean antifouling manufactured under licence.

Hauling Travel-hoists in Sidi Bou Said and El Kantaoui with hard standing. Large travel-hoists (up to 250 tons) in some of the fishing harbours (Tabarka, Kelibia, Monastir, and Sfax).

Gardiennage Services offered at Sidi Bou Said, El Kantaoui and Monastir. Ask around for recommendations.

Provisioning

Basic provisions can be found everywhere except for very small villages. In the cities there are French *Monoprix* supermarkets and in most places there are local supermarkets or general shops. All the cities and towns have excellent markets for local produce including fruit and vegetables, meat, fish, cheeses, and herbs and spices. Shopping hours vary but generally are 0830–1200 and 1600–2000 Mon–Sat except Tuesdays.

Charts and pilots

Mediterranean Pilot Vol 1 (NP45) (Admiralty). Covers Tunisia.

North Africa Hans van Rijn, revised by Graham Hutt (RCC Pilotage Foundation/Imray). Detailed pilotage for Tunisia including off-lying islands.

Charts Admiralty charts for the area are only just adequate. French Hydrographic (SHOM) charts give the best coverage of the area.

13.22 ALGERIA
TIME ZONE UT+1 ☎ IDD +213

Note Since 1992 there has been a violent internal dispute between the government and the GSPC (Algeria's main terrorist group) who began terrorist actions after the fundamentalist Muslim party was banned from participating in elections. In June 2004 the GSPC issued a statement declaring their intent to target any foreign individuals or interests in Algeria. It is not recommended a yacht visit Algeria at present except in an emergency or other exceptional circumstances. Once in Algeria do not venture inland, especially to known GSPC areas. The latest travel advice is available on the FCO website www.fco.gov.uk

Area 919,696M² (2,381,740km²)

Frontiers Total 6343km. Libya 982km, Niger 956km, Tunisia 965km, Mali 1376km, Mauritania 463km, Western Sahara 42km, Morocco 1559km

Coastline 648M (1043km)

Maritime claims 12M

Population 31·8M. Growth rate 2·8%

Government Nominally multi-party democracy, although when it looked like the Muslim fundamentalists would win in the last elections the party was banned by the (then) government.

Disputes Libya claims a large part (19,400km²) of SE Algeria. Current internal disputes and terrorism by the GSPC (mostly directed at foreigners and intellectuals) who were barred from taking part in the last elections

Capital Algiers

Time zone UT. DST Apr–Sep

Language Arabic. Berber dialects. French widely spoken

Ethnic groups 99% Arab-Berber. Less than 1% European (rapidly declining)

Religion 99% Muslim (Sunni)

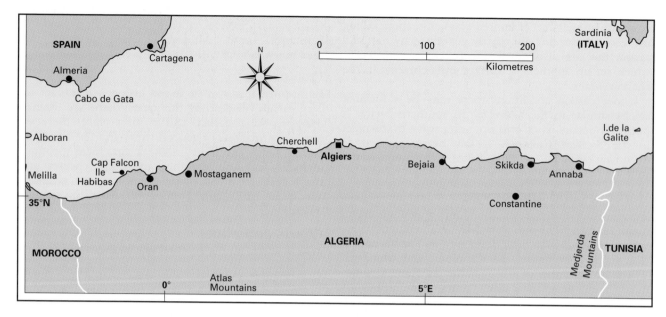

Economy Oil and natural gas based. Attempts to promote agriculture and industry have largely failed. Work force is 30% in agriculture, forestry and fisheries, 30% in industry, 27% in government and services.

Exports Oil and natural gas (98%).

Imports Food products, machinery, vehicles, consumer goods.

Minerals Oil, natural gas, iron, phosphates, lead, zinc, mercury, uranium.

Crops Cereals, citrus, olives, grapes.

Environment and pollution Oil pollution is heavy along the coast, especially around Annaba and Skikda. Other industrial pollution with waste products dumped directly into the sea. Sewage runs off untreated into the sea. Four coastal and wetland reserves although they are inadequately policed.

Internal travel Internal flights to the cities. Limited rail network. Buses run to all destinations but are often crowded. Taxis.

International travel Some international flights from Algiers (mostly to European and Maghreb countries). Ferries to Marseille and Sète.

Mail Generally reliable. Poste restante service.

Telecommunications Automatic dialling to Algiers and the cities. Country code +213. Most calls are routed via Algiers so it can take time to get through to some places. Calls can be made from the Post Office to outside Algeria.

Currency Dinar (D).

Banks Open 0800–1200 Sun to Thur. Traveller's cheques or cash accepted. Cash advances against major credit cards at the Credit Populaire Algerienne. Exchange regulations are strict: all foreign currency must be declared on a special form on which exchange of currency is noted and which is checked on departure. Although there is a thriving black market in currency exchange, much care is needed when using it.

Medical Just adequate in Algiers, rudimentary in most other places. Private insurance essential.

Electricity 220V 50Hz AC.

Geography

The Algerian coast is a fairly straight coastline with only a few small natural indentations. From the W roughly up to Oran, the coast is made up of steep hills with several uninhabited islets and the Habibas Islands a short distance offshore. From Oran to Algiers green wooded hills slope gently towards the shore. From Algiers eastwards the coast becomes increasingly mountainous towards Bejaia until Annaba, where the coast becomes lower until the Tunisian border. Few yachts cruise the coast and most usually put into one of the major ports while on passage to or from Gibraltar.

Seismic activity Low level seismic activity along the top of the African plate. Major quake in May 2003 struck the Algiers area killing 2,200 and injuring 10,000.

Weather The climate is of the North African type with very hot dry summers and mild winters. Most of the rainfall occurs in winter along the narrow coastal strip or over the Atlas Mountains.

Prevailing winds For most of the coast the prevailing winds are a NE–E sea breeze that blows for roughly 25M off the coast. It generally gets up about mid-morning and dies at night. It can blow up to Force 4–6. The direction close to the coast is altered by the local topography to blow from NE–SE. From Oran to the Moroccan border there are also W winds in the summer with about an equal mix of E and W overall.

Gales Most gales occur in the winter and are associated with a depression coming through the Strait of Gibraltar or over Tunisia. Gales can deepen around the Atlas mountains and may then veer off over the Algerian coast, although most frequently they go E out over the E coast of Tunisia. Gale force winds are most frequently from the N or S.

Tides

Tidal differences are hardly noticeable and for all practical purposes can be ignored.

Currents

The main E–going stream of the anticlockwise Mediterranean current runs along the Algerian coast at around 0·5–1·0 knot. It is less in the summer when the prevailing E winds cause surface drift currents and strongest in winter when winds are less constant in direction.

Harbours and anchorages

There is one marina at Sidi Ferruch. Apart from that there are a large number of commercial and fishing ports along the coast providing good shelter. There are few good anchorages.

Facilities

Yacht facilities are virtually non-existent. Basic engine repairs. Basic engineering repairs.

Provisioning

Basic items, (bread, fruit and vegetables, staples, meat and fish), are fairly widely available although there are periodic shortages. Imported items are rare except in the large cities. Carry a good stock of your preferred 'little luxuries' with you.

Charts and pilots

Mediterranean Pilot Vol 1 (NP45) (Admiralty). Covers Algeria.
North Africa Hans van Rijn, revised by Graham Hutt. (RCC Pilotage Foundation/Imray). Detailed pilotage for Algeria.
Charts Admiralty charts are adequate. French Hydrographic (SHOM) charts give the best coverage of the area.

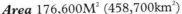
Area 176,600M² (458,700km²)
Frontiers Total 2002km. Algeria 1559km, Western Sahara 443km.
Coastline Total 991M (1835km). Mediterranean 270M 500km
Maritime claims 12M. 24M fishing zone
Population 30·5M. Growth rate 2·2%
Government Constitutional monarchy. Elected government with the sovereign as head of government. 36 provinces
Disputes Claims part of Western Sahara where there is armed conflict over the area. Spain controls two *presidos* (Ceuta and Melilla) on the coast
Capital Rabat
Time zone UT
Language Arabic (official). Berber dialects. French commonly spoken. Some Spanish and English.
Ethnic groups 99% Berber
Religion 98·7% Muslim. 1·1% Christian
Public holidays
Mar 3 Independence Day
May 1 Labour Day
Jul 9 Youth Festival
Moveable
Ras el Am
New Year's Day
Ashoura
Memorial Day
Mouloud
Birth of Mohammed
Aid-es-Seghir
End of Ramadan
Aid-el-Kebir
Economy Mixed economy of industry, mining, agriculture and fishing. The economy has suffered in recent years with declining prices for phosphates, competition for its manufactured goods, and declining fish catches. Tourism is important. Work force is 39% in agriculture and fisheries, 20% in services, 17% in industry.
Exports Phosphates, fruit, fish, textiles, refined petroleum.
Imports Oil, food products, iron, steel, machinery, vehicles.
Minerals Phosphates (75% of world reserves), lead, cobalt, manganese, copper.
Crops Cereals, citrus, fruit, dates, grapes.
Environment and pollution Most industrial pollution is along the Atlantic coast. Fish stocks are declining. Oil pollution mostly from passing tankers. Overall pollution is low along the Mediterranean coast.
Internal travel Internal flights to the cities. Rail network between the major cities. Buses serve all destinations. There are two classes of bus: CTM luxury buses which are more expensive but less crowded and the normal service which is often overcrowded. *Grands taxis* run regular routes in the country and *Petits taxis* run local routes in the cities

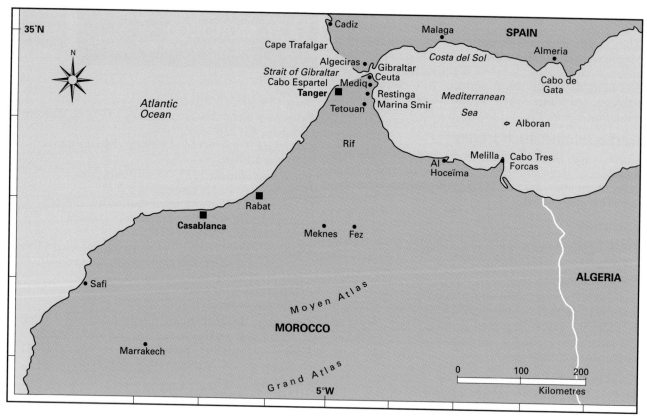

and towns for a fixed price. Taxis. Hire cars in the cities and larger resorts.

International travel Casablanca is the centre for international flights. European flights to Tanger, Rabat, Fez, and Marrakech. Ferries from Tanger to Gibraltar and Algeciras. Ferry from Ceuta to Algiceras. Ferry from M'Diq to Gibraltar. Ferry from Melilla to Malaga. Ferry from Toulon to Tanger.

Mail Usually reliable. Send mail to a private address if possible. Poste restante service.

Telecommunications Automatic dialling to the cities. Country code +212. Telephone calls can be made from the Post Office or from hotels or travel agents. GSM capability.

Currency Dirham (Dh) = 100 centimes.

Banks Open 0830–1130 and 1500–1630 Mon–Fri. Major credit cards and charge cards accepted in the cities and larger resorts. Traveller's cheques widely accepted.

Medical Adequate in the cities but poor in the country. Medical fees are moderate to high. Private insurance is essential. If possible go to Gibraltar for treatment.

Electricity 220V 50Hz AC.

Geography

Most of the Mediterranean coast is flanked by the steep-to Rif mountains. Several offshore islands and the enclaves of Ceuta and Melilla which are in Spanish hands.

Seismic activity The Rif mountains are prone to seismic activity and there have been a number of sizeable earthquakes in Morocco and the immediate sea area. The last major quake occurred on 28 February 1969, causing substantial damage.

Weather The climate along the coast is of the Mediterranean type with hot dry summers and mild wet winters. Inland the climate becomes more extreme with very hot dry summers and dry winters over the Sahara. In the Atlas mountains the winters are harsh and cold with substantial rainfall and snow.

Prevailing winds For most of the coast winds are from either the W or E with about an equal frequency. There are often days of calm in the summer. Around the Strait of Gibraltar winds are as for Gibraltar, see *13.2*.

Tides

For most of the coast tides are negligible. For the coast around the Strait of Gibraltar there are significant tides and tidal streams, see *13.2*.

Currents

The incoming current from the Strait of Gibraltar causes a SW–W–going counter-current along much of the Mediterranean Moroccan coast. The rate is variable around 0·5 knots. In the Strait of Gibraltar there is a constant E–going current of varying strength depending on the tidal stream. See *Imray Mediterranean Almanac*.

Harbours and anchorages

There are three marinas at Kabila, Marinasmir and Melilla with further developments along the Atlantic coast. There are also a number of commercial and fishing ports including those in the Spanish enclaves at Ceuta and Melilla. There are few secure anchorages.

Facilities

Everyday

Water Usually available but the water point may be a

long way away from a yacht berth. Fill up at Tanger, Marinasmir, Ceuta or Al Hoceima. Potable unless marked otherwise.

Fuel Easily obtained at Marinasmir, Ceuta or M'diq. Elsewhere it can be delivered by drum.

Electricity At Marinasmir, Ceuta and M'diq.

Gas All bottles can be refilled in Tanger and Ceuta. Elsewhere it may be possible to send the bottle away to be filled.

Boat repairs

Engines Limited spares for some of the major marine engines at Marinasmir. Otherwise spares are virtually non-existent. However it is relatively easy to get to Gibraltar to obtain them. Basic workshops.

Engineering Basic steel fabrication.

Wood and GRP Basic wood repairs. Basic GRP repairs at Marinasmir.

Paints and antifouling Available at Marinasmir.

Gardiennage Can be arranged at Marinasmir.

Provisioning

Good shopping for provisions in even quite small villages. Most larger villages and towns will have a market where good fruit and vegetables, herbs and spices, meat and poultry can be found. Ceuta is a duty free port and has a variety of products at cheap prices in the shops.

Charts and pilots

Mediterranean Pilot Vol I (NP45) (Admiralty). Covers Morocco.

North Africa Hans van Rijn, revised by Graham Hutt. (RCC Pilotage Foundation/Imray). Detailed pilotage for the Moroccan coast.

Charts Admiralty charts provide just adequate coverage of the coast. Spanish and French charts provide more detail and a better scale as well as being more up-to-date than the Admiralty charts.

14. Useful books

The following is a small selection of books relating to the Mediterranean that you may find useful. At the end of the sections on the countries there is a list of useful books for that country and these are not listed here.

History

The Mediterranean and the Mediterranean World in the Age of Philip II Fernand Braudel (Fontana). Two volumes.
The Penguin Atlas of Ancient History and *The Penguin Atlas of Medieval History* Colin McEvedy
The First Merchant Venturers William Culican (Thames and Hudson)
Sailing to Byzantium Osbert Lancaster (Murray)
Man and the Sea Philip Banbury (Adlard Coles)
Eothen A W Kinglake (Century)
The World of Odysseus M I Finley (Pelican)
Mankind and Mother Earth Arnold Toynbee
The Ancient Mariners Lionel Casson (Gollancz)
Long Ships and Round Ship John Morrison (The Stationery Office)
The Mediterranean: Portrait of a Sea Ernle Bradford
In Search of the Trojan War Michael Wood (BBC publications)
Beyond the Grand Tour Hugh Tregaskis (Ascent)

General

Harvest of Journeys Hammond Innes (Fontana)
Fool's Paradise Brian Moynaham (Pan)
Ulysses Found Ernle Bradford (Sphere)
A Money-wise Guide to the Mediterranean Michael von Haag (Travelaid)
Lugworm Homeward Bound Ken Duxbury (Pelham)
The Plundered Past Karl E Meyer (Penguin)
The Traveller's Handbook ed. Ingrid Cranfield (Futura)
On the Shores of the Mediterranean Eric Newby (Harvill)
Larousse Encyclopaedia of Mythology (London)
Corsair Country Xan Fielding (Secker & Warburg). OP.
Mariner in the Mediterranean John Marriner (Adlard Coles). OP.
Black Sea and Blue River John Marriner (Rupert Hart Davis). OP.
The Innocents Abroad Mark Twain (Signet)
Mediterranean Sailing Rod Heikell (Nautical)
Isabel and the Sea George Millar (Century)

Flora

Flowers of the Mediterranean Anthony Huxley and Oleg Polunin
The Oxford Concise Flowers of Europe Oleg Polunin
The Natural History of the Mediterranean Tegwyn Harris (Pelham)

Marine Life

Hamlyn Guide to the Flora and Fauna of the Mediterranean Sea A C Campbell
Hamlyn Guide to the Seashore and Shallow Seas of Britain and Europe A C Campbell
The Yachtsman's Naturalist M Drummon and P Rodhouse (Angus and Robertson)
Dangerous Marine Animals Bruce Halstead

Food

Food in History Reay Tannahill (Paladin)
A Book of Mediterranean Food Elizabeth David (Penguin)
A Book of Middle Eastern Food Claudia Roden (Penguin)

Admiralty Publications

The following UK Hydrographic Office publications are relevant. They are available from Admiralty Chart Agents and Imray, Laurie Norie & Wilson Ltd, Wych House, The Broadway, St Ives, Cambs, PE27 5BT England ☎ 01480 462114 *F* 01480 496109 *E* orders@imray.com

Charts The complete index is in the Catalogue of Admiralty Charts and other hydrographic publications (NP131). Issued annually.

List of Lights and Fog Signals
Vol E (NP78) Mediterranean and Black Sea

Sailing Directions – Mediterranean Pilot
Vol 1 (NP45) Covers West Mediterranean to the heel of Italy excluding France, Corsica, Sardinia and West Italy
Vol II (NP46) Covers France, Corsica, Sardinia and West Italy
Vol III (NP47) Cover the Adriatic and Ionian Seas
Vol IV (NP48) Covers the Aegean Sea
Vol V (NP49) Covers Libya, Egypt, Middle East and Southern Turkey

Radio Publications
Vol 1 Part 1 (NP281 (1)) Coast Radio Stations
Vol 2 (NP282) Radio navigational aids. Radiobeacons.
Vol 3 Part 1 (NP 283 (1)) Radio Weather Services and Navigational Warnings
Vol 5 (NP285) Global Maritime Distress & Safety Systems

Index